VISUALIZING TECHNOLOGY

INTRODUCTORY

VISUALIZING TECHNOLOGY

Fifth Edition

Debra Geoghan

Bucks County Community College

PEARSON

Boston   Columbus   Indianapolis   New York   San Francisco   Hoboken   Amsterdam
Cape Town   Dubai   London   Madrid   Milan   Munich   Paris   Montreal   Toronto
Delhi   Mexico City   Sao Paulo   Sydney   Hong Kong   Seoul   Singapore   Taipei   Tokyo

Vice President of Career Skills: Andrew Gilfillan
Executive Editor: Jenifer Niles
Team Lead, Project Management: Laura Burgess
Project Manager: Laura Karahalis
Development Editor: Cheryl Slavik
Editorial Assistant: Michael Campbell
Vice President Digital Strategy Workforce Readiness: Jason Fournier
Product Strategy Manager: Eric Hakanson
Production Media Project Manager: John Cassar
Director of Product Marketing: Maggie Waples
Director of Field Marketing: Leigh Ann Sims
Product Marketing Manager: Kaylee Carlson
Field Marketing Managers: Molly Schmidt & Joanna Sabella
Program Manager: Emily Biberger
Efficacy Curriculum Manager: Jessica Sieminski
Senior Operations Specialist: Diane Peirano
Senior Art Director: Diane Ernsberger
Cover Art: Gray Wall Studio/Fotolia and Kletr/Fotolia
Cover Design: Lumina Datamatics, Inc.
Composition and Full-Service Project Management:
   Lumina Datamatics, Inc.
Lumina Datamatics Project Manager: Sarah Vostok
Cover Printer: Lehigh-Phoenix Color/Hagerstown
Printer/Binder: RR Donnelley/Kendallville
Text Font: 10/12 Helvetica Neue LT W1G Roman

Credits and acknowledgments borrowed from other sources and reproduced, with permission, in this textbook appear on the appropriate page within text.

Library of Congress Cataloging-in-Publication Data
Names: Geoghan, Debra, author.
Title: Visualizing technology. Introduction / Debra Geoghan, Bucks County
   Community College.
Description: Fifth edition. | Boston : Pearson, [2017]
Identifiers: LCCN 2015050359| ISBN 9780134474519 (pbk.) | ISBN
0134474511
   (pbk.)
Subjects: LCSH: Microcomputers--Textbooks. | Computer science—Textbooks.
Classification: LCC QA76.5 .G3766 2017 | DDC 004--dc23
LC record available at http://lccn.loc.gov/2015050359

ISBN 10: 0-13-447451-1
ISBN 13: 978-0-13-447451-9

Brief Contents

Contents

CHAPTER 3

File Management   112

CHAPTER 6

Digital Devices and Multimedia   274

CHAPTER 9

Networks and Communication   436

What's New in This Edition?

Visualizing Technology is a highly visual, engaging computer concepts textbook. Filled with all the important topics you need to cover, but unlike other textbooks, you won't find pages full of long paragraphs. Instead, you'll find a text written the way students are hardwired to think: it has smaller sections of text that use images creatively for easier understanding, and chapters are organized as articles with catchy headlines. For the fifth edition, we have completely updated the design, so that students encounter content in a more linear, yet engaging way—just as they see on their favorite websites.

Visualizing Technology provides a hands-on approach to learning computer concepts in which students learn a little and then apply what they are learning in a project, simulation, or watch a Viz Clip video to dive deeper. Each chapter has two *How-To* projects focused on *Digital Literacy* and (*Essential Job Skills*) Job Skills so that students are gaining the skills needed for professional and personal success. They learn about the important topics of ethics, green computing, and careers in every chapter. And, the content is all up to date with the latest in technology, including Windows 10 and Mac OS X El Capitan.

The optimal way to experience *Visualizing Technology* is with MyITLab. All of the instruction, practice, review, and assessment resources are in one place, allowing you to arrange your course from an instructional perspective that gives students a consistent, measurable learning experience from chapter to chapter.

INSTRUCTION

Prepare visual and kinesthetic learners with a variety of instructional resources

- **Integrated Etext** provides an environment in which students can interact with the learning resources directly
- **Viz Intro Videos** provide an overview of the objectives covered in the chapter
- **Viz Clip Videos** dig deeper into key topics in the chapter in an engaging, YouTube-like approach
- **PowerPoint Presentation** – can be used in class for lecture, or assigned to students, particularly online students for instruction and review
- **Audio PowerPoint Presentation** deliver audio versions of the PowerPoint presentation - an excellent lecture-replacement option for online students
- **TechBytes Weekly** provides a timesaving news site that allows instructors to add pre-curated, interesting, timely, and relevant news items to their weekly lectures without having to search themselves. TIA Weekly also features valuable links and other resources, including discussion questions and course activities.

PRACTICE

Engage students with hands-on activities and simulations that demonstrate understanding

- **NEW How-To Projects these** active-learning projects are now delivered in two versions per chapter a *Digital Literacy* Project and an *Essential Job Skill* Project. Each project focuses on the skills students need for personal and professional success. Topics include, basic website creation, mobile application creation, video creation, and using social media for brand marketing.
  - **How-To Videos accompany each project to** *show* student how to complete the hands-on projects
- **IT Simulations** provide 12 newly revised and redesigned, individual scenarios that students work through in an active learning environment.
- **Windows 10 high-fidelity training simulations** allow students to explore Windows in a safe, guided environment that provides feedback and Learning Aids (Watch and Practice) to assist them if they need help.

REVIEW

Self-check and review resources keep learning on track

- **Viz Check Quiz Parts 1 & 2** provide a self-check of 3-4 objectives, so that students can see how well they are learning the content. (Feeds *grade* to MIL gradebook)
- **Viz Intro videos can also be used for review, as they provide an overview of what is covered in the chapter.**
- **Adaptive Dynamic Study Modules** are adaptive flashcards that provide students with personalized review based on their strengths and weaknesses
- **Jeopardy! Game** and **Crossword Puzzles** are a fun, engaging way for students to challenge knowledge

    Other in-book, end-of-chapter projects and resources: Mind-map visual review; Objective recaps; Key Terms; Summary; Review Exercises—Multiple Choice, True or False, and Fill in the Blank.

CHANGES BY CHAPTER

Chapter 1 What Is a Computer?

Added coverage of:
- Ergonomics How To actively
- Drones, Apple Watch

Chapter 2 Application Software

- Updated all software versions
- Mobile app How to activity

Chapter 3 File Management

- Updated to Windows 10 and OS X El Capitan

Chapter 4 Hardware

- Added coverage of USB-C and DisplayPort
- Power settings How to activity

Chapter 5 System Software

- Updated all content and figures to Windows 10 and OS X El CApitan
- Back up How To activity

ASSESSMENT

Measure performance with ready-to-use resources

- **End-of-Chapter Quiz** this is a comprehensive chapter quiz that covers all of the objectives from the chapter.
- **Application Projects** *(MyITLab Grader project)* and solution files. Projects are written to Windows 10 and Office 2016, but Grader projects are compatible with Office 2013 and 2016.
- **Testbank exam** customizable prebuilt, autograded, objective-based questions covering the chapter objectives
- **Other In-Book, End-of-Chapter projects:** Running Project; Critical Thinking; Do It Yourself; Ethical Dilemma; On The Web; Collaboration

Chapter 6 Multimedia and Digital Devices

- Screen capture How To activity

Chapter 7 The Internet and World Wide Web

- Added coverage of Microsoft Edge
- Build a website How to activity

Chapter 8 Communicating and Sharing

- Added new objective - Develop a Brand Marketing Strategy

Chapter 9 Networks and Communication

- Security software How to activity

Appendix A Microsoft® Office 2016 Applications Projects

Appendix B Using Mind Maps

Visual Walkthrough

VISUALIZING TECHNOLOGY HALLMARKS

- **Addresses visual and kinesthetic learners**—images help students to learn and retain content while hands-on projects allow students to practice and apply what they learned.
- **Easy to read**—it has the same amount of text as other concepts books but broken down into smaller chunks of text to aid in comprehension and retention.

- **Clear, easy-to-follow organization**—each chapter is broken into a series of articles that correspond to chapter objectives.
- **Highly visual**—students will want to read!

Learning Objectives clearly outlined in chapter opener and restated at the beginning of each article

Learning Outcomes are clearly defined at the beginning of each chapter.

Chapter Intro Video introduces the main concepts of the chapter

Explanation of the **Running Project** for that chapter

CHAPTER

2

Application Software

In This Chapter

A computer is a programmable machine that converts raw data into useful information. Programming—in particular, **application software**—is what makes a computer a flexible and powerful tool. After reading this chapter, you will recognize various types of software applications for both business and personal use.

Objectives

1. Identify Types and Uses of Business Productivity Software
2. Identify Types and Uses of Personal Software
3. Assess a Computer System for Software Compatibility
4. Compare Various Ways of Obtaining Software
5. Discuss the Importance of Cloud Computing
6. Install, Uninstall, and Update Software

Running Project

In this chapter, you'll learn about different kinds of application software and how to obtain it. Look for instructions as you complete each article. For most articles, there's a series of questions for you to research. At the conclusion of this chapter, you'll submit your responses to the questions raised.

52

53

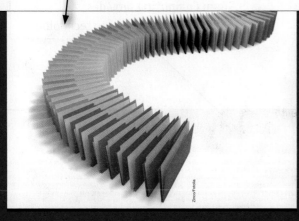

Catchy headlines begin each article

A Place for Everything

Objective
1

Create Folders to Organize Files

One of the most important things that you need to do when working with computers is called **file management**: opening, closing, saving, naming, deleting, and organizing digital files. In this article, we discuss organizing your digital files, creating new folders, and navigating through the folder structure of your computer.

File Management

The second part of the file name is the **file extension**. In this example, .docx is the extension. The extension is assigned by the program that's used to create the file. Microsoft Word files have the extension .docx. Windows maintains an association between a file extension and a program, so double-clicking on a .docx file opens Microsoft Word. The extension helps the operating system determine the type of file. If you change the file extension of a file, you may no longer be able to open it. **Table 3.4** lists some common file types and the programs associated with them.

TABLE 3.4 Common File Extensions and Default Program Associations

Extension	Type of File	Default Program Association (Windows)	Default Program Association (OS X)
.docx	Word document	Microsoft Word	Microsoft Word
.rtf	Rich text format document	WordPad or Word	TextEdit
.pages	Pages document	—	Pages
.xlsx	Excel workbook	Excel	Excel
.pptx	PowerPoint presentation	PowerPoint	PowerPoint
.bmp	Bitmap image	Paint	Preview
.jpeg/.jpg	Image file (Joint Photographic Experts Group)	Photos	Preview
.mp3	Audio file (Moving Picture Experts Group Audio Layer III)	Windows Media Player	iTunes
.aac	Audio file (Advanced Audio Coding)	iTunes	iTunes
.mov	Video file (QuickTime)	QuickTime	QuickTime
.wmv	Video file (Windows Media Video)	Windows Media Player	—
.pdf	Portable document format	Adobe Acrobat and Reader	Preview

Geoghan, Debra. Visualizing Technology Complete, 4e. Pearson Education, 2014.

FIND OUT MORE

The characters \ / ? : * " > < | can't be used in a file name because they each have a special meaning in Windows. For example, the colon (:) is used to indicate the letter of a drive (such as C: for your hard drive). Use the Internet to research the remaining illegal characters. What does each symbol represent?

IT Simulations—take students through a hands-on activity covering a key topic in the chapter

Find Out More—prompts for additional research on a given topic

Images are used to represent concepts that help students learn and retain ideas

Green Computing provides eco-friendly tips for using technology

Moore's Law

In 1965, Intel cofounder Gordon Moore observed that the number of transistors that could be placed on an integrated circuit had doubled roughly every two years. This observation, known as **Moore's Law**, predicted this exponential growth would continue. The current trend is closer to doubling every 18 months. As a result of new technologies, such as building 3D silicon processors or using carbon nanotubes in place of silicon (Figure 1.7), this pace will likely continue for another 10 to 20 years. The increase in the capabilities of integrated circuits directly affects the processing speed and storage capacity of modern electronic devices.

Moore stated in a 1996 article: "More than anything, once something like this gets established, it becomes more or less a self-fulfilling prophecy. The Semiconductor Industry Association puts out a technology road map, which continues this [generational improvement] every three years. Everyone in the industry recognizes that if you don't stay on essentially that curve they will fall behind. So it sort of drives itself.*" Thus, Moore's Law became a technology plan that guides the industry. Over the past several decades, the end of Moore's Law has been predicted. Each time, new technological advances have kept it going. Moore himself admits that exponential growth can't continue forever.

In less than a century, computers have gone from being massive, unreliable, and costly machines to being an integral part of almost everything we do. As technology has improved, the size and costs have dropped as the speed, power, and reliability have grown. Today, the chip inside your cell phone has more processing power than that first microprocessor developed in 1971. Technology that was science fiction just a few decades ago is now commonplace.

*Moore, Gordon E. 1996. "Some Personal Perspectives on Research in the Semiconductor Industry," in Rosenbloom, Richard S. and William J. Spencer (Eds.). Engines of Innovation: U.S. Industrial Research at the End of an Era. Harvard College

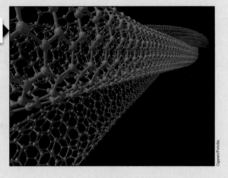

FIGURE 1.7 Carbon nanotubes may someday replace silicon in integrated circuits.

GREEN COMPUTING
Smart Homes

The efficient and eco-friendly use of computers and other electronics is called **green computing**. Smart homes and smart appliances help save energy and, as a result, are good for both the environment and your pocketbook.

Smart homes use home automation to control lighting, heating and cooling, security, entertainment, and appliances. Such a system can be programmed to turn various components on and off at set times to maximize energy efficiency. If you're away on vacation or have to work late, you can remotely activate a smart home by phone or over the Internet. Some utility companies offer lower rates during off-peak hours, so programming your dishwasher and other appliances to run during those times can save you money and help energy utility companies manage the power grid, potentially reducing the need for new power plants.

Smart appliances plug into the **smart grid**—a network for delivering electricity to consumers that includes communication technology to manage electricity distribution efficiently. Smart appliances monitor signals from the power company, and when the electric grid system is stressed, can react by cutting back on their power consumption.

Adrian Sherratt/Alamy

Running Project

Use the Internet to look up current microprocessors. What companies produce them? Visit **computer.howstuffworks.com/microprocessor.htm** and read the article. How many transistors were found on the first home computer processor? What was the name of the processor, and when was it introduced?

5 Things You Need To Know	Key Terms
• First-generation computers used vacuum tubes.	central processing unit (CPU)
• Second-generation computers used transistors.	ENIAC (Electronic Numerical Integrator and Computer)
• Third-generation computers used integrated circuits (chips).	integrated circuit
• Fourth-generation computers use microprocessors.	microprocessor
• Moore's Law states that the number of transistors that can be placed on an integrated circuit doubles roughly every two years—although today it is closer to every 18 months.	Moore's Law
	transistor
	vacuum tube

Subtopics have same color background as main topics—makes it easy to follow each piece

Ethics boxes provide thought-provoking questions about the use of technology

Social Review Sites

Social review sites such as TripAdvisor and epinions let users review hotels, movies, games, books, and other products and services. Yelp allows users to review local businesses and places with physical addresses such as parks. Figure 8.23 shows a Yelp map of Times Square restaurants on the iPad app. The reviews are from regular people, not expert food critics, and can help you decide where to eat. You can use the Yelp app on a mobile device to get information when you are right in the area.

FIGURE 8.23 Searching for a Place to Eat in Times Square Using the Yelp App on an iPad

Social Bookmarking and News Sites

Social bookmarking sites allow you to save and share your bookmarks or favorites online. Delicious allows you to not only save and share your bookmarks online but also search the bookmarks of others. It's a great way to quickly find out what other people find interesting and important right now. The links are organized into topics, or tags, to make it easier for you to find links. You can click the *Follow* button if you have a Delicious account, but you don't need an account to browse Delicious.

Pinterest allows you to create virtual cork boards around topics of interest and pin webpages to them (Figure 8.24). You can share your boards with others, and you can follow other people to see what they have pinned. StumbleUpon discovers websites based on your interests. When you sign up, you indicate topics that interest you. Then, as you visit websites, you can click the *StumbleUpon* button to be taken to a similar site. You can click *I like this* to improve the selection of pages you stumble onto.

Social news sites are different from traditional mass media news sites in that at least some of the content is submitted by users. Social news is interactive in a way that traditional media isn't. It's like having millions of friends sharing their finds with you. Content that's submitted more frequently or gets the most votes is promoted to the front page.

FIGURE 8.24 Pinterest

414 CHAPTER 8

Three of the most popular social news sites are reddit, Digg, and Slashdot. Digg doesn't publish content but allows the community to submit content they discover on the web and puts it in one place for everyone to see and to discuss. reddit (Figure 8.25) allows community members to submit content and to vote that content up or down, as well as discuss it. reddit is organized into categories called subreddits. Celebrities often participate in AMA—ask me anything—interviews on reddit. Slashdot, which focuses primarily on technology topics, produces some content but also accepts submissions from its readers. Whatever your interests, there's probably a social news site for you.

FIGURE 8.25 reddit

ETHICS

Some people create multiple accounts on social bookmarking and news sites so they can promote their own content. For example, a blogger might create several accounts on Digg and use each one to Digg a blog post, artificially raising its popularity on Digg and driving more traffic to it. This violates the Digg terms of use. But what if the blogger had all his friends and family members create accounts and Digg his post? Is it ethical? Does it violate the terms of use? Is it fair to other bloggers?

Running Project

Go to the Wikipedia article "Reliability of Wikipedia" at wikipedia.org/wiki/Reliability_of_Wikipedia. How does Wikipedia ensure that the content is correct? What procedures are in place to remove or correct mistakes? How does Wikipedia compare to other online sources of information?

3 Things You Need To Know	Key Terms
• Social media relies on the wisdom of the crowd rather than that of an expert.	crowdsourcing
• Anybody can edit a wiki.	social bookmarking site
• Social bookmarking and news sites help users find content that others recommend.	social news site
	social review site
	wiki

Objective 5 **415**

Running Project—Specific instructions are provided for compiling information for the Running Project

Things You Need to Know—Key takeaway points are provided for each article

Key Terms—Students are reminded of the key terms they should understand after reading each article

How To?
Digital Literacy Skill

Capture a Screenshot of Your Desktop

 HOW TO VIDEO

Throughout this book, you will be directed to provide screenshots of the work you have done. This is quite easy to do and is useful in other situations. For example, it's helpful for providing directions on how to do something or for keeping a record of an error message that appears on your screen. Windows includes a program called the

Snipping Tool that you can use to capture a screenshot. Macs include the Grab tool.

The Windows Snipping Tool can capture four types of snips:
- **Free-form Snip:** Allows you to draw boundaries around an object for a snip
- **Rectangular Snip:** Allows you to draw a rectangle around an object for a snip
- **Window Snip:** Captures a selected window for a snip

- **Full-screen Snip:** Captures the whole screen for a snip

You can save your screenshots, email them, paste them into documents, and annotate and highlight them by using the buttons on the Snipping Tool toolbar. If necessary, download the student data files from **pearsonhighered.com/viztech**. From your student data files, open the *vt_ch01_howto1_answersheet* file and save the file as **lastname_firstname_ch01_howto1_answersheet**

> Students get prepared for professional and personal success with these **Digital Literacy** and **Essential Job Skills** How-To projects.

> **Career Spotlight**—Each chapter provides an interesting career option based on chapter content

---

To create a Facebook Page, you need a personal Facebook account. Facebook's Terms of Service permit you to have only one personal Facebook account, but you can create multiple Facebook Pages. So, for example, a college representative might create a page for each department, club, or office. Once you are logged in to your personal account, the option *Create Page* can

be found in the menu options. You can choose from several page categories (Figure 8.30). A page for a business or an organization will have different features than a page for a person or cause. When you create a page, read the Facebook Pages terms carefully. Customize your page with a profile picture and header image that represents your brand.

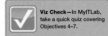
FIGURE 8.30 Create a Page Categories

 CAREER SPOTLIGHT
JOBS

BLOGGER—Although many blogs are personal in nature and earn the writer no compensation, some lucky folks are professional bloggers. These bloggers may be paid by a company to blog about a product or provide news or reviews, and their blogs are usually part of a bigger website. Some professional bloggers use their blogs to drive customers to their other products. Successful bloggers monetize the content on their sites in several ways, including placing ads and links to other sites. A professional blog may earn money by using Google AdSense to place ads and links on it. It takes a lot of time and work to write a good blog and even more to make money doing it.

Running Project

Select a local business that you regularly patronize or are interested in learning about, and search the web for evidence of online brand marketing. Does this business have a social media presence on Facebook, Google, Yahoo!, Twitter? How easy is it for a potential customer to locate information about the business? What advice would you give to this business to improve its online presence?

2 Things You Need To Know	Key Terms
• Organizations should maintain an online presence that includes both a traditional website and social media.	hashtag
• Successful search engine optimization (SEO) makes a website easier to find.	search engine optimization (SEO)

 Viz Check—In MyITLab, take a quick quiz covering Objectives 4–7.

> **Viz Check quizzes**—Each chapter includes two short online quizzes covering 3–5 objectives

How to Projects—Each chapter provides two step-by-step projects, complete with visual instructions, to complete interesting and useful items

How to Videos—Each How to Project has a corresponding video walk-through of the project

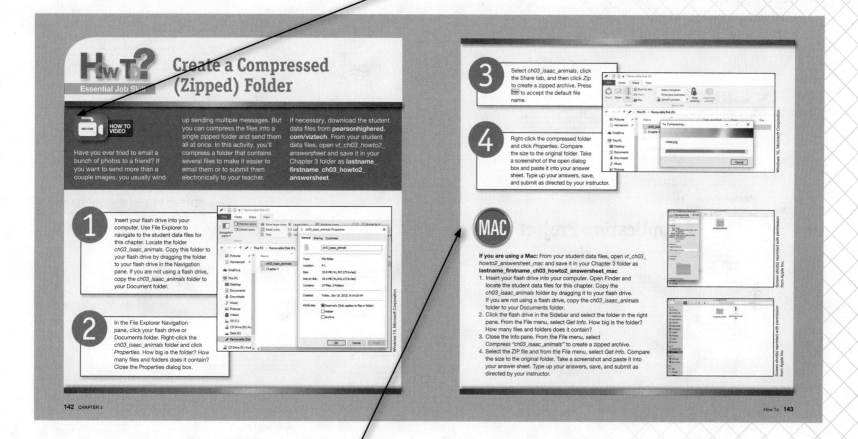

Mac coverage—Where appropriate, instructions and solutions are included so Mac users can complete the exercises

The **End-of-Chapter content** ranges from traditional review exercises to application and hands-on projects that have students working independently, collaboratively, and online

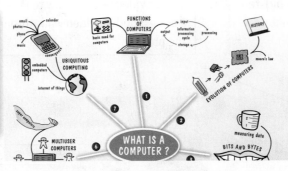

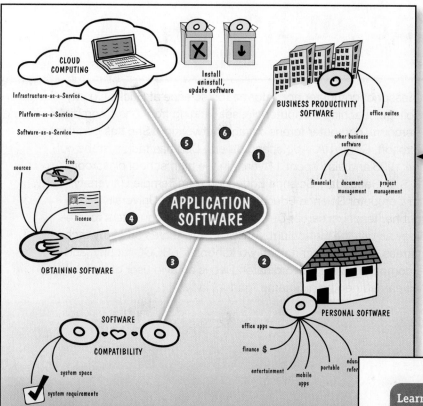

Mind maps are visual outlines of the chapter content, organized by objectives. They help students organize and remember the information they learned

Learn It Online

- Visit **pearsonhighered.com/viztech** for student data files
- Find simulations, VizClips, and additional study materials in **MyITLab**
- Be sure to check out the **Tech Bytes** weekly news feed for current topics to review and discuss

Objectives Recap

1. Identify Types and Uses of Business Productivity Software
2. Identify Types and Uses of Personal Software
3. Assess a Computer System for Software Compatibility
4. Compare Various Ways of Obtaining Software
5. Discuss the Importance of Cloud Computing
6. Install, Uninstall, and Update Software

Key Terms

application software 53
bug 99
cell 57
cloud 86
cloud computing 86
cloud service provider (CSP) 87
database 59
document management system (DMS) 61
donationware 83
EULA (end-user license agreement) 83
field 59
form 59
freeware 83
Gantt chart 62
hotfix 99
Infrastructure-as-a-Service (IaaS) 87
office application suite 55
open source 65

patch 99
personal information manager (PIM) 60
Platform-as-a-Service (PaaS) 87
platform neutral 95
portable apps 71
project management software 62
query 59
record 59
report 59
retail software 83
service pack 99
shareware 83
Software-as-a-Service (SaaS) 88
spreadsheet 57
system requirements 80
table 59
word processor 55

Summary

1. **Identify Types and Uses of Business Productivity Software**

   The most common business software is an office application suite—which may include a word processor, spreadsheet, presentation program, database, and personal information manager. Other business applications include financial software, document management, and project management software.

2. **Identify Types and Uses of Personal Software**

   Personal software includes office applications, especially word processors, spreadsheets, and presentation programs. Other personal applications include entertainment and multimedia software such as media managers, video and photo editing software, and video games. Financial and tax preparation software as well as educational and reference software are also popular. You can run portable apps from a flash drive and take them with you.

3. **Assess a Computer System for Software Compatibility**

   Before purchasing and installing software, you should research the system requirements needed to run the program and compare them to your system specifications using the System Control Panel.

4. **Compare Various Ways of Obtaining Software**

   You can obtain software from brick-and-mortar and online stores, publisher websites, and download websites. Download mobile apps only from trusted markets. It's important to read the EULA to understand the software license restrictions.

5. **Discuss the Importance of Cloud Computing**

   Cloud computing moves hardware and software into the cloud, or Internet. Cloud computing allows you to access applications and data from any web-connected computer. Some benefits include lower cost, easier maintenance, security, and collaboration.

6. **Install, Uninstall, and Update Software**

   Managing the programs on your computer includes installing, uninstalling, and updating the software. You can install programs through an app store, by using media, or by downloading it from a website. Updating software fixes bugs, adds features, or improves compatibility. You should uninstall software using the program's uninstaller.

About the Author

Debra is a professor of computer and information science at Bucks County Community College, teaching computer classes ranging from basic computer literacy to cybercrime, computer forensics, and networking. She has certifications from Microsoft, CompTIA, Apple, and others. Deb has taught at the college level since 1996 and also spent 11 years in the high school classroom. She holds a B.S. in Secondary Science Education from Temple University and an M.A. in Computer Science Education from Arcadia University.

Throughout her teaching career Deb has worked with educators to integrate technology across the curriculum. At BCCC she serves on many technology committees, presents technology workshops for BCCC faculty, and serves as the computer science coordinator. Deb is an avid user of technology, which has earned her the nickname "gadget lady."

Dedication

This project would not have been possible without the help and support of many people. I cannot express how grateful I am to all of you. Thank you.

My team at Pearson—Jenifer, Cheryl, Emily, Laura, and everyone else: you have been amazing, helping to bring my vision to reality and teaching me so much along the way.

My colleagues and students at Bucks County Community College: for your suggestions and encouragement throughout this process. You inspire me every day.

And most importantly—my family. My husband and sons for your patience, help, and love—even when it meant taking a photo "right this minute," or reading a chapter when you wanted to be doing something else, or missing me while I was away. And the rest of my family and friends who agreed to let me use their photos throughout the book. I couldn't have done this without your love and support.

And finally my dad—who taught me to love technology and not be afraid to try new things. I miss you and love you, daddy.

Reviewers of All Editions

Phil Valvalides   Guilford Technical Community College

Svetlana Marzelli   Atlantic Cape Community College

Pat Lyon   Tomball College

Arta Szathmary   Bucks County Community College

June Lane   Bucks County Community College

Ralph Hunsberger   Bucks County Community College

Sue McCrory   Missouri State

Laura White   University of West Florida

Karen Allen   Communtiy College of RI

Ralph Argiento   Guilford Technical Community College

Kuan Chen   Purdue University Calumet

Carin Chuang   Purdue University North Central

Christie Jahn Hovey   Lincoln Land Community College

Dr. Seth Powless   University of Toledo

Amiya K. Samantray   Marygrove College

**Special thanks to Lisa Hawkins,
Frederick Community College**

Mimi Spain   Southern Maine Community College

Kathie O'Brien   North Idaho College

Pat Franco   Los Angeles Valley College

Claire Amorde   Florida Institute Of Technology

Michael Haugrud   Minnesota State University Moorhead

Anjay Adhikari   Miami Dade College

Lynne Lyon   Durham College

Kate Le Grand   Broward College

Carolyn Barren   Macomb Community College

Bob Benavedis   Collins College

Theresa Hayes   Broward College

Mary Fleming   Ivy Tech Community College

Penny Cypert   Tarrant County College

Bernice Eng   Brookdale Community College

Deb Fells   Mesa Community College

Karen Allen   Bunker Hill Community College

Beverly Amer   Northern Arizona University

Michael Beddoes   Salt Lake Community College

Leilani Benoit   New Mexico State University

Gina Bowers   Harrisburg Area Community College

Linda Collins   Mesa Community College

Fred D'Angelo   Pima Community College

Robert Devoe Peterson   Fresno City College

Hedy Fossenkemper   Paradise Valley Community College

Rachelle Hall   Glendale Community College

Terri Helfand   Chaffey College

Ilga Higbee   Black Hawk College

Kay Johnson   Community College of Rhode Island

Darrel Karbginsky   Chemeketa Community College

Susan Katz   University of Bridgeport

Sherry Kersey   Hillsborough Community College

Ellen Kessler   Harrisburg Area Community College

Kate Legrand   Broward Community College

Mike Lehrfeld   Brevard Community College

Jian Lin   Eastern Connecticut State University

Nicole Lytle   California State University, San Bernadino

Peggy Menna   Community College of Rhode Island

Deborah Meyer   Saint Louis Community College, Forest Park

Pam Silvers   Asheville-Buncombe Technical Community College

Will Smith   Tulsa Community College

Lynne Stuhr   Trident Technical College

Ann Taff   Tulsa Community College

Jim Taggart   Atlantic Cape Community College

Michelle Vlaich Lee   Greenville Technical College

VISUALIZING
TECHNOLOGY

Blackday/Fotolia

What Is a Computer?

In This Chapter

If you've gone grocery shopping, put gas in your car, watched a weather report on TV, or used a microwave oven today, then you've interacted with a computer. Most of us use computers every day, often without even realizing it. Computers have become so commonplace that we don't even consider them computers. In this chapter, we discuss what a computer is and look at the development of computers in the past few centuries. After reading this chapter, you will recognize the different types of computing devices and their impact on everyday life.

Objectives

1 **Explain the Functions of a Computer**

2 **Describe the Evolution of Computer Hardware**

3 **Describe How Computers Represent Data Using Binary Code**

4 **List the Various Types and Characteristics of Personal Computers**

5 **Give Examples of Other Personal Computing Devices**

6 **List the Various Types and Characteristics of Multiuser Computers**

7 **Explain Ubiquitous Computing and Convergence**

Running Project

In this project, you'll explore computers used in everyday life. Look for instructions as you complete each article. For most articles, there is a series of questions for you to research. At the conclusion of the chapter, you'll submit your responses to the questions raised.

Sergey Nivens/Fotolia

What Does a Computer Do?

Explain the Functions of a Computer

A **computer** is a programmable machine that converts raw **data** into useful **information**. Raw data includes numbers, words, pictures, or sounds that represent facts about people, events, things, or ideas. A toaster can never be anything more than a toaster—it has one function—but a computer can be a calculator, a media center, a communications center, a classroom, and much more. The ability to change its programming distinguishes a computer from any other machine.

Necessity is the Mother of Invention

The original computers were people, not machines, and the mathematical tables they computed tended to be full of errors. The technical and scientific advancements of the Industrial Revolution at the end of the 19th century led to a growing need for this type of hand-calculated information and to the development of the first mechanical computers. Computers automated the tedious work of computing such things as tide charts and navigation tables.

In the early 19th century, mathematician Charles Babbage designed a mechanical computer called an **Analytical Engine**, which could be programmed using punch cards. **Punch cards** are stiff pieces of paper that convey information by the presence or absence of holes. Punch cards were developed by Joseph Marie Jacquard, as part of the Jacquard loom, to manufacture textiles with complex patterns (Figure 1.1). The Analytical Engine would have been the first mechanical computer, but the technology didn't exist at the time to build it. In his 1864 book *Passages from the Life of a Philosopher*, Babbage wrote, "The whole of the development and operations of analysis are now capable of being executed by machinery. As soon as an Analytical Engine exists, it will necessarily guide the future course of science*." In 2011, a group of researchers at London's Science Museum began a project to build Babbage's computer. The project will take at least 10 years and cost millions of dollars.

Mathematician Ada Lovelace, a contemporary of Babbage, wrote a program for the Analytical Engine to calculate a series of Bernoulli numbers—a sequence of rational numbers used in number theory. Because of her efforts, many consider her the first computer programmer. Lovelace never tested the program because there were no machines capable of running it; however, when run on a computer today, her program yields the correct mathematical results. In 1979, the Ada computer language was named in her honor.

In 1936, mathematician Alan Turing wrote a paper titled *On Computable Numbers*, in which he introduced the concept of machines that could perform mathematical computations—later called **Turing machines**. In 1950, he developed the **Turing test**, which tests a machine's ability to display intelligent behavior. It took 64 years for the first computers to pass the Turing test, but it happened in 2014. Many consider Alan Turing to be the father of computer science and **artificial intelligence**—the branch of science concerned with making computers behave like humans. In 2014, the film *The Imitation Game* chronicled Alan Turing and other mathematicians' attempts during World War II to crack the Enigma code used by the Germans to encrypt communications.

Mark Scheuern/Alamy

FIGURE 1.1 Punch cards used to create textile patterns in a Jacquard loom.

*Babbage, Charles. Passages from the Life of a Philosopher. Longman, Green, Longman, Roberts, & Green. London. 1864.

Geoghan, Debra. Visualizing Technology Complete, 4e. Pearson Education, 2014.

STORAGE: The raw data is stored temporarily until it can be processed. The processed information is stored for later retrieval.

INPUT: Data is collected from a customer order form.

OUTPUT: The processed data—now information—is output to the store employee to fulfill the order.

PROCESSING: The data is manipulated, or processed, so it can be used to evaluate the customer's order.

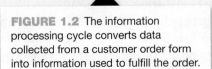

FIGURE 1.2 The information processing cycle converts data collected from a customer order form into information used to fulfill the order.

THE INFORMATION PROCESSING CYCLE

Computers convert data into information by using the **information processing cycle (IPC)**. The four steps of the IPC are input, processing, storage, and output. Raw data entered into the system during the input stage is processed, or manipulated, to create useful information. The information is stored for later retrieval and then returned to the user in the output stage. Figure 1.2 shows an example of how this works.

It was nearly a century after Babbage designed his Analytical Engine before the first working mechanical computers were built. From that point, it took only about 40 years to go from those first-generation machines to the current fourth-generation systems.

Running Project

Many developments of the Industrial Revolution helped pave the way for modern computers, such as the Jacquard loom. Use the Internet to find out how the following people also contributed: George Boole, Vannevar Bush, Nikola Tesla, and Gottfried Wilhelm Leibniz.

4 Things You Need to Know

- Computers are programmable machines.
- The four steps of the information processing cycle are input, processing, storage, and output.
- The IPC converts raw data into useful information.
- Artificial intelligence is the science of making computers behave like humans.

Key Terms

Analytical Engine

artificial intelligence

computer

data

information

information processing cycle (IPC)

punch card

Turing machine

Turing test

Capture a Screenshot of Your Desktop

HOW TO VIDEO

Throughout this book, you will be directed to provide screenshots of the work you have done. This is quite easy to do and is useful in other situations. For example, it's helpful for providing directions on how to do something or for keeping a record of an error message that appears on your screen. Windows includes a program called the Snipping Tool that you can use to capture a screenshot. Macs include the Grab tool.

The Windows Snipping Tool can capture four types of snips:
- **Free-form Snip:** Allows you to draw boundaries around an object for a snip
- **Rectangular Snip:** Allows you to draw a rectangle around an object for a snip
- **Window Snip:** Captures a selected window for a snip
- **Full-screen Snip:** Captures the whole screen for a snip

You can save your screenshots, email them, paste them into documents, and annotate and highlight them by using the buttons on the Snipping Tool toolbar. If necessary, download the student data files from **pearsonhighered. com/viztech**. From your student data files, open the *vt_ch01_howto1_answersheet* file and save the file as **lastname_firstname_ch01_howto1_answersheet**

1 From your student data files, right-click the file *vt_ch01_friend*, point to *Open with*, and then click *Windows Photo Viewer* or *Photo Gallery*.

2 In the Windows search box, type **snip** and then, in the search results, click *Snipping Tool*.

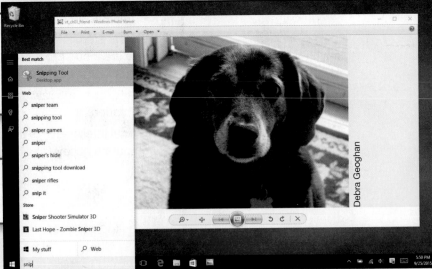

Windows Photo Viewer, Windows 10, Microsoft Corporation

Debra Geoghan

3 In the Snipping Tool window, click the drop-down arrow next to *New* and click *Free-form Snip*. Drag the mouse to draw a line around the dog's head with the Snipping Tool scissors. Switch to your answer sheet and paste the snip under **Free-form Snip**. You can resize the image to fit your answer sheet.

Debra Geoghan

4 In the Snipping Tool window, click the drop-down arrow next to *New* and click *Rectangular Snip*. Drag the box around the dog's head and release the mouse button. Paste the rectangular snip into your document under **Rectangular Snip**. Use the Snipping Tool to capture a Window Snip and a Full-screen Snip of the dog and paste both in your document. In a paragraph, describe the difference between the snips you took. Save the file and submit your file as directed by your instructor.

If you are using a Mac:

1. From your student data files, double-click the file *vt_ch01_friend* to open it in Preview. (Note: If the image opens in another program, it is still okay.)
2. Use Launchpad to open Grab, located in the *Other* folder.
3. From the *Capture* menu, click *Selection*, *Window*, or *Screen*, as appropriate. Follow the onscreen directions to take each capture. Once you have captured each image, use the *Edit* menu to copy the capture and paste it into your answer sheet. In a paragraph, describe the difference between the grabs you took. Save the file and submit your file as directed by your instructor.

Debra Geoghan

BillionPhotos.com/Fotolia

A Brief History of Computers

2 Describe the Evolution of Computer Hardware

In this article, we look at the evolution of computers in the past century—from the massive first-generation machines of the 1930s and 1940s to the modern fourth-generation devices—and how Moore's Law has predicted the exponential growth of technology.

History of Computers

Computers have come a long way since Babbage and Turing. Between the mid-19th and mid-20th centuries, the Industrial Revolution gave way to the Information Age. Since that time, the pace of technology has grown faster than it ever has before. **ENIAC (Electronic Numerical Integrator and Computer)**, built at the University of Pennsylvania from 1943 to 1946, is considered the first working, digital, general-purpose computer (Figure 1.3).

FIGURE 1.3 ENIAC was the first working, digital, general-purpose computer.

Pictorial Press/Alamy

FIRST-GENERATION COMPUTERS

During the 1930s and 1940s, several electromechanical and electronic computers were built. These first-generation computers were massive in size and used vacuum tubes and manual switches to process data. **Vacuum tubes**, which resemble incandescent lightbulbs, give off a lot of heat and are notoriously unreliable. ENIAC used about 18,000 vacuum tubes, weighed almost 30 tons, and occupied about 1,800 square feet. Originally created to calculate artillery firing tables, ENIAC wasn't completed until after the war ended and was reprogrammed to solve a range of other problems, such as atomic energy calculations, weather predictions, and wind-tunnel design. The programming was done by manipulating switches and took six programmers several days to complete.

The Harvard Mark I, also known as the IBM Automatic Sequence Controlled Calculator, was a general-purpose digital calculator used by the U.S. Navy toward the end of World War II. It was 51 feet long and 8 feet tall. Grace Hopper worked on the Mark I and was one of the first computer programmers. Hopper is credited with coining the term *bug* to refer to a glitch in a computer program.

Important first-generation computers include the Z1 and Z3 built in Germany; the Colossus machines in the United Kingdom; and the Atanasoff–Berry Computer (ABC), the Harvard Mark 1, ENIAC, and UNIVAC in the United States (Table 1.1).

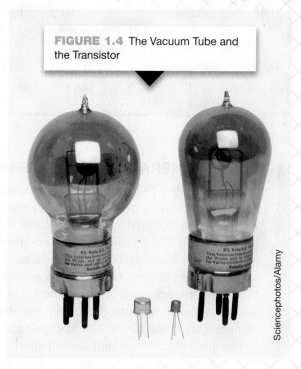

FIGURE 1.4 The Vacuum Tube and the Transistor

Sciencephotos/Alamy

SECOND-GENERATION COMPUTERS

Invented in 1947, **transistors** are tiny electronic switches. The use of transistors in place of vacuum tubes enabled second-generation computers in the 1950s and 1960s to be more powerful, smaller, more reliable, and reprogrammed in far less time than first-generation computers. Figure 1.4 illustrates the difference between the size of a vacuum tube and a transistor.

TABLE 1.1 Important First-Generation Computers

Date	Computer	Origin	Creator	Description
1936–1941	Z1–Z3	Germany	Konrad Zuse	The Z1 through Z3 were mechanical, programmable computers. Working in isolation in Germany, Konrad Zuse didn't receive the support of the Nazi government, and his computers were destroyed during the war.
1942	Atanasoff–Berry Computer (ABC)	United States	Professor John Atanasoff and graduate student Clifford Berry at Iowa State College	The ABC was never fully functional, but Atanasoff won a patent dispute against John Mauchly (ENIAC), and Atanasoff was declared the inventor of the electronic digital computer.
1944	Colossus	United Kingdom	Tommy Flowers	Used by code-breakers to translate encrypted German messages, these computers were destroyed after the war and kept secret until the 1970s.
1944	Harvard Mark 1	United States	Designed by Howard Aiken and programmed by Grace Hopper at Harvard University	The Mark 1 was used by the U.S. Navy for gunnery and ballistic calculations until 1959.
1946	ENIAC	United States	Presper Eckert and John Mauchly at the University of Pennsylvania	ENIAC was the first working, digital, general-purpose computer.
1951	UNIVAC	United States	Eckert/Mauchly	The world's first commercially available computer, UNIVAC was famous for predicting the outcome of the 1952 presidential election.

Geoghan, Debra. Visualizing Technology Complete, 4e. Pearson Education, 2014.

THIRD-GENERATION COMPUTERS

Developed in the 1960s, **integrated circuits** are chips that contain large numbers of tiny transistors fabricated into a semiconducting material called silicon (Figure 1.5). Third-generation computers used multiple integrated circuits to process data and were even smaller, faster, and more reliable than their predecessors, although there was much overlap between second- and third-generation technologies in the 1960s. The Apollo Guidance Computer, used in the moon landing missions, was designed using transistors, but over time, the design was modified to use integrated circuits instead. The 2000 Nobel Prize in physics was awarded for the invention of the integrated circuit.

FIGURE 1.5 Integrated Circuits on a Circuit Board

Brian Kinney/Fotolia

FOURTH-GENERATION COMPUTERS

The integrated circuit made the development of the **microprocessor** possible in the 1970s. A microprocessor is a complex integrated circuit that contains the **central processing unit (CPU)** of a computer (Figure 1.6). The CPU functions as the brain of a computer. The first microprocessor, developed in 1971, was as powerful as ENIAC. Modern fourth-generation personal computers use microprocessors. Microprocessors are found in everything from smartphones to automobiles and refrigerators.

Singkham/Fotolia

FIGURE 1.6 Fourth-generation computers use microprocessors.

FIND OUT MORE

Integrated Circuits

Play the integrated circuit game nobelprize.org/educational/physics/integrated_circuit to learn more about this invention. Who invented the integrated circuit? Where might you still find a vacuum tube today? How did the invention of the transistor affect the radio? What's the significance of the handheld calculator?

Nobel Media AB

Moore's Law

In 1965, Intel cofounder Gordon Moore observed that the number of transistors that could be placed on an integrated circuit had doubled roughly every two years. This observation, known as **Moore's Law**, predicted this exponential growth would continue. The current trend is closer to doubling every 18 months. As a result of new technologies, such as building 3D silicon processors or using carbon nanotubes in place of silicon (Figure 1.7), this pace will likely continue for another 10 to 20 years. The increase in the capabilities of integrated circuits directly affects the processing speed and storage capacity of modern electronic devices.

Moore stated in a 1996 article: "More than anything, once something like this gets established, it becomes more or less a self-fulfilling prophecy. The Semiconductor Industry Association puts out a technology road map, which continues this [generational improvement] every three years. Everyone in the industry recognizes that if you don't stay on essentially that curve they will fall behind. So it sort of drives itself.*" Thus, Moore's Law became a technology plan that guides the industry. Over the past several decades, the end of Moore's Law has been predicted. Each time, new technological advances have kept it going. Moore himself admits that exponential growth can't continue forever.

In less than a century, computers have gone from being massive, unreliable, and costly machines to being an integral part of almost everything we do. As technology has improved, the size and costs have dropped as the speed, power, and reliability have grown. Today, the chip inside your cell phone has more processing power than that first microprocessor developed in 1971. Technology that was science fiction just a few decades ago is now commonplace.

*Moore, Gordon E. 1996. "Some Personal Perspectives on Research in the Semiconductor Industry," in Rosenbloom, Richard S., and William J. Spencer (Eds.). Engines of Innovation: U.S. Industrial Research at the End of an Era. Harvard College

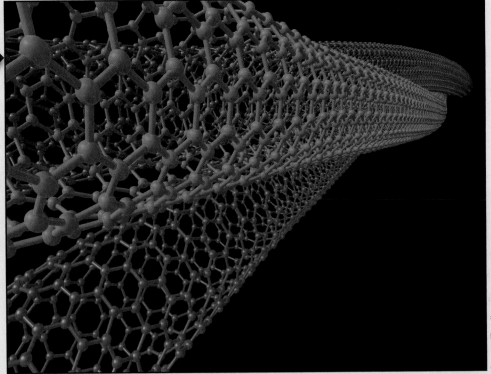

FIGURE 1.7 Carbon nanotubes may someday replace silicon in integrated circuits.

Ogwen/Fotolia

GREEN COMPUTING
Smart Homes

The efficient and eco-friendly use of computers and other electronics is called **green computing**. Smart homes and smart appliances help save energy and, as a result, are good for both the environment and your pocketbook.

Smart homes use home automation to control lighting, heating and cooling, security, entertainment, and appliances. Such a system can be programmed to turn various components on and off at set times to maximize energy efficiency. If you're away on vacation or have to work late, you can remotely activate a smart home by phone or over the Internet. Some utility companies offer lower rates during off-peak hours, so programming your dishwasher and other appliances to run during those times can save you money and help energy utility companies manage the power grid, potentially reducing the need for new power plants.

Smart appliances plug into the **smart grid**—a network for delivering electricity to consumers that includes communication technology to manage electricity distribution efficiently. Smart appliances monitor signals from the power company, and when the electric grid system is stressed, can react by cutting back on their power consumption.

Adrian Sherratt/Alamy

Running Project

Use the Internet to look up current microprocessors. What companies produce them? Visit **computer.howstuffworks.com/microprocessor.htm** and read the article. How many transistors were found on the first home computer processor? What was the name of the processor, and when was it introduced?

5 Things You Need To Know

- First-generation computers used vacuum tubes.
- Second-generation computers used transistors.
- Third-generation computers used integrated circuits (chips).
- Fourth-generation computers use microprocessors.
- Moore's Law states that the number of transistors that can be placed on an integrated circuit doubles roughly every two years—although today it is closer to every 18 months.

Key Terms

central processing unit (CPU)

ENIAC (Electronic Numerical Integrator and Computer)

integrated circuit

microprocessor

Moore's Law

transistor

vacuum tube

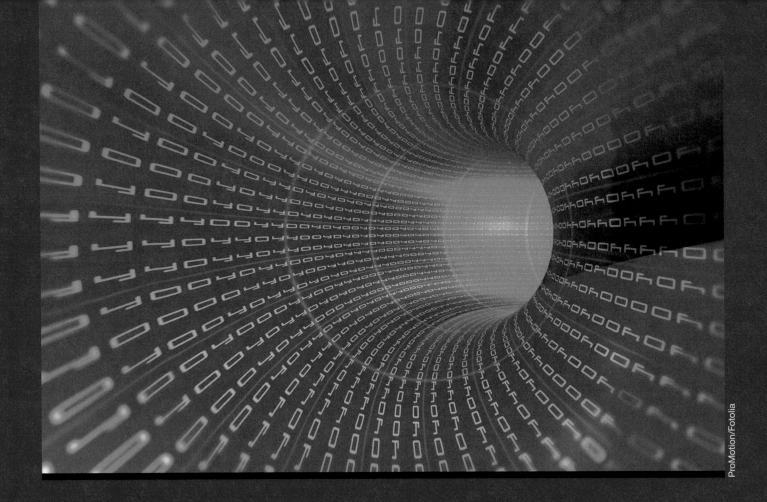

ProMotion/Fotolia

Bits and Bytes

3

Describe How Computers Represent Data Using Binary Code

Humans have 10 digits, which is why we find the decimal, or base 10, number system to be natural. Remember how you used your fingers and toes to do math when you were a kid? Computers don't have fingers; they have switches and use the **binary**, or **base 2, number system**, which has only two digits: 0 and 1.

VIZ CLIP

Bits and Bytes

Binary Code

Computers don't speak English—or Spanish, Chinese, or Greek, for that matter—so how does a computer understand what you enter? On a typewriter, when you press the *A* key, you get an A on the paper, but computers only understand 0s and 1s, so when you press the *A* key, it must somehow be represented by 0s and 1s. Digital data is represented using **binary code**.

Binary code works like a bank of light switches. If you have only a single light switch in a room, there are two possible states: The light can be on, or it can be off. This code works in situations with only two possibilities, such as yes/no or true/false, but it fails when there are more than two choices, such as with vanilla/chocolate/strawberry. Adding another switch increases the possible combinations by a factor of two, which equals four possibilities. A third switch, or bit, gives us eight possibilities, and so on (Table 1.2). A **bit**, short for binary digit, is the smallest unit of digital information. Eight bits equal a **byte**, which gives us 256 possibilities. A byte is used to represent a single character in modern computer systems. For example, when you press the *A* key, the binary code 01000001

(65 in decimal) is sent to the computer.

ASCII (American Standard Code for Information Interchange) was developed in the 1960s using a 7-bit system that represented 128 characters and included English upper- and lowercase alphabet symbols, numbers 0 through 9, punctuation, and a few special characters. ASCII was later expanded to an 8-bit extended set with 256 characters, but ASCII needed to be adapted to be used for other languages, and many extended sets were developed. The most common extended ASCII set is **Unicode**. Unicode is the standard on the Internet and includes codes for most of the world's written languages, mathematical systems, and special characters. It has codes for more than 100,000 characters. The first 256 characters are the same in both ASCII and Unicode; however, the characters in the last rows in Table 1.3 include Latin, Greek, and Cyrillic symbols, which are represented only in Unicode.

TABLE 1.2 A binary code using 8 switches, or bits, has 256 different possible combinations.

Number of Bits (switches)	Possibilities	Power of Two
1	2	2^1
2	4	2^2
3	8	2^3
4	16	2^4
5	32	2^5
6	64	2^6
7	128	2^7
8	256	2^8

Geoghan, Debra. Visualizing Technology Complete, 4e. Pearson Education, 2014.

TABLE 1.3 ASCII and Unicode Representations

Character	ASCII (in decimal)	Unicode (in decimal)	Binary Code
#	35	35	00100011
$	36	36	00100100
0	48	48	00110000
1	49	49	00110001
A	65	65	10000001
B	66	66	1000010
a	97	97	1100001
b	98	98	1100010
œ		339	
r'		341	
		945	

Geoghan, Debra. Visualizing Technology Complete, 4e. Pearson Education, 2014.

Measuring Data

Bits (b) are used to measure data transfer rates such as an Internet connection, and bytes (B) are used to measure file size and storage capacity. The decimal prefixes of *kilo*, *mega*, *giga*, *tera*, *peta*, and so on are added to the base unit (*bit* or *byte*) to indicate larger values. Binary prefixes *kibi*, *mebi*, and *gibi*, have been adopted, although their use isn't widespread. A megabyte (MB) is equal to 1,000,000 bytes, and a mebibyte (MiB) is equal to 1,048,576 bytes, a slightly larger value. Tables 1.4 and 1.5 compare the two systems.

A megabyte (MB) can hold about 500 pages of plain text, but a single picture taken with a digital camera can be more than 25 megabytes in size. As the types of files we save have changed from plain text to images, music, and video, file sizes have become larger, and the need for storage has grown dramatically—but, fundamentally, all files are still just 0s and 1s.

TABLE 1.4 Decimal Storage Capacity Prefixes

Decimal Prefix	Symbol	Decimal Value	
		Exponential	Numeric
kilo	K or k	10^3	1,000
mega	M	10^6	1,000,000
giga	G	10^9	1,000,000,000
tera	T	10^{12}	1,000,000,000,000
peta	P	10^{15}	1,000,000,000,000,000
exa	E	10^{18}	1,000,000,000,000,000,000
zetta	Z	10^{21}	1,000,000,000,000,000,000,000
yotta	Y	10^{24}	1,000,000,000,000,000,000,000,000

Geoghan, Debra. Visualizing Technology Complete, 4e. Pearson Education, 2014.

TABLE 1.5 Binary Storage Capacity Prefixes

Binary Prefix	Symbol	Binary Exponent	Decimal Value
kibi	Ki	2^{10}	1,024
mebi	Mi	2^{20}	1,048,576
gibi	Gi	2^{30}	1,073,741,824
tebi	Ti	2^{40}	1,099,511,627,776
pebi	Pi	2^{50}	1,125,899,906,842,624
exbi	Ei	2^{60}	1,152,921,504,606,846,976
zebi	Zi	2^{70}	1,180,591,620,717,411,303,424
yobi	Yi	2^{80}	1,208,925,819,614,629,174,706,176

Geoghan, Debra. Visualizing Technology Complete, 4e. Pearson Education, 2014.

Alen D/Fotolia

CAREER SPOTLIGHT

BIOINFORMATICS—Computers have become integral in almost every modern career. Nowhere is this more evident than in the field of biology. **Bioinformatics** is the application of information technology to the field of biology. Computers are used to analyze data, predict how molecules will behave, and maintain and search massive databases of information. The rapid growth of biological information over the past few decades has created a demand for new technologies and people who know how to use them. This field requires at least a four-year degree. If you have a strong interest in science and technology, bioinformatics might be a good career choice for you.

Alexander Raths/Shutterstock

Running Project

Use the Internet to research the usage of decimal and binary prefixes discussed in this chapter. Describe two instances when binary prefixes are more commonly used.

4 Things You Need to Know

- Computers use the binary (base 2) number system.
- ASCII and Unicode are binary code character sets.
- A bit is the smallest unit of digital information.
- A byte is equal to 8 bits and represents one character.

Key Terms

ASCII (American Standard Code for Information Interchange)

binary code

binary (base 2) number system

bit

byte

Unicode

Let's Get Personal

Objective

4

List the Various Types and Characteristics of Personal Computers

A **personal computer (PC)** is a small microprocessor-based computer used by one person at a time. Today, the term *personal computer* usually refers to a computer running a Windows operating system; however, Mac computers and those running Linux operating systems are also personal computers.

SIMULATION

What Is a Computer?

Desktop Computers

A **desktop computer** is a personal computer that fits into a workspace, such as a desk or counter. Desktops range in price from under $300 for basic personal systems, to thousands of dollars for cutting-edge machines used for video editing, gaming, and number crunching. Desktop computers offer the most speed, power, and upgradability for the lowest cost. A **workstation** is a high-end desktop computer or one that's attached to a network in a business setting.

An **all-in-one computer** is a compact desktop computer with an integrated monitor and system unit (Figure 1.8). Some all-in-ones are wall-mountable. All-in-ones save desktop real estate but may be difficult to upgrade because of their small size. They are popular in places where space is at a premium, such as emergency rooms, bank teller windows, and classrooms.

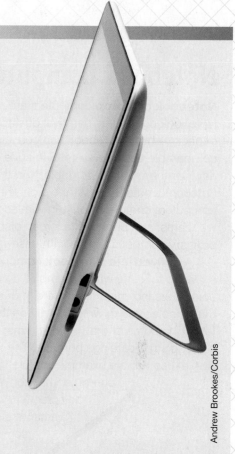

FIGURE 1.8 An all-in-one desktop computer with the components mounted behind the monitor is popular in settings in which desktop space is limited.

Andrew Brookes/Corbis

Xy/Fotolia

Notebook Computers

Notebook or **laptop** computers are portable personal computers. Notebook computers can rival desktops in power and storage capacity—but a notebook can cost significantly more than a comparable desktop system. In spite of the higher cost, notebooks have become more affordable, and thus more popular. In 2015, notebooks outsold desktops more than 2:1. Modern notebook computers come with built-in wireless networking capabilities, webcams, and bright widescreen displays, and can handle most ordinary computing tasks with ease.

A **convertible notebook** computer has a screen that can swivel to fold into what resembles a notepad or tablet. These computers include a touch screen or a special digital pen or **stylus** that enables you to write directly on the screen, making them useful for taking notes or drawing diagrams, and for making information such as sales catalogs portable. The Windows Continuum and Apple iPad Pro are examples of two-in-one notebooks—a portable computer that converts to a tablet by detaching the screen from the keyboard. A **tablet** is a handheld mobile device that falls somewhere between a notebook and a smartphone. A tablet has an LCD—liquid-crystal display—screen, a long battery life, and built-in wireless connectivity. Tablets are a good choice for travel. A tablet may have a detachable keyboard, making it more notebook-like with the keyboard in place. Tablets come with a variety of preinstalled **mobile applications**, or **mobile apps**—programs that extend the functionality of mobile devices. Thousands of apps can be downloaded and installed to make the device even more versatile. With these devices, you can edit documents, take photographs, surf the web, send and receive email, and watch videos. Cellular-enabled tablets use the same network as your smartphone to access the Internet. You need to purchase a data plan from your cellular carrier to use this feature.

The smallest type of notebook computer is a **netbook**. These lightweight, inexpensive computers are designed primarily for Internet access. Low-cost notebooks and subnotebooks have largely replaced netbooks. A **subnotebook** is a notebook computer that is thin and light, has high-end processing and video capabilities, and has a higher price tag to match. The screen on a subnotebook is typically larger than on a netbook, in the range of 13–15 inches. Ultrabooks that run Windows, Chromebooks, and Apple's Macbook Air are examples of subnotebooks (Figure 1.9).

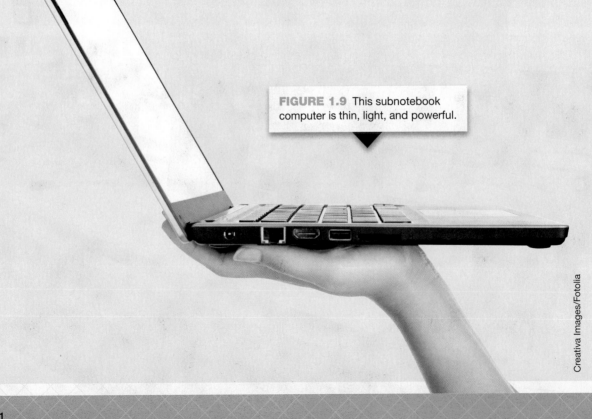

FIGURE 1.9 This subnotebook computer is thin, light, and powerful.

Creativa Images/Fotolia

MAC OR PC?

In the personal computer market, there are two main platforms of personal computers to choose from: Macs and PCs. A computer platform includes both the hardware and software that make up a computer system. What's the difference between the two, and which one should you choose? Most of the configurations of computers discussed in this chapter are available in both platforms. The primary difference between them is the operating system they run. An **operating system** is software that provides the user with an interface to communicate with the hardware and software on a computer. A computer can't run without an operating system installed. Operating systems are discussed in detail in another chapter.

Mac computers are built by Apple and run the OS X operating system. Using a program called Boot Camp that's included with OS X, users can also run Microsoft Windows on a Mac. Macs have a reputation for being secure, stable, and fun. They come with a variety of useful programs already installed and are very user-friendly. Macs are often used in creative businesses, such as advertising and graphic design, and are growing in popularity in the home market.

PCs can be built by any number of companies, including Sony, Asus, Lenovo, and Toshiba. PCs that run some version of the Windows or Linux operating systems constitute over 90 percent of the U.S. market share. Because PCs are produced by many manufacturers, they are available in numerous models, configurations, and price ranges. PCs can also run a vast selection of available software.

The type of computer you choose depends on many factors, including personal preferences, the types of software you use, compatibility with school or work computers, and cost. Figure 1.10 highlights some of the features of Macs and PCs.

Personal computers have become so commonplace that roughly 80 percent of U.S. households have at least one personal computer. In addition, tablet sales are soaring—and by 2014 they rivaled PC sales.

FIGURE 1.10 Comparing Macs and PCs

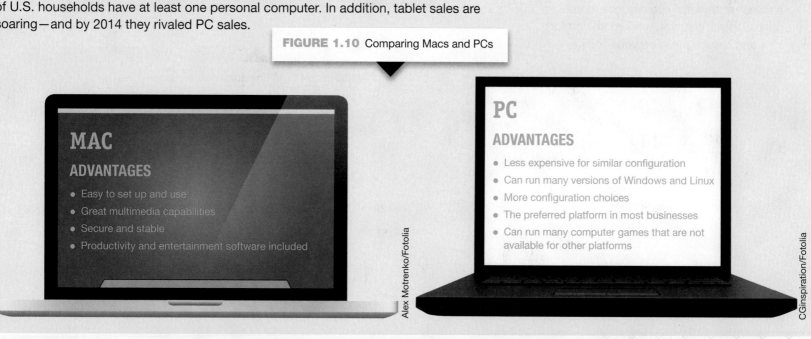

MAC
ADVANTAGES
- Easy to set up and use
- Great multimedia capabilities
- Secure and stable
- Productivity and entertainment software included

PC
ADVANTAGES
- Less expensive for similar configuration
- Can run many versions of Windows and Linux
- More configuration choices
- The preferred platform in most businesses
- Can run many computer games that are not available for other platforms

Ergonomics

Ergonomics is the study of the relationship between workers and their workspaces. An improperly set up workspace can affect your health, comfort, and productivity. Ergonomic design creates a work environment designed to reduce illnesses and musculoskeletal disorders. The furniture you use, the lighting in the room, and the position of your equipment all affect your work environment.

Your goal should be to keep your body in a neutral position, without twisting or turning to reach or see your screen. You should not need to lean forward, and your feet should be flat on the ground or on a footrest. Your monitor should be at or below eye level so you don't need to tilt your neck to see it, and the lighting shouldn't cause glare on your screen. The keyboard and mouse should be positioned so your arms are in a relaxed position, as shown in Figure 1.11. One important step that many people forget is to take regular breaks to stretch and move around. Whether you're writing a report for school, doing your income taxes, or playing a video game, following ergonomic design principles will help you work more comfortably and reduce strain on your body.

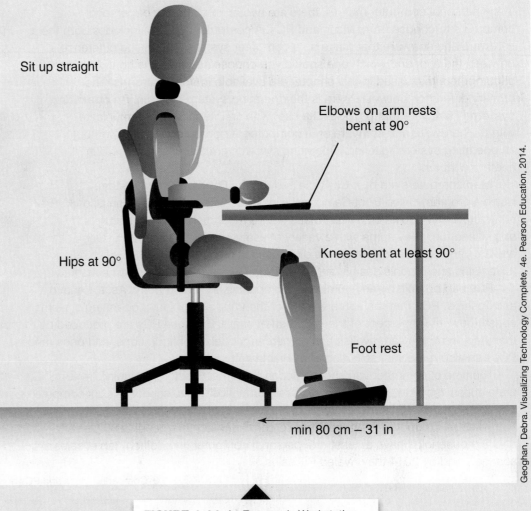

Sit up straight

Elbows on arm rests bent at 90°

Hips at 90°

Knees bent at least 90°

Foot rest

min 80 cm – 31 in

FIGURE 1.11 An Ergonomic Workstation

Geoghan, Debra. Visualizing Technology Complete, 4e. Pearson Education, 2014.

UNIVERSAL DESIGN

Universal design principles not only help create environments that accommodate people with disabilities, but also benefit those with no special needs. For example, wider doorways allow wheelchairs and walkers through and also make it easier to carry merchandise and move furniture. In technology, applying universal design means designing spaces that are easily accessible. This term also refers to input and output devices that can be used and adjusted by everyone. Devices should be simple and intuitive to use for everyone.

Running Project

It's hard to imagine a job that doesn't require a working knowledge of personal computers. Look up the term *digital literacy*. Use several different websites to get an idea of what this term means and then write up a description of digital literacy for the career that you plan to pursue.

5 Things You Need to Know

- Desktop computers give you the most bang for your buck.
- Notebook or laptop computers are portable PCs.
- Subnotebooks and netbooks are specialized notebook computers.
- Tablets fall somewhere between notebooks and smartphones.
- The primary difference between a Mac and a PC is the software.

Key Terms

all-in-one computer

convertible notebook

desktop computer

ergonomics

laptop

Mac

mobile application (mobile app)

netbook

notebook

operating system

personal computer (PC)

stylus

subnotebook

tablet

Universal design

workstation

 Viz Check—In MyITLab, take a quick quiz covering Objectives 1–4.

Ergonomics

Essential Job Skill

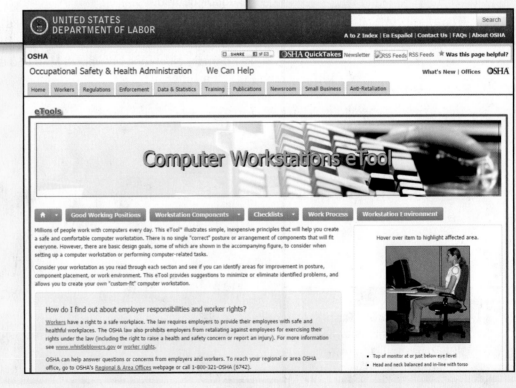
HOW TO VIDEO

Ergonomic design creates a work environment designed to reduce illnesses and musculoskeletal disorders. The OSHA website has a computer workstation checklist. In this activity, you will use the checklist to evaluate your workspace at home or school. If necessary, download the student data files from **pearsonhighered. com/viztech**. From your student data files, open the *vt_ch01_ howto2_answersheet* file and save the file as **lastname_firstname_ ch01_howto2_answersheet**

1 Open your browser and go to **www.osha.gov/SLTC/etools/ computerworkstations**.

UNITED STATES DEPARTMENT OF LABOR

Search

A to Z Index | En Español | Contact Us | FAQs | About OSHA

OSHA

SHARE | OSHA QuickTakes Newsletter | RSS Feeds RSS Feeds ★ Was this page helpful?

Occupational Safety & Health Administration   We Can Help

What's New | Offices OSHA

Home | Workers | Regulations | Enforcement | Data & Statistics | Training | Publications | Newsroom | Small Business | Anti-Retaliation

eTools

Computer Workstations eTool

🏠 | Good Working Positions | Workstation Components | Checklists | Work Process | Workstation Environment

Millions of people work with computers every day. This eTool* illustrates simple, inexpensive principles that will help you create a safe and comfortable computer workstation. There is no single "correct" posture or arrangement of components that will fit everyone. However, there are basic design goals, some of which are shown in the accompanying figure, to consider when setting up a computer workstation or performing computer-related tasks.

Consider your workstation as you read through each section and see if you can identify areas for improvement in posture, component placement, or work environment. This eTool provides suggestions to minimize or eliminate identified problems, and allows you to create your own "custom-fit" computer workstation.

Hover over item to highlight affected area.

How do I find out about employer responsibilities and worker rights?

Workers have a right to a safe workplace. The law requires employers to provide their employees with safe and healthful workplaces. The OSHA law also prohibits employers from retaliating against employees for exercising their rights under the law (including the right to raise a health and safety concern or report an injury). For more information see www.whistleblowers.gov or worker rights.

OSHA can help answer questions or concerns from employers and workers. To reach your regional or area OSHA office, go to OSHA's Regional & Area Offices webpage or call 1-800-321-OSHA (6742).

• Top of monitor at or just below eye level
• Head and neck balanced and in-line with torso

U.S Department of Labor, Occupational Safety & Health Administration - Computer Workstation Tool

2 Click **Good Working Positions** and read the information on this page. What does neutral body positioning mean, and what are the four reference postures?

U.S Department of Labor, Occupational Safety & Health Administration - Computer Workstation Tool

🏠 ▾ | **Good Working Positions** | **Workstation Components** ▾ | **Checklists** ▾ | **Work Process** | **Workstation Environment**

Good Working Positions

To understand the best way to set up a computer workstation, it is helpful to understand the concept of neutral body positioning. This is a comfortable working posture in which your joints are naturally aligned. Working with the body in a neutral position reduces stress and strain on the muscles, tendons, and skeletal system and reduces your risk of developing a musculoskeletal disorder (MSD). The following are important considerations when attempting to maintain neutral body postures while working at the computer workstation:

- *Hands, wrists,* and *forearms* are straight, in-line and roughly parallel to the floor.
- *Head* is level, or bent slightly forward, forward facing, and balanced. Generally it is in-line with the *torso*.
- *Shoulders* are relaxed and *upper arms* hang normally at the side of the body.
- *Elbows* stay in close to the body and are bent between 90 and 120 degrees.
- *Feet* are fully supported by the floor or a footrest may be used if the desk height is not adjustable.
- *Back* is fully supported with appropriate lumbar support when sitting vertical or leaning back slightly.
- *Thighs* and *hips* are supported by a well-padded seat and generally parallel to the floor.
- *Knees* are about the same height as the hips with the *feet* slightly forward.

3 Click the **Checklists** arrow and click **Evaluation**. Complete the checklist to evaluate your workspace. For each question that you answer no to, click the appropriate link to read the information on how to correct the problem. How did your workstation fare? What are some areas for improvement? How could you improve your score? When you have finished the checklist, click the link to Print Checklist. Save the checklist as a PDF file or Microsoft XPS file, depending on your browser and operating system configuration. Save the file as **lastname_firstname_ch01_howto2_checklist** Submit both the answer sheet and checklist files as directed by your instructor.

U.S Department of Labor, Occupational Safety & Health Administration - Computer Workstation Tool

🏠 ▾ | **Good Working Positions** | **Workstation Components** ▾ | **Checklists** ▾ | **Work Process** | **Workstation Environment**

Checklists » Evaluation

This checklist can help you create a safe and comfortable computer workstation. You can also use it in conjunction with the purchasing guide checklist. A "no" response indicates that a problem may exist. Refer to the appropriate section of the eTool for assistance and ideas about how to analyze and control the problem.

🖨 Print Checklist | Clear Form

☑ **WORKING POSTURES** - The workstation is designed or arranged for doing computer tasks so it allows your...

1. **Head** and **neck** to be upright, or in-line with the torso (not bent down/back). If "no" refer to Monitors, Chairs and Work Surfaces.
   ○ Yes   ○ No

2. **Head, neck,** and **trunk** to face forward (not twisted). If "no" refer to Monitors or Chairs.
   ○ Yes   ○ No

☑ **MONITOR** - Consider these points when evaluating the monitor. The monitor is designed or arranged for computer tasks so the...

1. **Top** of the screen is at or below eye level so you can read it without bending your head or neck down/back.
   ○ Yes   ○ No

2. **User with bifocals/trifocals** can read the screen without bending the head or neck backward.
   ○ Yes   ○ No

Stefano Garau/Fotolia

Beyond the Desktop

5 Give Examples of Other Personal Computing Devices

Today, the term *computer* no longer refers only to desktops used for office work. Many of us carry computers with us everywhere we go. In fact, mobile devices have become the primary computing devices for many people.

Mobile Devices

Mobile devices are portable, handheld computers used for business and entertainment and come in many different shapes and sizes—from smartphones to fitness monitors that you wear on your wrist. Some of these devices serve specialized functions, such as GPS navigation, while others, such as smartphones, are more general-purpose devices.

Oleksiy Mark/Fotolia

SMARTPHONES AND TABLETS

Mobile devices such as smartphones and tablets combine features such as Internet and email access, digital cameras, GPS and mapping tools, the ability to edit documents, and access to thousands of mobile apps. Mobile devices are useful when carrying a regular notebook computer isn't practical. Once primarily the tool of business professionals, smartphones have become indispensable to the rest of us as well. Mobile devices are the fastest-growing segment of personal computers.

WEARABLES AND GPS

Computers worn on the body are known as **wearables**. These hands-free computers are used for health monitoring, communications, military operations, and entertainment. Apple Watch is a general-purpose wearable computer (Figure 1.12).

Originally built by the military, the **Global Positioning System** or **GPS**, consists of 24 satellites operating at all time, plus several spares (Figure 1.13). These satellites transmit signals that are picked up by a GPS receiver on the ground, to determine the receiver's current location, time, and velocity through triangulation of the signals. Since the mid-1990s, GPS devices have been available for civilian use. There are scientific applications for GPS technology, such as surveying, map making, self-navigating robots, and clock synchronization. GPS is used in automobiles, airplanes, and boats for navigation and tracking. Many mobile apps use GPS for navigation, location services, and just plain fun. For example, some apps use your location to determine what information to display, such as discounts, local weather, or nearby restaurant recommendations.

FIGURE 1.12
The Apple Watch is a wearable computer.

Jacek Lasa/Alamy

FIGURE 1.13 The Global Positioning System (GPS) is a satellite-based navigation system composed of a network of 24 satellites placed into orbit by the U.S. Department of Defense.

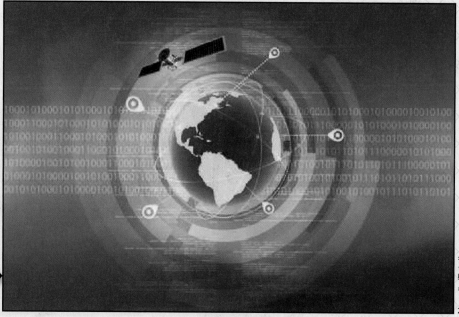

Nmedia/Fotolia

Umnola/Fotolia

Video Game Systems and Simulations

A **video game system** is a computer designed primarily to play games. The first arcade video games were released in the early 1970s, and video game systems for the home soon followed. Magnavox released its Odyssey game console in 1972. It was programmed to play 12 different games. Atari released a home version of Pong for the 1975 holiday season. Sold exclusively through Sears, Pong was the hottest gift of the year. For many people, video game systems were the first computers they had in their homes.

Current eighth-generation video game systems have high-end processing and graphics capabilities, and the abilities to play movies and music, enable online game play, and browse the Internet. Game consoles such as Microsoft Xbox One and Sony PlayStation 4 have built-in hard drives, can play DVDs and Blu-rays, and display high-definition video. Kinect for Xbox has motion and voice sensors that enable you to play certain games without holding a **game controller**—a device used to interact with a video game. Nintendo's Wii U is less powerful and less expensive than either the Xbox or the PlayStation. The Wii has motion-sensing controllers that give players unique gameplay experiences and interactivity.

The Wii has reached out to nontraditional markets, such as senior citizens and families with young children, by offering such games as bowling, tennis, Wii Fit, and Brain Age.

Handheld video games, such as the Nintendo 3DS XL and 2DS and NVIDIA SHIELD Portable, enable you to take your games wherever you go. You can download and watch movies, view photos and listen to music, and chat with friends over cellular or Wi-Fi wireless networks. Such systems include Internet capabilities, HD graphics, and a multicamera system that lets you take photos. The popularity of smartphones and tablets has reduced this market dramatically.

Video game systems aren't just for entertainment. In healthcare, medical students use video game simulations to learn to be better doctors, simulations help stroke patient rehab to improve fine motor reflexes, and surgeons use simulations to practice intricate techniques. In other applications, pilots train on flight simulators, business students solve complex problems, and biology students dissect virtual frogs. Simulations enable you to immerse yourself in a situation that may not be safe or accessible otherwise.

Rido/Fotolia

Geocaching

Geocaching is an electronic scavenger hunt played around the world. Geocachers hide geocaches and post GPS coordinates on the Internet. Other geocachers can then find geocaches using their own GPS devices. The geocaches have logbooks to sign and, often, small prizes. Geocachers who find a prize leave something else in return, and you never know what you'll find!

Visit geocaching.com to find geocaches near you. How many geocaches are there near you? Are they in an urban or rural area? How many are there globally? On your mobile device, search the app store for GPS. How many hits did you get? What types of apps are listed?

Groundspeak, Inc.

Running Project

Use the Internet to find out how medical students are using video game simulations. What are some of the medical schools using such systems? How are these systems used? How do professors and students feel about them? What other fields use simulators to train students?

4 Things You Need to Know	Key Terms
• Smartphones and tablets are handheld mobile devices. • GPS is a satellite-based navigation system. • Wearables are computers worn on the body. • Today's video game consoles are eighth-generation systems with high-end graphics and processing.	game controller geocaching GPS (global positioning system) mobile device video game system wearable

Boscorelli/Fotolia

Multiuser Computers

6 List the Various Types and Characteristics of Multiuser Computers

Multiuser computers are systems that allow multiple, simultaneous users to connect to them. The advantages of multiuser systems include centralized resources and security. Multiuser computers are more powerful than personal computers.

Servers

Servers are computers that provide services, such as Internet access, email, or file and print services, to client systems such as your home or office computer. A **client** is a computer that connects to or requests services from a server. Servers range in size and cost, from very small servers costing a few hundred dollars to massive enterprise servers costing hundreds of thousands of dollars (Figure 1.14).

The smallest multiuser computers are **minicomputers**, which support fewer than 200 users. Users connect to minicomputers via dumb terminals, which have no processing capabilities of their own. Minicomputers have widely been replaced by **midrange servers** that users connect to via personal computers. Midrange servers can perform complex calculations, store customer information and transactions, or host an email system for an organization. They can support hundreds of simultaneous users and are scalable, allowing for growth, as a company's needs change.

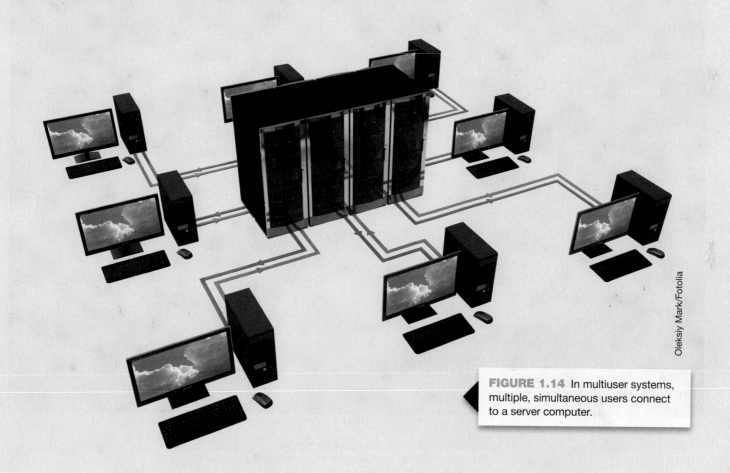

Oleksiy Mark/Fotolia

FIGURE 1.14 In multiuser systems, multiple, simultaneous users connect to a server computer.

Mainframes are large computers that can perform millions of transactions in a day. These are most commonly found in businesses that have massive amounts of data or transactions to process, such as banks and insurance companies. Mainframe computers have largely been replaced by **enterprise servers**, and the terms are sometimes used synonymously (Figure 1.15). These systems allow thousands of users to utilize the system concurrently.

Oleksiy Mark/Fotolia

FIGURE 1.15 Enterprise servers can allow thousands of simultaneous users and perform millions of transactions every day.

Supercomputers

Supercomputers are very expensive computer systems designed to perform a limited number of tasks as quickly as possible. They perform complex mathematical calculations, such as those used in weather forecasting and medical research. Visit the website of the Los Alamos National Laboratory, **lanl.gov,** for more photos like this one (Figure 1.16). A supercomputer can consist of a single computer with multiple processors or can be a group of computers that work together. The world's top supercomputers are found at major universities and research institutes around the world. Table 1.6 provides a sampling from the listing of the top 500 supercomputers, which is located at **top500.org**.

FIGURE 1.16 Sara Del Valle in front of the Powerwall (at the Los Alamos National Laboratory).

Image courtesy of Los Alamos National Library

TABLE 1.6 Key Supercomputers

Research Institute	Location	Uses
Los Alamos National Laboratory	United States	• National security and energy challenges
RIKEN Advanced Institute for Computational Science (AICS)	Japan	• Simulation research • Human resource development programs
Shanghai Supercomputer Center	China	• Weather forecasts • Oil exploration • Biomedical research • Gene research • Aviation and aeronautics
NASA/Ames Research Center/NAS	United States	• Critical NASA missions • Scientific discoveries for the benefit of humankind
Amazon Web Services	United States	• High-performance computing (HPC) for complex science, engineering, and business problems

Geoghan, Debra. Visualizing Technology Complete, 4e. Pearson Education, 2014.

Distributed and Grid Computing

Distributed computing distributes the processing of a task across a group of computers. Distributed computing using a group of computers in one location is **grid computing**. On a much larger scale, **volunteer computing** projects harness the idle processing power of hundreds or thousands of personal computers. At **boinc.berkeley.edu**, a volunteer can choose from a variety of projects to join. A volunteer interested in astronomy might join SETI@home. One of the first volunteer computing projects, SETI@home has had more than 6 million participants since 1999. A volunteer downloads and installs a program that runs as a screensaver when the computer is idle which allows SETI (Search for Extraterrestrial Intelligence) to utilize the processing abilities of your computer when it is idle, without having to pay for processing time. The SETI screensaver is actually a complex piece of software that downloads and analyzes radio telescope data to SETI. Folding@home is another volunteer computing project that works to fight diseases by studying protein folding (Figure 1.17). Volunteer computing project websites have active communities where volunteers can talk to the scientists and to each other.

Multiuser systems enable users to leverage the power of computers that far exceed what a PC can do. Centralized information management, security, and distributed processing across multiple systems have given the scientific and business communities the power to solve many of society's most pressing problems in an extremely short amount of time.

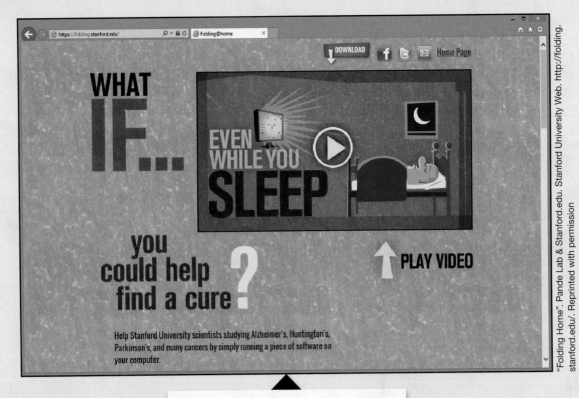

FIGURE 1.17 The Folding@home website

Fotolia

UNMANNED AIRCRAFT SYSTEMS

Just a few years ago, aircrafts piloted by remote control or onboard computers or **unmanned aircraft systems (UAS)**, also known as drones, were used only by the military. Today, commercial applications are being developed. Drones are useful in agriculture, land management, energy, and construction industries; for example, to inspect the underside of bridges and other locations where it is difficult or unsafe for people to go. Amazon plans to develop a drone delivery service. Drones carrying cameras are helpful in search and rescue missions, and could replace traffic and news helicopters (Figure 1.18). As technology improves, many more drone applications will surely be developed.

There are, however, privacy and safety concerns about the proliferation of UAS in our skies. The Federal Aviation Administration (FAA) has implemented some rules for non-military UAS users, **faa.gov/uas**. "The FAA reviews and approves UAS operations over densely-populated areas on a case-by-case basis." The FAA estimates that as many as 7,500 small commercial UAS may be in use by 2018.

Alexander Kolomietz/Shutterstock

FIGURE 1.18
A UAS records video of icebergs and glaciers.

Running Project

Use the Internet to learn about current volunteer computing projects. Select one that you are interested in and write two or three paragraphs highlighting the project and some of its achievements.

5 Things You Need to Know

- Servers provide services such as file and print sharing and email to client computers.
- Minicomputers have largely been replaced by midsized servers that can support hundreds of concurrent users.
- Mainframes and enterprise servers can process millions of transactions in a day.
- Supercomputers perform complex mathematical calculations for such things as weather forecasting and medical research.
- Distributed, grid, and volunteer computing distribute processing tasks across multiple computers.

Key Terms

client

distributed computing

enterprise server

grid computing

mainframe

midrange server

minicomputer

multiuser computer

server

supercomputer

volunteer computing

unmanned aircraft systems (UAS)

Computers are Everywhere

Objective 7

Explain Ubiquitous Computing and Convergence

Computers have become so commonplace that sometimes the technology isn't recognized as being a computer. **Ubiquitous computing (ubicomp)**, also referred to as invisible computing, means technology recedes into the background. The technology actually becomes part of the environment. Digital signage is replacing traditional billboards, you can pay for gas with the wave of a credit card, and you can upload pictures to Facebook from your mobile phone. Smart homes—in which the lights, climate, security, and entertainment are automated—are examples of ubiquitous computing.

VIZ CLIP

Ubiquitous Computing

Embedded Computers

Embedded computers are present at gasoline pumps, in home appliances, traffic lights, and self-checkout lines at supermarkets. Computer chips can monitor your vital signs and calories burned when exercising, regulate the flow of gas in your car, and regulate the temperature of water in your dishwasher. Embedded computers make modern lives easier. These specialized computers have become so common that it would be hard to imagine living without them (Figure 1.19).

The **Internet of Things (IoT)** is the connection of the physical world to the Internet. Objects are tagged and can be located, monitored, and controlled using small, embedded electronics. Some examples of IoT devices you may already use include fitness and health trackers, smart thermostats, and monitors for babies or the elderly. These devices have existed for some time, but adding the IoT features means they can be monitored and controlled remotely via a web browser or mobile app. The Internet of Things Consortium is an organization of companies driving the IoT revolution. You can visit their website **iofthings.org** to learn about the latest development in IoT.

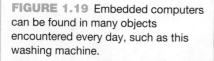

FIGURE 1.19 Embedded computers can be found in many objects encountered every day, such as this washing machine.

Convergence

The **convergence**, or integration, of technology on multifunction devices, such as smartphones, has accustomed us to carrying technology with us. You no longer need to carry around several different devices because convergence devices now incorporate cell phones, personal information management tools, email, web browsing, document editing, MP3 players, cameras, GPS, games, and more (Figure 1.20). In some parts of the world, there are more mobile phones than people, and this has resulted in the rapid development of technologies such as mobile payment systems. In many cases, mobile phones have replaced personal computers.

As we rely more and more on technology, we expect it to work. We take for granted that traffic light timing will protect us, the GPS will guide us to our destination, and the ATM will dispense our funds only to us. Ubiquitous computing is only in its infancy, and it is already an integral part of our lives. It will be interesting to see where ubicomp takes us in the not-too-distant future.

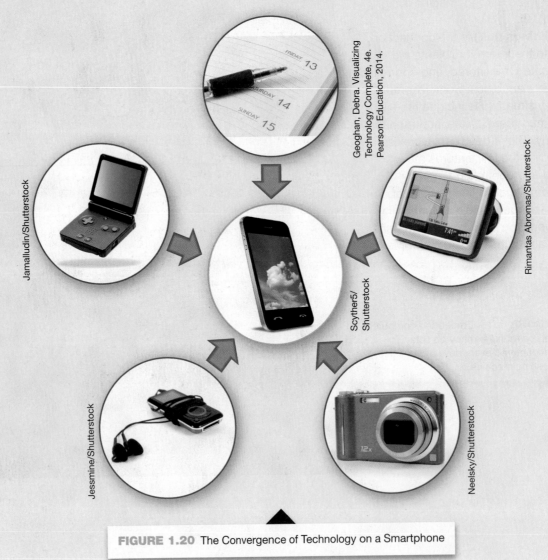

Geoghan, Debra. Visualizing Technology Complete, 4e. Pearson Education, 2014.

Jamalludin/Shutterstock

Rimantas Abromas/Shutterstock

Scyther5/Shutterstock

Jessmine/Shutterstock

Neelsky/Shutterstock

FIGURE 1.20 The Convergence of Technology on a Smartphone

ETHICS

The Internet of Things

IoT may make modern life more convenient and comfortable, but at the cost of some of your privacy. Retailers can track you in their stores by the location of your cell phone, noticing what aisles you visit and avoid, helping plan the store layout and targeted advertising presented to you. Personal health trackers record your vital statistics, and promise not to share your personal information. The built-in camera on your Smart TV that enables you to use Skype or play interactive content, can be used to record your actions and audio, even when you are not using it. And all Internet-connected devices—yes even your refrigerator—are potential hacker targets. Is the potential loss of privacy worth the convenience of the technology?

Running Project

Science fiction meets science fact. Many modern devices were envisioned by famous science fiction writers, such as Gene Rodden-berry. Use the Internet to research some of the *Star Trek* technologies that exist today. Write a paragraph about at least three of them.

4 Things You Need to Know

- Ubiquitous computing is technology that's invisible to us.
- Embedded computers are found in everything from traffic lights to dishwashers.
- The Internet of Things (IoT) connects the physical world to the Internet.
- The convergence of technology allows us to carry a single multifunction device that can do the job of many separate devices.

Key Terms

bioinformatics

convergence

embedded computer

green computing

Internet of Things (IoT)

smart appliance

smart grid

smart home

ubiquitous computing (ubicomp)

Viz Check—From MyITLab, take a quick quiz covering Objectives 5–7.

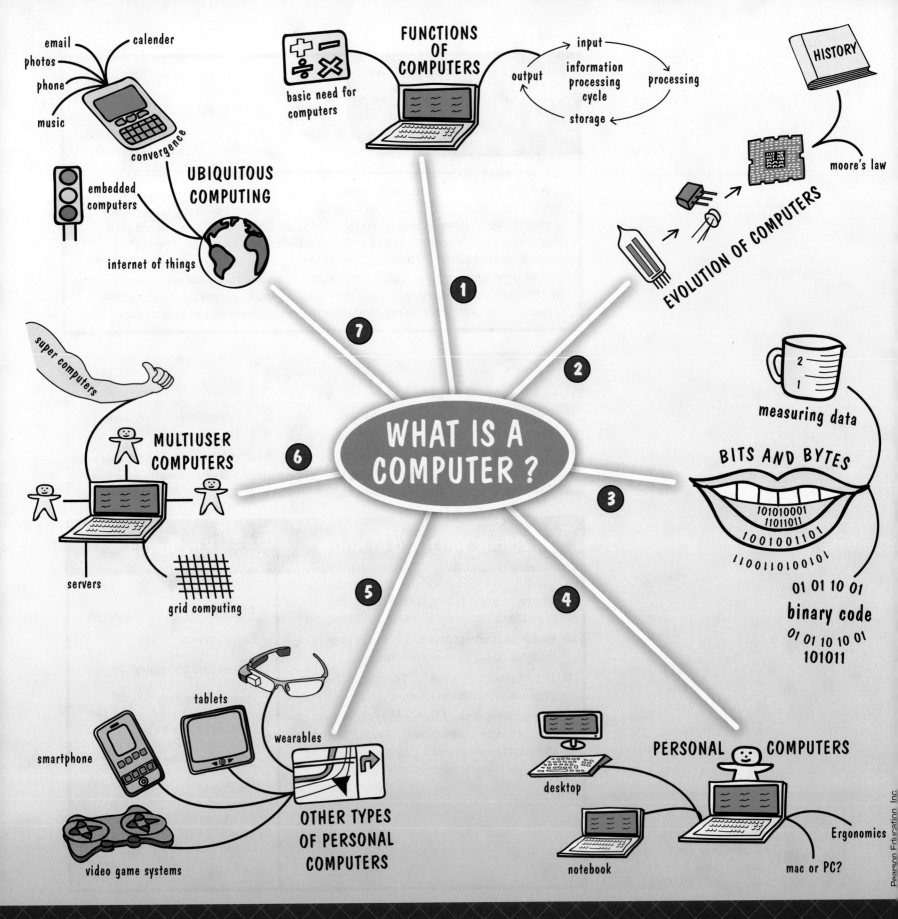

email
calender
photos
phone
music
convergence

FUNCTIONS OF COMPUTERS

basic need for computers

input
information processing cycle
output
processing
storage

HISTORY

moore's law

EVOLUTION OF COMPUTERS

UBIQUITOUS COMPUTING

embedded computers

internet of things

super computers

MULTIUSER COMPUTERS

WHAT IS A COMPUTER ?

measuring data

BITS AND BYTES

101010001
11011011
1001001101
110011010010

01 01 10 01

binary code

01 01 10 10 01
101011

servers

grid computing

tablets

wearables

smartphone

OTHER TYPES OF PERSONAL COMPUTERS

video game systems

desktop

PERSONAL COMPUTERS

notebook

Ergonomics

mac or PC?

1
2
3
4
5
6
7

Objectives Recap

1. Explain the Functions of a Computer
2. Describe the Evolution of Computer Hardware
3. Describe How Computers Represent Data Using Binary Codes
4. List the Various Types and Characteristics of Personal Computers
5. Give Examples of Other Personal Computing Devices
6. List the Various Types and Characteristics of Multiuser Computers
7. Explain Ubiquitous Computing and Convergence

Key Terms

all-in-one computer **21**
Analytical Engine **5**
artificial intelligence **5**
ASCII (American Standard Code for Information Interchange) **17**
binary code **17**
binary (base 2) number system **16**
bioinformatics **19**
bit **17**
byte **17**
central processing unit (CPU) **13**
client **33**
computer **4**
convergence **40**
convertible notebook **22**
data **4**
desktop computer **21**

distributed computing **36**
embedded computer **39**
ENIAC (Electronic Numerical Integrator and Computer) **11**
enterprise server **34**
ergonomics **24**
game controller **30**
geocaching **31**
GPS (global positioning system) **29**
green computing **15**
grid computing **36**
information **4**
information processing cycle (IPC) **7**
integrated circuit **12**
Internet of Things (IoT) **39**
laptop **21**
Mac **23**
mainframe **34**

microprocessor **13**
midrange server **33**
minicomputer **33**
mobile application (mobile app) **22**
mobile device **29**
Moore's Law **14**
multiuser computer **32**
netbook **22**
notebook **22**
operating system (OS) **23**
personal computer (PC) **20**
punch card **5**
server **33**
smart appliance **15**
smart grid **15**
smart home **15**
stylus **22**

subnotebook **22**
supercomputer **35**
tablet **22**
transistor **11**
Turing machine **5**
Turing test **5**
ubiquitous computing (ubicomp) **38**
Unicode **17**
Universal design **25**
unmanned aircraft system (UAS) **37**
vacuum tube **11**
video game system **30**
volunteer computing **36**
wearable **29**
workstation **21**

Summary

1. Explain the Functions of a Computer

A computer is a device that converts raw data into information using the information processing cycle. The four steps of the IPC are: input, processing, storage, and output. Computers can be programmed to perform different tasks.

2. Describe the Evolution of Computer Hardware

The earliest computers used vacuum tubes, which are inefficient, large, and prone to failure. Second-generation computers used transistors, which are small electric switches. Third-generation computers used integrated circuits, which are silicon chips that contain multiple tiny transistors. Fourth-generation computers use microprocessors, which are complex integrated circuits that contain the central processing unit (CPU) of a computer.

Moore's Law states that the number of transistors that can be placed on an integrated circuit has doubled roughly every two years. The increase in the capabilities of integrated circuits directly affects the processing speed and storage capacity of modern electronic devices.

3. Describe How Computers Represent Data Using Binary Codes

A single bit (or switch) has two possible states—on or off—and can be used for situations with two possibilities such as yes/no or true/false. Digital data is represented by 8-bit binary code on most modern computers. The 8-bit ASCII system originally had binary codes for 256 characters. Unicode is an extended ASCII set that has codes for more than 100,000 characters.

Summary continues on the next page

Summary *continued*

4. List the Various Types and Characteristics of Personal Computers

Personal computers include desktop computers, which offer the most speed, power, and upgradability for the lowest cost; workstations, which are high-end desktop computers; and all-in-ones, which are compact desktop computers with the computer case integrated into the monitor. Portable personal computers include notebooks and tablets.

5. Give Examples of Other Personal Computing Devices

Other computing devices include smartphones, wearables, GPS, video game systems, and simulators.

6. List the Various Types and Characteristics of Multiuser Computers

Multiuser computers allow multiple simultaneous users to connect to the system. They include servers, minicomputers and midrange servers, and mainframe computers and enterprise servers. Supercomputers perform complex mathematical calculations. They perform a limited number of tasks as quickly as possible. Distributed computing uses the processing of multiple computers to perform complex tasks.

7. Explain Ubiquitous Computing and Convergence

Ubiquitous computing means the technology recedes into the background so you no longer notice it as you interact with it. The Internet of Things is the connection of the physical world to the Internet. Convergence is the integration of multiple technologies, such as cell phones, cameras, and MP3 players, on a single device.

Multiple Choice

Answer the multiple-choice questions below for more practice with key terms and concepts from this chapter.

1. The _____ is a measure of a computer's ability to display intelligent behavior.
   a. Analytical Engine
   b. Artificial intelligence
   c. Bernoulli numbers
   d. Turing test

2. First-generation computers used _____ to process data.
   a. integrated circuits
   b. microprocessors
   c. transistors
   d. vacuum tubes

3. A _____ is a complex, integrated circuit that contains the central processing unit (CPU) of a computer.
   a. microprocessor
   b. silicon
   c. transistor
   d. vacuum tube

4. What is the binary code that can represent most currently used language characters and is the standard used on the Internet?
   a. ASCII
   b. Base 2
   c. International standards
   d. Unicode

5. What are desktop computers attached to a network in a business setting called?
   a. Dumb terminals
   b. Mainframes
   c. Minicomputers
   d. Workstations

6. What type of portable computer is thin and light, has high-end processing and video capabilities, and a 13–15 inch screen?
   a. Convertible notebook
   b. Netbook
   c. Subnotebook
   d. Tablet

7. _____ consists of 24 satellites that transmit signals to determine the receiver's current location, time, and velocity through triangulation of the signals.
   a. Geocaching
   b. GPS
   c. A wearable system
   d. A flight simulator

8. _____ perform complex mathematical calculations, such as those used in weather forecasting and medical research.
   a. Enterprise servers
   b. Mainframes
   c. Minicomputers
   d. Supercomputers

9. _____ is a field of study in which information technology is applied to the field of biology.
   a. Bioinformatics
   b. Distributed computing
   c. Ergonomics
   d. Ubicomp

10. A(n) _____ is an example of convergence.
   a. smart grid
   b. smartphone
   c. traffic light
   d. ubicomp

True or False

Answer the following questions with *T* for true or *F* for false for more practice with key terms and concepts from this chapter.

_____ 1. Computers convert data into information using the Information Processing Cycle.

_____ 2. Third-generation computers used vacuum tubes.

_____ 3. Today's computers use transistors and integrated circuits.

_____ 4. Moore's Law states that the number of transistors that can be placed on an integrated circuit will double roughly every 18 years.

_____ 5. Unicode contains codes for most of the languages in use today.

_____ 6. Bioinformatics allows you to design a workspace for your comfort and health.

_____ 7. All-in-one is another name for a tablet computer.

_____ 8. Users connect to servers via clients.

_____ 9. Volunteer computing projects harness the idle processing power of hundreds or thousands of personal computers.

_____ 10. The idea that computers are all around us is called convergence.

Fill in the Blank

Fill in the blanks with key terms from this chapter.

1. A computer is a programmable machine that converts raw _____ into useful _____.

2. The _____ was a mechanical computer designed, but not built, in the early nineteenth century by mathematician Charles Babbage.

3. _____ is the branch of science concerned with making computers behave like humans.

4. Developed in the 1960s, _____ are chips that contain large numbers of tiny transistors fabricated into a semiconducting material called silicon.

5. _____ design creates a work environment designed to reduce illnesses and musculoskeletal disorders.

6. _____ is a system that represents digital data as a series of 0s and 1s that can be understood by a computer.

7. A _____ consists of 8 bits and is used to represent a single character in modern computer systems.

8. _____ are computers that provide services, such as Internet access, email, or file and print services, to client systems.

9. _____ shares the processing of a task across a group of computers.

10. A _____ is a network for delivering electricity to consumers that includes communication technology to manage electricity distribution efficiently.

Running Project...

...The Finish Line

Use your answers from the previous sections of the chapter project to discuss the evolution of computers in the past few centuries. Write a report responding to the questions raised throughout the chapter project. Save your file as **lastname_firstname_ch01_project** and submit it to your instructor as directed.

Do It Yourself 1

Consider the features available on the personal computing device that you use the most. From your student data files, open the file *vt_ch01_DIY1_answersheet* and save the file as **lastname_firstname_ch01_DIY1_answersheet**

What device did you choose? Is it a desktop, notebook, tablet, or some other type of system? Where is it located? How long have you had it? Did you research the computer before you made your purchase? What made you purchase it?

What do you use the computer for the most? What are five features you use most frequently? Why? What are three you use the least? Why? How could this device be improved to make your life more convenient? Describe one way life would be easier and one way your life would be more difficult without this device. Save your answers and submit it as directed by your instructor.

Do It Yourself 2

Use an online mind mapper tool such as Mindomo (**mindomo.com**), Mindmeister (**mindmeister.com**) or Coggle (**coggle.it**) to create a mind map to compare desktop, notebook, and mobile devices. A mind map is a visual outline. More information about using mind maps can be found in Appendix B. From your student data files, open the file *vt_ch1_DIY2_answersheet* and save the file as **lastname_firstname_ch1_DIY2_answersheet**

Your map should have three main branches: desktop, notebook, and mobile devices. Each branch should have at least three leaves: characteristics, advantages, and disadvantages.

When you have finished your map, take a screenshot of this window and paste it into your answer sheet, or, if available, export your mind map as a PNG or JPG file.

Critical Thinking

Convergence has led to smaller devices that cost less and do more. From your student data files, open the file *vt_ch01_CT_answersheet* and save the file as **lastname_firstname_ch01_CT_answersheet**

Research three of the newest smartphones or tablets on the market—one from each mobile platform: iOS, Android, and Windows. Complete the following table, comparing the features of each device. Use this research to decide which device would best meet your personal needs. Which device should you buy and why? What other accessories will you need to purchase? Do you need to purchase a service plan to take advantage of all the device's features? Save your file and submit both your table and essay as directed by your instructor.

	Device 1 - iOS	Device 2 - Android	Device 3 - Windows
Website or store			
Brand			
Model			
Price			
Phone			
Calendar			
Camera/video			
GPS			
Games			
Video player			
MP3 player			
Internet			
Downloadable apps			
Additional features			
Additional purchases required			

Ethical Dilemma

The term *digital divide* refers to the gap in technology access and literacy. There have been many types of programs designed to close this gap. One current trend is to put tablets in the hands of every student. From your student data files, open the file *vt_ch01_ethics_answersheet* and save the file as **lastname_firstname_ch01_ethics_answersheet**

Use the Internet to find a school program that supplies all students with tablets or notebooks. What are the goals of the program? How was it funded? Has it been successful? How has its success or failure been measured? Do you think programs like this one can really solve the digital divide? Why or why not? Type up your answers; be sure to cite your sources. Save the file and submit your work as directed by your instructor.

On the Web

There are many important people and events that led to our modern computers. In this exercise, you will create a timeline that illustrates the ones you feel are most significant. From your student data files, open the file *vt_ch01_web_answersheet* and save the file as **lastname_firstname_ch01_web_answersheet**

Visit **computerhope.com/history** and under *Timeline* click the link to open the time period that includes the year you were born. Create a timeline showing five to seven important milestones in the development of computers that occurred in this decade. Use a free online timeline generator, such as Dipity (**dipity.com**) or TimeGlider (**timeglider.com**), or online presentation tool (such as Prezi or PowerPoint) to create your timeline. Share the URL and present your findings to the class. Prepare a summary of your timeline and include the URL where it can be viewed. Save the file, and submit your work as directed by your instructor.

Collaboration

With a group of three to five students, research a famous computer pioneer. Write and perform a news interview of this person. If possible, video record the interview. Present your newscast to the class.

Instructors: Divide the class into groups of three to four students, and assign each group a famous computing pioneer from the list **computerhope.com/people**.

The Project: As a team, prepare a dialog depicting a news reporter interviewing this person. Use at least three references. Use Google Drive or Microsoft Office to prepare the presentation and provide documentation that all team members have contributed to the project.

Outcome: Perform the interview in a newscast format using the dialog you have written. The interview should be 3 to 5 minutes long. If possible, record the interview, and share the newscast with the rest of the class. Save this video as **teamname_ch01_video** Turn in a final text version of your presentation named **teamname_ch01_interview** Be sure to include the name of your presentation and a list of all team members. Submit your presentation to your instructor as directed.

Application Project

Office 2016 Application Projects
Word 2016: Intern Report

Project Description: In the following Microsoft Word project, you will create a letter telling your new boss about the things you have learned in this class. In the project you will enter and edit text, format text, insert graphics, check spelling and grammar, and create document footers. *If necessary, download the student data files from **pearsonhighered.com/viztech***.

Anna Sanchez
670 Pembroke Ave
Unit 26
Frederick, MD 21703

March 6, 2016

Jones Consulting
Mr. Martin Rogert
275 Regency Sq.
Frederick, MD 21703

Dear Mr. Rogert:

Subject: Eager intern

Thank you so much for giving me the opportunity to work with you as an intern this semester. I have learned a lot about computers in my class at school and I'm eager to share my knowledge with you at *Jones Consulting*. For example, I have learned about the different types of personal computers and other devices.

Thank you so much for this amazing opportunity. I am eager to get started and believe that I can really help you effectively leverage technology in the office.

Sincerely,

Anna Sanchez, Intern

lastname_firstname_ch01_word.docx

Step	Instructions
1	Start Word. From your student data files, open the file named *vt_ch01_word* Save the document as **lastname_firstname_ch01_word**
2	On the last line of the document, type **Anna Sanchez, Intern** to complete the letter.
3	Select the first four lines of the document containing the name and street address. Apply the No Spacing style.
4	Format the entire document as Times New Roman, 12 pt.
5	In the first body paragraph, format *Jones Consulting* as italic.
6	Place the insertion point before *Anna* on the last line of the document. Insert the picture of a QR code *vt_ch01_image1*
7	Change the text wrapping style of the picture to Top and Bottom.
8	Use the shortcut menu to correct the misspelling of the word *semsester* to *semester*.
9	Using the Spelling and Grammar dialog box, accept the suggested correction for the repeated word.
10	Use the Spelling and Grammar dialog box to correct the misspelling of the word *beleive* to *believe*. Ignore all other spelling and grammar suggestions.
11	Insert the file name in the footer of the document using the FileName field.
12	Save the document and then close Word. Submit the document as directed.

Application Project

Office 2016 Application Projects
PowerPoint 2016: Business Technology Plan

Project Description: Your new boss has asked you to help her create a PowerPoint presentation discussing technology needs at Clearview Medical Supplies. In this project, you will edit and format text and bullets, insert and format pictures, check spelling, add new slides and change slide layout, apply transitions, and add speaker notes. *If necessary, download the student data files from **pearsonhighered.com/viztech**.*

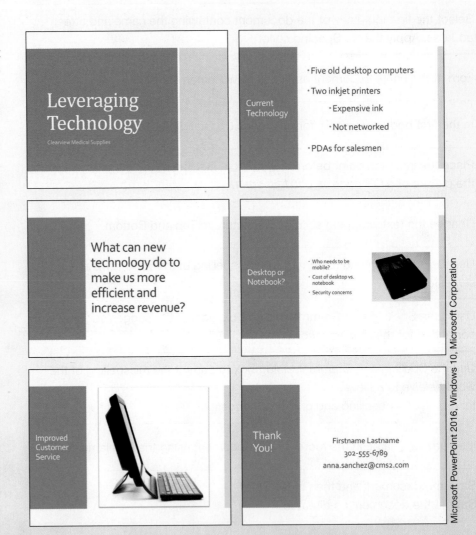

Step	Instructions
1	Start PowerPoint. From your student data files, open the file *vt_ch01_ppt* Save the presentation as **lastname_firstname_ch01_ppt**
2	On Slide 1, change the subtitle text *(Clearview Medical Supply)* to **Clearview Medical Supplies**
3	On Slide 1, use the shortcut menu to correct the spelling of *Technology*. Change the font of the title text, *Leveraging Technology,* to Cambria and change the size to 72.
4	On Slide 2, change the font size of the title text to 32. Change the line spacing of the bullets on Slide 2 to 1.5 and the font size to 32.
5	Insert a new Title and Content slide after Slide 3 and add **Improved Customer Service** as the title text.
6	On the new Slide 4, in the content placeholder, insert the picture *vt_ch01_image2*
7	On Slide 4, apply the Simple Frame, White picture style to the picture.
8	Find and replace the word *sales* with **revenue**
9	Use the Spelling tool to check the spelling in the document. Correct the spelling errors on Slide 2, but ignore all instances of the spelling of *Clearview.*
10	Change the layout of Slide 5 to Two Content. In the right placeholder, insert the picture *vt_ch01_image3*
11	Switch to Slide Sorter view and delete Slide 6. Move Slide 5 into the Slide 4 position. Switch back to Normal view.
12	On Slide 6, replace *Anna Sanchez* with your name.
13	In the Notes Pane on Slide 2, add the following speaker note (include the period): **Clearview needs to be a forward-thinking company.**
14	Apply the Fade transition with a duration of 01.00 to all of the slides in the presentation.
15	Insert the page number and the footer **Firstname Lastname** using your name, on the notes and handouts pages for all slides in the presentation. View the presentation in Slide Show view from beginning to end, and then return to Normal view.
16	Save the presentation and then close PowerPoint. Submit the presentation as directed.

CHAPTER
2

Application Software

In This Chapter

A computer is a programmable machine that converts raw data into useful information. Programming—in particular, **application software**—is what makes a computer a flexible and powerful tool. After reading this chapter, you will recognize various types of software applications for both business and personal use.

Objectives

1 **Identify Types and Uses of Business Productivity Software**

2 **Identify Types and Uses of Personal Software**

3 **Assess a Computer System for Software Compatibility**

4 **Compare Various Ways of Obtaining Software**

5 **Discuss the Importance of Cloud Computing**

6 **Install, Uninstall, and Update Software**

Running Project

In this chapter, you'll learn about different kinds of application software and how to obtain it. Look for instructions as you complete each article. For most articles, there's a series of questions for you to research. At the conclusion of this chapter, you'll submit your responses to the questions raised.

Devrim Pinar/Fotolia

Making Business Work

1 Identify Types and Uses of Business Productivity Software

Companies of all sizes rely on computers for many aspects of running a business—from billing to inventory to payroll to sales. Most businesses depend on a variety of software applications to complete tasks.

Office Suites

The most commonly used application software in business is an **office application suite**, such as Microsoft Office, Apple Productivity Apps (Figure 2.1), or Apache OpenOffice. These suites include several applications that are designed to work together to manage and create different types of documents and include features that enable multiple users to collaborate. In a business environment, Microsoft Office is the standard, but most programs have the ability to save a file in multiple formats, making them compatible with other products or backward compatible with older software versions.

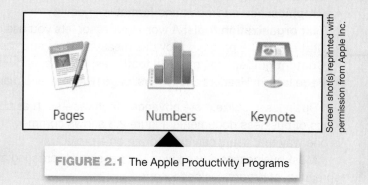

FIGURE 2.1 The Apple Productivity Programs

WORD PROCESSING

A **word processor** is an application that's used to create, edit, and format text documents; the documents can also contain images. A full-featured word processor, such as Microsoft Word, Pages, or Apache OpenOffice Writer, can create everything from simple memos to large, complex documents.

Figure 2.2 shows a Word document created using some of the most commonly used features of a word processor. The page number was inserted in the header, and a word processor renumbered the document pages as the content changed. The *Title* style was used to format the title. Styles enable you to apply a predefined set of formatting steps to text. The image is centered on the page, but the body text is left-aligned. The spellchecker displays a red squiggly line under the word *Appy*, indicating that the word wasn't found in the spellchecker dictionary. It's possible to add words not found in the spellchecker dictionary and create a custom dictionary so that these additional words (such as your last name or industry-specific terms and brand names) aren't flagged for incorrect spelling.

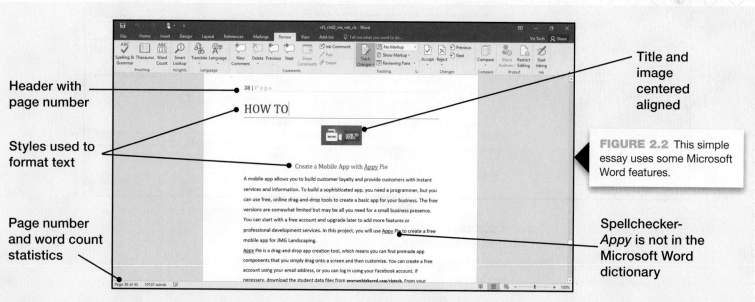

Header with page number

Styles used to format text

Page number and word count statistics

Title and image centered aligned

FIGURE 2.2 This simple essay uses some Microsoft Word features.

Spellchecker-*Appy* is not in the Microsoft Word dictionary

Some standard features of modern word processors include:

- **What you see is what you get:** The layout on the computer screen shows the document layout as it would appear when printed.
- **Formatting styles:** You can change the formatting by changing text styles, fonts, colors, sizes, and alignments.
- **Spelling and grammar checkers:** You can check for common grammar errors and misspelled words.
- **Graphics:** You can insert and format images.
- **Text organization tools:** A word processor lets you use organization tools like tables, bullets, and lists.
- **Statistics:** The program provides measurements such as word count and reading level.
- **Content guides:** You can add footnotes, indexes, and tables of contents.
- **Page layout:** Headers and footers, page numbers, and margins all improve your page layout.

Businesses utilize more advanced features—such as track changes, mail merge, and document protection—to create many kinds of business documents. Figure 2.3 shows comments and edits from multiple reviewers working on the same document. This is one way that users can collaborate on a project.

Most businesses rely on word processing for creating all types of documents; however, when calculations are involved, a spreadsheet program is necessary.

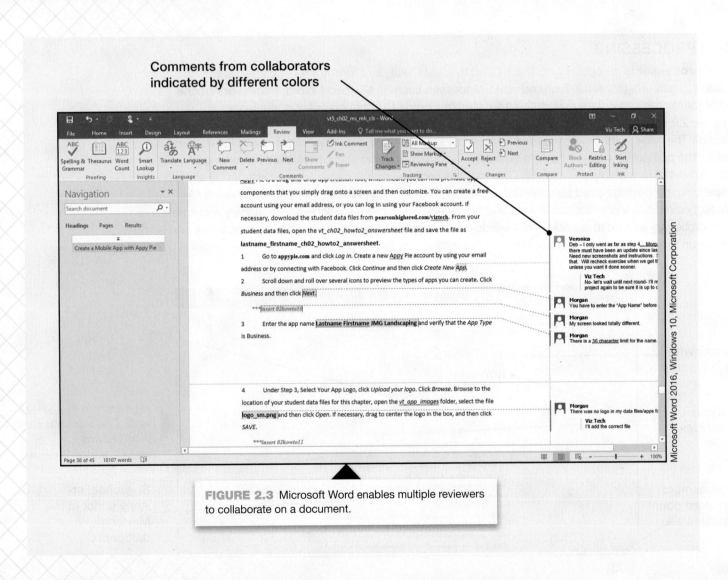

FIGURE 2.3 Microsoft Word enables multiple reviewers to collaborate on a document.

SPREADSHEET SOFTWARE

A **spreadsheet** application, such as Numbers or Microsoft Excel, creates electronic worksheets composed of rows and columns. Spreadsheets are used for applications such as budgeting, grade books, and inventory. Spreadsheets are critical to researchers in both the natural and social sciences as a statistical analysis tool. They are useful tools for managing business expenses, payroll, and billing, although there are also tools that are specifically made for such tasks.

In a spreadsheet, the intersection of a row and a column is called a **cell**. Cells can contain numbers, text, or formulas. Three-dimensional spreadsheets can have multiple worksheets that are linked together, making them very flexible and powerful. Spreadsheet applications have the ability to create charts or graphs to represent data visually. Although there are other spreadsheet programs available, in a business environment, Microsoft Excel is used almost exclusively.

Spreadsheets are also very good at organizing data, by sorting, filtering, and rearranging, making them useful for things that don't involve calculations at all—such as address lists and schedules. Figure 2.4 shows a spreadsheet created for a U.S. history course that lists all the U.S. presidents and their political parties. The number of presidents in each party was calculated, and a pie chart showing that information was created.

One advantage to using a spreadsheet program is that it can be customized. For example, a teacher might use a spreadsheet to create custom formulas and calculations rather than having to adjust grading methods to fit into a commercial grade book program's format. Another advantage is cost savings. Because most office computers already have a spreadsheet program installed as part of an office suite, there's no need to purchase additional software. Programs that are part of an office suite have a similar interface, so users will have some familiarity with the program interface and need less training to use the individual programs.

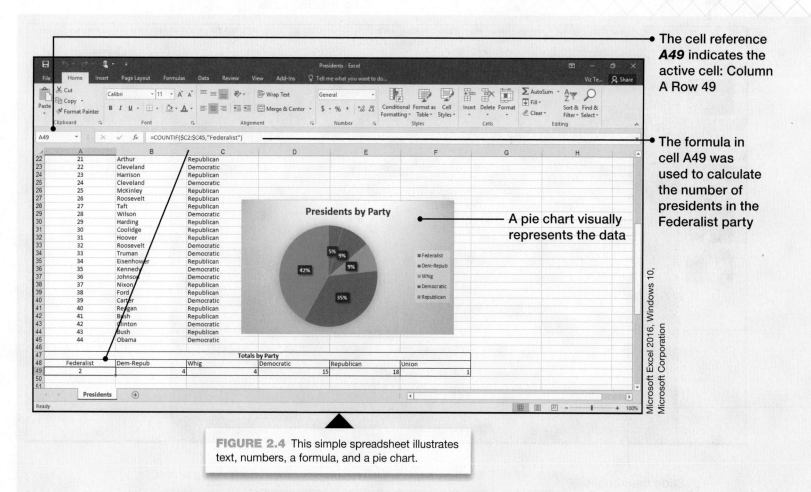

FIGURE 2.4 This simple spreadsheet illustrates text, numbers, a formula, and a pie chart.

PRESENTATION SOFTWARE

A presentation application, such as Microsoft PowerPoint, Keynote on a Mac, or the online tools Prezi or Sway, is used to create electronic presentations. If you want to present facts, figures, and ideas and engage your audience at the same time, you need visual aids. With presentation software, it's easy to create them. Each slide can contain text, graphics, video, audio, or any combination of these, making your visual aids dynamic and enhancing your presentation. A good speaker creates a presentation that audiences will be interested in and will remember.

Figure 2.5 shows a Keynote presentation on animals. The presentation here is shown in Navigator view, which enables the author to see the slide order and easily make changes by dragging the slides into position. This presentation contains four slides—some containing images—and uses a built-in design template with predefined colors, fonts, and layouts. Good design principles for presentations include using easy-to-see color schemes and large font sizes, limiting the amount of text on each slide, limiting the use of slide transitions and animations, and using images to enhance your words.

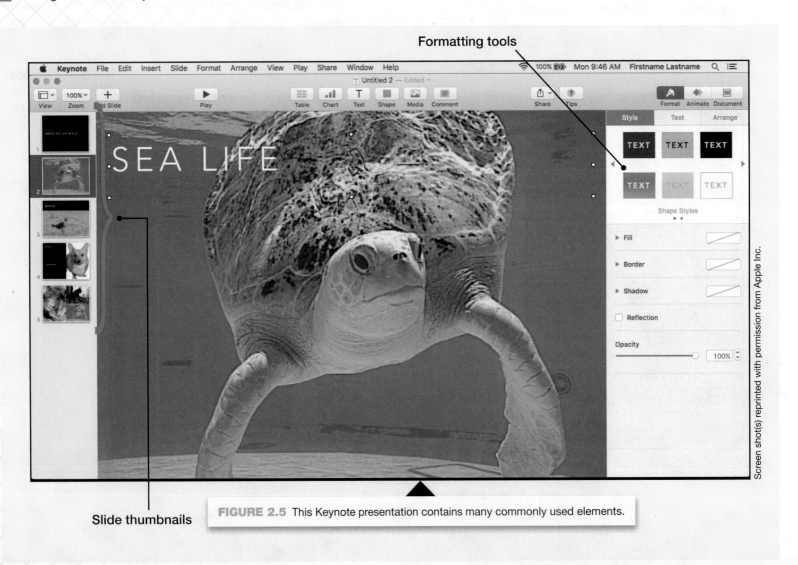

FIGURE 2.5 This Keynote presentation contains many commonly used elements.

Slide thumbnails

Formatting tools

Screen shot(s) reprinted with permission from Apple Inc.

DATABASE SOFTWARE

A database program such as Microsoft Access is used to create and manage a database. A **database** is a collection of information that is organized in a useful way. Your telephone book or email contact list is a simple database. A library catalog, patient records in a doctor's office, and Internet search engines are all examples of commonly used databases. You can use a desktop database application to create small databases for contact management, inventory management, and employee records.

A database is a collection of related records organized into a **table**. More complex databases include multiple tables. A **record** in a database contains information about a single entry, such as a customer or product. Other objects can be generated to organize the data, including forms, reports, and queries.

Using a contact list as an example, each contact has a record. Every record consists of fields of information. A **field** is a single piece of information in a record in a database. In this case, each record would contain fields for name, address, email, phone, etc. Although a simple database like this could also be created in a spreadsheet, using a database program gives you more options. **Forms** can be created for easy data entry. **Reports** can be generated to display selected information. Figure 2.6 shows a contact list database that consists of five records in a table and a phone list report created from the table. Most flexible of all, **queries** can be created to pull out records that meet specific criteria.

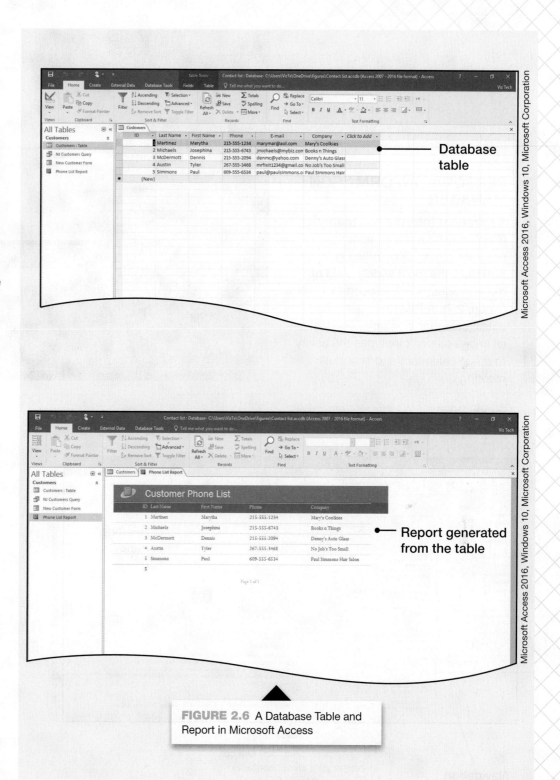

Database table

Report generated from the table

FIGURE 2.6 A Database Table and Report in Microsoft Access

Rawpixel/Fotolia

PERSONAL INFORMATION MANAGER

A **personal information manager (PIM)** may be a stand-alone program or part of an office suite. In business, the most widely used of these programs is Microsoft Outlook (Figure 2.7). A PIM manages your email, calendar, contacts, and tasks—all in one place. It includes the ability to share calendars and schedule meetings.

Navigation pane

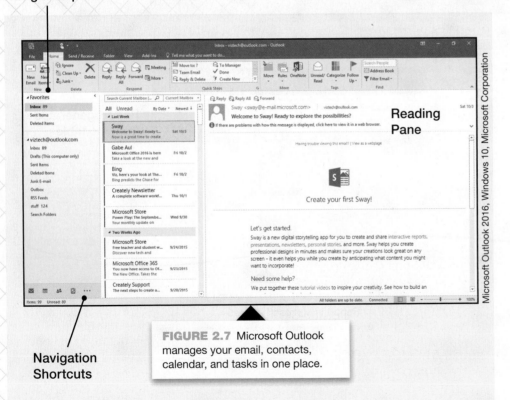

Microsoft Outlook 2016, Windows 10, Microsoft Corporation

Navigation Shortcuts

FIGURE 2.7 Microsoft Outlook manages your email, contacts, calendar, and tasks in one place.

Other Types of Business Software

Although office suites cover the majority of business documents, other software is often used for more complex and large-scale management and projects. Keeping track of finances, projects, and the sheer number of documents even the smallest business might have can be a daunting task. Specialized software can help make these tasks easier and more efficient.

FINANCIAL

Even the smallest business has to keep track of expenses and taxes. An Excel spreadsheet system might work for very simple situations, but most businesses need to use basic accounting software such as Intuit QuickBooks (Figure 2.8) or Sage Peachtree. Accounting software helps track business finances and generate reports and graphs that can be used to make business decisions. You can use accounting software for expense tracking, invoicing, payroll, and inventory management. Organizing all your financial information in one place makes it easy to see the big picture and to handle year-end tasks such as income tax returns.

FIGURE 2.8 The Homepage of Intuit QuickBooks

DOCUMENT AND PROJECT MANAGEMENT

For practical and often also legal reasons, businesses need document management capabilities—the ability to save, share, search, and audit electronic documents throughout their life cycle. Keeping track of all the documents in a business, ensuring that the right people have access to them, and ensuring that the correct version is available are all part of a **document management system (DMS)** such as Microsoft SharePoint, KnowledgeTree, or Alfresco. One of the keys to using a DMS is storage. Rather than keeping files on local drives, the files are stored on a server or on the web, making them more accessible and secure.

Project management software helps you complete projects, keep within your budget, stay on schedule, and collaborate with others. The most popular project management program is Microsoft Project, and the leading web-based application is Basecamp. Both of these tools excel at helping keep your projects running smoothly. Figure 2.9 shows a workshop planning project in Microsoft Project. The left column contains the tasks and dates for the project, and the right side shows the schedule and progress of the project in a graphic known as a **Gantt chart**.

Thousands of software applications are used in businesses, including some that are created in-house or made for a specific type of business, but the programs discussed in this article are universal. Modern businesses depend on both people and technology to remain competitive.

Gantt chart

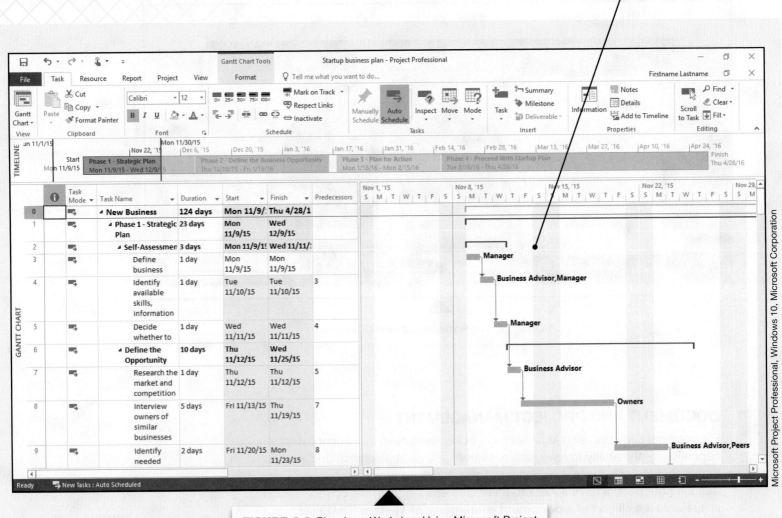

FIGURE 2.9 Planning a Workshop Using Microsoft Project

Microsoft Project Professional, Windows 10, Microsoft Corporation

Running Project

Microsoft Office is a full suite of programs, but not every user needs the whole package. Use the Internet to research the current versions of Microsoft Office that are available. If you use a Mac, be sure to include the Mac version. Write a two- to three-paragraph essay comparing the versions. Explain which applications are in each, the cost, the number of licenses available, and any other details you deem important.

Chad McDermott/Fotolia

4 Things You Need to Know

- Office application suites may include word processing, spreadsheet, presentation, and database software.
- Personal information manager software manages email, contacts, calendars, and tasks.
- Document management systems enable businesses to save, share, search, and audit electronic documents.
- Project management software helps businesses keep projects on schedule.

Key Terms

application software

cell

database

document management system (DMS)

field

form

Gantt chart

office application suite

personal information manager (PIM)

project management software

query

record

report

spreadsheet

table

word processor

Efks/Fotolia

Making It Personal

2

Identify Types and Uses of Personal Software

Software is what makes a computer useful. The variety of software available today is vast, but it takes only a couple programs to make a computer indispensable—and even fun to use. In this article, we look at some of the software you might want to install on your own system.

Office Applications

A full office application suite, which includes word processing, spreadsheet, database, presentation, and personal information management applications, may be more than the average home user needs or wants. A basic word processor and perhaps a spreadsheet and presentation program are often included in home or student versions of an office suite. Microsoft Office comes in several different versions, including a monthly subscription plan called Office 365, allowing you to purchase just the applications you actually need. For the Mac, Pages, Numbers, and Keynote are built-in apps. Nevertheless, commercial software can be expensive. There are many free or low-cost alternatives if you're willing to spend some time finding them and learning how to use them. These alternative programs have the ability to save files in common file formats so you can move your work between programs and across platforms.

Apache OpenOffice is a free, open source alternative office suite available in Windows, Mac, and Linux versions. **Open source** means that the source code is published and made available to the public, enabling anyone to copy, modify, and redistribute it without paying a fee. Some open source websites, such as Apache OpenOffice, ask for donations to support the development of the product. Apache OpenOffice contains word processor, spreadsheet, presentation, drawing, database, and formula writer applications. It can open and work with documents created in other programs, such as Microsoft Office, and can save files in its own format or common formats such as Microsoft Word or Rich Text Format so you can work with your files in other programs and across platforms. Figure 2.10 shows the welcome screen of Apache OpenOffice.

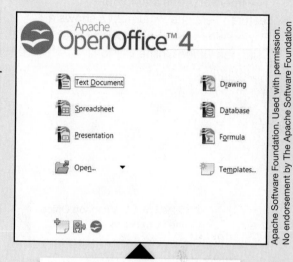

FIGURE 2.10 Apache OpenOffice Welcome Screen

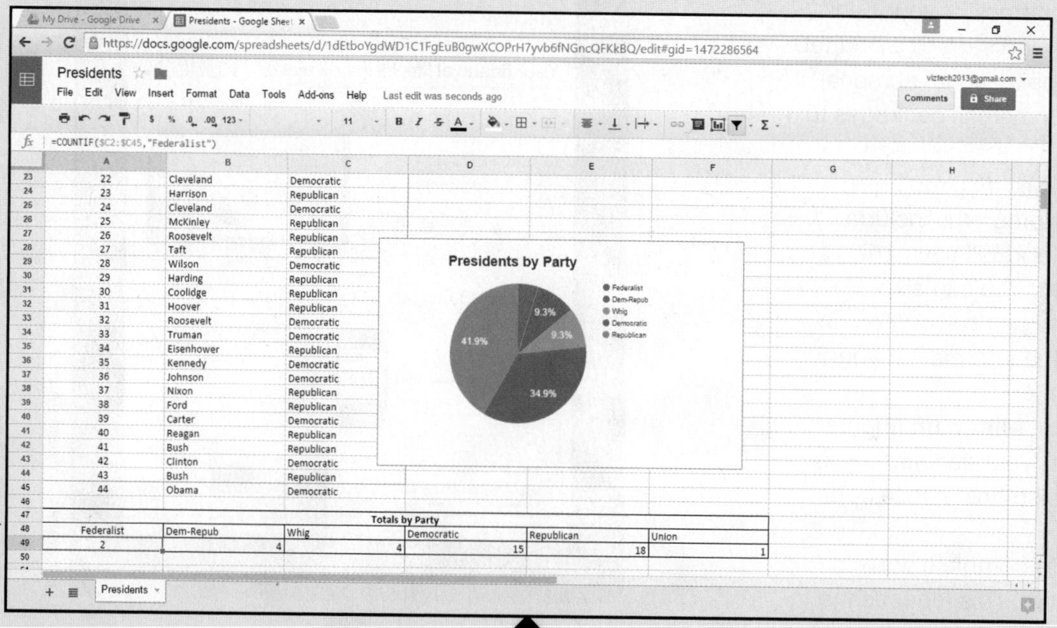

FIGURE 2.11 Google Drive Spreadsheet

Online alternative office suites are another solution. Some of the most popular are Microsoft Office Online, Google Drive, and Zoho Docs. These free websites offer easy-to-use interfaces, with word processing, spreadsheet, presentation, and communication applications. You access them through a browser and don't need to install anything on your computer. The beauty of these websites is that you can access and edit your files from anywhere, including many mobile devices, and easily collaborate and share with others. Figure 2.11 shows a spreadsheet in Google Drive.

Microsoft Office Online includes Word, Excel, PowerPoint, and OneNote. The free web apps are not full-featured versions. Figure 2.12 shows a PowerPoint presentation being edited using the Office Online version.

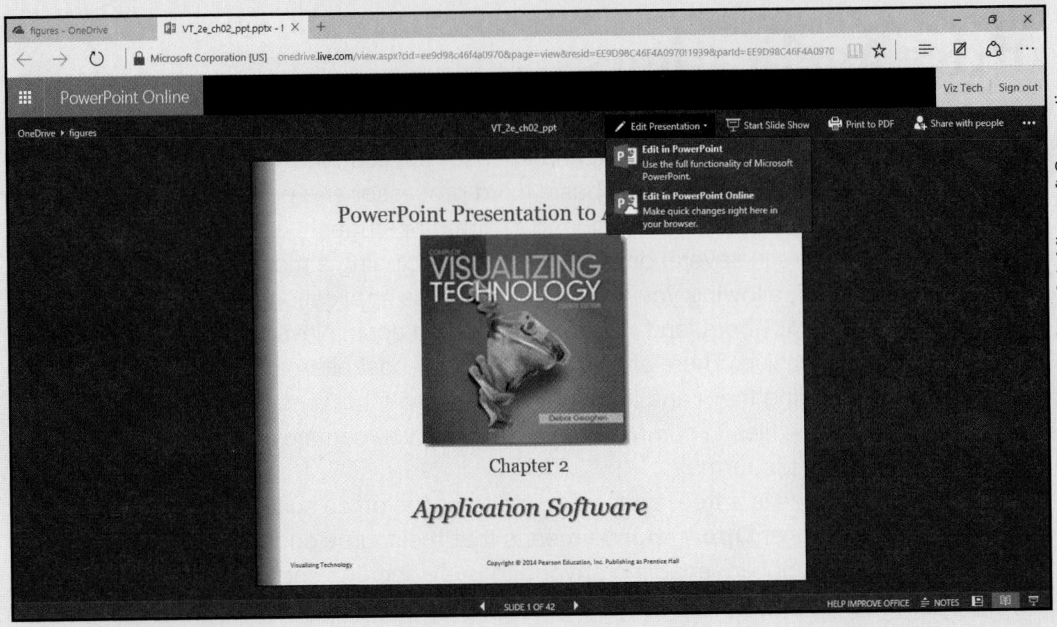

FIGURE 2.12 Microsoft Office Online PowerPoint

Microsoft PowerPoint 2013, Windows 8.1, Microsoft Corporation.

Finance and Tax Preparation Software

Personal finance software can help you keep track of your bank accounts, monitor your investments, create and stick to a budget, and file your income taxes. As with office applications, personal finance software ranges from expensive commercial packages to free and online options.

Some commercial packages are Intuit Quicken, You Need a Budget (YNAB), and MoneyDance. These programs include advanced features, such as online banking and bill payment, investment portfolio tracking, and budgeting. You can also generate reports, calculate loan interest, and pay bills. When tax time comes around, you can easily gather the information you need from these applications.

If you prefer to use an online application, **Mint.com** (Figure 2.13) is a popular choice. Once you enter all your accounts, you can use Mint to track your spending. Mint also has mobile apps for iOS, Android, and Windows.

Tax preparation software enables you to complete your income tax returns yourself on your computer. This reduces the chance of making errors in your calculations and makes it easy to save—and later retrieve—your returns. You can file your return electronically or print and mail it. You can also import previous returns into a new return and generate year-to-year comparisons.

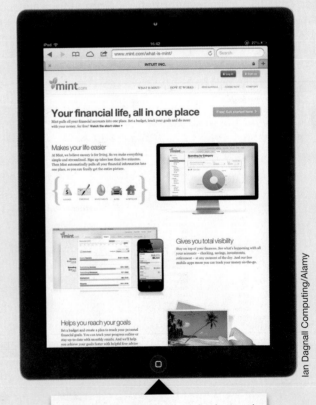

FIGURE 2.13 Track your budget and spending on Mint.com.

Ian Dagnall Computing/Alamy

Tax preparation programs walk you through the process step by step and provide you with suggestions and help throughout. The two main tax preparation programs are TurboTax from Intuit and H&R Block At Home. For simple tax returns, there are free online options. For more complex returns, you can install the full programs on your computer or use the online version. In general, the more complicated your return, the more expensive the software you need. If you start a free return and later discover that you need to upgrade to a full version, you can do so without losing any of the information you have already input (Figure 2.14).

No matter how simple or complex your financial situation, there's a financial software solution that you can use.

FIGURE 2.14 H&R Block Tax Prep

NetPhotos/Alamy

Google and the Google logo are registered trademarks of Google Inc., used with permission.

Debra Geoghan

Entertainment and Multimedia Software

Entertainment and multimedia software makes computers fun to use for education and entertainment. You can edit and organize your photos (Figure 2.15), movies, and music; play games; or learn a new skill.

FIGURE 2.15 Editing a Photo in Picasa

FIND OUT MORE

One place to learn about free software alternatives is MakeUseOf. This website is a daily blog that includes a directory of hundreds of useful websites and apps. Go to makeuseof.com, click *TOP LIST*, and select a category that interests you. Select two articles to read, and write a one- to two-paragraph summary of one of the articles. Did you decide to try the application described? If so, why? Did you find it useful? Would you recommend it to a friend?

MakeUseOf

VIDEO AND PHOTO EDITING

Video and photo editing software enables you to create masterpieces from your personal photos and videos. You can spend hundreds of dollars for professional programs, but you can also find free or low-cost alternatives that have almost all the features you need.

Using a free program such as Picasa that you can download from Google, a photo editing app on your mobile device, or an online tool, you can edit your images. You can crop, straighten, adjust contrast and color, and apply various effects, such as sepia or black and white—most of the adjustments you'd want to accomplish. One useful feature is facial recognition or face matching. In Figure 2.16, Picasa suggests matches based upon the tags that have been applied to other images containing the same person.

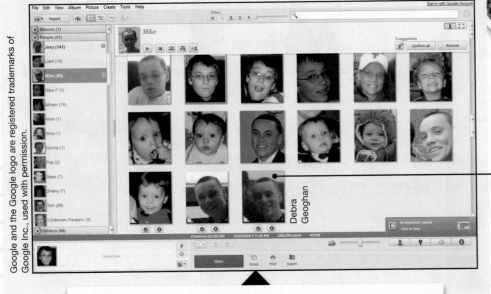

Picasa suggests an image based on facial recognition

FIGURE 2.16 Picasa's facial recognition identifies a possible match.

FIGURE 2.17 Creating a Video with iMovie

You can also create some interesting projects, such as a screensaver, a gift CD, a movie, or a collage. You can upload your images to the web and easily share them with others.

Photo software may give you some limited ability to organize and work with your videos, but you need a true video editing program to really edit and create the movies you want. Windows Movie Maker is a free download, and Apple iMovie comes preloaded on Mac computers. Figure 2.17 shows a movie being created using iMovie. In addition, several commercial products are available for about $100. Two of the most popular are Sony Vegas Movie Studio and Adobe Premiere Elements. Because video editing requires a lot of system resources, there are few online options available, but WeVideo is one of the best online alternatives.

MEDIA MANAGEMENT

Media management software is used to keep track of and play multimedia files—music, TV shows, and videos—on your computer. Media player software, such as Windows Media Player, Apple iTunes, and Winamp, are all examples of media management software. With iTunes, you can organize your music and videos and watch TV shows and movies (Figure 2.18).

GAMES

When you think of someone who plays video games, do you picture a young man shooting aliens? Games and simulations are more than just first-person shooters, and they're played by all sorts of people. Video game sales in 2013 reached $15.4 billion, with computer games sales accounting for about $220 million of that total. According to the Entertainment Software Association, 59 percent of Americans play video games, the average age of a video game player is 31, 71 percent are over 18, and about 48 percent are female. So much for stereotypes.

Games are one type of software for which you really need to pay attention to the system requirements for installation. They take a lot of processing, memory, and video power to run well and display complex graphics (Figure 2.19), and trying to play a game on an inadequate system will just frustrate you.

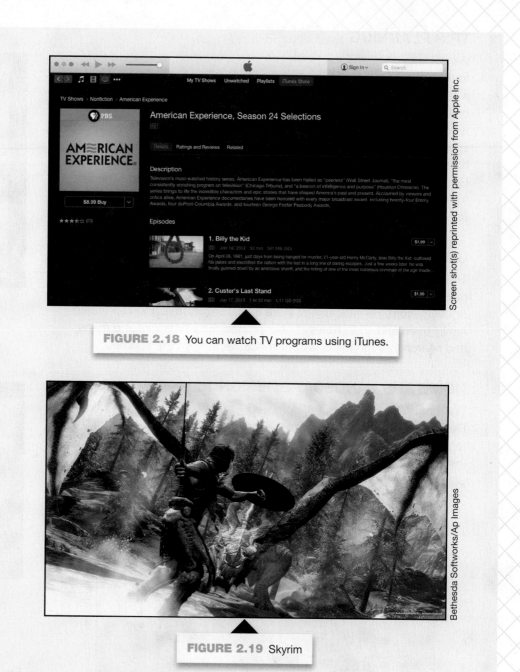

FIGURE 2.18 You can watch TV programs using iTunes.

FIGURE 2.19 Skyrim

Educational and Reference Software

Educational and reference software is a broad category of software. The increase in tablets and other mobile devices has driven the development of thousands of apps to study, plan, design, and create just about anything you could imagine. More than any other category we have discussed, educational and reference software options are mobile and cloud-based applications. Let's look at a few of the most popular offerings.

TRIP PLANNING

When I was a kid and the family planned a vacation, we had to go to the store to buy maps, tour books, and yellow highlighters. We would spend hours mapping out our route, planning our stops based on the outdated information in the tour books, and hoping the food would be decent and the hotel rooms would be clean. Today, I still spend hours researching and planning our trips, but I use mobile apps or online mapping software, such as Bing Maps (Figure 2.20) or Google Maps, and I read online reviews from other travelers. Thanks to the software available, I can easily reroute a trip if something unexpected happens.

GENEALOGY

There are many genealogy tools on the market today. One of the most popular is Family Tree Maker (Figure 2.21), which integrates with Ancestry.com. For Mac users, there is MacFamilyTree. You can create family trees and slideshows of your photos, view timelines and maps, and search through millions of historical records on the Internet.

HOME AND LANDSCAPE DESIGN

Want to build a deck? Plant a garden? Remodel your kitchen? Rearrange your furniture? Paint the dining room? Home and landscape design software has you covered. Free or retail, online or installed on your system, there are programs to help you design and plan all your home improvement projects.

FIGURE 2.20 Windows Maps App

FIGURE 2.21 Ancestry.com

FIGURE 2.22 Paint your house with Colorjive.

Several online apps allow you to compare paint colors. Just upload a picture and experiment with the color choices until you find your favorites. Behr Paint (behr.com), Sherwin-Williams Color Visualizer (sherwin-williams.com), and Benjamin Moore Personal Color Viewer (benjaminmoore.com) all allow you to upload and color your own photos for free and select colors from their particular paint lines. Colorjive (colorjive.com) includes colors across multiple brands (Figure 2.22). You should use whatever program has the color codes for the brand of paint you plan to buy.

Portable Apps

You may sometimes find yourself without your own computer—at work, school, travel, or a friend's house. **Portable apps** are programs that you can carry and run from a flash drive. They need no installation, so you can run them on just about any computer system. Your settings and data are on your flash drive—not the host computer—and when you remove your drive, there's no personal information left behind. One place to find portable apps is at portableapps.com. The Portable Apps platform is open source, and the apps are free. The same apps you use on your computer—office applications, web browsers, email clients, games, and utilities—can be run as portable apps (Figure 2.23).

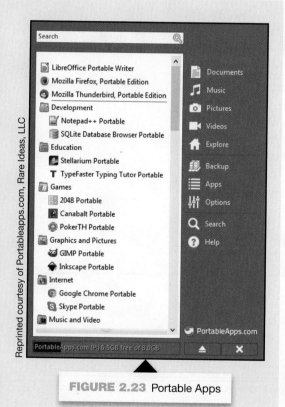

FIGURE 2.23 Portable Apps

Running Project

Use the Internet to learn about Apache OpenOffice. Is it available in different versions? What applications are included? Compare it to the Microsoft Office versions you researched in the previous project. Does Apache OpenOffice offer everything that Microsoft Office does? If not, what is missing?

4 Things You Need To Know

- Personal productivity software includes office applications as well as financial and reference software.
- Entertainment software includes media management software, photo and video editing software, and games.
- Educational and reference software is available for a variety of interests, including trip planning, genealogy, and landscaping.
- Portable apps can be stored on and run from a flash drive.

Key Terms

open source

portable apps

Digital Literacy Skill

Create a Document Using WordPad or TextEdit

HOW TO VIDEO

Microsoft Windows includes a word processing application called WordPad. OS X includes TextEdit. These are basic programs that can be used to create simple documents, such as homework assignments, even if you don't have a full word processor, such as Microsoft Word, installed.

The figure below identifies the parts of the WordPad window:
- The File menu contains commands to open, save, print, and email your documents.
- The Quick Access toolbar has buttons for save, undo, and redo by default, but you can customize it by clicking the arrow on the right.
- The ribbon has two tabs: Home and View. The Home tab contains the commands for formatting the document and inserting objects; the View tab contains commands to change the way the document displays on your screen.

1

To start WordPad, from the Windows Start menu or Search bar, begin to type **wordpad**. In the Search results, click *WordPad*. In the blank document area of the WordPad screen, type **Chapter 2 How to Use WordPad** and press Enter. On the next line, type your name and press Enter twice.

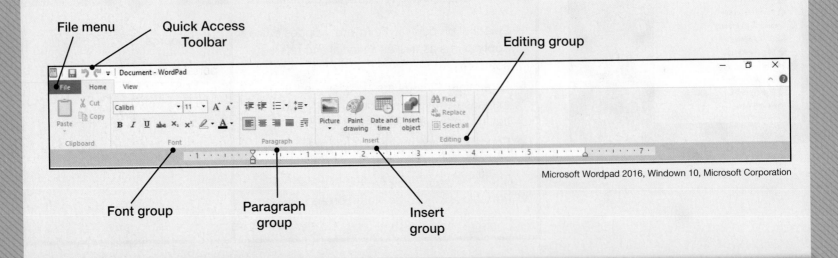

File menu Quick Access Toolbar Editing group

Font group Paragraph group Insert group

Microsoft Wordpad 2016, Window 10, Microsoft Corporation

2 Type the following paragraph:
WordPad is a basic word processor that is included with Windows. I can use it to type homework assignments and other documents that are compatible with most word processing programs.

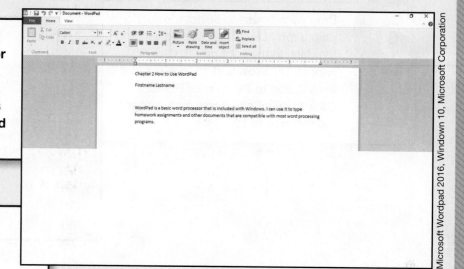

3 Press Enter. On the Home tab, in the Paragraph group, click the *Start a list* button and type the following three bullet points (press Enter after each):

Free

Easy to use

Compatible

4 Press Enter again to exit the bulleted list. In the Insert group, click the *Date and time* button; select a date format that includes the day of the week. Click *OK*.

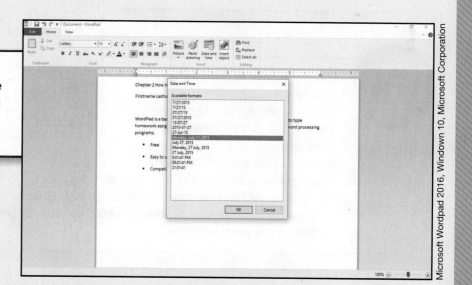

5 Drag your mouse to select the paragraph of text, the bulleted list, and the date. In the Font group, click the *Font family* arrow and change the font from Calibri to Times New Roman. Click the *Font size* arrow and change the font size to 12.

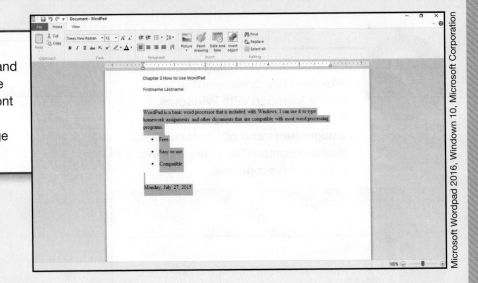

6 Select the first two lines and, in the Paragraph group, click the *Center* button. In the Font group, change the font size to 14 and click the *B* button to make the text bold.

7 Click *File*, point to *Save as*, and choose the appropriate format. The default format is *Rich Text document*, which is compatible with all word processors. If you're required to submit your work in the Microsoft Word format, select *Office Open XML document* from the list instead. Navigate to the folder where you are saving your Chapter 2 work and save the file as **lastname_firstname_ch02_howto1**. Submit this file as directed by your instructor.

If you are using a Mac:

In OS X, TextEdit has a menu bar with six menu choices:

The TextEdit menu includes options to customize the program.

- The File menu includes items such as Open, Close, Save, and Print.
- The Edit menu is where you find options to edit the text in your document, such as Cut, Copy, Insert, and the Spelling and Grammar checker.
- The Format menu has tools to format text, tables, lists, etc.
- The View menu enables you to zoom in and out.
- The Window menu enables you to modify how a document displays on your screen.

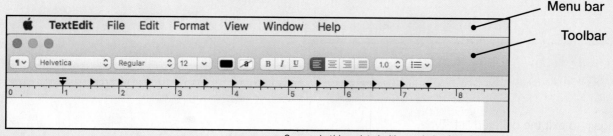

Menu bar

Toolbar

Screen shot(s) reprinted with permission from Apple Inc.

1. Open *TextEdit* from the Launchpad. If necessary, in the TextEdit dialog box, click *New Document*. Click the *Format* menu and then click *Wrap to Page*. In the blank document area of the TextEdit document, type **Chapter 2 How to Use TextEdit** and press Enter. On the next line, type your name and press Enter twice.
2. Type the following paragraph:

   TextEdit is a basic word processor that is included with OS X. I can use it to type homework assignments and other documents that are compatible with most word processing programs.

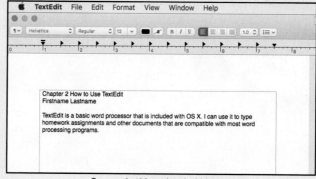

Screen shot(s) reprinted with permission from Apple Inc.

3. Press Enter. Click the *List bullets and numbering* button. Below *None*, click the second (round) bullet choice, and type the following three bullet points (press Enter after each):

Free
Easy to use
Compatible

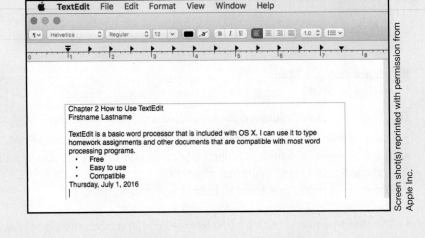

4. Press Enter again to exit the bulleted list. Type the current date, using the format *Thursday, July 1, 2016*, and press Enter.
5. Drag your mouse to select the paragraph of text, the bulleted list, and the date. Click the *Choose the font family* arrow and change the font from Helvetica to Times. Verify the font size is set to 12.

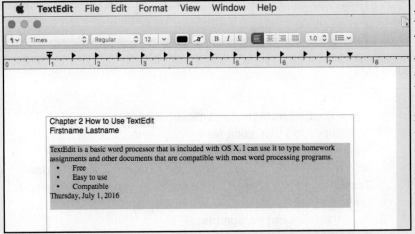

6. Select the first two lines and click the *Center text* button. Set the font size to 14 and click the *B* button to make the text bold.

7. Click *File*, click *Save*, and choose the appropriate format. The default format is *Rich Text Document*, which is compatible with all word processors. If you're required to submit your work in the Microsoft Word format, select *Word 2007 (.docx) Document* from the list instead. Click the Where arrow, navigate to the folder where you are saving your Chapter 2 work, and save the file as **lastname_firstname_ch02_howto1**. Submit this file as directed by your instructor.

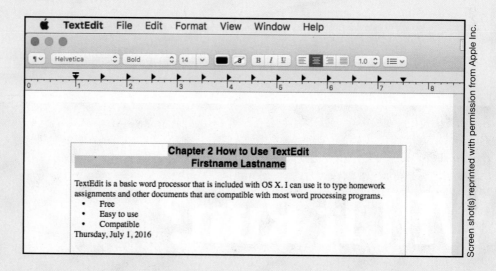

Tsiumpa/Fotolia

Will It Run?

Assess a Computer System for Software Compatibility

Your best friend just told you about an awesome new game she bought. Should you run right out and buy it, too? At $60, the game is an investment that warrants at least a little bit of research on your part, as do most other software purchases. So what do you need to know?

Your System Specs

Before you rush out—or go online—to buy software, you need to do a little bit of work. You need to document your system specs so you can compare them to the system requirements of the software. That is the only way you'll know whether your system can run the program.

Most store-bought software requires a DVD drive to do the installation. Although a few programs will run from a DVD or flash drive, most programs are installed on your computer's hard drive. Many newer, lighter notebook computers no longer include a DVD drive. To install software on a system without a DVD drive, you can purchase an external drive, but the easiest thing to do is to install software that you download directly from the web. The amount of drive space required for the installed software is listed in the system requirements. You can verify that you have enough free space by opening File Explorer. The Windows computer in Figure 2.24 has a CD drive. It has 45.3 GB of free space on the hard drive (C:) labeled OS, and 146 GB free on the second drive (E:) labeled Data. There is also a removable disk with 407 MB free.

On a Windows computer, obtain the other information you need by using the System control panel. To do this, open *File Explorer*, right-click *This PC*, and then click *Properties*. (Note: On earlier versions of Windows, right-click *Computer*.) Most of the information you need is found on this page: operating system version, processor type and speed, and amount of memory installed (Figure 2.25).

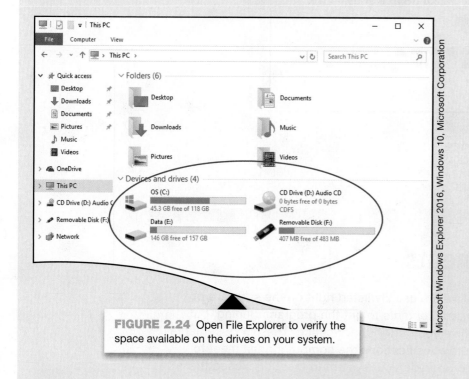

FIGURE 2.24 Open File Explorer to verify the space available on the drives on your system.

Microsoft Windows Explorer 2016, Windows 10, Microsoft Corporation

Windows System Information

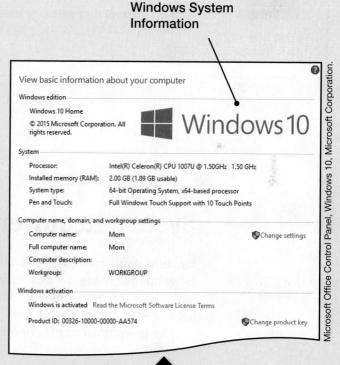

Microsoft Office Control Panel, Windows 10, Microsoft Corporation.

FIGURE 2.25 You can use the System control panel window to determine whether a computer meets the system requirements for a particular software application.

To find this information on a Mac, click the *Apple* menu and then click *About This Mac*. On the About This Mac screen, click *More Info*. The Storage tab (Figure 2.26) lists disk drive information. The other system specs, such as processor speed, memory, and operating system version, are located in the other tabs in this window.

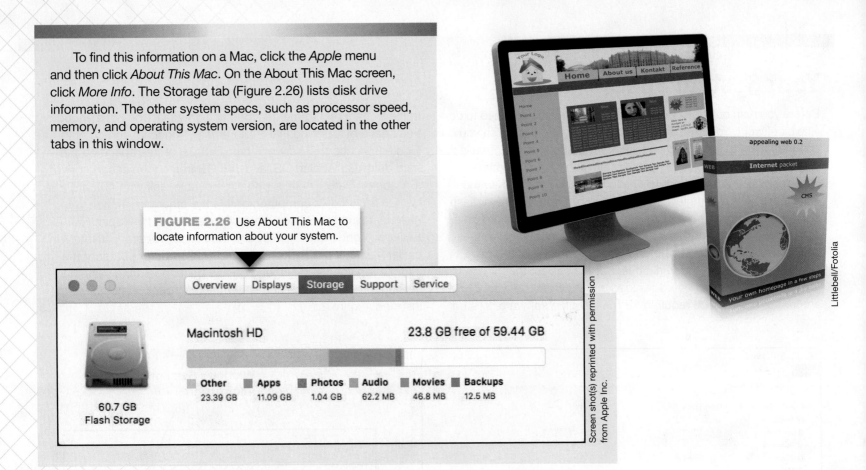

FIGURE 2.26 Use About This Mac to locate information about your system.

Screen shot(s) reprinted with permission from Apple Inc.

Littlebell/Fotolia

System Requirements

System requirements for software are usually listed right on the software box or webpage. These are *minimum requirements* to get the program running, but exceeding the requirements will give you better performance. These requirements list both the hardware and software specifications the computer must meet to run the program. You may need to upgrade your system to meet or exceed these requirements. As software becomes more sophisticated, the system requirements go up.

It's important to know the system requirements for a program before you buy it so you're not stuck with a purchase that you can't use. Spending a few minutes verifying that your system meets the requirements will help ensure that you can actually use the software you buy or let you know if a system upgrade is necessary.

CAREER SPOTLIGHT

SOFTWARE TRAINERS—Software trainers—sometimes called corporate trainers—are in demand as companies deploy more software programs. This high-paying career may involve some travel and requires good computer skills, organization, and communication skills. Software trainers usually have at least a bachelor's degree and on-the-job training. Some companies offer train-the-trainer courses that can lead to certification. You might work for a training company, in the training department of a large company, or as a consultant to many companies.

Running Project

Research a game or program that you would like to run on your computer. What are the system requirements for the program? Does your computer meet the minimum requirements? In what ways does it exceed them?

Viz Check—In MyITLab, take a quick quiz covering Objectives 1–3.

3 Things You Need to Know

- File Explorer can help you determine the drives and storage space available on your computer.
- You can find out your system specifications by using the System control panel or the About This Mac window.
- System requirements are the minimum requirements needed to run software and include hardware and software specifications.

Key Term

system requirements

Natalia Merziyakova/Fotolia

Where To Get It

4 Compare Various Ways of Obtaining Software

There are several different ways to obtain software. You can go out to a store and buy it, order it online and have it shipped to you, or download it from a website or app store. In this article, we look at software licensing and how to obtain software.

Licensing

When you purchase and install software on your computer, you may not actually own the program. Instead, you license it. The software is owned by the company that created it. There are several different software license types. Carefully read the **EULA (end-user license agreement)**—the agreement between the user and the software publisher—on all software to know your rights before you install it, including the number of computers you can legally install it on, the length of time you have access to it, and any privacy notices (Figure 2.27). You should also look for important hidden information in the fine print. For example, by clicking *I Agree* on some EULAs, you allow the installation of additional "features" such as toolbars and spyware on your computer.

The two most common software licenses are:

- **Proprietary software license:** Grants a license to use one or more copies of software, but ownership of those copies remains with the software publisher. This is the type of license found on most commercial software and is the most restrictive in terms of your rights to distribute and install the software.
- **Open source software license:** Grants ownership of the copy to the end user. The source code for that software must be made freely available. The end user has the right to modify and redistribute the software under the same license. Open source software is growing in popularity, and there are more offerings available all the time.

In both cases, there may or may not be a fee for the use of the software. The cost of software is a big factor in choosing which programs to install.

Free or Fee

The cost of software is determined by the publisher. Not all proprietary software has a fee, and not all open source software is free. There are four basic models for software distribution:

- **Retail software:** The user pays a fee to use the software. Microsoft Office, Adobe Photoshop, and TurboTax are all examples of retail software.
- **Freeware:** The software can be used at no cost for an unlimited period of time. Popular freeware includes Apple iTunes, Evernote, and 7-Zip.
- **Shareware:** Software may be offered in trial form or for a limited period that allows you to try it out before purchasing a license. It's sometimes referred to as trialware. This marketing model of selling software has become so popular that you can purchase most retail software this way. You can download a 30- or 60-day free trial of products from Microsoft, Adobe, and many other publishers. New computers often come preloaded with lots of trialware.
- **Donationware:** With this form of freeware, the developers accept donations, either for themselves or for a nonprofit organization. Apache OpenOffice is an example of donationware.

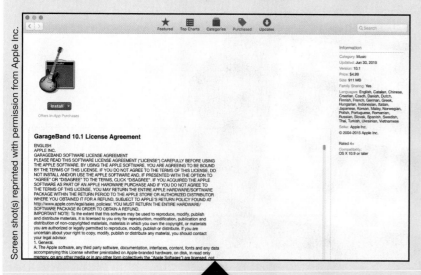

FIGURE 2.27 The GarageBand Software License Agreement

Sources of Software

Software is available in a variety of places. Where you choose to obtain it depends on the type of software you're looking for and the time frame in which you need it. You can purchase software in specialized computer and electronics stores, office supply stores, and discount and mass merchandise stores. The price and variety of programs available in these places will vary widely. If you're looking for a popular piece of software, such as game or tax preparation software, then you'll likely find it for a good price, but if you're looking for something less popular, you may have a hard time finding it on the shelf.

A much larger selection of software is available through online retailers, such as **Amazon.com**. These sites sell the same software in a box and ship it to you. Some software may also be available for immediate download. Online retailers often have a larger selection of software than retail stores, and prices are comparable. When you purchase software directly from the software publisher's website, you can immediately download it. The cost can be competitive with retailers, but it pays to shop around.

Helen Sessions/Alamy

Websites such as **cnet.com**, **tucows.com**, and **zdnet.com** have huge libraries of freeware and shareware to download. For open source software, go to **sourceforge.net**. An advantage to using sites like these is that they include editor and user reviews to help you choose the program that is right for you. Also, these websites test the programs for malicious intent, but it still makes sense to be careful. Read the reviews and look out for any suspicious terms in the licenses and installers.

The Mac App Store is part of OS X (Figure 2.28) and gives you access to thousands of programs for your Mac. Software apps for mobile devices should be downloaded from trusted sources. It is safest if you use the recommended app store or marketplace for your device. The apps must pass through rigorous testing to be placed in the market, thus reducing the risk of malicious or harmful code running on your device.

When you download software from a website, it's good practice to back up the downloaded file and license in case you ever need to reinstall the program. Wherever you finally decide to purchase software, be sure that you understand the license terms before you click the *I Accept* button.

FIGURE 2.28 Mac App Store Best New Apps

Running Project

Use the Internet to find out what the terms *volume license* and *single-seat license* mean. What are they? How are they alike? How are they different?

3 Things You Need to Know

- When you purchase software, you don't own it but are only licensing it—unless it's open source.
- You should read the EULA (end-user license agreement) to determine the restrictions and potential add-on features related to the software before you install it.
- Not all proprietary software has a fee, and not all open source software is free.

Key Terms

donationware

EULA (end-user license agreement)

freeware

retail software

shareware

Dragonstock/Fotolia

Your Head in the Cloud

Objective 5

Discuss the Importance of Cloud Computing

You may have heard the term *cloud computing*. The term **cloud** refers to the Internet. **Cloud computing** takes processing and storage off your desktop and business hardware and puts it in the cloud. As the need for storage, security, and collaboration has grown, cloud computing has become an important part of business and personal systems.

Cloud Computing

Three types of services can be delivered through the cloud: Infrastructure-as-a-Service, Platform-as-a-Service, and Software-as-a-Service (Figure 2.29). Together, these three services can provide a business with an integrated system for delivering applications and content using the cloud. The companies that deliver these cloud services, such as Amazon, Google, and Salesforce, are known as **cloud service providers (CSPs)**. Cloud solutions save money in software, hardware, and personnel costs; increase standardization; and increase efficiency and access to technology. CSPs can build huge datacenters in remote locations near cheap and green power supplies, such as hydroelectric plants, which is impractical for most businesses.

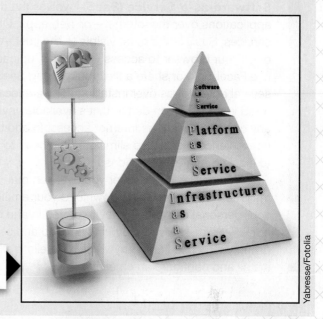

FIGURE 2.29 Cloud Computing Services

Yabresse/Fotolia

INFRASTRUCTURE-AS-A-SERVICE (IaaS)

Cost of infrastructure, such as computer hardware, cabling, and cooling, can be as much as 80 percent of a typical IT budget. With **Infrastructure-as-a-Service (IaaS)**, a company uses servers in the cloud instead of purchasing and maintaining them. This reduces costs for hardware, software, and support personnel. Companies that don't have the expertise in-house can have sophisticated servers to house large databases, centralized document management, and security, using and paying for just what they need, so they can increase their usage during surges in demand, such as holiday or tax season, and decrease it during lulls. A commonly used IaaS service is off-site backup services.

Mathias Rosenthal/Fotolia

PLATFORM-AS-A-SERVICE (PaaS)

Platform-as-a-Service (PaaS) provides a programming environment to develop, test, and deploy custom web applications. This gives businesses the ability to build, deploy, and manage SaaS applications. PaaS also makes collaboration easier and requires less programming knowledge than traditional programming tools. Three popular PaaS programs are AppEngine from Google, Force.com from SalesForce, and Microsoft Azure Services Platform.

Mathias Rosenthal/Fotolia

SOFTWARE-AS-A-SERVICE (SaaS)

Software-as-a-Service (SaaS) involves the delivery of applications over the Internet—or web apps. Of the cloud services, SaaS is the most visible to the user. Any time you open your browser to access your email, upload photos, use Facebook, or share a file, you're using SaaS. SaaS has several advantages over installing software locally. Because SaaS is delivered on demand, it's available anytime from any computer that has Internet access. In addition to the convenience, SaaS also eliminates the need to apply updates to local software installations.

You use SaaS whenever you use web mail. Using web mail means that you don't download your email messages to your personal computer. They're stored in and accessed from a hosted email server, providing backup and security for you, giving you access from anywhere, and eliminating the need to install and configure an email program on your computer.

Mathias Rosenthal/Fotolia

Microsoft Office Online and Google Drive are examples of personal SaaS. For businesses, there are more powerful, fee-based tools. Google Apps for Business and Microsoft Office 365 include collaboration tools, email, calendar, and documents. Table 2.1 compares the costs of using Microsoft Office 2016, Google Apps, and Microsoft Office 365 for a small business with 10 users.

TABLE 2.1 Small Business Costs

Cost Comparison for a Small Business	Microsoft Office Home and Business 2016	Google Apps for Business	Microsoft Office 365 Business Premium	Microsoft Office 365 Business Essentials
Initial cost	$229.99 per license	—	—	—
Price per user per year	—	$50	$150	$60
Annual cost for 10 users	$2,299 for the first year (or $766 per year for three years*) plus support costs	$500	$1,500	$600
Cost for three years	$2,299	$1,500	$4,500	$1,800
Support/updates	Local updates must be done on-site by users or IT Microsoft community support	24/7 phone and email support; self-serviced online support	Microsoft community support Apps always up to date	Telephone and online answers, how-to resources
		Web apps only—no desktop applications	Includes web apps and desktop applications and Office on Demand streaming of full-featured versions of Office on Windows computers	Web apps only—works with your existing versions of desktop applications

*There is a new Microsoft Office release about every three years.

Geoghan, Debra. Visualizing Technology Complete, 4e. Pearson Education, 2014.

Applying an update to an application on each computer can be a costly, time-consuming process. However, with a SaaS solution, updates happen on the remote system and do not affect local users. Users instantly have access to new features as soon as they log into their account on a SaaS site. No local configuration is needed.

For businesses, using the cloud to deliver apps offers several benefits: a simple and quick way of accessing applications from anywhere, a relatively small cost per user, and the elimination of the need to maintain and support the applications on site. SaaS may not be a term most people use very often, but the services it provides are used every day by individuals and businesses alike. As cloud computing continues to mature, you'll find more and more of your computing up in the cloud.

Running Project

Does your school use cloud computing—also known as above-campus computing? If so, which services (e.g., email, apps) do you access from the cloud? Give two examples of your personal use of cloud computing.

3 Things You Need to Know	Key Terms
<ul><li>The cloud is the Internet.</li><li>Cloud computing uses hardware and software resources that are in the cloud instead of local.</li><li>Cloud computing consists of three types of services: Infrastructure-as-a-Service (IaaS), Platform-as-a-Service (PaaS), and Software-as-a-Service (SaaS).</li></ul>	cloud cloud computing cloud service provider (CSP) Infrastructure-as-a-Service (IaaS) Platform-as-a-Service (PaaS) platform-neutral Software-as-a-Service (SaaS)

How To?

Essential Job Skill

Create a Mobile App with Appy Pie

HOW TO VIDEO

A mobile app allows you to build customer loyalty and provide customers with instant services and information. To build a sophisticated app, you need a programmer, but you can use free, online drag-and-drop tools to create a basic app for your business. The free versions are somewhat limited but may be all you need for a small business presence. You can start with a free account and upgrade later to add more features or professional development services. In this project, you will use Appy Pie to create a free mobile app for JMG Landscaping.

Appy Pie is a drag-and-drop app creation tool, which means you can find premade app components that you simply drag onto a screen and then customize. You can create a free account using your email address, or you can log in using your Facebook account. If necessary, download the student data files from pearsonhighered.com/viztech. From your student data files, open the *vt_ch02_howto2_answersheet* file and save the file as **lastname_firstname_ch02_howto2_answersheet**.

---

1 Go to **appypie.com** and click *Free Sign Up*. Create a new Appy Pie account by using your email address. Click *Sign Up* and then, on the Dashboard, click *Create New App*.

2 Scroll down and roll over several icons to preview the types of apps you can create. Enter the app name **Lastname Firstname App** Click *Business* and then click *Next*.

Courtesy of AppyPie.com

3 On the Build tab, Under App Pages, under Recommended, click the *About* icon to add this page to your app. In the *Description* box, type **We are JMG Landscaping, family-owned and operated since 1985.** (include the period). Enter your name as the *Founder*, and in the *Founded* box type **1985**. At the bottom of the page, click *Add Page*.

Courtesy of AppyPie.com

4 Under Recommended, click *Contacts* and enter the following information in the appropriate fields: *Name* **JMG Landscaping**, *Call* **215-555-4566**, *Email* **info@jmglandscaping.net**, *Website* **http://jmglandscaping.net**. Leave the remaining fields blank. At the bottom of the page, click *Add Page*.

Courtesy of AppyPie.com

5

Under Social, click *Facebook*. In the *Enter Facebook URL* box, type **https://facebook.com/visualizingtechnology** and then click *Preview* to verify that the link works. If the preview does not work, verify that the URL protocol you typed is *https*. Take a screenshot of this page and paste it into your answer sheet. Click *Add Page*.

6

Under *Commerce*, click *Coupon*. In the *Heading* box, type **Pre-season Clean-up**. In the *Date Of Issue* box, click the date picker and select today's date. Change the *Valid Till* date to the end of the following month. Verify that the Scanner Code Type is set to *QR code*, enter **PRE20** in the *Coupon Code* box, and then click **GENERATE**. Take a screenshot of this page and paste it into your answer sheet. Click *Add Page*.

QR code generated

7 Click the Style & Navigation tab. Click *App Icon*. Click the *Upload New* tab. Click the existing icon, browse to the location of your student data files for this chapter, select the file **logo_sm.png**, and then click *Open*. If necessary, drag to center the logo in the box, and then click *SAVE*.

Courtesy of AppyPie.com

8 Click *Splash Screen* and then click the *Upload Splash Screen* tab. Under For Portrait, click the existing image, browse to the location of your student data files for this chapter, select the file **splash.jpg**, and then click *Open*. If necessary, drag the sizing handle of the image selection box to make the image fill the box. Select *Use the same image for both Portrait and Landscape modes* and then click *SAVE*.

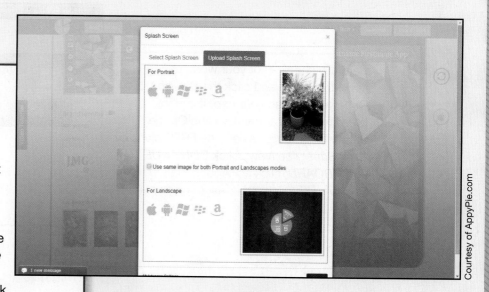

Courtesy of AppyPie.com

9 Under App Background, browse the images and select a suitable background image. Scroll down, and under Select Navigation Layout, select *Bottom.* Under App Overlay, select the green (first) theme.

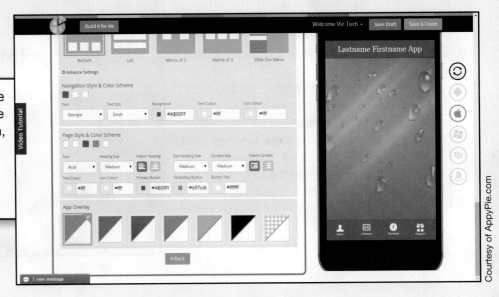

Courtesy of AppyPie.com

10 Carefully check all of your work, and then scroll to the top and click the *Publish* tab. Once you publish your app, it cannot be edited using a free account. On the Subscription page, select the FREE plan. Click *Subscribe Now*. Click *CONTINUE TO DASHBOARD*, click *My Apps*.

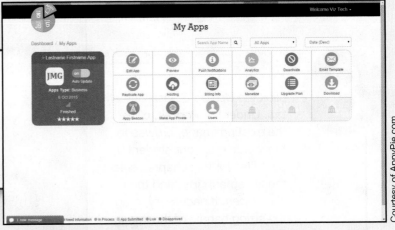

Courtesy of AppyPie.com

11 Click the *Download* link for your app. Take a screenshot of the *Download Your Apps* page and paste it into your answer sheet. Copy the URL of the page from the browser address bar (not the app package), paste it into your answer sheet, and submit it as directed by your instructor.

You have created an app that can be downloaded and used on a mobile device. Return to your dashboard and wait 5–10 minutes before proceeding (Note: It may take up to 2 hours before your app is available). On the Dashboard, click *My Apps*. You can preview the app using the simulator in your browser. Click the *Download* button and read about the options to download your app. The URL and QR code provided can be embedded in your website or other media to share your app with customers. Appy Pie uses HTML5 to build apps, which is a **platform-neutral** language that works on all modern personal computing systems. That means you can create one app that can be used on the web and on iOS, Android, and Windows devices. To create apps for some platforms requires a paid Appy Pie account.

Psphotography/Fotolia

Managing Software on Your System

6 Install, Uninstall, and Update Software

Some specialized devices have their instructions coded into the firmware, but most programs must be installed on a computer. Managing the programs on your computer includes installing, uninstalling, and updating the software. It is important to keep software current and to uninstall unneeded programs to keep your system running efficiently, free up disk space, and prevent flawed software from enabling malware or hacker attacks.

Installing Software

The process of installing software copies files to the computer and may alter system settings and create new folders. The installation process might require you to enter administrator credentials to proceed. There are three ways to install software on a personal computer: through an app store, by using media such as a flash drive or DVD, or by downloading it from a website.

When you purchase an app from the Windows Store (Figure 2.30), click *Buy*, *Try*, or *Install*, depending on the type of app you want, and the installation will proceed automatically. If it is a paid app, you will have to complete the purchase before you install the program. A message will appear in the upper-right corner of the screen, indicating that the program is being installed, and a notification will pop up when the installation is finished. From the Mac App Store, for a free app, click *Get* and then click *Install App*. For a paid app, click the price and then click *Buy App*. You must enter your Apple ID and password to complete the purchase and installation.

To install from a CD or DVD, insert the disc in the drive and follow the instructions on the screen. If the installation does not begin automatically, open File Explorer, click the disc in the Navigation pane, and then double-click the setup or installation file. On a Mac, double-click the disc image that appears on the desktop. Installing from a disc will likely require you to enter a product key to validate the software. Many notebook computers no longer include an optical drive for installing software in this manner.

To install a program from a website, click the link to download the file. If the file is zipped, you might need to unzip or extract it before you can install the program. You may be given the option to run or save the file. The advantage of saving the file is that you can use it to reinstall the program if the need arises. Locate and double-click the installer file, which is usually named Setup.

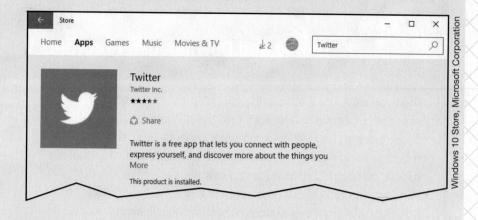

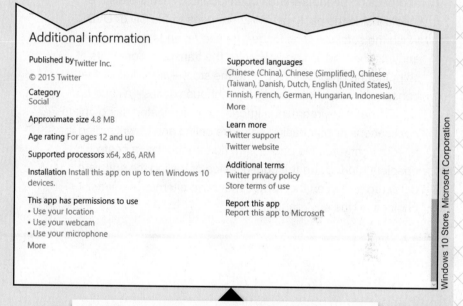

FIGURE 2.30 Install an app through the Windows Store.

GREEN COMPUTING
Online and Downloaded Programs Vs. Store-Bought Software

When you walk into a store and pick up software in a box or order from an online retailer and have the package shipped to you, there are several environmental impacts. First, there's product packaging and the packaging material used to ship the product. Although cardboard and paper are recyclable, the EPA estimates that only about 70 percent of it is actually recycled. The rest of it—and other materials, such as plastic shrink-wrap and packing peanuts—ends up in landfills. Then there's the media inside the package. What happens to the CD or DVD when the software is no longer needed? It ends up in the trash—and into the landfill it goes. Finally, the transportation costs of shipping the product to you or to the store—air pollution, fuel consumption, and emission of greenhouse gases—all add up.

All these environmental impacts are eliminated using online applications or purchasing software online and downloading it to your computer. No packaging, no transportation costs, no obsolete media, and the convenience of having the software delivered to you on the spot make these alternatives better choices for the environment.

Pablo Eder/Shutterstock

Updating and Uninstalling Software

Software publishers regularly release updates to their programs. These updates can address security holes, or **bugs**—flaws in the programming. An update might add new features, compatibility with new devices or file formats, or more levels to a game. A **patch**, or **hotfix**, addresses individual problems as they are discovered. A **service pack** is a larger, planned update that addresses multiple problems or adds multiple features. The previous patches and hotfixes are included in the service pack.

Updating software requires an Internet connection. Apps purchased through an app store can be updated through the store (Figure 2.31). Other programs require files to be downloaded from the web. You can configure software to check for updates automatically, or you can search for updates yourself. In a business environment, computers are generally not set to update software automatically because updates are centrally managed by the IT department.

When you no longer need a program on your computer, you should uninstall it by using the proper uninstaller to ensure that all files and settings are properly removed. Troubleshooting computer problems sometimes involves uninstalling and reinstalling software or updates. To view or uninstall the programs on a Windows computer, open File Explorer, in the Navigation pane click *This PC*, and then, on the Computer tab of the ribbon, click *Uninstall or change a program*. You can then run the uninstaller for the selected application.

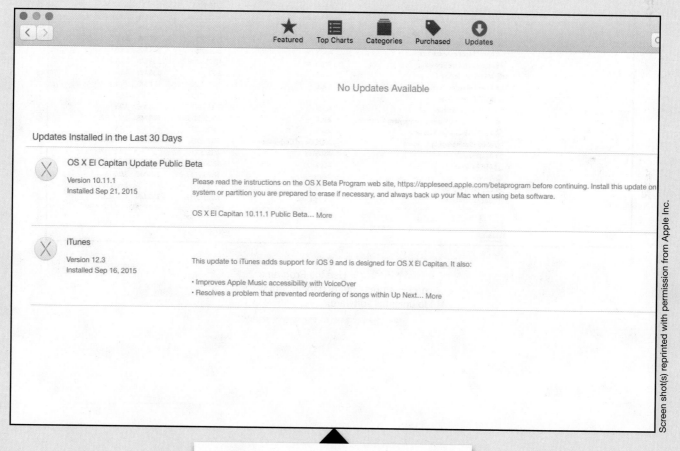

FIGURE 2.31 Update Apps through the App Store

In the Programs and Features window (Figure 2.32), locate the program that you want to uninstall. Click the program name and then click either the *Uninstall* or *Uninstall/Change* button that appears above the program list. The options available will vary depending on the program. To uninstall a program from the Start menu, right-click an app and then click *Uninstall*, which will open the Programs and Features window. To uninstall a program on a Mac, if no uninstaller is provided, simply drag the program from the Applications folder to the trash.

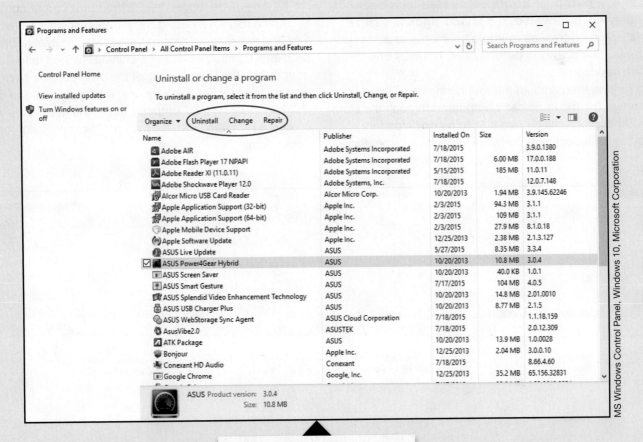

FIGURE 2.32 Use the Programs and Features control panel window to uninstall software.

ETHICS
Sharing Software

Jacob and Thomas share a dorm room, and each has his own notebook computer. The college provides students in the Computer Science department with several programs for their class work. One of the programs that Jacob receives as a part of his major is an expensive drawing program. Thomas has always wanted to learn the drawing program, but because it is so expensive he has not had a chance to try it out, so he asks Jacob to lend him a copy to install on his own computer. Jacob is unwilling to do so, because he knows the software license only allows him to install one copy of the program on his own computer, specifically for his class work. What should Jacob do? Is there a legal way for the guys to share the program?

Running Project

On your computer, open the Programs and Features control panel window (on a Mac, open the Applications folder). How many programs are installed on your system? What are they? How many do you use on a regular basis? Which ones do you think should be uninstalled and why?

3 Things You Need to Know

- Programs can be installed through an app store, using media such as a flash drive or DVD, or by downloading from a website.
- Software publishers regularly release updates to their programs.
- When you no longer need a program on your computer, you should uninstall it by using the proper uninstaller.

Key Terms

bug

hotfix

patch

service pack

Viz Check—In MyITLab, take a quick quiz covering Objectives 4–6.

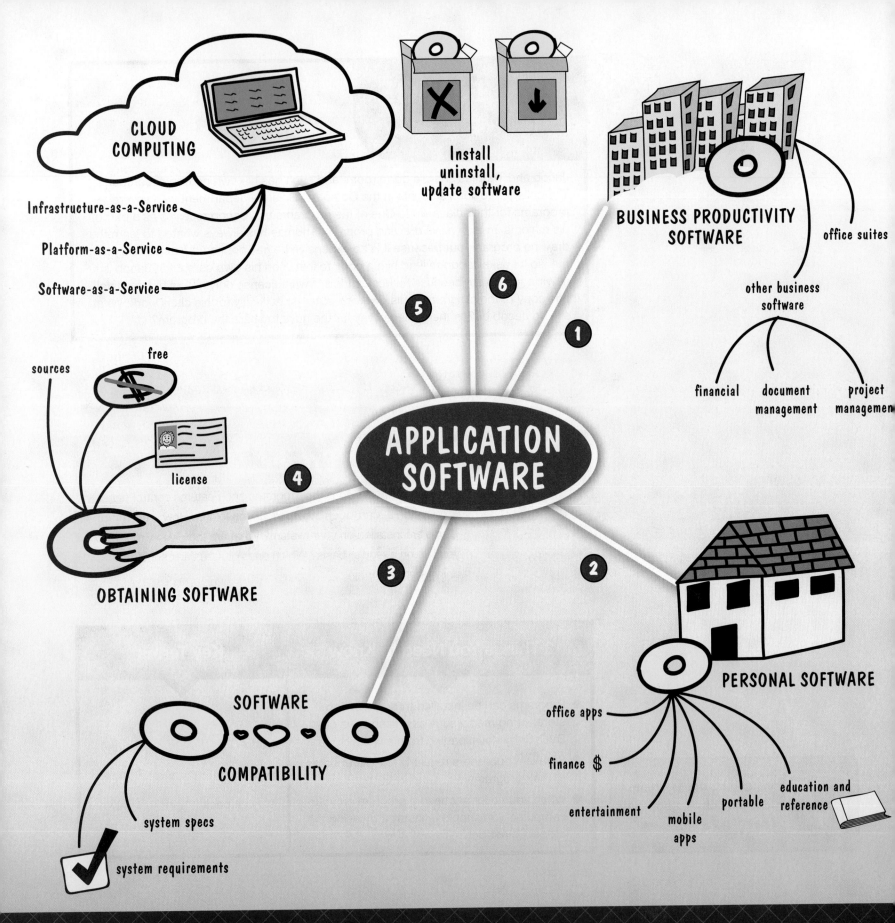

CLOUD COMPUTING

Infrastructure-as-a-Service

Platform-as-a-Service

Software-as-a-Service

Install uninstall, update software

BUSINESS PRODUCTIVITY SOFTWARE

office suites

other business software

financial   document management   project management

APPLICATION SOFTWARE

6

5

1

4

3

2

sources

free

license

OBTAINING SOFTWARE

SOFTWARE

COMPATIBILITY

system specs

system requirements

PERSONAL SOFTWARE

office apps

finance $

entertainment

mobile apps

portable

education and reference

Objectives Recap

1. Identify Types and Uses of Business Productivity Software
2. Identify Types and Uses of Personal Software
3. Assess a Computer System for Software Compatibility
4. Compare Various Ways of Obtaining Software
5. Discuss the Importance of Cloud Computing
6. Install, Uninstall, and Update Software

Key Terms

application software 53
bug 99
cell 57
cloud 86
cloud computing 86
cloud service provider (CSP) 87
database 59
document management system (DMS) 61
donationware 83
EULA (end-user license agreement) 83
field 59
form 59
freeware 83
Gantt chart 62
hotfix 99
Infrastructure-as-a-Service (IaaS) 87
office application suite 55
open source 65

patch 99
personal information manager (PIM) 60
Platform-as-a-Service (PaaS) 87
platform neutral 95
portable apps 71
project management software 62
query 59
record 59
report 59
retail software 83
service pack 99
shareware 83
Software-as-a-Service (SaaS) 88
spreadsheet 57
system requirements 80
table 59
word processor 55

Summary

1. Identify Types and Uses of Business Productivity Software

The most common business software is an office application suite—which may include a word processor, spreadsheet, presentation program, database, and personal information manager. Other business applications include financial software, document management, and project management software.

2. Identify Types and Uses of Personal Software

Personal software includes office applications, especially word processors, spreadsheets, and presentation programs. Other personal applications include entertainment and multimedia software such as media managers, video and photo editing software, and video games. Financial and tax preparation software as well as educational and reference software are also popular. You can run portable apps from a flash drive and take them with you.

3. Assess a Computer System for Software Compatibility

Before purchasing and installing software, you should research the system requirements needed to run the program and compare them to your system specifications using the System Control Panel.

4. Compare Various Ways of Obtaining Software

You can obtain software from brick-and-mortar and online stores, publisher websites, and download websites. Download mobile apps only from trusted markets. It's important to read the EULA to understand the software license restrictions.

5. Discuss the Importance of Cloud Computing

Cloud computing moves hardware and software into the cloud, or Internet. Cloud computing allows you to access applications and data from any web-connected computer. Some benefits include lower cost, easier maintenance, security, and collaboration.

6. Install, Uninstall, and Update Software

Managing the programs on your computer includes installing, uninstalling, and updating the software. You can install programs through an app store, by using media, or by downloading it from a website. Updating software fixes bugs, adds features, or improves compatibility. You should uninstall software using the program's uninstaller.

Multiple Choice

Answer the multiple-choice questions below for more practice with key terms and concepts from this chapter.

1. Which application would be the best choice for creating a budget?
   a. Database
   b. Personal information manager
   c. Spreadsheet
   d. Word processor

2. Software that has the source code published and made available to the public—enabling anyone to copy, modify, and redistribute it without paying a fee—is called _____ software.
   a. freeware
   b. open source
   c. trial version

3. Which object displays selected information?
   a. Field
   b. Form
   c. Record
   d. Report

4. _____ is an online alternative to office application suites.
   a. Google Drive
   b. OpenOffice
   c. TextEdit
   d. WordPad

5. _____ software helps you manage email, calendars, and tasks.
   a. Document management
   b. Personal information management
   c. Project management
   d. Word processing

6. Programs that can run from a flash drive are known as _____.
   a. open source software
   b. portable apps
   c. SaaS
   d. suites

7. The system requirements for software include the _____.
   a. amount of free drive space
   b. amount of RAM
   c. operating system version
   d. all of the above

8. _____ can be used for a limited period that allows the user to try it out before purchasing a license.
   a. Donationware
   b. Freeware
   c. Retail software
   d. Shareware

9. Which cloud computing service enables a company to use servers in the cloud instead of purchasing and maintaining them?
   a. IaaS
   b. PaaS
   c. SaaS

10. A(n) _____ is a large, planned software update that addresses multiple problems or adds multiple features.
    a. bug
    b. hotfix
    c. patch
    d. service pack

True or False

Answer the following questions with T for true or F for false for more practice with key terms and concepts from this chapter.

1. In a business environment, Microsoft Excel is the most popular spreadsheet application.

2. A field is the intersection of a row and a column in a spreadsheet.

3. Apache OpenOffice can open and work with documents created in Microsoft Office.

4. Documents created with a word processor can also contain images.

5. A project management system enables a company to save, share, search, and audit electronic documents throughout their life cycle.

6. A Gantt chart shows the schedule and progress of a project.

7. If your computer doesn't meet the minimum system requirements for a piece of software, it will probably still run on your system.

8. Trialware is a form of freeware where the developers accept donations, either for themselves or for a nonprofit organization.

9. Web mail is an example of PaaS.

10. It is generally safe to download mobile apps from unknown sources.

Fill in the Blank

Fill in the blanks with key terms from this chapter.

1. A(n) _____ is an application that creates electronic worksheets composed of rows and columns.

2. A(n) _____ is a row of data in a database table that describes a particular entry in the database.

3. A(n) _____ is a database object used to enter data into a database table.

4. A(n) _____ is used to save, share, search, and audit electronic documents throughout their life cycle.

5. _____ software has its source code published and made available to the public, enabling anyone to copy, modify, and redistribute it.

6. _____ are the minimum hardware and software specifications required to run a software application.

7. _____ is a form of freeware where the developers accept donations, either for themselves or for a nonprofit organization.

8. The license agreement between the software user and the software publisher is the _____.

9. Part of cloud computing, _____ is the delivery of applications—or web apps—over the Internet.

10. A(n) _____ is a flaw in software programming.

Running Project...

...The Finish Line

Assume that you just got a new computer with no software on it. Use your answers to the previous sections of the project to help you select five pieces of software that you consider indispensable to have. Which programs did you pick and why? If you could only afford to buy one program, which would it be? Which would you likely use a web-based tool for?

Write a report describing your selections and responding to the questions raised throughout the chapter. Save your file as **lastname_firstname_ch02_project** and submit it to your instructor as directed.

Do It Yourself 1

System requirements for new software often require a computer system with lots of available processing power, storage space, and memory. In this activity, examine your own computer to help you make smart software purchases. Windows and OS X provide many details about your computer through built-in utilities. For this exercise, use the File Explorer window. For a Mac, use the About This Mac window to complete the table. From your student data files, open the file *vt_ch02_DIY1_answersheet* and save the file as **lastname_firstname_ch02_DIY1_answersheet**

Open File Explorer. If necessary, click *This PC*. In the right pane is a listing of all the drives available on your computer. If you are using a Mac, open the *About This Mac* window from the Apple menu and click the *Storage* tab. Complete the table below to record details about your system—include the name, capacity, and free space for each drive. Save the file and submit the assignment as directed by your instructor.

Hard Disk Drives	Other Devices	Network Locations

Do It Yourself 2

Windows and OS X come with several applications. In this activity, you'll examine these accessories. From your student data files, open the file *vt_ch02_DIY2_answersheet* and save the file as **lastname_firstname_ch02_DIY2_answersheet**

1. From the Windows 10 Start menu, click *All apps*. (From the Windows 8 Start Screen, in the bottom left corner, click the down arrow to display all apps. If necessary, click the arrow next to Apps to display by name.) Scroll to display Windows Accessories. For a Mac, click the *Launchpad* and review the programs on the first screen, then click *Other*. What programs are listed? Which of these programs have you used in the past? Are there any that you are unfamiliar with?

2. Use Windows Help to learn about Calculator, Math Input Panel, Paint, and Sticky Notes. If you are using a Mac, on the Finder menu bar, click *Help*, and search for Apps included with your Mac. Look up Calculator, Solver, Preview, and Stickies. Write a one- to two-paragraph summary of each application. Save the file and submit it as directed by your instructor.

Critical Thinking

You're starting a small photography business. You need an inexpensive but powerful photo editing program to touch up your Images. Compare two photo editing programs in the $75–$200 range. From your student data files, open the file *vt_ch02_CT_answersheet* and save the file as **lastname_firstname_ch02_CT_answersheet**

1. Evaluate two photo editing programs from online retailers and compare them with respect to your requirements. Complete the table below, comparing the features of each program, to organize your research.

	Program 1	Program 2
Name of program		
Cost		
Local install or online?		
Important features		
Online ratings (website)		
Support		

2. Write your conclusion in a two- to three-paragraph essay. Which program should you buy and why? Is there anything else (hardware, software, office supplies) that you'll need to purchase to use the program? Save your file and submit both your table and essay as directed by your instructor.

Ethical Dilemma

You decided to buy an expensive video editing program and look online for a good deal. You find a listing from a seller that has good ratings, so you buy the software. When the software arrives, you're disappointed to find that it is a pirated copy and includes a program to generate a license key to unlock the program—a key gen program. From your student data files, open the file *vt_ch02_ethics_answersheet* and save the file as **lastname_firstname_ch02_ethics_answersheet**

You bought the software in good faith and really need it to complete your homework assignment. What do you do? Would you install the software? Why or why not? Is it acceptable to install the software for the assignment and uninstall it when you're finished? Save the file and submit it as directed by your instructor.

On the Web

The SourceForge website is a great place to find open source software. From your student data files, open the file *vt_ch02_web_answersheet* and save the file as **lastname_firstname_ch02_web_answersheet**

1. Go to **sourceforge.net**. What are the projects of the month and editor's choices? Click the title of each project to view the webpage of the project. Complete the following table.

Project	Brief Description	Rating	Last Updated

2. Select an application category from the menu on the left. Choose one application that looks interesting and that you do not already use. Read the description and reviews. What are the strengths and weaknesses of the program? Save the file and submit it as directed by your instructor.

Collaboration

Instructors: Divide the class into five groups, and assign each group one software license topic for this project. The topics include freeware, shareware, donationware, open source software, and EULAs.

The Project: As a team, prepare a multimedia presentation for your license type. The presentation should be designed to educate consumers about the license type. Use at least three references, only one of which may be this textbook. Use Google Docs or Microsoft Office to plan the presentation, and provide documentation that all team members have contributed to the project.

Outcome: Prepare a multimedia presentation on your assigned topic, using Prezi or another tool approved by your instructor, and present it to your class. The presentation may be no longer than 3 minutes. Turn in your file showing your collaboration named **teamname_ch02_collab** Include the URL to your presentation. Submit your presentation to your instructor as directed.

Application Project

myitlab grader

Office 2016 Application Projects
PowerPoint 2016: Introduction to PowerPoint Design

Project Description: Your boss has asked you to edit a PowerPoint presentation discussing good PowerPoint design. In this project, you will edit and format text and bullets, insert and format pictures, check spelling, add new slides and change slide layout, apply transitions, and add speaker notes. If necessary, download the student data files from **pearsonhighered.com/viztech**.

PowerPoint Design

Firstname Lastname

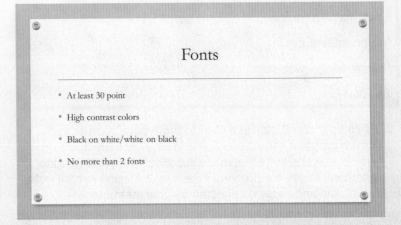

Fonts

- At least 30 point
- High contrast colors
- Black on white/white on black
- No more than 2 fonts

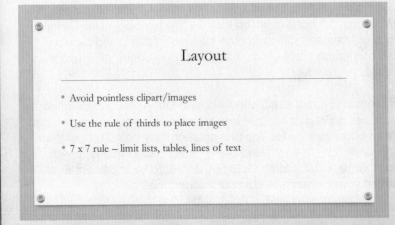

Layout

- Avoid pointless clipart/images
- Use the rule of thirds to place images
- 7 x 7 rule – limit lists, tables, lines of text

Images

Inserted Picture   Online Search

Step	Instructions
1	Start PowerPoint. From your student data files, open the file *vt_ch02_ppt*. Save the presentation as lastname_firstname_ch02_ppt
2	On Slide 1, using your own name, type the subtitle text **Firstname Lastname** Change the font of the title text, *PowerPoint Design,* to Cambria and change the size to 48.
3	On Slide 2, change the line spacing of the bullets to 1.5 and the font size to 28.
4	On Slide 3, use the shortcut menu to correct the spelling of *Layout*. Change the line spacing of the bullets to 1.5 and the font size to 28.
5	Insert a new Comparison slide after Slide 3 and add the title text **Images**
6	On the new Slide 4, in the bottom left content placeholder, insert the picture *vt_ch02_image2* In the content place holder, type **Inserted Picture**
7	On the new Slide 4, in the bottom right content placeholder, search for and insert an online image of a cat. In the content place holder, type **Online Search**
8	Format both images to a height of **2.5″** Align the middle of the images.
9	Switch to Slide Sorter view and delete Slide 5. Switch back to Normal view.
10	In the Notes pane on Slide 2, add the following speaker note: **Keep your fonts simple and easy to read.**
11	In the Notes pane on Slide 3, add the following speaker note: **Your layout should focus the viewer's attention.**
12	In the Notes pane on Slide 4, add the following speaker note: **Images should enhance what you have to say.**
13	Apply the Wipe transition with a duration of **01.50** to all of the slides in the presentation.
14	Insert the page number and then type your name as the footer on the notes and handouts pages for all slides in the presentation. View the presentation in Slide Show view from beginning to end, and then return to Normal view.
15	Save the presentation and close PowerPoint. Submit the presentation as directed.

Application Project

myitlab grader

Office 2016 Application Projects

Excel 2016: Comparing Office Application Suite Costs

Project Description: In this Microsoft Excel project, you will format cells and a worksheet. You will create a formula and insert a header and footer. *If necessary, download the student data files from* **pearsonhighered.com/viztech**.

Comparisons

Cost Comparison for a Small Business

	Google Apps for Business with Vault	MS Office 365 Small Business plan
Initial Cost - per license	-	-
Price Per User Per Month	10.00	12.50
Annual Cost for 10 Users	$ 100.00	$ 125.00
Apps included	Docs, Sheets, Slides, Mail, Calendar, Chat, Drive, Sites, Groups	Word, Excel, PowerPoint, Outlook, OneNote, Publisher, Access, Lync
Live Support/Updates	24/7 phone and email support	Telephone and online answers
		How-to resources, connections
Online Support	Self-service online support	with other Office 365 customers
Reliability	99.9% uptime guarantee	Guaranteed 99.9% uptime

Step	Instructions
1	Start Excel. From your student data files, open the Excel file named *vt_ch02_excel*. Save the workbook as **lastname_firstname_ch02_excel**
2	Apply the Berlin theme to the workbook.
3	Merge and center the text in cell A1 over columns A:C. Change the cell style to Heading 1.
4	Set the width of columns A:C to 30. Wrap text in cells B7:C10.
5	Apply the Comma cell style to the range B3:C4. Apply the Currency and Total cell styles to the range B5:C5.
6	Select the range A2:C2 and set the text to wrap in the cells. Center and middle align the text in the selected range. Change the cell style to Heading 3.
7	In cell B5, create a formula to calculate the annual cost of Google Apps for 10 users. Copy the formula to cell C5.
8	Change the orientation of the Sheet 1 worksheet to Landscape.
9	Center the worksheet horizontally on the page.
10	Rename the Sheet1 tab as **Comparisons**
11	Insert a header with the sheet name in the center cell. Insert a footer with the file name in the left cell.
12	Save the workbook and close Excel. Submit the workbook as directed.

Massimo G/Fotolia

File Management

In This Chapter

The concepts of file management are not unique to computing. We use file cabinets, folders, boxes, drawers, and piles to manage our paper files. These files can contain anything from bills to photographs to homework assignments to coupons. In this chapter, we look at managing electronic files. After you complete this chapter, you will be able to organize and manage your files to make working more efficient.

Objectives

1 **Create Folders to Organize Files**

2 **Explain the Importance of File Extensions**

3 **Explain the Importance of Backing Up Files**

4 **Demonstrate How to Compress Files**

5 **Use Advanced Search Options to Locate Files**

6 **Change the Default Program Associated with a File Type**

Running Project

In this chapter, you'll learn about the importance of file management. Look for instructions as you complete each article. For most articles, there's a series of questions for you to research or a set of tasks to perform. At the conclusion of this chapter, you'll submit your responses to the questions raised and the results of the tasks you've performed.

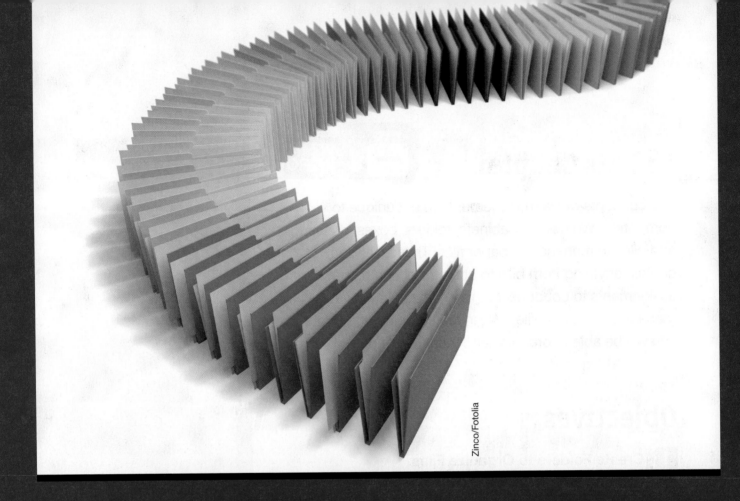

Zinco/Fotolia

A Place for Everything

Objective 1

Create Folders to Organize Files

One of the most important things that you need to do when working with computers is called **file management**: opening, closing, saving, naming, deleting, and organizing digital files. In this article, we discuss organizing your digital files, creating new folders, and navigating through the folder structure of your computer.

File Management

Navigating Your Computer

Before you can create files, you need a place to put them. You can start with the existing folder structure of your computer that is created by the operating system and customize it to fit your needs. **Folders** are containers that organize files on your computer. Windows comes with some folders already created, organized in a **hierarchy**. There are folders within folders, known as subfolders or children, which enable you to further organize your files. The sequence of folders to a file or folder is known as its **path**. Some versions of Windows use **libraries** to organize similar files located in different locations. There are four libraries: Documents, Music, Pictures, and Videos.

FILE EXPLORER

On a computer running Microsoft Windows, the window you use to navigate the file system is called **File Explorer**. In older versions of Windows, the tool was called Windows Explorer. You can use File Explorer to navigate through your system and to handle most file management tasks. Open File Explorer by clicking the *File Explorer* icon on the taskbar on the desktop or from the Windows Start menu. Figure 3.1 identifies some of the parts of the File Explorer window.

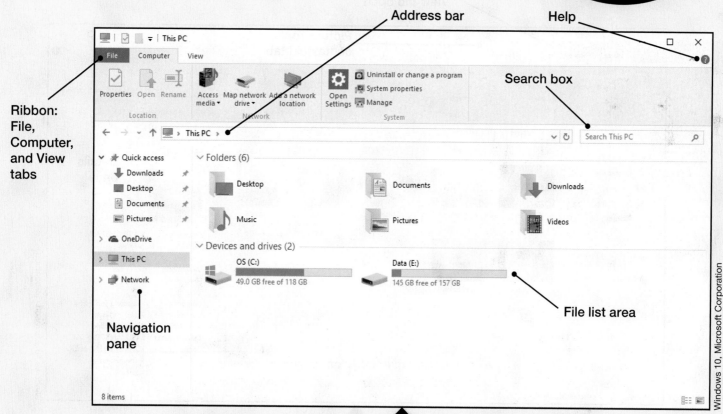

FIGURE 3.1 Parts of File Explorer

File Explorer includes the following items:

- **Quick Access Toolbar:** Contains icons for frequently used commands. The icons displayed can be customized to the way you work.
- **Ribbon:** Use to perform common tasks on the items in the file list area. The tabs change depending on the objects displayed.
- **Address bar:** Contains the path to the current location in the File Explorer window and is used to navigate through folders and libraries. You can move down in the folder hierarchy by clicking the arrow after your location. You can move back up in the folder hierarchy by clicking the arrows or links in the Address bar.
- **Search box:** Use to search for files located in the current File Explorer window.
- **Help:** Found under the File tab or by clicking the ? icon in the upper right corner.

- **Navigation pane:** Use to navigate the folders and drives available on a computer. The Navigation pane is divided into several sections: Quick Access, OneDrive, This PC, and Network. Clicking on any of these sections changes the contents in the right pane. Clicking the small triangle before an item in the Navigation pane expands it to display the locations it contains. You can customize what displays in this pane using the View tab.
- **File list area:** Displays the contents of the current location selected in the File Explorer window.
- **File tab:** Contains commands to open and close the windows and provides access to system Help.
- **Computer tab:** Contains commands to navigate your computer and access system settings and the Control Panel.
- **View tab:** Contains commands that enable you to change the way objects in the file list are displayed. For picture files, choosing *Large Icons*, as shown in Figure 3.2, displays a small preview, or thumbnail, of the image. Displaying the Details pane shows you more information about a selected file.

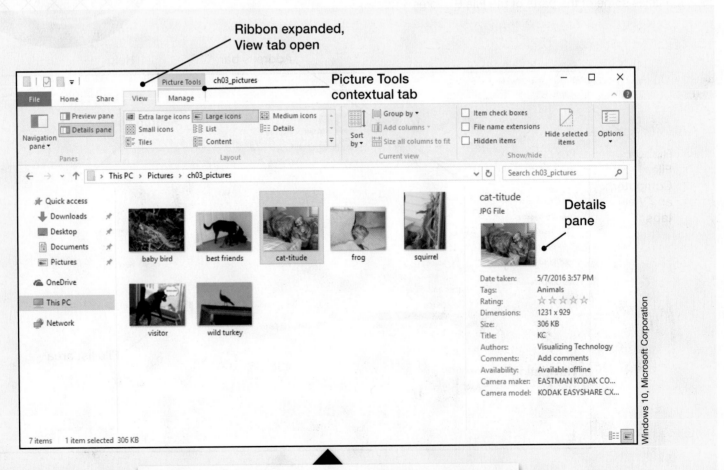

FIGURE 3.2 The Large Icon view displays small previews of image files.

THE WINDOWS USER FOLDER

When a user account is added to a Windows computer, Windows automatically creates a personal user folder for that account, along with subfolders inside it (Figure 3.3). To see your user folder through File Explorer, click *This PC*, click the up arrow (↑), and then double-click the folder with your user name. Your user folder items are normally accessible only by you. If another person logs on to the computer using a different account, that person won't see your files.

What folders are located under your user name? The Documents folder is the place to store files such as word processing files, spreadsheets, presentations, and text files. There are also folders set up for pictures, music, and videos. These specialized folders are the best places to save your pictures, music, and videos so they're easy to find. Without this folder structure, all your files would be lumped together, making it much harder to keep track of what you have; it would be like dumping all your snapshots into a shoebox.

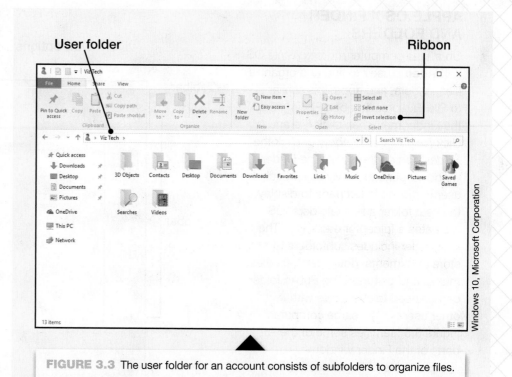

FIGURE 3.3 The user folder for an account consists of subfolders to organize files.

QUICK ACCESS

In Windows 10, File Explorer includes Quick access items on the Navigation pane to help you work more easily. By default, this section includes shortcuts to Downloads, Desktop, Documents, and Pictures, and as you work, it adds recent and frequently used locations to the list. In Figure 3.4 the Homework folder has been added. You can modify this behavior by using *Change folder and search options* in the File menu, and you can customize Quick access by adding other locations. In File Explorer, simply right-click the location and click *Pin to Quick access*.

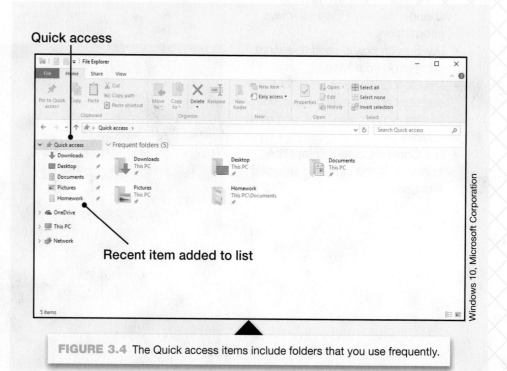

FIGURE 3.4 The Quick access items include folders that you use frequently.

APPLE OS X FINDER AND FOLDERS

On a Mac computer running Apple OS X, **Finder** is used to find and organize files, folders, and apps. It is similar to File Explorer. To open Finder, from the Finder menu bar, click *File* and click *New Finder Window* or click the *Finder* icon on the dock. The Finder window opens to All My Files. Click the user name in the left pane to display the user folder and subfolders. OS X creates a folder for each user. The user folder includes subfolders to store documents, downloads, movies, music, and pictures. The Public folder can be used to share files with other users of the same computer. Figure 3.5 identifies some of the parts of the Finder window.

Elements of Finder include the following:

- The Toolbar contains buttons to change the way Finder behaves.
- The View options on the toolbar change the way Finder displays information.
- The Search box is used to search for files on your Mac.
- The Sidebar contains icons for things you frequently use, such as disks, folders, shared resources, and other devices.
- The Contents area displays the contents of the currently selected location.

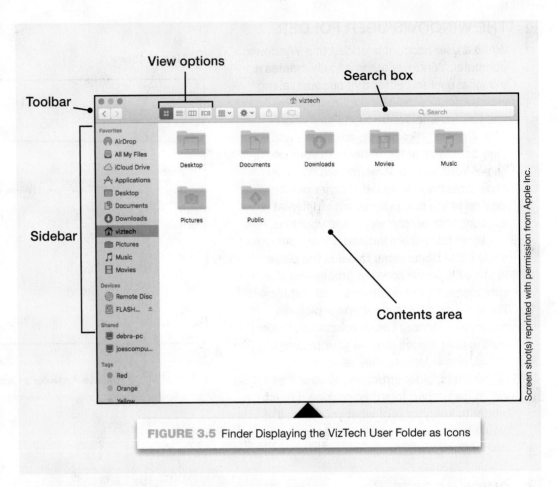

FIGURE 3.5 Finder Displaying the VizTech User Folder as Icons

Screen shot(s) reprinted with permission from Apple Inc.

Naypong/Fotolia

MOBILE DEVICES AND FILE STORAGE

Mobile devices are meant to be mobile—fast and light—and don't have a lot of room to store files. For larger storage, they rely on using the Internet, or cloud, to organize and store your files—making your mobile files accessible on all of your devices, not just the one in your hand. Cloud storage is discussed later in this chapter.

Creating and Using Folders

You're not limited to using the folder structure that's automatically created by Windows or OS X. You can create your own organizational scheme to fit your needs. This is especially useful when you use flash drives and other locations that aren't part of the user folder hierarchy. Suppose you print 25–30 photos a month (or 300–360 photos a year). How would you keep track of them? If you put them in a big box, in a few years you'd have thousands of photos in the box. It would be nearly impossible to keep track of them or find anything unless you organized them into photo albums. The same is true with the files on your computer. Creating folders to organize your files makes storing and finding them much easier. You can create a new folder when you save a file. This enables you to organize your files as they're created instead of after the fact. The Save As dialog box that opens when you save a file looks very much like File Explorer and includes the *New folder* button (Figure 3.6). Figure 3.7 demonstrates how to create a new folder on a flash drive.

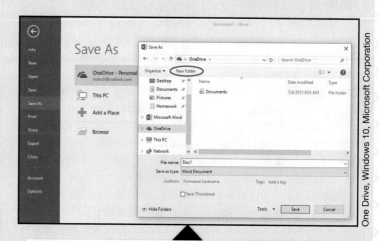

One Drive, Windows 10, Microsoft Corporation

FIGURE 3.6 Create a new folder when saving a file in Word.

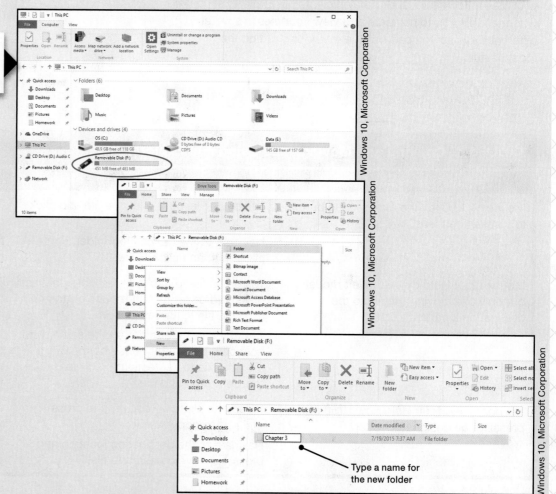

FIGURE 3.7 Steps to Create a New Folder on a Flash Drive (Windows)

Windows 10, Microsoft Corporation

Type a name for the new folder

1. Insert the flash drive into the computer. Close any windows that open automatically. Open File Explorer and, if necessary, click *This PC*. You should see the flash drive listed under Devices and drives. The drive letter will vary depending on the other drives on the system.
2. Double-click the icon for the flash drive to open it. Right-click a blank area of the window, point to *New*, and click *Folder*. (Another way–on the ribbon, click New Folder)
3. Type **Chapter 3** to name the folder and press Enter. You have created a new folder on your flash drive to store your files.

To create a new folder on a Mac, use the File menu in Finder or press ⇧ Shift + ⌘ Command + N (Figure 3.8).

Organizing your files into folders is easy once the folders have been created. You can use File Explorer or Finder to copy and move files to different locations on your computer. When you copy a file, you make a duplicate that can be put in another location, leaving the original file intact; moving a file changes the location of the file. Both of these tasks can be accomplished in several ways, as explained in **Table 3.1** and **Table 3.2**. To select multiple files to copy or move, hold down the Ctrl key in Windows as you click on each file. If the files are adjacent, in Windows you can click the first file, hold down the Shift key, and click the last file. To select all the files in a window, press Ctrl + A. In OS X, use the Command ⌘ or Shift key to select multiple files, or use Command ⌘ + A to select all.

Learning to work with folders will make organizing your files much easier and more efficient. File Explorer and Finder enable you to navigate and view your files in several different ways so you can use the methods you find the most useful.

Screen shot(s) reprinted with permission from Apple Inc.

FIGURE 3.8 Create a new folder in OS X.

TABLE 3.1 Copying and Moving Files Using File Explorer

Method	Copy	Move
Mouse click: Click the right mouse button to display the menu.	To copy a file, right-click the file and click *Copy*. Navigate to the destination folder, right-click on it, and click *Paste*.	To move a file, right-click the file and click *Cut*. Navigate to the destination folder, right-click on it, and click *Paste*.
Mouse drag: Hold down the left mouse button while moving the file to the destination location.	To copy a file to a folder on a different disk, hold down the left mouse button and drag the file to its destination. To copy a file to a folder on the same disk, hold down the right mouse button and drag the file to its destination. Release the mouse button and click *Copy here*.	To move a file to a folder on the same disk, hold down the left mouse button and drag the file to its destination. To move a file to a folder on a different disk, hold down the right mouse button and drag the file to its destination. Release the mouse button and click *Move here*.
Keyboard shortcut: Hold down Ctrl while pressing the designated letter.	Select the file to be copied and press Ctrl + C to copy the file. Navigate to the destination location and press Ctrl + V to paste the file.	Select the file to be moved and press Ctrl + X to move the file. Navigate to the destination location and press Ctrl + V to paste the file.

Geoghan, Debra. Visualizing Technology Complete, 4e. Pearson Education, 2014.

TABLE 3.2 Copying and Moving Files Using Finder

Method	Copy	Move
Mouse click: Press Ctrl and click the mouse button to display the menu.	To copy a file, press Ctrl + click and select *Copy*. Navigate to the destination folder, press Ctrl + click, and click *Paste Item*.	Follow the steps to copy a file and then drag the original file to the trash.
Mouse drag: Hold down the mouse button while moving the file to the destination location.	To copy a file to a folder on a different disk, hold down the mouse button and drag the file to its destination.	To move a file to a folder on the same disk, hold down the mouse button and drag the file to its destination.
Keyboard shortcut: Hold down Command ⌘ while pressing the designated letter.	Select the file to be copied and press Command ⌘ + C to copy the file. Navigate to the destination location and press Command ⌘ + V to paste the file.	Follow the steps to copy a file and then drag the original file to the trash.

Pearson Education, Inc.

Running Project

Using File Explorer or Finder, look at the user folder on your system. What is the user name? What subfolders are displayed for this user in addition to the Documents, Music, and Pictures folders? Take a screenshot of the user folder and paste it into your answer sheet.

3 Things You Need To Know

- Windows and OS X create a folder hierarchy for storing files.
- Each user has his or her own folder structure for storing documents, pictures, music, videos, and more.
- File Explorer in Windows and Finder in OS X are used to navigate through folders and drives.

Key Terms

File Explorer

file management

Finder

folder

hierarchy

library

path

Organize Your Files

Digital Literacy Skill

 **HOW TO VIDEO**

In this activity you will use File Explorer or Finder to view various file types and folders. If necessary, on your flash drive, create a folder for Chapter 3 (refer to Figure 3.6 for help). Use this folder to save your work for this chapter. If necessary, download the student data files from **pearsonhighered. com/viztech**. From your student data files, open *vt_ch03_howto1_answersheet* and save it in your Chapter 3 folder as **lastname_firstname_ch03_howto1_answersheet**

1 In File Explorer, navigate to the student data files for this chapter. If necessary, click ▶ to expand *This PC* in the Navigation pane. Drag the *ch03_pictures* folder from the file list in the right pane to the *Pictures* folder in the Navigation pane. Drag the *ch03_music* folder to the *Music* folder. Drag the *ch03_documents* folder to the *Documents* folder.

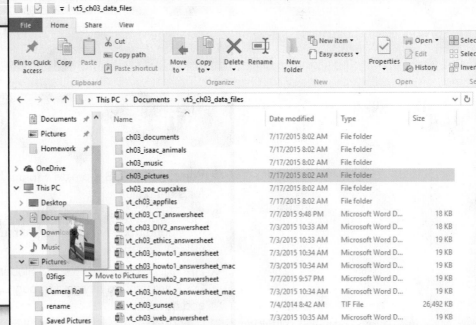

Windows 10, Microsoft Corporation

2

In the Navigation pane, under This PC, click *Music*. In the file list on the right, double-click the *ch03_music* folder. If it has not been customized, the default view is Music Details. Click the *View* tab, and if necessary, in the Layout group, click *Details*. What are the headings of the columns in this view? Click the *Title* column heading. What happens to the files in the window? Click the *Name* column heading. What happens? Take a screenshot and paste it into your answer sheet.

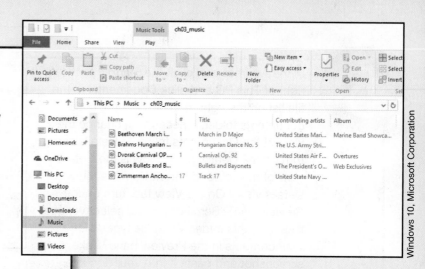

3

In the Navigation pane, click *Pictures*. In the file list on the right, double-click the *ch03_pictures* folder. The default view for this folder is Large Icons. Use the View tab, if necessary, to change the view to Large Icons. How is the view in this folder different from the Music folder? Take a screenshot and paste it into your answer sheet.

4

Click the *View* tab and in the Panes group, if necessary, select the *Details* pane. Select one image (but do not open it) and look at the Details pane. What information is found in this pane? Change the rating of the file. What other information can you change? Take a screenshot and paste it into your document.

5 In the Address bar, click the **>** arrow to the right of This PC and click Documents. In the file list on the right, double-click the *ch03_documents* folder. If necessary, change the view of the Documents folder to Details and turn off the Details pane. How is the Details view of this folder different from the Music Details view? On the View tab, turn on the *Preview* pane. Scroll down and select various files from this folder. What file types display their contents in the Preview pane? Take a screenshot and paste it into your document. Type your answers, including the appropriate screenshots, save your file, and submit as directed by your instructor.

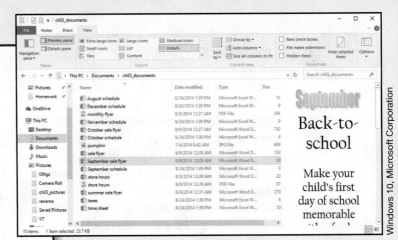

MAC

List view

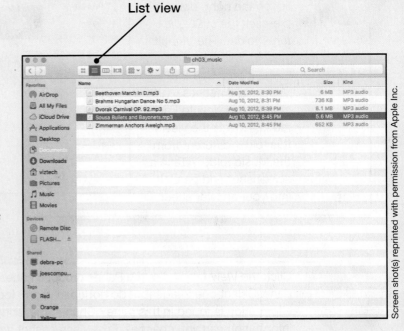

If you are using a Mac: From your student data files, open *vt_ch03_howto1_answersheet_mac* and save it in your Chapter 3 folder as **lastname_firstname_ch03_howto1_answersheet_mac**

1. Open Finder. If the Music and Pictures folders are not visible in the Sidebar, from the Finder menu, open *Preferences* and click the *Sidebar* tab to display them. Navigate to the student data files for this chapter. Drag the *ch03_pictures* folder to Pictures and the *ch03_music* folder to Music in the sidebar. Drag the *ch03_documents* folder to the Documents folder.

2. Display the contents of *ch03_music* in List view using the button on the toolbar or the View menu. What are the headings of the columns in this view? Click the *Name* column heading. What happens to the files in the window? Click the *Name* column heading again. What happens? Take a screenshot and paste it into your answer sheet.

3. Display the contents of the *ch03_pictures* folder in Cover Flow view using the button on the toolbar or the View menu. How is the view in this folder different from the Music folder? Take a screenshot and paste it into your answer sheet.

4. Select one image (but do not open it). Select *Get Info* from the File menu. What information is found in this pane? What information can you change? Take a screenshot and paste it into your answer sheet. Close the Get Info pane.

5. Display the contents of the *ch03_documents* folder in Column view using the button on the toolbar or the View menu. How is the Column view of this folder different from List view? Select various files from this folder. What file types display their contents in the Preview pane? Take a screenshot and paste it into your answer sheet. Type up your answers, including the appropriate screenshots, save your file, and submit as directed by your instructor.

Cover Flow view

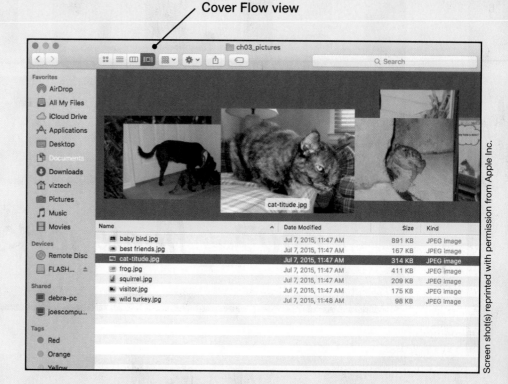

Column view

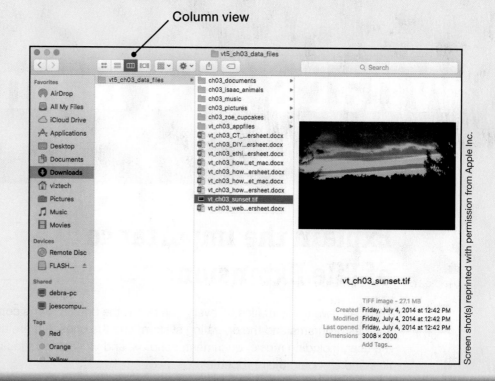

HELLO

my name is

ch03__homework.docx

What's in a Name?

Explain the Importance of File Extensions

There are two types of files on every computer: the ones that the computer uses to function, such as programs and the operating system, and the ones that are used and created by you, the user, including music, documents, photos, and videos. Let's look at a few of these user files and compare their properties.

File Names and Extensions

Every file has a **file name** that consists of a name and a file extension. The name is useful to the user and describes the contents of the file. When creating your own files, you decide the name. In the example in Figure 3.09, *ch03_homework* is the name of the file. On early PCs, file names were limited to eight characters with a three-letter extension and were often cryptic. Today, file names on Windows computers can be up to 260 characters long, including the file extension and the path to the file, and can include spaces and special characters. Table 3.3 shows illegal characters in a Windows file name. OS X file names can be up to 255 characters long, and the only illegal character is the colon (:).

TABLE 3.3 Illegal Characters in Windows File Names

Character	Description
\	Back slash
/	Forward slash
?	Question mark
:	Colon
*	Asterisk
"	Quotation marks
>	Greater than
<	Less than

Geoghan, Debra. Visualizing Technology Complete, 4e. Pearson Education, 2014.

FIGURE 3.9 A file name includes a name and an extension to identify the contents and type of file.

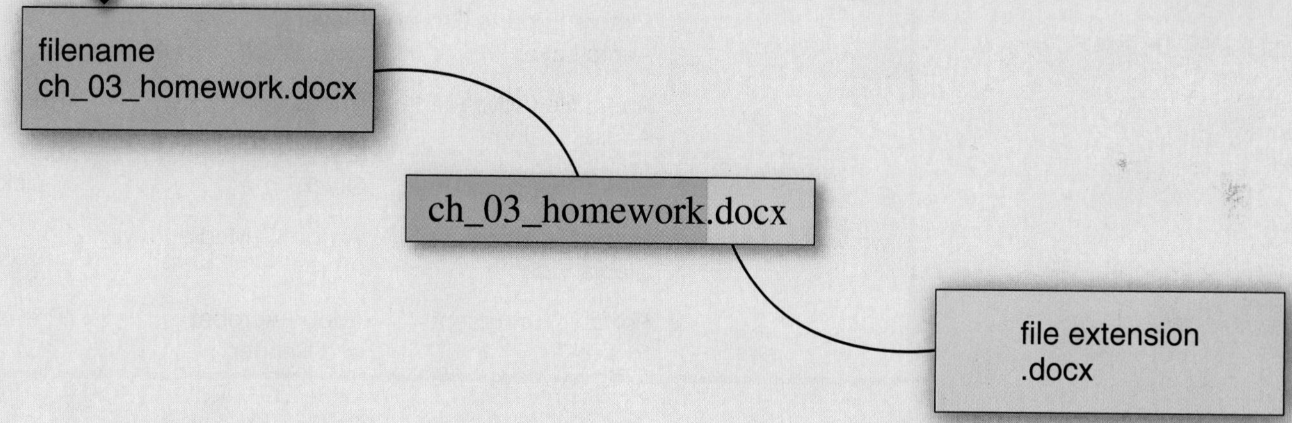

filename
ch_03_homework.docx

ch_03_homework.docx

file extension
.docx

Geoghan, Debra. Visualizing Technology Complete, 4e. Pearson Education, 2014.

The second part of the file name is the **file extension**. In this example, .docx is the extension. The extension is assigned by the program that's used to create the file. Microsoft Word files have the extension .docx. Windows maintains an association between a file extension and a program, so double-clicking on a .docx file opens Microsoft Word. The extension helps the operating system determine the type of file. If you change the file extension of a file, you may no longer be able to open it. **Table 3.4** lists some common file types and the programs associated with them.

TABLE 3.4 Common File Extensions and Default Program Associations

Extension	Type of File	Default Program Association (Windows)	Default Program Association (OS X)
.docx	Word document	Microsoft Word	Microsoft Word
.rtf	Rich text format document	WordPad or Word	TextEdit
.pages	Pages document	—	Pages
.xlsx	Excel workbook	Excel	Excel
.pptx	PowerPoint presentation	PowerPoint	PowerPoint
.bmp	Bitmap image	Paint	Preview
.jpeg/.jpg	Image file (Joint Photographic Experts Group)	Photos	Preview
.mp3	Audio file (Moving Picture Experts Group Audio Layer III)	Windows Media Player	iTunes
.aac	Audio file (Advanced Audio Coding)	iTunes	iTunes
.mov	Video file (QuickTime)	QuickTime	QuickTime
.wmv	Video file (Windows Media Video)	Windows Media Player	—
.pdf	Portable document format	Adobe Acrobat and Reader	Preview

Geoghan, Debra. Visualizing Technology Complete, 4e. Pearson Education, 2014.

FIND OUT MORE

The characters \ / ? : * " > < | can't be used in a file name because they each have a special meaning in Windows. For example, the colon (:) is used to indicate the letter of a drive (such as C: for your hard drive). Use the Internet to research the remaining illegal characters. What does each symbol represent?

File Properties

Each file includes **file properties**, which provide information about the file. You can use these properties to organize, sort, and find files more easily. Some file properties, such as type, size, and date, are automatically created along with the file. Others, such as title, tags, and authors, can be added or edited by the user.

Figure 3.10 shows the properties of a file in the Details pane of File Explorer. The Details pane of the File Explorer window displays more information about a file. You can modify some of these properties, such as Title and Authors, directly in the Details pane.

When the files are displayed in the Details view, as they are in this figure, you can use the column headings to sort files by their properties. For example, clicking on the *Name* column heading lists the files in alphabetical order. The properties that display in this view depend on the type of files in the folder.

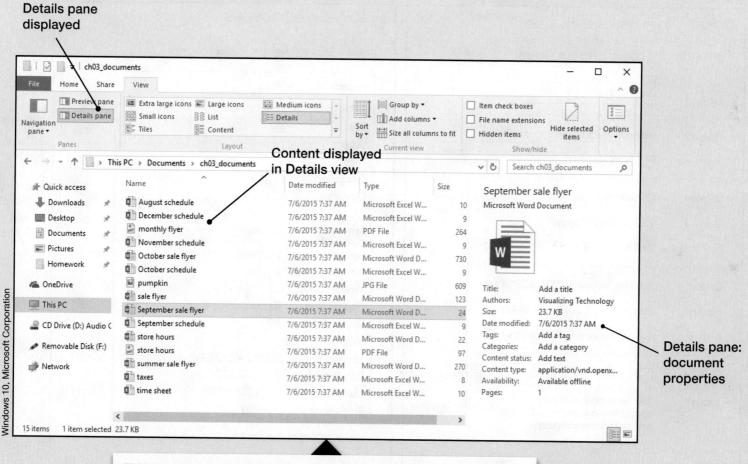

FIGURE 3.10 File Explorer enables you to view and modify some file properties.

You can view more information about a file by right-clicking the file in File Explorer and clicking *Properties*. This opens the Properties dialog box for the file. The tabs of the Properties dialog box contain a lot of information, and the tabs you see will depend on the configuration of your system and the type and location of the file or folder you are viewing. The General tab makes it easy to change the name of a file and the program that opens it. The Details tab lists information about the content of the file, such as word count. Figure 3.11 shows these two tabs for the same file. Notice that the Details tab contains too much information to display on the page, so you need to scroll down to see the rest of it. The type of information that's displayed depends on the type of file you're viewing.

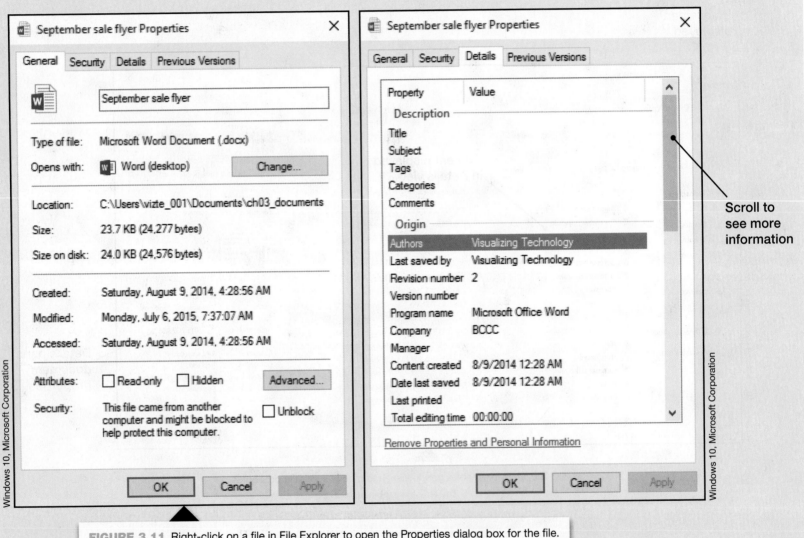

FIGURE 3.11 Right-click on a file in File Explorer to open the Properties dialog box for the file.

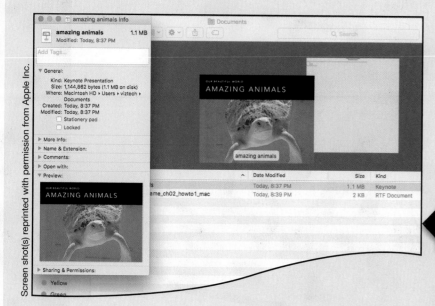

To view and modify file properties in OS X, in Finder, select the file, click *File*, and then click *Get Info*. This will open the Info pane for the file, where you can view and change some of the file properties such as the file name, sharing permissions, Spotlight comments, and the program that open it (Figure 3.12).

File names and other properties provide you with more information about files, making them more useful and easier to manage and locate. They also save you time and give you more control over your computer systems.

FIGURE 3.12 The Info box in OS X displays file properties.

Running Project

This article discussed how to add properties to a file, but how would you remove them? Which properties can you remove? Use Windows Help and Support, OS X Spotlight, or the Internet to find the answers.

4 Things You Need To Know

- Windows file names can be up to 260 characters long, including the path. OS X file names can be up to 255 characters long.
- Windows file names can't include the \ / ? : * " < > | characters, and OS X file names can't include the colon.
- The file extension indicates the type of file.
- File properties, such as size, type, date, and author, can be used to sort and search for files.

Key Terms

file extension

file name

file property

Kikkerdirk/Fotolia

Back It Up

Explain the Importance of Backing Up Files

It's something many people don't think about until it's too late: losing files on a computer system that wasn't backed up. One simple step to take is to periodically **back up** or copy your files to another drive or the cloud. In this article, we look at how easy it is to automatically back up your files for protection.

VIZ CLIP

Online Storage

Windows Backup

Windows includes a backup utility called File History, which is not turned on by default. You can access File History from the System and Security control panel (Figure 3.13). To use File History, you must have an external drive or network location accessible for the copies to be stored. To reduce the size of the File History saved, you can exclude specific folders or libraries.

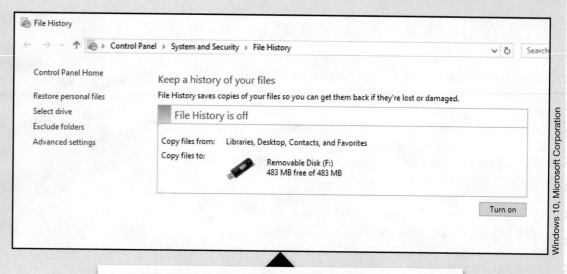

FIGURE 3.13 Windows File History is one way to back up your files.

Windows 10, Microsoft Corporation

OS X Time Machine

OS X includes a backup utility called Time Machine. You can open Time Machine from the Launchpad to configure it (Figure 3.14). Alternatively, you can connect a new disk, such as an external hard drive, to your Mac, and Time Machine will ask you if you want to use the disk to back up your files. Time Machine keeps three types of backups: hourly backups for the previous 24 hours, daily backups for the past month, and weekly backups for all previous months. The oldest backups are deleted as the disk fills up. Time Machine backs up everything on your computer: your personal files, as well as system files, applications, and settings.

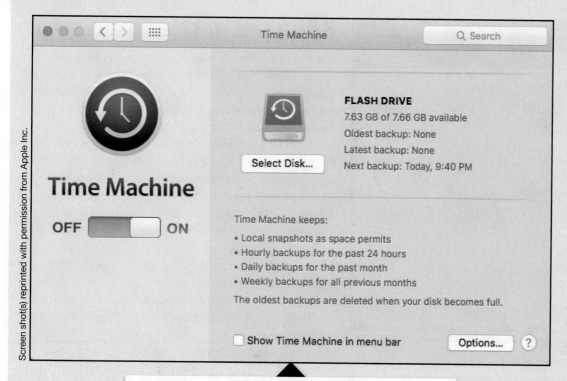

Screen shot(s) reprinted with permission from Apple Inc.

FIGURE 3.14 Time Machine backs up everything on a Mac.

Other Backup Software

External hard drives are an inexpensive place to back up your files (Figure 3.15). These drives often include a backup program that you can use for automatic or one-touch backups of your system. For example, Seagate FreeAgent external drives include Seagate Manager, and Western Digital's Passport drives include WD SmartWare. You can purchase a large-capacity external hard drive for less than $100.

Another alternative is commercial backup software. There are numerous programs on the market, including many that are free or cost less than $50. DVD-burning software, such as Roxio Creator and Nero BackItUp, also include backup features.

Nomad Soul/Fotolia

FIGURE 3.15 Back up to an external drive

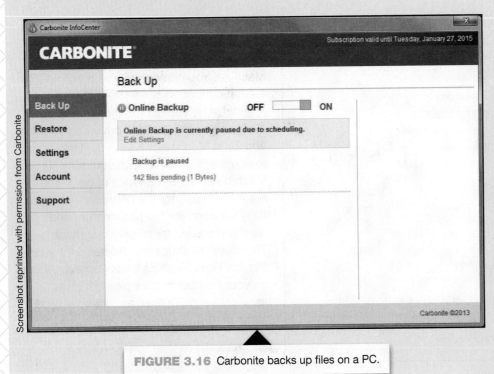

Screenshot reprinted with permission from Carbonite

FIGURE 3.16 Carbonite backs up files on a PC.

BACKUP to the Cloud

The use of Internet, or **cloud**, backup services is another option. Many sites offer free personal storage of 1 or 2 GB or unlimited storage for a monthly or annual subscription fee. Business solutions can cost thousands of dollars, depending upon the amount of storage needed.

Using an online or cloud backup service has the advantage of keeping your backups at another location—but easily accessible—and protecting your files from fire, flood, or damage to your main location. Cloud backups are automatic and accessible from any computer with an Internet connection, so you can access your backed-up files even if you're not using the same device. Companies like Mozy and Carbonite (Figure 3.16) offer plans for home users that include desktop software to automatically back up your files.

Professional backup companies make setup easy, and their services are very safe and reliable. Once the initial setup is complete, the backup process is automatic, and your backed-up files are accessible from any Internet-connected computer. As with any other service, you should do your homework before trusting online backup services with your files.

Cloud Storage

What is the difference between cloud backups and cloud storage? Cloud storage allows you to store working files in a convenient place. Although this also serves to back them up, cloud storage is generally more limited than a backup in what and how much you can store.

When you sign up for a free Microsoft account, it includes free online storage, called **OneDrive** (Figure 3.17). If you are logged in to your Windows computer using a Microsoft account, the default save location for Microsoft Office applications is your OneDrive, and you can save to your OneDrive from other programs using the Save As dialog box. Older Windows computers, OS X, Windows Phone, iOS, and Android devices can connect to OneDrive by using a OneDrive app or the OneDrive website, so you can store files, photos, and favorites in the cloud and access and share them from any Internet-connected device. OneDrive also has the advantage of being integrated with Office Online web apps, which enable you to create and edit Microsoft Office documents in your browser.

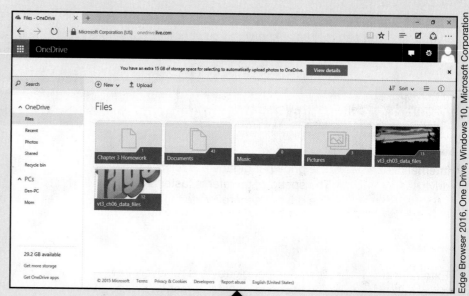

FIGURE 3.17 OneDrive Online Storage

FIGURE 3.18 iCloud can automatically back up your files and sync them with other devices.

Apple OS X and iOS devices include a free online storage and sync service known as **iCloud**. iCloud can be set to automatically sync your personal files on all your devices and to the cloud (Figure 3.18). It comes with 5 GB of free storage, and there is a version that you can download and install on your Windows computers, so you can share your files between all your devices. iCloud uploads and stores your photos and pushes them to your My Photo Stream album on your connected devices. To access your photos on a Mac, enable iCloud in iPhotos or Aperture. For music, apps, books, and videos, enable automatic download in iTunes. iCloud also includes free web versions of Pages, Numbers, and Keynote that you can use to create and edit documents.

Other popular cloud storage services include Dropbox, Google Drive, ADrive, Box, MediaFire, and Amazon Cloud.

Some mobile apps automatically upload photos to websites such as OneDrive, Dropbox, Flickr, Instagram, or Facebook. Because many people rely on the camera in their mobile devices for capturing life's important (and not-so-important) moments, as well as storing all their contacts and calendars, it is wise to regularly back up these devices.

Table 3.5 compares various types of backup solutions. However you choose to back up your files, you can rest easy knowing that your files are safe and that if the inevitable hard drive failure strikes, you won't lose your important work and precious photos.

TABLE 3.5 Comparing Backup Storage Types

Storage Type	Pros	Cons
Internal hard drive	• The price per gigabyte is relatively low. • The speed of transfer is fastest. • The drive is secure inside the system unit.	• You need to open the system unit to install an internal drive. • Because it's in the same physical location as the original files, backing up to the internal hard drive doesn't keep files safe from fire, flood, or other damage.
External hard drive	• The price per gigabyte is relatively low. • The speed of transfer is fast. • The drive is easy to move and secure in another location.	• If the external hard drive is stored in another location, it must be transported back to the system location to perform a backup. • If the backup storage device is left in the same physical location as the original files, the files aren't safe from fire, flood, or other damage.
Optical drive (CD/DVD/Blu-ray)	• Media (discs) are inexpensive and easy to purchase. • Media is easy to move to store in another location. • Using new discs for each backup means the discs don't have to be returned to the system to complete future backups.	• Disc capacity is small compared to hard drives and may require several (or many) discs to complete a backup.
Network	• A shared folder or drive on another computer can be used for backup. • Placing the files on another system protects them.	• Using a network as a backup location requires some advanced setup of the network. • The network location must be available when the backup runs.
Cloud backup	• Files are stored off-site, so they're protected from fire, flood, or other damage. • Files are accessible from other devices and locations.	• Subscriptions can be expensive. • Cloud backup requires an active Internet connection. • Restoring files can be time-consuming.
Cloud storage	• Files are stored off-site, so they're protected from fire, flood, or other damage. • Files are accessible from other devices and locations.	• Storage capacity and types of files allowed may be limited.

Geoghan, Debra. Visualizing Technology Complete, 4e. Pearson Education, 2014.

GREEN COMPUTING

The Paperless Office

Advancing Sustainable Materials Management: 2013 Fact Sheet. Assessing Trends in Material Generation, Recycling and Disposal in the United States June 2015. Figure 5, pp7. U.S. Environmental Protection Agency

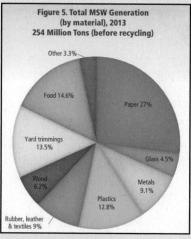

Figure 5. Total MSW Generation (by material), 2013 254 Million Tons (before recycling)

Other 3.3%
Paper 27%
Food 14.6%
Yard trimmings 13.5%
Glass 4.5%
Wood 6.2%
Metals 9.1%
Plastics 12.8%
Rubber, leather & textiles 9%

Source: **www.epa.gov/wastes/ nonhaz/municipal/**

The promise of the paperless office hasn't quite become a reality. In fact, we're buried under more paper today than ever before. According to the U.S. Environmental Protection Agency (EPA), in 2013 (the most recent figures available), paper made up 27 percent of our municipal solid waste.

The process of making paper uses water and energy in addition to trees, and it results in greenhouse gas emissions and air and water pollution. Reduce your paper usage to help the environment.

The prospect of going paperless has advantages for the environment and for your bottom line. So, how do you achieve it? The reality is that you probably can't go totally paperless, but here are a few ways to reduce your paper usage:

- Send email and make phone calls instead of sending greeting cards and letters.
- Pay your bills online and opt for paperless billing from your billers and banks.
- Don't print out electronic documents unless absolutely necessary.
- Read magazines and books in electronic formats.
- Opt out of receiving junk mail at the DMA website (**www.dmachoice.org**) and catalogs at Catalog Choice (**www.catalogchoice.org**).

 Direct Marketing Association

 TrustedID

Running Project

Research two online backup sites and investigate their cost, reliability, storage size, and features. Write a brief report to convince your boss of the importance of backing up files and how backups should be handled. Should the company use online storage? Explain your thoughts. In the report, be sure to describe the type and size of the business you're working for.

Viz Check—In MyITLab, take a quick quiz covering Objectives 1–3.

4 Things You Need To Know

- You should regularly back up your important files.
- Keep your backup files in a different physical location than your working files.
- Back up (verb) is the process of creating a backup (noun).
- Cloud backup services store files using the Internet.

Key Terms

back up

cloud

iCloud

OneDrive

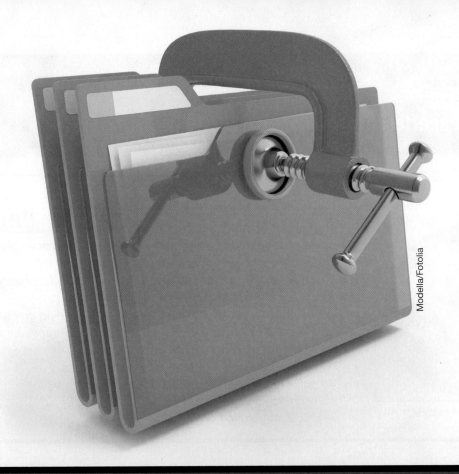

Modella/Fotolia

Shrink It

Demonstrate How to Compress Files

Some of the files used today can be rather large, especially media files such as photos, music, and videos. File **compression** is the process of making files smaller to conserve disk space and make the files easier to transfer.

Types of File Compression

There are two types of file compression: lossless and lossy. An **algorithm** is a procedure for solving a problem. The compression algorithm used depends on the type of file being compressed. **Lossless compression** takes advantage of the fact that files contain a lot of redundant information. With lossless compression, the compressed file can be decompressed with no loss of data. A lossless compression algorithm looks for the redundancy in the file and creates an encoded file using that information to remove the redundant information. When the file is decompressed, all the information from the original file is restored.

A **lossy compression** algorithm is often used on image, audio, and video files. These files contain more information than humans can detect, and that extra information can be removed from the file. An image file taken with a digital camera on its highest setting may yield a file of 5 MB to more than 50 MB in size, but the normal quality setting yields a file of 1 to 2 MB. If the file is used to create a large, high-quality print or for medical images where every detail is critical, then the high-quality information is important. Most people, however, can't tell the difference between the two when viewing them on a computer screen or printing snapshots. The highest-quality settings result in an uncompressed file. BMP and TIF images are uncompressed image file types. An image taken at a lower quality setting results in a smaller file, compressed using a lossy compression algorithm. A JPG/JPEG image is a BMP image that has been compressed using lossy compression. It's possible to compress the file after it's been taken, but once the file is compressed using lossy compression, it can't be fully restored to the raw format.

Another type of file that is commonly compressed is video. Video files can be very large, making them difficult to transfer or upload or download to and from a website. YouTube accepts many video formats for upload, such as MPEG4, 3GPP, MOV, AVI, and WMV, but these files are then processed and converted to compressed formats such as Flash for viewing.

K-Photos/Alamy

Working with File Compression

Windows includes the ability to compress and decompress files using the ZIP format. This is a common format that's used to send files by email or download them from the Internet. A ZIP file, known as an archive, can contain multiple files zipped together. This makes transferring multiple files easier.

To zip a file or folder using File Explorer, with the file or folder selected, click the *Share* tab and then click *Zip*. Or you can right-click on the file or folder that you want to zip, point to *Send to*, and click *Compressed (zipped) folder*. In the example shown in Figure 3.19, the *ch03_zoe_cupcakes* folder was originally 712 KB,

or 0.712 MB, and was compressed down to 568 KB, or 0.568 MB. This ZIP file can more easily be sent as an email attachment or uploaded to the web, and it takes up less space on a disk. To compress a file or folder using a Mac, click *Compress* from the File menu in Finder.

Windows can open and browse the files in a ZIP archive. Figure 3.20 shows the *ch03_zoe_cupcakes.zip* file and the compression ratio for each file inside it. Because each file contains different types and amounts of information, the compression ratios vary.

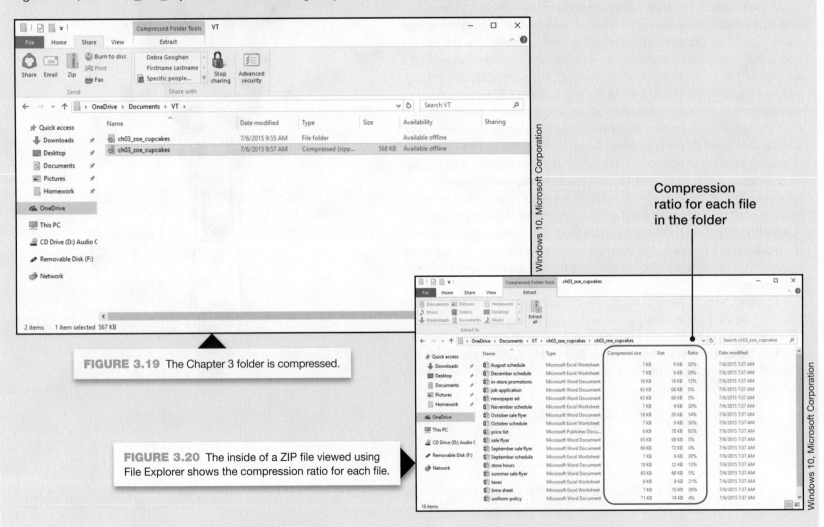

FIGURE 3.19 The Chapter 3 folder is compressed.

FIGURE 3.20 The inside of a ZIP file viewed using File Explorer shows the compression ratio for each file.

Compression ratio for each file in the folder

Windows 10, Microsoft Corporation

Windows can browse and use files inside a zipped folder, but sometimes you need to decompress or extract the files to work with them. In File Explorer, on the Compressed Folder Tools Extract tab, click the *Extract All* button or right-click the ZIP file and click *Extract All* (Figure 3.21). If you are using a Mac, just double-click the ZIP file to unzip it.

There are other programs that you can use to compress and decompress ZIP files, and there are other compressed formats, such as TAR and RAR, that Windows can't create or open. Some of the more popular programs available are 7-Zip, WinRAR, WinZip, and StuffIt.

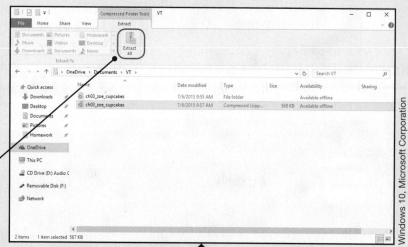

Windows 10, Microsoft Corporation

Click Extract all or right-click on the zipped folder and choose Extract All

FIGURE 3.21 Extracting Files from a ZIP Archive in Windows

Running Project

An MP3 file is a compressed audio file that uses a lossy compression algorithm. Many audiophiles say that they can hear a noticeable difference in the quality of the sound. Use the Internet to research ways to improve the quality of MP3 files.

4 Things You Need To Know	Key Terms
● File compression saves disk space and makes transferring files easier.	algorithm
● A file compressed with lossless compression can be decompressed back to the original file.	compression
● A file compressed with lossy compression can't be decompressed because information has been removed from the file.	lossless compression
● Windows and OS X have the ability to create and extract ZIP archives.	lossy compression

How To? Create a Compressed (Zipped) Folder

HOW TO VIDEO

Have you ever tried to email a bunch of photos to a friend? If you want to send more than a couple images, you usually wind up sending multiple messages. But you can compress the files into a single zipped folder and send them all at once. In this activity, you'll compress a folder that contains several files to make it easier to email them or to submit them electronically to your teacher.

If necessary, download the student data files from **pearsonhighered.com/viztech**. From your student data files, open *vt_ch03_howto2_answersheet* and save it in your Chapter 3 folder as **lastname_firstname_ch03_howto2_answersheet**

1 Insert your flash drive into your computer. Use File Explorer to navigate to the student data files for this chapter. Locate the folder *ch03_isaac_animals*. Copy this folder to your flash drive by dragging the folder to your flash drive in the Navigation pane. If you are not using a flash drive, copy the *ch03_isaac_animals* folder to your Document folder.

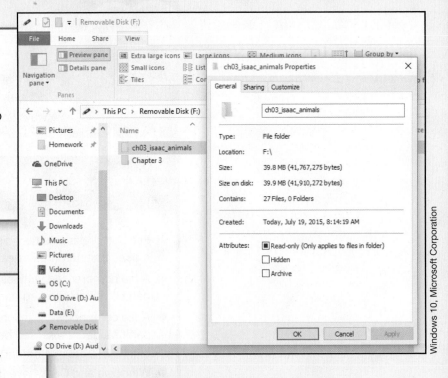

2 In the File Explorer Navigation pane, click your flash drive or Documents folder. Right-click the *ch03_isaac_animals* folder and click *Properties*. How big is the folder? How many files and folders does it contain? Close the Properties dialog box.

Windows 10, Microsoft Corporation

3 Select *ch03_isaac_animals*, click the *Share* tab, and then click *Zip* to create a zipped archive. Press Enter to accept the default file name.

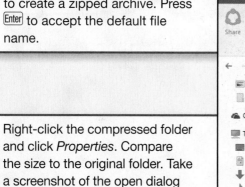

4 Right-click the compressed folder and click *Properties*. Compare the size to the original folder. Take a screenshot of the open dialog box and paste it into your answer sheet. Type up your answers, save, and submit as directed by your instructor.

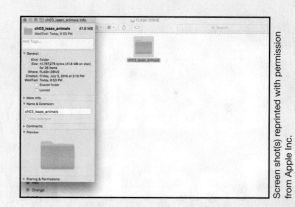

Windows 10, Microsoft Corporation

If you are using a Mac: From your student data files, open *vt_ch03_howto2_answersheet_mac* and save it in your Chapter 3 folder as **lastname_firstname_ch03_howto2_answersheet_mac**

1. Insert your flash drive into your computer. Open Finder and locate the student data files for this chapter. Copy the *ch03_isaac_animals* folder by dragging it to your flash drive. If you are not using a flash drive, copy the *ch03_isaac_animals* folder to your Documents folder.

2. Click the flash drive in the Sidebar and select the folder in the right pane. From the File menu, select *Get Info*. How big is the folder? How many files and folders does it contain?

3. Close the Info pane. From the File menu, select *Compress "ch03_isaac_animals"* to create a zipped archive.

4. Select the ZIP file and from the File menu, select *Get Info*. Compare the size to the original folder. Take a screenshot and paste it into your answer sheet. Type up your answers, save, and submit as directed by your instructor.

Screen shot(s) reprinted with permission from Apple Inc.

Screen shot(s) reprinted with permission from Apple Inc.

It's Always in the Last Place You Look

Objective 5

Use Advanced Search Options to Locate Files

A typical computer contains thousands of files, and finding what you need among them can be like looking for the proverbial needle in a haystack. If you follow the principles of good file management, create folders, and save your files in an organized way, then you'll have a much easier time keeping track of your materials. In this article, we look at how using search tools can help you find what you're looking for.

Using Windows to Search for Files

Files contain properties that you can use to help organize and find them. Using the Windows Search feature can help you do just that. There's a search box almost every place you go—in the Help and Support window, every Control Panel window, and every File Explorer window. When you begin to type something in the search box, Windows immediately begins searching (Figure 3.22). Just start typing from the Start menu or in the *Search the web and Windows* box on the taskbar to search apps, settings, files, and web images and video (in Windows 8, drag in from the right to open the Search charm). Windows maintains an **index** that contains information about the files located on your computer. This index makes searching for files very fast. You can include unindexed locations in your search, but it causes the search to be slower.

Clicking *My Stuff* at the bottom of the search results launches a search of your files and apps that include that term (Figure 3.23).

In Figure 3.24, beginning a search in File Explorer with the folder for the user Viz Tech displayed limits the search to files and folders within that user folder. The search begins as soon as the letter *f* is typed in the Search box. The search results include files in the current location and the folders below it in the hierarchy. Search results include files with the letter *f* in file names, file properties, and file contents. You can further refine the search results by typing more letters or by adding a search filter, such as Type or Name. You can also save a search to be repeated later. If you don't find what you're looking for in your initial search, adjust your criteria.

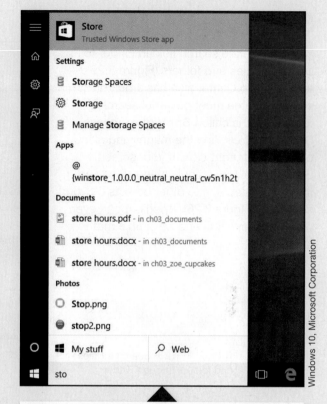

FIGURE 3.22 Windows Search locates programs and settings as well as files.

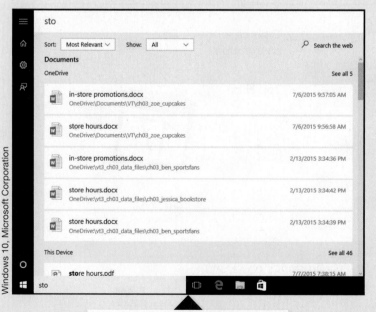

FIGURE 3.23 Clicking My Stuff at the Bottom of the Search Results

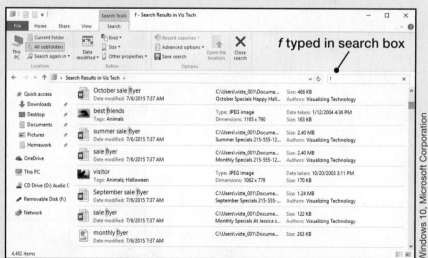

FIGURE 3.24 The search results in File Explorer show the *f* found in file names, content, and other file properties.

Searching in OS X

You can use the search field in Finder to search for files and folders (Figure 3.25), and the Help Center also has a built-in search, but the most powerful search tool in OS X is called **Spotlight**. Access Spotlight by clicking the magnifying glass on the upper right side of your screen. Spotlight searches applications, files and folders, contacts, and other objects on your computer (Figure 3.26). Spotlight can even provide a definition and do simple math calculations.

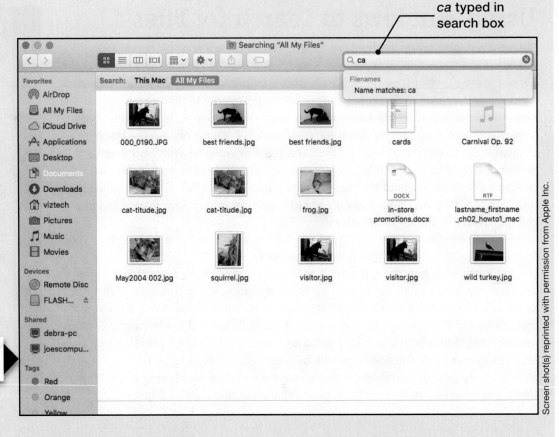

ca typed in search box

FIGURE 3.25 Search for files and folders through Finder.

Screen shot(s) reprinted with permission from Apple Inc.

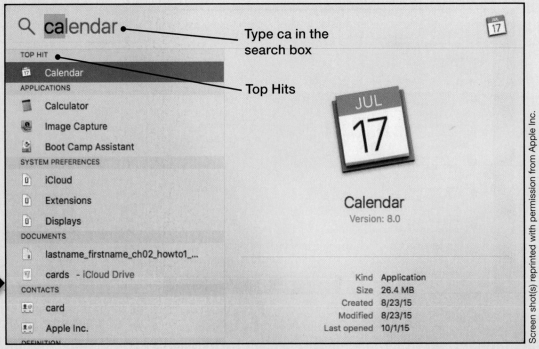

Type ca in the search box

Top Hits

FIGURE 3.26 OS X Spotlight searches for many types of objects on your computer.

Screen shot(s) reprinted with permission from Apple Inc.

Using Boolean Logic to Refine Searches

You can further refine your searches by using Boolean filters. George Boole was a 19th-century mathematician who created this system. There are three **Boolean operators** that define the relationships among words or groups of words: AND, OR, and NOT. Notice that they're written in all uppercase. You can use these operators to create search filters or queries in most searches, including databases and web searches. Figure 3.27 illustrates the effect of Boolean filters on the search using the terms John and Kennedy:

- **AND:** Search results must include both words: John AND Kennedy. This filter excludes files that don't include both terms.
- **OR:** Search results must include either word: John OR Kennedy. This filter includes all files that contain either or both terms.
- **NOT:** Search results must include the first term and must not include the second term: John NOT Kennedy. This filter excludes files that include the term *Kennedy*.

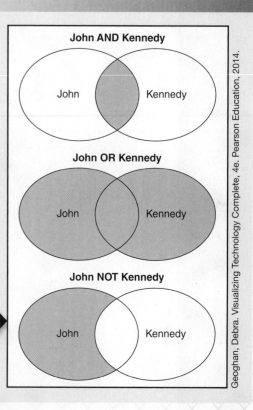

FIGURE 3.27 Boolean operators can be used to filter search results. The shaded areas represent the search results for each Boolean filter.

Geoghan, Debra. Visualizing Technology Complete, 4e. Pearson Education, 2014.

Using the Search feature of Windows or OS X can make locating a file or program quick and easy, saving you both time and aggravation. Good file management and searching techniques are important skills to have.

Running Project

Use the Internet to research *natural language search*. What is it, and how does it change the way you can search your computer?

4 Things You Need To Know

- There's a search box in most windows, control panels, and help screens.
- Windows maintains an index that contains information about the files located on your computer.
- The search tool in OS X is called Spotlight.
- The Boolean operators AND, OR, and NOT can be used to create search filters.

Key Terms

Boolean operator

index

Spotlight

Miya227/Fotolia

That's Not the Program I want to Open this File

6 Change the Default Program Associated with a File Type

Your operating system maintains a list of file extensions and associated **default programs** that enables it to automatically open the correct program when you click on a file. This is fine for file types that are specific to one program—such as .docx for Microsoft Word and .mov for Apple QuickTime—but it can be a problem with more generic file types that can be opened with several different programs. In this article, we look at how to manage default programs and file type associations in Windows and OS X.

Setting Program Defaults

In Windows you can manage default programs settings via Default apps settings (Figure 3.28). In File Explorer, click *This PC*, and on the ribbon, click *Settings*. In the Settings window, click *System*. Scroll down and click *Default apps*. In the right pane, scroll down and click *Set Defaults by app* to open the Set Default Programs control panel window (Figure 3.29). This window enables you to view and modify the file types the program opens by default.

To restore all the program's defaults at once, click the name of the program that you want to change and then click *Set this program as default* or click *Choose defaults for this program* to modify them individually. This enables you to specify which file types should be automatically opened by this program.

If you select the *Choose defaults for this program* option, a new window opens that enables you to pick items individually. For example, Photos is the default program for displaying many types of image files, such as JPG and GIF files. If you install Picasa on your computer, however, the default association for GIF files might change to Picasa Photo Viewer. You can use this dialog box to change the association back to Photos or to another program that you prefer.

FIGURE 3.28 The Default apps settings

FIGURE 3.29 The Set Default Programs Control Panel Window for Paint

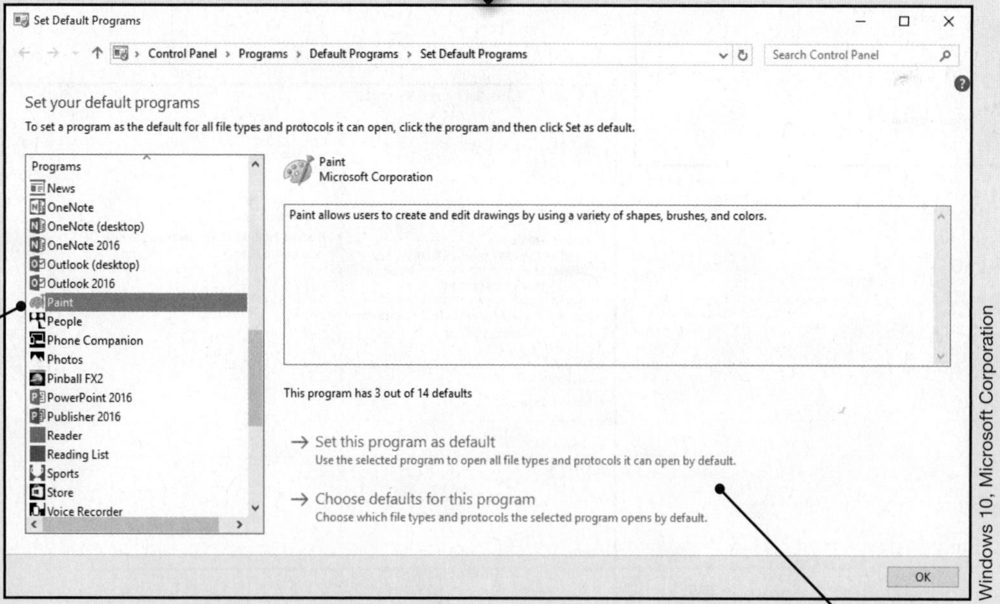

Select the program from the list to view information about the file types the program can open

Select the first option to set all the defaults, or the second option to select defaults individually

Managing File Type Associations

To manage individual file type associations, in the System Settings window, click *Default apps*, and then click *Choose default apps by file type*. Click the app or program name next to the file type you want to change and then click the new app or program Figure 3.30. This example shows *.bmp* files are currently associated with Photos and lists Paint, Photos, and Snagit Editor as other apps. The options you see will depend on the software installed on your system. You can also click *Look for an app in the Store* to open the Windows Store. Another way to change file type associations is to use the Default Programs control panel window; click *Associate a file type or protocol with a program*.

To change the program that opens a file in OS X, use Finder. Open Finder and select the file. From the File menu, select *Get Info*. In the Info pane, click *Open with* and choose the proper application from the list. To make sure that every file of that type uses the new application, click the *Change All* button (Figure 3.31).

Understanding file type associations will help you avoid frustration when an association is incorrect, and it will enable you to configure your programs the way that works best for you.

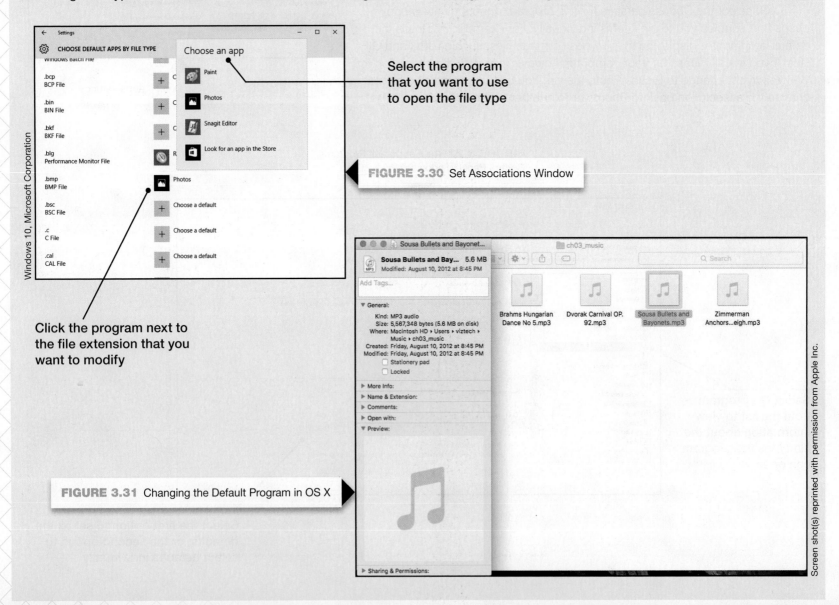

Select the program that you want to use to open the file type

FIGURE 3.30 Set Associations Window

Windows 10, Microsoft Corporation

Click the program next to the file extension that you want to modify

FIGURE 3.31 Changing the Default Program in OS X

Screen shot(s) reprinted with permission from Apple Inc.

CAREER SPOTLIGHT

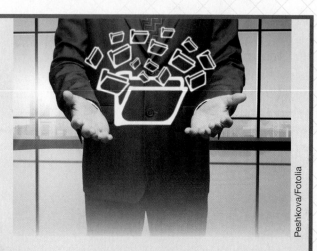

Peshkova/Fotolia

CERTIFICATION OF FEDERAL RECORDS MANAGEMENT—It's hard to imagine a career today that doesn't require you to have some file management skills. Any work that deals with documents—from traditional office work to doctor's offices, flower shops, contractors, and teachers—has files that need to be managed. Many industries, such as healthcare, finance, and government agencies, have document management regulations that require individuals with excellent file management skills.

The U.S. National Archives and Records Administration (NARA) offers a certification track for federal employees. To receive the Certification of Federal Records Management, you must complete five Knowledge Area courses and exams. The organization offers an overview course in records management that's optional. Required courses are Creating and Maintaining Agency Business Information, Records Scheduling, Records Schedule Implementation, Asset and Risk Management, and Records Management Program Development. The NARA certification focuses on federal record management and regulations.

Running Project

Use the Default Programs control panel or Finder on your computer to complete this section of the project. What program is currently associated with MP3 files? What other file types can this program open by default? What other programs are installed on your computer that can open MP3 files by default? Note: If you do not have an MP3 file on your computer, use one provided with your student data files.

Viz Check—In MyITLab, take a quick quiz covering Objectives 4–6.

2 Things You Need To Know

- Your operating system maintains a list of file extensions and associated default programs.
- You can use the System Settings, Default Programs control panel, or Finder to change these associations.

Key Term

default program

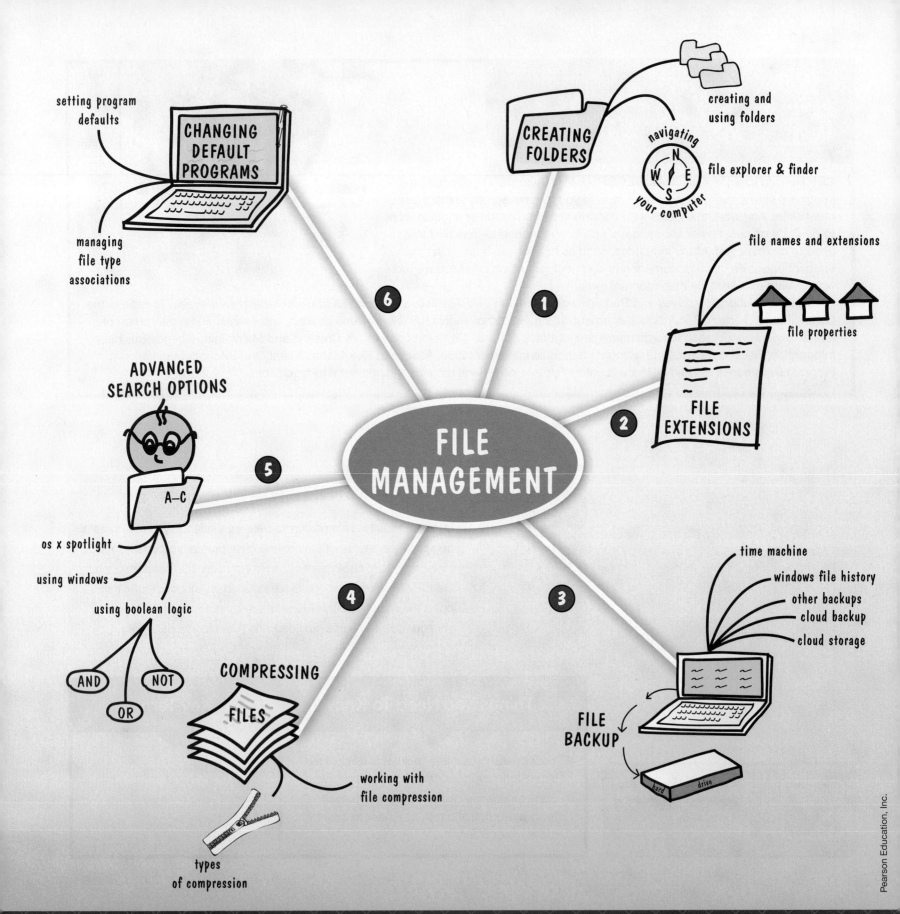

Objectives Recap

1. Create Folders to Organize Files
2. Explain the Importance of File Extensions
3. Explain the Importance of Backing Up Files
4. Demonstrate How to Compress Files
5. Use Advanced Search Options to Locate Files
6. Change the Default Program Associated with a File Type

Key Terms

algorithm **139**	Finder **118**
back up **132**	folder **115**
Boolean operator **147**	hierarchy **115**
cloud **134**	iCloud **135**
compression **138**	index **145**
default program **148**	library **115**
File Explorer **115**	lossless compression **139**
file extension **128**	lossy compression **139**
file management **114**	OneDrive **135**
file name **127**	path **115**
file property **129**	Spotlight **146**

Summary

1. **Create Folders to Organize Files**

   Windows and OS X create a user folder hierarchy for you to use to store your files. You can create new folders in this hierarchy and in other locations, such as a flash drive or cloud storage, to organize and store your files. Windows Explorer and OS X Finder are tools you can use to work with these folders and files.

2. **Explain the Importance of File Extensions**

   A file name consists of two parts: the name that's used by people to describe the contents of the file and the extension that's used by the operating system to identify the type of file and determine which program should be used to open it.

3. **Explain the Importance of Backing Up Files**

   Scheduling a regular, automatic backup of important files ensures that you won't lose your files if something happens to your computer. For the greatest protection, keep the backup files in a different physical location.

4. **Demonstrate How to Compress Files**

   Files can be compressed using several methods. An easy method on a Windows computer is to select a file or folder in File Explorer, click the *Share* tab, and then click the *Zip* button. In OS X, the *Compress* option is in the Finder File menu.

5. **Use Advanced Search Options to Locate Files**

   Windows creates an index of files found on your computer that's used when you use search. The search tool in OS X is called Spotlight. When searching, you can add filters, such as Type and Date modified, to your search as well as use Boolean operators (AND, OR, or NOT) to further refine it.

6. **Change the Default Program Associated with a File Type**

   Windows provides a Default Programs control panel that can be used to modify the programs associated with specific file types. This tool allows you to control which program opens automatically when you double-click a file. The Info pane in OS X contains the Open with option.

Multiple Choice

Answer the multiple-choice questions below for more practice with key terms and concepts from this chapter.

1. The sequence of folders to a file or folder is known as its _____.
   a. Home folder
   b. library
   c. path
   d. subfolder

2. Which part of a File Explorer window contains commands to open and close the windows, as well as access to system Help?
   a. Address bar
   b. File tab
   c. Ribbon
   d. Views button

3. What tool is used to find and organize files on a Mac?
   a. File Explorer
   b. Finder
   c. Library
   d. User folder

4. Which of the following isn't a legal Windows file name?
   a. hello.goodbye.hello.txt
   b. homework 11-04-15.docx
   c. homework:ch_03.xlsx
   d. make_my_day.bmp

5. Which file extension indicates a Word document?
   a. .docx
   b. .rtf
   c. .txt
   d. .wrd

6. The backup utility included with Windows is called _____.
   a. BackItUp
   b. File History
   c. OneDrive
   d. Time Machine

7. Which type of image uses lossy compression to reduce file size?
   a. BMP
   b. JPG
   c. TIF
   d. ZIP

8. Which search utility is included on a Mac?
   a. Explorer
   b. Cover Flow
   c. Finder
   d. Spotlight

9. Which Boolean operator excludes certain words from the search results?
   a. AND
   b. EXCLUDE
   c. OR
   d. NOT

10. What is the default program association for JPG files on a Windows computer?
    a. Explorer
    b. Photos
    c. Picasa
    d. Preview

True or False

Answer the following questions with T for true or F for false for more practice with key terms and concepts from this chapter.

_____ 1. Folders are containers that are used to organize files on your computer.

_____ 2. Folders within folders are also called paths.

_____ 3. The folder structure created by Windows is a library.

_____ 4. Windows File Explorer is a tool used to navigate the Internet.

_____ 5. You can change some of the properties of a file.

_____ 6. If you change the file extension of a file, you may be unable to open it.

_____ 7. The Finder is a tool used in OS X to work with files and folders.

_____ 8. A file compressed with a lossless compression algorithm can be decompressed to its original form.

_____ 9. Searching using the Boolean operator AND limits the search results.

_____ 10. The default program that opens a file can't be changed.

Fill in the Blank

Fill in the blanks with key terms from this chapter.

1. The processes of opening, closing, saving, naming, deleting, and organizing digital files are collectively called _____.

2. The folder structure created by Windows is a(n) _____.

3. A(n) _____ is used to gather files that are located in different locations on a Windows computer.

4. The second part of the file name is the _____, which is assigned by the program that is used to create a file.

5. A(n) _____ is information about a file, such as authors, size, type, and date, which can be used to organize, sort, and find files more easily.

6. You should regularly _____ your files for ease of recovering files in case of computer damage.

7. A(n) _____ is a procedure for solving a problem.

8. Windows maintains a(n) _____ of files on your computer to speed up searching.

9. The _____ AND, OR, and NOT are used to create search filters.

10. The _____ is the program that's associated with a particular file type and that automatically opens when a file of that type is double-clicked.

Running Project...

...The Finish Line

Using your answers to the previous projects' questions, write a report describing the importance of file management. Explain how to organize, protect, and manage the files you save on your computer. Save your file as **lastname_firstname_ch03_project** and submit it to your instructor as directed.

Do It Yourself 1

In this activity you will set up folders you can use to store the work you complete in this class. This activity assumes you're using a USB flash drive to save your work for this class. If you're storing your files on your own computer, you can store them in the Documents folder. If you didn't complete the steps in the Running Project to create a class folder and a Chapter 3 folder, do so now. Open a new, blank document in your word processor.

1. In your word processor, click *File* and click *Save As*. If necessary, click *Browse*. In the Save As dialog box, in the left pane, click your flash drive. Open the class folder and the Chapter 3 folder. In the File name text field, save your work as **lastname_firstname_ch03_DIY1_answersheet**

2. Navigate to the folder that you created for this class using File Explorer or Finder. Create new folders for each chapter in this book. Take a screenshot of the window showing these folders. Paste the screenshot into your answer sheet. Write a brief note to a friend explaining how to create a folder and why it is useful. Save your file, close your word processor, and submit the file as directed by your instructor.

Do It Yourself 2

Lossy compression is used when a BMP or TIF file is converted into a JPG file. Most people can't tell the difference between the two when viewing them on the computer screen. To complete this exercise, you need to have a photo editing program such as Windows Photo Gallery installed on your Windows computer. If you have a Mac, you can use Preview to complete this exercise. You can also use a different program, such as Paint, iPhoto, or Picasa. From your student data files, open the file *vt_ch03_DIY2_answersheet* and save the file as **lastname_firstname_ch03_DIY2_answersheet**

1. Open File Explorer and navigate to the data files folder for this chapter. Locate the *vt_ch03_sunset* image file. This is a photo taken with the camera's highest setting. Drag this file to your Pictures folder. Open the Pictures folder and locate the sunset file. Select the file, and if necessary, use the View tab to display the Details pane. Look at the properties in the Details pane of the window. How big is the image file? What are the dimensions of the image? What is the file type?

2. Right-click the image, point to *Open with*, and then click *Paint*. Click *File,* point to *Save As*, and then click *JPEG picture*. With the file type in the Save As dialog box as JPEG, save the file with the suggested name. In File Explorer, navigate to the location where you saved the image, and select the new .jpg version of the file. Use the Details pane to determine the new file size, dimensions, and file type. How much was the file compressed by converting it from a TIF to a JPG? Open the image files and look at them carefully. Compare both files. Can you tell the difference? If so, what differences do you notice? Is the JPG file acceptable for viewing on the screen, or is the image quality too poor? Save your answers and submit the file as directed by your instructor.

If you are using a Mac:

1. Open Finder and navigate to the data files folder for this chapter. Locate the *vt_ch03_sunset* image file. This is a photo taken with the camera's highest setting. Drag this file to your Pictures folder. Open the Pictures folder and locate the sunset file. Select the file and choose *Get Info* from the File menu. How big is the image file? What are the dimensions of the image? What is the file type?

2. Double-click the file to open Preview. From the File menu, choose *Export.* With the file type in the Export As dialog box as JPEG, save the file with the suggested name. Navigate to the location where you exported the image, and select the new .jpg version of the file. In Finder, click the *File menu* and click *Get Info*. How much was the file compressed by converting it from a TIF to a JPG? Open the image files and look at them carefully. Compare both files. Can you tell the difference? If so, what differences do you notice? Is the JPG file acceptable for viewing on the screen, or is the image quality too poor? Save your answers and submit the file as directed by your instructor.

Critical Thinking

Your friend Zoe is starting her own cupcake business. She's overwhelmed by all the information she has to keep track of and has asked you to help her get organized. All her files are stored on one flash drive, and she needs you to sort them for her. From your student data files, open the file *vt_ch03_CT_answersheet* and save the file as **lastname_firstname_ch03_CT_answersheet**

1. Locate the data files for this course. Copy the folder *ch03_zoe_cupcakes* to your flash drive or Documents folder. Examine the file names to determine the contents of each. Complete the table that follows. Label columns with three or four appropriate categories (such as flyers, recipes, and so on) to organize the files on the disk. In each column, list the files that belong in each category. Add columns and rows as needed to fit your organizational plan.

2. Use File Explorer or Finder to create a folder that represents each category. Move the files into the appropriate folders. Take screenshots that show the contents of each folder you create and paste these into your answer sheet. Save your file and submit it as directed by your instructor.

Flyers	Category 2	Category 3	Category 4
sale flyer			

Ethical Dilemma

Depending upon the system configuration, you may have public folders that are accessible to all users of a computer system and provide an easy way to share files among them. From your student data files, open the file *vt_ch03_ethics_answersheet* and save the file as **lastname_firstname_ch03_ethics_answersheet**

You log into the computer in the lab at school and notice that another student has stored his or her homework assignments in the Public folder. It's the same class that you're taking, so the work could help you. What is the ethical thing to do? If the work was for a different course, what would you do? Type up your answers, save the file, and submit it as directed by your instructor.

On the Web

There are few careers today that don't require some file management skills. From your student data files, open the file *vt_ch03_web_answersheet* and save the file as **lastname_firstname_ch03_web_answersheet**

Use the Internet to search for jobs that have file management listed as a required skill. Use at least two websites. What websites did you use? How many jobs were listed with your criteria? What were some of the industries that require this skill? Type up your answers, save the file, and submit it as directed by your instructor.

Collaboration

With your group, research the differences between two media file types and create a poster that illustrates the comparison.

Instructors: Divide the class into five groups, and assign each group one topic for this project. The topics include WMA and MP3; TIF and JPG; MP4 and WMV; AAC and MP3; and MOV and AVI.

The Project: As a team, create a poster comparing file types. The poster should explain both the pros and cons of each file type and include examples of when it's appropriate to use them. Use at least three references. Use Google Drive or Microsoft Office to prepare your poster, and provide documentation that all team members have contributed to the project.

Outcome: Prepare a poster on your assigned topic and present it to your class. Turn in a final version of your poster named **teamname_ch03_poster** and your file showing your collaboration named **teamname_ch03_collab** and submit your poster to your instructor as directed.

Application Project

Office 2016 Application Projects
Excel 2016: Municipal Waste

Project Description: In this Microsoft Excel project, you will format cells and a worksheet. You will create a formula and insert a header and footer. *If necessary, download the student data files from* **pearsonhighered.com/viztech**.

2012

Municipal Solid Waste Generation, Recycling, and Disposal in the United States

Facts and Figures for 2012

Material	Weight Generated	Weight Recovered	Recovery as Percent of Generation	Weight Discarded
Paper and paperboard	68.62	44.36	64.6%	24.26
Glass	11.57	3.2	27.7%	8.37
Ferrous	16.8	5.55	33.0%	11.25
Aluminum	3.58	0.71	19.8%	2.87
Other nonferrous metals†	2	1.36	68.0%	0.64
Plastics	31.75	2.8	8.8%	28.95
Rubber and leather	7.53	1.35	17.9%	6.18
Textiles	14.33	2.25	15.7%	12.08
Wood	15.82	2.41	15.2%	13.41
Other materials	4.6	1.3	28.3%	3.3
Total materials in products	**176.6**	**65.29**	**37.5%**	**111.31**
Other wastes				
Food, other‡	36.43	1.74	4.8%	34.69
Yard trimmings	33.96	19.59	57.7%	14.37
Miscellaneous inorganic wastes	3.9 Negligible		Negligible	3.9
Total other wastes	**74.29**	**21.33**	**28.0%**	**52.96**
Total municipal solid waste	250.89	86.62	34.5%	164.27

Generation, Recovery, and Discards of Materials in MSW, 2012*
(in thousands of tons and percent of generation of each material)

Source- U.S. Environmental Protection Agency (EPA)

lastname_firstname_ch03_excel

Step	Instructions
1	Start Excel. From your student data files, open the Excel file named *vt_ch03_excel*. Save the workbook as lastname_firstname_ch03_excel
2	Increase the width of columns B:E to 15.
3	Select the text in the range B4:E4 and set the text to wrap. Center and middle align the text in the selected range. Change the cell style to Heading 4.
4	Merge and center the text in cell A1 over columns A:E. Change the cell style to Heading 2. Merge and center the text in cell A2 over columns A:E. Change the cell style to Heading 3.
5	Change the cell style in cell A16 to Heading 4.
6	Format the range D5:D23 as percentage, 1 decimal place.
7	Delete row 7. Delete row 10.
8	Change the cell style of the range A15:E15 to Total. Change the cell style of the range A20:E20 to Total.
9	In cell B21, create a formula to calculate the total municipal solid waste by adding the values for total materials in products and total other wastes. Copy the formula to cell C21 and E21.
10	In cell D21, create a formula to calculate the percentage of municipal waste that is recovered by dividing the weight recovered by the weight generated.
11	Rename the Sheet1 tab as 2012
12	Insert a header with the Sheet name in the center cell. Insert a footer with the file name in the left cell. Center the worksheet horizontally on the page and change the orientation to landscape. Save the workbook and exit Excel. Submit the workbook as directed.

Application Project

Office 2016 Application Projects
Word 2016: Importance of File Management

Project Description: In the following Microsoft Word project, you will create a report about the importance of file management. In the project you will enter and edit text, format text, insert graphics, check spelling and grammar, and create document footers. *If necessary, download the student data files from* **pearsonhighered.com/viztech**.

File Management Primer

Have you ever saved a file on your computer and then lost it? Is your email inbox full? Is your desktop covered with icons and files? Have you downloaded a file from the Internet or email and been unable to locate it? *All of these are symptoms of poor file management.* Poor file management causes frustration, inefficiency, lost productivity, and duplication of effort. So, it is critical to practice good file management—and it's easy too.

First, get to know your folder hierarchy. Both Windows and OS X create your user folder for you—with folders for documents, pictures, music, videos, and downloads. This is a great start. It gives you logical places to put things. But if you have a lot of files or want to save them on other disks or in another structure, you'll need to do more.

Second, learn to navigate your file system. On a Windows computer, learn to use **File Explorer**. On a Mac, get friendly with **Finder**. These tools are your best friends when it comes to finding and organizing your files.

Third, organize your files into folders. Create the folders that make sense to you. Consider creating folders for each class you take, or each project you work on.

Finally, remember to use your new organization scheme. Save your files in the right place, and you will always be able to find them!

PS- I mentioned email in the first paragraph. Well guess what, same rules apply. Create folders or labels in your email program to organize your email messages—and file or delete them as soon as you have finished with them. Nothing is more satisfying at the end of the day than an empty inbox!

lastname_firstname_ch03_word

Step	Instructions
1	Start Word. From your student data files open the file named *vt_ch03_word*. Save the document as **lastname_firstname_ch03_word**
2	Select the first line of the document and apply the Title style.
3	Format the rest of the document as Times New Roman, 12 pt.
4	In the first body paragraph, format *All of these are symptoms of poor file management.* as italic.
5	In the third body paragraph, format *File Explorer* and *Finder* as bold.
6	Place the insertion point at the end of the third body paragraph (begins with Second), and then press *Enter*. Insert the picture of File Explorer *vt_ch03_image1*.
7	Resize the image to a height of 2.8' and center it.
8	Use the Spelling and Grammar checker to correct the misspelling of the word *lables* to *labels* and correct the misspelling of the word *delte* to *delete*.
9	Using the Spelling and Grammar dialog box, accept the suggested correction for the grammar error *n*. Ignore all other spelling and grammar suggestions.
10	Insert the file name in the footer of the document using the File Name field. Save the document and exit Word. Submit the document as directed.

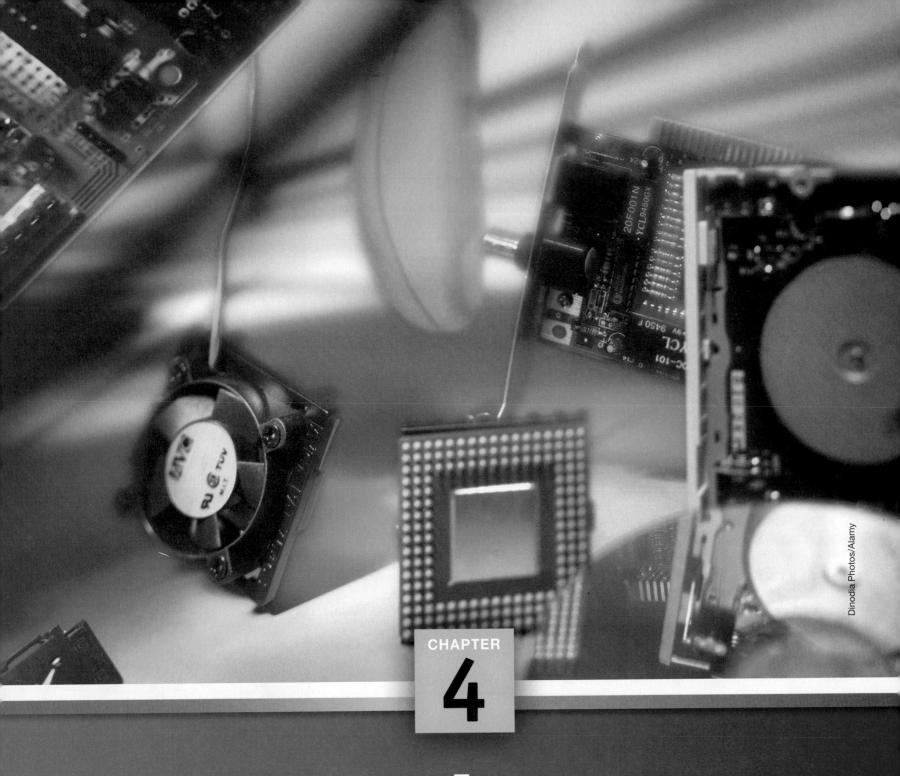
Dinodia Photos/Alamy

Hardware

In This Chapter

VIZ INTRO

Computers perform four tasks: input, processing, output, and storage. A computer consists of components that process data. **Hardware** refers to the physical components of a computer. The components that serve the input, output, and storage functions are called **peripheral devices**. Peripherals can be external devices, or they can be integrated into the system unit. After reading this chapter, you will be able to identify common input and output devices and their uses.

Objectives

1 Explain the Functions of a CPU

2 Identify the Parts of a System Unit and Motherboard

3 Compare Storage Devices

4 List and Describe Common Input Devices

5 List and Describe Essential Video and Audio Output Devices

6 Compare Various Types of Printers

7 Explain and Provide Examples of Adaptive Technology

8 Discuss Communication Devices

Running Project

In this chapter, you'll explore the key hardware components of a computer, which can be put together to create a system that fits your needs. Look for instructions as you complete each article. For most articles, there's a series of questions for you to research. At the conclusion of the chapter, submit your responses to the questions raised and present and justify your selections.

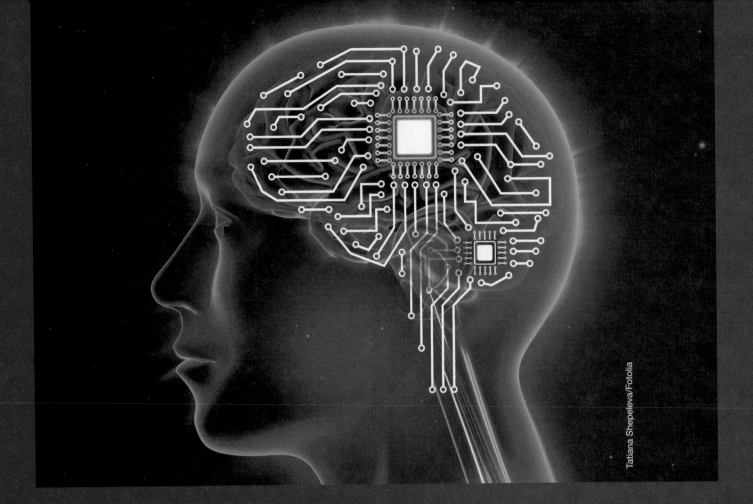

The CPU: The brains of the operation

Explain the Functions of a CPU

The brain of a computer is called the **central processing unit (CPU)**, or **processor**, and it is housed on the motherboard—the main circuit board of a computer (Figure 4.1). The CPU consists of two parts: the arithmetic logic unit and the control unit.

The **arithmetic logic unit (ALU)** performs arithmetic and logic (AND, OR, and NOT) calculations. The **control unit** manages the movement of data through the CPU. Together, these units perform three main functions: executing program instructions (control unit), performing calculations (ALU), and making decisions (control unit).

How Processors Work

Andrey Armyagov/Fotolia

FIGURE 4.1 The central processing unit fits into the motherboard inside the system unit.

Instruction Cycle

In order to perform the three functions, the CPU utilizes the **instruction cycle**, which is also known as the fetch-and-execute cycle, or the machine cycle (Figure 4.2). There are four steps of the instruction cycle:

- **Fetch:** The instruction is retrieved from the main memory.
- **Decode:** The control unit translates the instruction into a computer command.
- **Execute:** The ALU processes the command.
- **Store:** The results are written back to memory (stored).

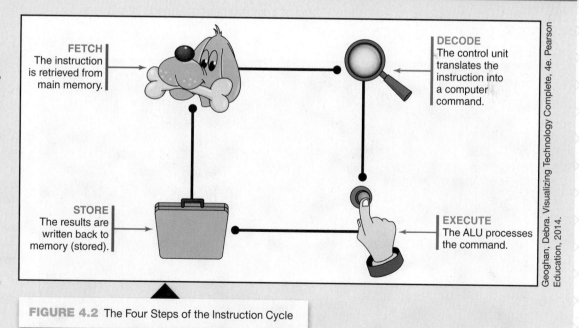

FETCH
The instruction is retrieved from main memory.

DECODE
The control unit translates the instruction into a computer command.

STORE
The results are written back to memory (stored).

EXECUTE
The ALU processes the command.

Geoghan, Debra. Visualizing Technology Complete, 4e. Pearson Education, 2014.

FIGURE 4.2 The Four Steps of the Instruction Cycle

CPU Performance

The processor executes billions of cycles each second. When you evaluate processors for performance, one of the variables to look at is **clock speed**, which is the speed at which the processor executes the cycles. Today, that speed is measured in **gigahertz (GHz)**—billions of cycles per second. A 3 GHz processor has 3 billion data cycles per second. Modern computers are capable of processing multiple instructions simultaneously rather than executing only one instruction at a time, which increases the efficiency of the processor and the performance of the computer.

MULTI-CORE AND MULTIPLE PROCESSORS

A **multi-core processor** consists of two or more processors that are integrated on a single chip. Multi-core processing increases the processing speed over single-core processors and reduces energy consumption over multiple separate processors. Today, dual-core, quad-core, and even six-core processors are found on most personal computers. A video card may have its own processor called a **GPU (graphics-processing unit)**, which can contain multiple cores. The GPU reduces the processing required of the system CPU for graphics-intensive processes.

Multiple processors are found in servers, which may have anywhere from two to several hundred processors (Figure 4.3). Supercomputers are considered *massively multiprocessor* computers and may have thousands of processors, just as the massively multiplayer online game *World of Warcraft* has thousands of players.

FIGURE 4.3
Multiple Processors on a Server Motherboard

Demarcomedia/Shutterstock

PARALLEL PROCESSING

Parallel processing uses multiple processors, or multi-core processors, to divide up processing tasks (Figure 4.4). It can dramatically increase computer performance when running processor-intensive programs such as system scans or when running multiple programs at the same time.

Parallel processing is most effective when software developers write programs that take advantage of multiple processors. Modern operating systems, such as Microsoft Windows, Mac OS X, and Linux, are optimized for parallel processing.

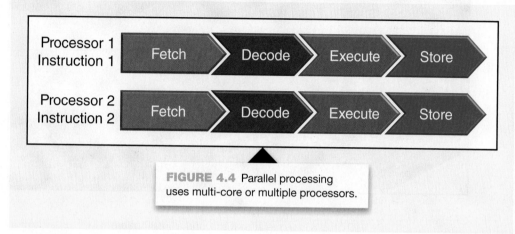

FIGURE 4.4 Parallel processing uses multi-core or multiple processors.

Geoghan, Debra. Visualizing Technology Complete, 4e. Pearson Education, 2014.

PIPELINING

Pipelining is a method used by a single processor to improve performance. As soon as the first instruction has moved from the fetch stage to the decode stage, the processor fetches the next instruction (Figure 4.5). The process is much like an assembly line in a factory. In a multi-core or multiple processor system, each processor may also use pipelining to further boost processing efficiency.

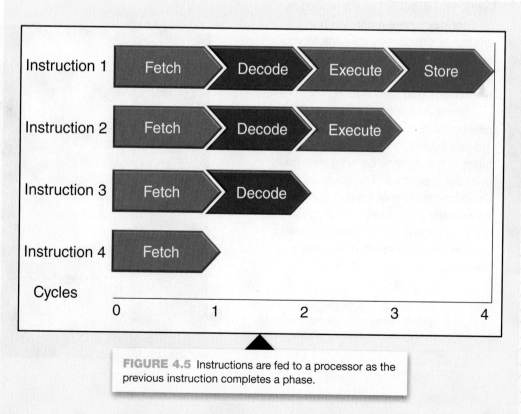

FIGURE 4.5 Instructions are fed to a processor as the previous instruction completes a phase.

Geoghan, Debra. Visualizing Technology Complete, 4e. Pearson Education, 2014.

COOLING SYSTEM: AIR CONDITIONING FOR THE PROCESSOR

Working quickly and using multiple processors or processing paths generates a great deal of heat. Excessive heat can damage a processor or cause it to fail, so modern computers need cooling systems for their CPUs.

To keep a processor from overheating, a **heat sink** and cooling fan are installed above the processor to dissipate the heat the processor produces (Figure 4.6). The heat sink is composed of metal or ceramic and draws heat away from the processor. In addition to the fan above the processor, most computer system units have at least one case fan to exhaust hot air and keep the entire system cool.

When using a notebook computer, you should place it on a hard surface and make sure not to block the air vents. You shouldn't use a notebook on your lap, where it can get hot enough to cause skin damage to you and overheat your computer. You can purchase a USB-powered cooler for a notebook that runs hot.

Some computers have a liquid cooling system that works like a car radiator by circulating liquid through tubes in the system, carrying heat away from the processor. The advantage to liquid cooling is that it's more efficient and quieter than a fan. The biggest disadvantage is that the liquid cooling system takes up much more space in the system unit (Figure 4.7).

Markd800/Fotolia

FIGURE 4.6 A metal heat sink and a small fan are installed above the CPU to keep it cool.

Getty Images

FIGURE 4.7 In this high-performance system, tubes from the liquid cooling system can be seen inside the case.

FIND OUT MORE

One way to improve processor performance is to overclock the processor. This means forcing it to run at speeds higher than it was designed to perform. Use the Internet to research overclocking. How is this possible? Is it legal? Why might you consider overclocking your CPU? What are the risks? Where did you find this information?

Running Project

Use the Internet to research current processors. What companies are the two main manufacturers of processors today? What is the fastest processor available today for desktop computers? What about notebooks? Other mobile devices?

4 Things You Need to Know

- The CPU consists of the arithmetic logic unit (ALU) and the control unit.
- The four steps of the instruction cycle are fetch, decode, execute, and store.
- Modern processors use pipelining and parallel processing to improve performance.
- A multi-core processor consists of more than one processor on a single chip.

Key Terms

arithmetic logic unit (ALU)

central processing unit (CPU)

clock speed

control unit

gigahertz (GHz)

GPU (graphics-processing unit)

hardware

heat sink

instruction cycle

multi-core processor

overclock

parallel processing

peripheral device

pipelining

processor

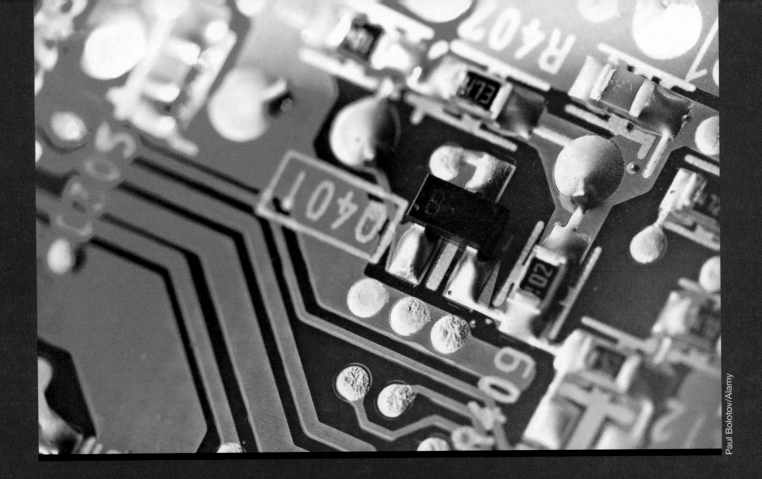

Paul Bolotov/Alamy

Getting to Know Your System Unit and Motherboard

Identify the Parts of a System Unit and Motherboard

VIZ CLIP

Setting Up a Computer System

The **system unit** is the case that encloses and protects a computer's internal components, including the power supply, motherboard, CPU, and memory. It has drive bays to hold the storage devices and openings for peripheral devices to connect to expansion cards on the motherboard (Figure 4.8). All-in-one systems and notebook computers have the keyboard and monitor integrated into the system unit. The system unit holds everything together.

Power supply

Processor and cooling fan

Expansion slots

Drive bays

Vetkit/Fotolia

FIGURE 4.8 In this desktop system unit with the cover removed, the processor is hidden under the cooling fan. The motherboard is mostly obscured by the other components.

Ports and connectors

Memory

Expansion slots

Shutterstock

Drive controllers

The Motherboard

The main circuit board of a computer is the **motherboard** (Figure 4.9). In addition to housing the CPU, it contains drive controllers and interfaces, expansion slots, data buses, ports and connectors, BIOS, and memory. A motherboard may also include integrated components, such as video, sound, and network adapters. The motherboard provides a way for devices to attach to the computer.

FIGURE 4.9 A Modern Motherboard

DRIVE CONTROLLERS AND INTERFACES

A **drive controller** on the motherboard provides a drive interface, which connects disk drives to the processor. **SATA (Serial Advanced Technology Attachment)** is the standard internal drive interface, but the **EIDE (Enhanced Integrated Drive Electronics)** interface is still found on older computers. SATA is up to three times faster than EIDE and has smaller, thinner cables that take up less room and enable better airflow inside the system unit (Figure 4.10).

FIGURE 4.10 A SATA cable (red) takes up less room in the system unit than does an EIDE cable (gray).

Alberto PÃ©rez Veiga/Shutterstock

EXPANSION CARDS

Also called **adapter cards**, **expansion cards** plug directly into **expansion slots** on the motherboard and enable you to connect additional peripheral devices to a computer. Video cards, sound cards, network cards, TV tuners, and modems are common expansion cards (Figure 4.11). Most expansion cards plug into a **PCI (Peripheral Component Interconnect)** slot on a motherboard. Video cards and some other devices use the faster **PCIe (PCI Express)** slots. Systems manufactured before 2009 used an **AGP (Accelerated Graphics Port)** for video.

DATA BUSES

Information flows between the components of a computer over wires on the motherboard called **data buses**. Local buses connect the internal devices on the motherboard, while external buses connect the peripheral devices to the CPU and memory of the computer. The speed of the data bus is an important factor in the performance of a system.

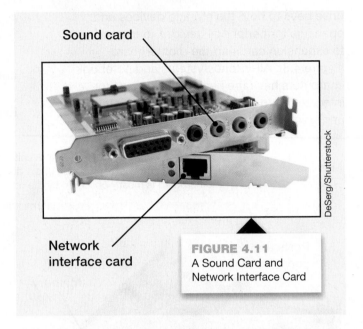

Sound card

Network interface card

FIGURE 4.11
A Sound Card and Network Interface Card

DeSerg/Shutterstock

Ports and Connectors

Ports are used to connect peripheral devices to a motherboard (Figure 4.12). The most common types of ports found today are USB and FireWire. **Serial and parallel ports** are legacy ports that aren't typically found on modern computers. **PS/2 ports**, which connect a keyboard and mouse, have also been widely replaced by USB. Bluetooth is a technology designed to connect peripherals wirelessly.

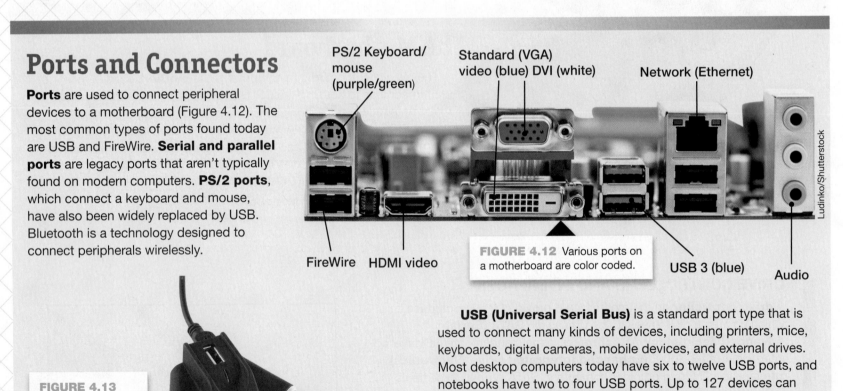

PS/2 Keyboard/ mouse (purple/green)

Standard (VGA) video (blue) DVI (white)

Network (Ethernet)

FireWire   HDMI video

FIGURE 4.12 Various ports on a motherboard are color coded.

USB 3 (blue)

Audio

Ludinko/Shutterstock

FIGURE 4.13
Multiple USB cables connected through a hub can share a single USB port on a computer.

Adrin Shamsudin/Fotolia

USB (Universal Serial Bus) is a standard port type that is used to connect many kinds of devices, including printers, mice, keyboards, digital cameras, mobile devices, and external drives. Most desktop computers today have six to twelve USB ports, and notebooks have two to four USB ports. Up to 127 devices can share a single USB port by using a **USB hub** (Figure 4.13). USB also provides power to some devices, which allows this type of connection to be used to charge a media player or smartphone and power devices such as webcams. Another advantage of USB devices is that they are **hot-swappable**, meaning they can be plugged in and unplugged without turning off the computer.

USB 1.0 was introduced in 1996 and was replaced by USB 2.0 in 2000. USB 2.0 is called Hi-Speed USB and is 40 times faster than its predecessor. The USB 3.0 SuperSpeed standard, released in 2008, is about 10 times faster than USB 2.0. This additional speed is particularly valuable for hard drives and digital video applications. The standard connection to the computer or hub is called USB-A. USB-B and various mini, micro, and proprietary formats are used to connect to USB devices (Figure 4.14). The newest version, USB-C, sometimes referred to as USB 3.1, is twice as fast as USB 3.0 and takes up much less space, so it is ideal for the thinnest notebook computers.

FireWire, also known as **IEEE 1394**, was originally released by Apple in 1995. FireWire is hot-swappable and can connect up to 63 devices per port. It also allows for peer-to-peer communication between devices, such as two video cameras, without the use of a computer. The original FireWire 400 is roughly equal to USB 2.0 in speed, and FireWire 800 is twice as fast. FireWire is primarily used to connect digital video cameras, which benefit from its superior speed. Figure 4.15 shows several USB and FireWire ports on a computer.

FireWire has largely been replaced by USB and the newer **Thunderbolt** technology. Thunderbolt was developed by IBM and Apple and is the standard on most Apple computers. It carries both PCIe and DisplayPort video signals on the same cable, so it can be used to connect many different types of peripherals to a computer. Thunderbolt combines two 10 Gbps channels, making it four times faster than USB 3.0 and 12 times faster than FireWire. You can connect up to six devices using one Thunderbolt connection.

Bluetooth is a short-range wireless technology that's used to connect many types of peripheral devices. It's commonly used to connect mice, keyboards, and printers to personal computers. A computer must have an adapter to communicate with Bluetooth-enabled devices. Bluetooth is also used in game consoles, such as the Nintendo Wii and Sony PlayStation 4, to connect game controllers, and in other applications, such as connecting a smartphone to a vehicle communication system.

Other ports that may be found on a computer include Ethernet ports to connect to a network, audio ports for speakers and microphones, and video ports to connect monitors and projectors. These are covered in more detail later in this chapter.

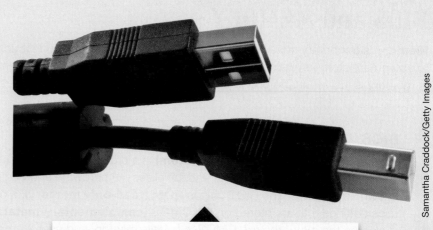

Samantha Craddock/Getty Images

FIGURE 4.14 USB connectors: Type A (top) connects to a computer or hub, and type B (bottom) connects to a USB device such as a printer or external drive.

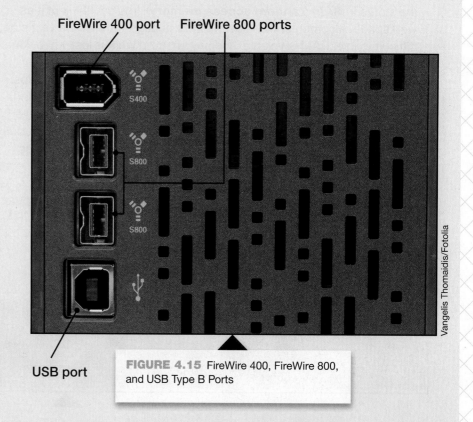

FireWire 400 port   FireWire 800 ports

USB port

Vangelis Thomaidis/Fotolia

FIGURE 4.15 FireWire 400, FireWire 800, and USB Type B Ports

BIOS and MEMORY

Memory is temporary storage that's used by the computer to hold instructions and data. Memory is also referred to as primary storage. Memory can be volatile or nonvolatile. **Volatile** memory requires power, any information left in memory is lost when the power is turned off. **Nonvolatile** memory does not need power to keep its data.

BIOS

The **BIOS (Basic Input/Output System)** is a program stored on a chip on the motherboard that's used to start up the computer. It tests and initializes the hardware and begins to load the operating system, also known as **booting**. The BIOS chip is **ROM (read-only memory)**, a nonvolatile form of memory. The BIOS uses settings that are stored on the **CMOS (complementary metal oxide semiconductor)** chip, which is also on the motherboard. CMOS is volatile memory and uses a small battery to provide it with power to keep the data in memory even when the computer is turned off.

RANDOM ACCESS MEMORY

The operating systems, programs, and data a computer is currently using are stored in **RAM (random access memory)**. You can think of it as your workspace. A computer that doesn't have enough RAM will be very slow and difficult to use. RAM is volatile, and any unsaved work is lost when you close a program or turn off your computer.

Memory boards are small circuit boards that contain memory chips. Most desktop memory uses a DIMM (dual in-line memory module), and notebooks use the SODIMM (small outline dual in-line memory module) configuration (Figure 4.16). There are several types of RAM available today. Older computers used SDRAM (synchronous dynamic random access memory), or DDR (double data rate) or DDR2 SDRAM. Newer computers use DDR3. Each type of memory is faster and more efficient than its predecessor.

RAM is fairly easy to install, and adding more memory to a computer is an inexpensive way to increase its performance. Installing additional RAM in an older computer can significantly extend its useful life.

Stocksnapper/Fotolia

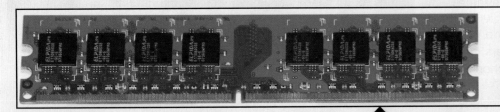

Joseph Geoghan

FIGURE 4.16 A desktop DIMM is about twice the physical size of a notebook SODIMM.

CACHE MEMORY

Most computers have a small amount of very fast memory that's used to store frequently accessed information close to the processor. This type of memory is called **cache memory**. Its location close to the processor greatly reduces the time it takes to access data and improves processor performance. Level 1 (L1) cache is built into the processor, and Level 2 (L2) cache is on a separate chip and takes slightly longer to access. Modern processors may have L2 cache built in and a Level 3 (L3) cache on the motherboard. Each progressive level of cache is farther from the CPU and takes longer to access.

Running Project

Use the Internet to research RAM. What's the fastest RAM available today for desktop computers? What about notebooks? Look at computer ads on some current retail websites. What is the average amount of RAM in desktop computers? In notebooks? What type of RAM is found in the most expensive systems?

5 Things You Need To Know

- The motherboard is the main circuit board in a computer. It provides a way for devices to attach to the computer.
- Ports and connectors attach peripheral devices to a motherboard.
- Information flows between the components of a computer over data buses.
- The BIOS is a program stored on a chip on the motherboard that's used to start up a computer.
- RAM is volatile memory that holds the operating systems, programs, and data the computer is currently using.

Key Terms

adapter card	memory
AGP (Accelerated Graphics Port)	motherboard
BIOS (Basic Input/Output System)	nonvolatile
Bluetooth	PCI (Peripheral Component Interconnect)
booting	PCIe (PCI Express)
cache memory	port
CMOS (complementary metal oxide semiconductor)	PS/2 port
data bus	RAM (random access memory)
drive controller	ROM (read-only memory)
EIDE (Enhanced Integrated Drive Electronics)	SATA (Serial Advanced Technology Attachment)
expansion card	serial and parallel ports
expansion slot	system unit
FireWire	Thunderbolt
hot-swappable	USB (Universal Serial Bus)
IEEE 1394	USB hub
	volatile

A Place for Everything

Objective 3

Compare Storage Devices

There are two ways to think about the storage of data: how it's physically stored on disks and how you organize the files you store. In this article, we'll look at physical storage devices. The capacity of storage has grown significantly over the past few years, as operating systems and software have gotten more sophisticated and files saved have become larger and more numerous. A decade ago, a floppy disk could hold 1.4 MB of information—roughly 750 pages of text. Today, a 1 terabyte hard drive in a personal computer can store about 500 million pages of text, 180 hours of high-definition video, or more than 280,000 high-quality photos.

SIMULATION **Hardware**

Optical Discs

Optical discs are a form of removable storage and include CDs, DVDs, and Blu-ray discs. The spelling *d-i-s-c* refers to optical discs, and *d-i-s-k* refers to magnetic disks. Data is stored on optical discs using a laser to either melt the disc material or change the color of embedded dye. A laser can read the variations as binary data (Figure 4.17).

An optical disc drive is mounted in the system unit in an external drive bay, which enables you to access the drive to insert or eject discs. Optical disc drives can also be peripheral devices connected by USB or FireWire. Optical discs can take several forms: read-only (ROM), recordable (+R/-R), or rewritable (+RW/-RW). The type of disc you should purchase depends on the type of drive you have. This is usually labeled on the front of the drive, as shown in Figure 4.18.

FIGURE 4.17 The data on an optical disc is read by a laser.

FIGURE 4.18 This drive can use R or RW discs.

CDS

A **CD (compact disc)** is the oldest type of optical disc in use today and has a storage capacity of about 700 MB. CDs are used to distribute software and music and to store photos and data, but they have been replaced by larger-capacity DVDs to distribute movies and some software.

DVDS

A **digital video disc** or **digital versatile disc**, more commonly known as a **DVD**, has the same physical dimensions as a CD but stores more than six times as much data. Single-layer (SL) DVDs can hold about 4.7 GB of information. Double-layer (DL) DVDs have a second layer to store data and can hold about 8.5 GB. DVDs are used to distribute movies and larger software programs.

BLU-RAY

A **Blu-ray disc (BD)** is an optical disc with about five times the capacity of a DVD, which it was designed to replace. The single-layer disc capacity is 25 GB, and the double-layer disc capacity is 50 GB. Because of this larger storage capacity, Blu-ray is used for high-definition video and data storage. BD-R discs are recordable, and BD-RE discs can be erased and re-recorded multiple times. Table 4.1 provides a comparison of the storage capacities of various optical media.

Table 4.1 Comparison of the Capacities of Optical Disc Formats

Optical Disc	Capacity	Number of 3.5 MB Photos	Video	High-Definition Video
CD-ROM	700 MB	200	35 minutes	—
DVD, single layer	4.7 GB	1,343	2 hours	—
DVD, dual layer	8.5 GB	2,429	4 hours	—
Blu-ray, single layer	25 GB	7,143	—	4.5 hours
Blu-ray, dual layer	50 GB	14,286	—	9 hours

Geoghan, Debra. Visualizing Technology Complete, 4e. Pearson Education, 2014.

Flash Memory

Unlike optical and magnetic storage, **solid-state storage** is non-mechanical. The data is stored using **flash memory** on a chip. Flash memory is used in solid-state drives, flash drives, memory cards, and mobile devices. Because there are no moving parts, a **solid-state drive (SSD)** is fast, quiet, and durable (Figure 4.19). SSDs are used in small electronic devices, such as media players, as well as in notebooks and desktops. Solid-state drives can use the same controllers as hard drives and can be either internal or external. Because SSDs are more expensive than similar-capacity hard drives, they are used primarily where speed and durability are necessary.

FIGURE 4.19 An Assortment of SSD Drives

Oleksiy Mark/Fotolia

FLASH DRIVES

Sometimes called key drives, thumb drives, pen drives, or jump drives, **flash drives** are small, portable, solid-state drives that can hold up to 1 TB of information, although the largest capacities are very expensive. Flash drives connect to a computer via a USB port and come in a variety of shapes and sizes (Figure 4.20). Flash drives are also used as internal storage in tablets and mobile devices.

Antonsov85/Fotolia

FIGURE 4.20 An Assortment of USB Flash Drives

MEMORY CARDS

You can expand the storage of digital cameras, video games, and other devices with **memory cards**—a storage medium that uses flash memory to store data. The type of memory card you use is dependent upon the device. The most common formats include Secure Digital (SD), CompactFlash (CF), Memory Stick (MS), and Extreme Digital xD-Picture Card (xD). Card readers are used to transfer data, such as photos and music, between a card and a computer or printer. Personal computers and photo printers may have built-in card readers, or you can use USB card readers on computers that don't have them.

Hard Drives

Hard drives are the main mass-storage devices in a computer. They are sometimes called hard disks or hard disk drives. Hard drives are a form of nonvolatile storage; when the computer is powered off, the data isn't lost. The primary hard drive holds the operating system, programs, and data files. Hard drives are measured in hundreds of gigabytes or terabytes and can hold hundreds of thousands of files.

Hard drives store data magnetically on metal platters. The platters are stacked, and read/write heads move across the surface of the platters, reading data and writing it to memory (Figure 4.21). The drives spin at up to 15,000 revolutions per minute, allowing for very fast data transfer.

Hard drives can be either internal or external. Internal drives are located inside the system unit in an internal drive bay and are not accessible from the outside. An external drive may be attached as a peripheral device using a USB or FireWire connection. The advantages of external drives are that they can be installed without opening the system unit and can be easily moved to another computer.

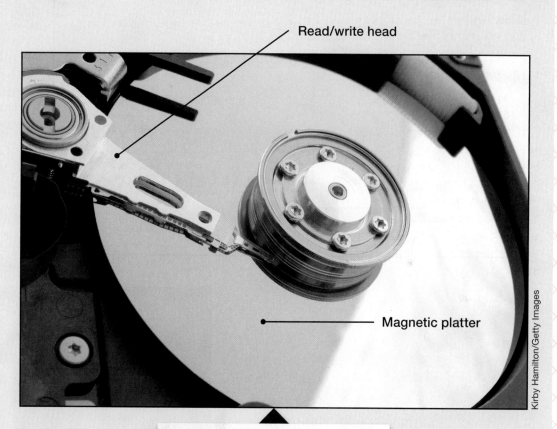

Read/write head

Magnetic platter

Kirby Hamilton/Getty Images

FIGURE 4.21 The read/write head is visible above the disk surface in this view of the inside of a hard drive.

Disconnecting An External Drive

Removable drives that connect to your computer via USB, such as flash drives or external hard drives, need special steps to be disconnected from a computer. It is important to be sure that Windows has finished writing to a drive before you unplug it. Open File Explorer, in the Navigation pane click *This PC*, right-click the drive, and then click *Eject* (Figure 4.22a). Once Windows has finished with the device, you will see a message that tells you it is safe to remove the device. Another way – in the Notification area of the taskbar, click the icon to Safely Remove Hardware and Eject Media, and then click to eject the appropriate item (Figure 4.22b). If you are using a Mac, drag the drive from the desktop to the trash to eject it, press Control + click and choose *Eject* from the shortcut menu (Figure 4.22c), or click the *Eject* button next to the drive's icon in the Navigation pane of Finder.

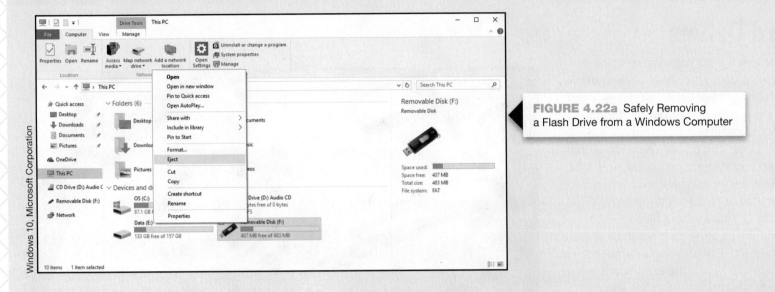

FIGURE 4.22a Safely Removing a Flash Drive from a Windows Computer

Windows 10, Microsoft Corporation

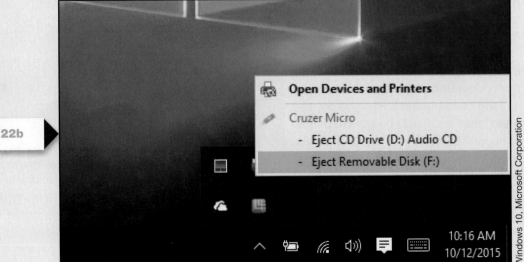

FIGURE 4.22b

Windows 10, Microsoft Corporation

FIGURE 4.22c Ejecting a Flash Drive from a Mac

Windows 10, Microsoft Corporation

Running Project

Look at computer ads on some current retail websites. What is the average size of a hard drive in desktop computers? In notebooks? What type of optical disc drive is found in most desktops? Notebooks? What type and capacity of storage is found in most tablets? Think about your needs. What types of storage do you need and how much? Can you easily add more storage later?

3 Things You Need To Know

- Lasers read the data on optical discs (CDs, DVDs, and Blu-ray discs).
- Hard drives store data magnetically on metal platters.
- Flash memory stores data on a chip.

Key Terms

Blu-ray disc (BD)

CD (compact disc)

DVD (digital video disc/digital versatile disc)

flash drive

flash memory

hard drive

memory card

optical disc

solid-state drive (SSD)

solid-state storage

Assess Your Computer Hardware

Digital Literacy Skill

HOW TO VIDEO

Computer performance is affected by many things. In this activity, you'll learn a little bit about your own computer. Your operating system can provide many details about your computer's hardware through a variety of built-in utilities. If necessary, download the student data files from **pearsonhighered. com/viztech**. From your student data files, open the *vt_ch04_ howto1_answersheet* file and save the file as **lastname_firstname_ ch04_howto1_answersheet**

1 Open File Explorer. If necessary, in the Navigation pane click *This PC*; and then on the Computer tab of the ribbon, click *System properties*.

2 In the middle of the screen, under System, is the information about your processor and memory. What type of processor do you have? What is its clock speed? How much RAM do you have?

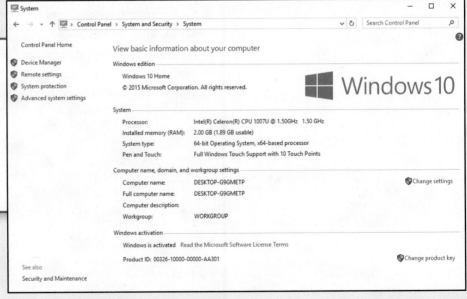

3 Click the back arrow and return to the File Explorer window. If necessary, click *This PC*. List all the devices and drives that are displayed. Include any additional information, such as size and free space, for each.

4 Type up your answers, save the file, and submit it as directed by your instructor.

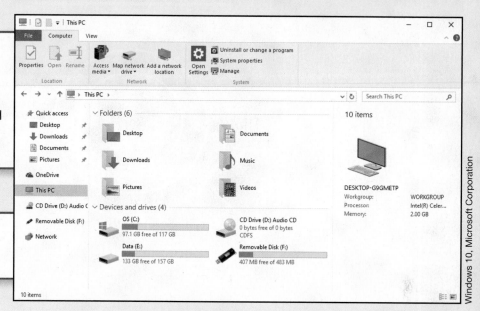

MAC

If you are using a Mac:

From your student data files, open the *vt_ch04_howto1_answersheet_mac* file and save the file as **lastname_firstname_ch04_howto1_answersheet_mac**

1. Click the *Apple* menu, click *About This Mac*.
2. On the Overview tab you'll find information about your processor and memory. What type of processor do you have? What is its clock speed? How much RAM do you have?
3. Click the *Storage* tab. List all disks that are displayed. Include any additional information, such as size and free space, for each.
4. Type up your answers, save the file, and submit it as directed by your instructor.

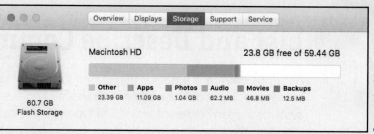

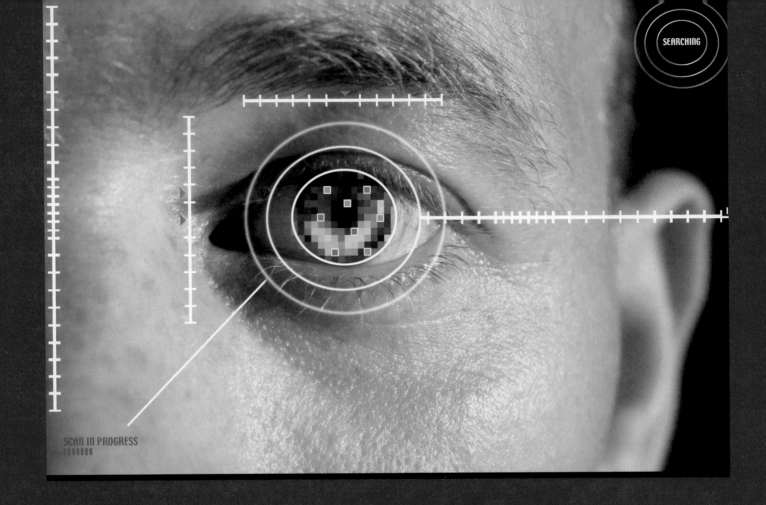

SEARCHING

SCAN IN PROGRESS

What Goes In...

List and Describe Common Input Devices

An **input device** is a device that's used to enter data into a computer system so that it can be processed. Input devices come in all shapes and sizes and enable you to interact with computer systems in many different ways. The type of input device you use depends on many factors, including the type of data to be input, the type of computer the input device is connected to, and the application you're using. Whether you're narrating a PowerPoint presentation, drawing a picture, or writing an email, you use input devices to get the data into the computer system so it can be processed. In this article, we'll look at some of the many input devices available.

Keyboards

The primary input device to enter text is a **keyboard** that consists of alphabet keys, numeric keys, and other specialized keys. A keyboard translates keystrokes into a signal a computer understands. This sounds pretty basic, but there are many different types of keyboards available. The most common type of keyboard is the standard QWERTY format, so called because *Q-W-E-R-T-Y* are the first alphabetic keys on the keyboard. The QWERTY design was originally developed by Christopher Sholes in 1873 to reduce the number of key jams on a mechanical typewriter, which can occur when adjacent keys on the keyboard are pressed quickly and interfere with each other. Although it may reduce the interference, it's an inefficient typing layout that's no longer needed because computer keyboards aren't mechanical. We have become so accustomed to the QWERTY layout that even virtual keyboards use it (Figure 4.23).

In addition to the alphabet and number keys, most standard keyboards have specialized keys (Table 4.2). Some keys, such as Esc and the Function keys, have specific actions associated with them. Other keys, such as Ctrl, Alt, and Shift, are modifiers and are pressed in conjunction with other keys. Toggle keys, such as CapsLock and NumLock, turn a feature on or off when pressed. Full-sized keyboards contain 101 or 104 keys; notebook computer keyboards are smaller and may not include a separate numeric keypad.

FIGURE 4.23 A Virtual QWERTY Keyboard on a Tablet

Mihai Simonia/Shutterstock

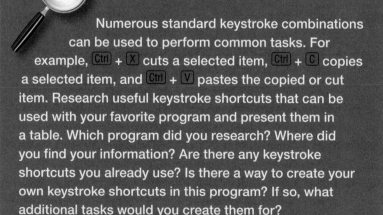

FIND OUT MORE

Numerous standard keystroke combinations can be used to perform common tasks. For example, Ctrl + X cuts a selected item, Ctrl + C copies a selected item, and Ctrl + V pastes the copied or cut item. Research useful keystroke shortcuts that can be used with your favorite program and present them in a table. Which program did you research? Where did you find your information? Are there any keystroke shortcuts you already use? Is there a way to create your own keystroke shortcuts in this program? If so, what additional tasks would you create them for?

TABLE 4.2 Special Keys on a Keyboard

Key	Type	Action
Esc	Normal	Cancel
CapsLock	Toggle	Turns capitalization on/off
Shift	Modifier—pressed with at least one other key	Activates uppercase or alternate-key assignment
Ctrl (Windows)/ Command ⌘ (Mac)	Modifier—pressed with at least one other key	Modifies the behavior of a key press
Alt (Windows)/ Option (Mac)	Modifier—pressed with at least one other key	Modifies the behavior of a key press
⊞	Normal	Opens the Windows Start menu

Geoghan, Debra. Visualizing Technology Complete, 4e. Pearson Education, 2014.

Keyboards can also have alternate layouts or be customized for a particular application. The Dvorak Simplified Keyboard was designed to put the most commonly used letters where they're more easily accessed to increase efficiency and reduce fatigue (Figure 4.24). Most modern operating systems include support for the Dvorak layout, but it's not been widely adopted.

Ergonomic keyboards are full-sized keyboards that have a curved shape and are designed to position the wrists in a more natural position to reduce strain (Figure 4.25). They may look funny, but many people who spend a lot of time on the computer rely on ergonomic keyboards to prevent injuries.

QWERTY Keyboard

DVORAK Keyboard

Geoghan, Debra. Visualizing Technology Complete, 4e. Pearson Education, 2014.

FIGURE 4.24 The QWERTY Keyboard Layout (top) and the Dvorak Keyboard Layout (bottom)

Creativa Images/Shutterstock

FIGURE 4.25 The curved shape of an ergonomic keyboard reduces wrist strain.

FIGURE 4.26 A USB keypad can be attached to a notebook computer.

Roman A. Kozlov/Fotolia

Another alternative keyboard is a **keypad**, a small keyboard that has a limited set of keys. This type of input device is typically found in point-of-sale (POS) terminals. People who enter a lot of numbers, such as teachers, accountants, and telemarketers, might find it useful to attach a USB keypad to a notebook computer (Figure 4.26). Many computer gamers find that a dedicated game keypad makes game play easier and more fun.

The Mouse and Other Pointing Devices

Pointing devices, such as mice and touchpads, are input devices that enable a user to interact with objects by moving a pointer, also called a cursor, on the computer screen. Many different versions of each of these devices are available. They enable you to point and click instead of typing text commands.

Szasz Fabian Jozsef/Fotolia

MOUSE AND TOUCHPAD

A **mouse** may include one or more buttons and a scroll wheel and works by moving across a smooth surface to signal movement of the pointer. Older mechanical mice had a ball that rolled across the surface. The ball tended to get dirty, which caused the mouse to become difficult to use. Modern optical mice detect motion by bouncing light from a red LED (light-emitting diode) off the surface below it. Because they have fewer moving parts, optical mice are less prone to failure than mechanical mice.

Most notebook computers include a built-in **touchpad** (also called a track pad) instead of a mouse (Figure 4.27). With this device, you move a finger across the touch-sensitive surface, and the computer detects and translates your motion. Touchpads also have buttons that function like mouse buttons and special areas that enable you to quickly scroll through documents, webpages, and images.

FIGURE 4.27 A Touchpad on a Notebook Computer

By Studio/Fotolia

TOUCH INPUT

Tablets, graphic design tablets (Figure 4.28), cell phones, handheld game consoles, and other devices have **touchscreens** that can accept input from a finger or a stylus. A **stylus** is a special pen-like input tool. Resistive touchscreens sense pressure and can be used with a finger or an ordinary stylus. A resistive screen could be used by someone wearing gloves. A capacitive screen senses the conductive properties of an object such as your finger or a specially designed conductive stylus. Interactive whiteboards are large interactive displays used in classrooms and businesses. They have touch-sensitive surfaces and enable the user to control the computer from the screen as well as capture what's written on the screen with special pens.

Denis Pepin/Shutterstock

FIGURE 4.28 A graphic design tablet with a stylus is a specialized input device used in graphic arts, CAD (computer-aided design), and other applications.

Digital Cameras and WEBCAMS

Digital cameras can capture still images or video. The cameras can be built in, directly connected to a computer by USB or FireWire cable, or transfer files to the computer via a removable flash card. **Webcams** are specialized video cameras that provide visual input for online communication, such as web conferencing or video chatting, as shown in Figure 4.29.

ArtFamily/Fotolia

FIGURE 4.29 Video Chatting Using a Tablet Webcam

Scanners

Scanners have many uses, from archiving old documents to checking out customers in grocery stores to organizing libraries to assisting law enforcement. The use of **scanners** increases the speed and accuracy of data entry and converts information into a digital format that can be saved, copied, and manipulated.

OPTICAL SCANNERS

You can convert a photo or document into a digital file by using an optical scanner. Flatbed scanners are the most common type of optical scanner used in homes and offices. You place the document or photo you wish to scan on a glass screen, and the scanner head moves underneath the glass to convert the image to a digital file. Business card readers and photo scanners typically have a sheet-feed format that moves the page to be scanned and keeps the scanner head stationary. Handheld scanners such as bar code readers are small and portable (Figure 4.30). You see these in supermarket checkout lines, library circulation desks, and shipping operations.

QR code reader and bar code readers on smartphones have turned shopping into an interactive activity. Many retail stores and magazines include **QR (Quick Response) codes**, two-dimensional bar codes, in ads and on merchandise tags that the shopper can scan to learn more about the item. Using bar code scanners, shoppers can scan an item in a mall and quickly determine which store or website has the lowest price. Website analytics can track webpages accessed from QR codes, providing useful information to the retailer about its shoppers.

QR and bar codes are used to share information in digital business cards and to ensure packages are delivered to the correct address. A mobile boarding pass includes traveler and flight information encoded in a QR or bar code that can be scanned by an attendant at the gate. (Figure 4.31)

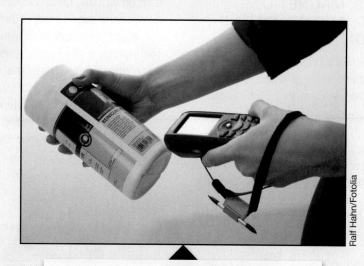

FIGURE 4.30 A bar code reader quickly scans the label, saving time and reducing data entry errors.

FIGURE 4.31 A QR code on this mobile boarding pass eliminates the need to print out the pass.

RFID SCANNERS, MAGNETIC STRIP READERS, AND NEAR FIELD COMMUNICATION

An RFID scanner can read the information in an **RFID tag**, which contains a tiny antenna for receiving and sending a radio-frequency signal. RFID (radio-frequency identification) is used in inventory tracking, electronic toll collection, contactless credit card transactions, and passports.

Another common scanner is a magnetic strip reader, which can read information encoded in the magnetic strip on a plastic card, such as a driver's license, gift card, library card, credit card, or hotel door key.

Near field communication (NFC) is a technology that enables devices to share data with each other by touching them together or bringing them within a few centimeters of each other. Interaction is possible between two NFC-enabled devices or between an NFC device and an NFC tag (Figure 4.32). For example, a tablet can be configured to use a wireless printer by tapping an NFC tag that has the configuration encoded in it.

FIGURE 4.32 NFC is used in a mobile payment system.

AA W/Fotolia

BIOMETRIC SCANNERS

Used in banks to identify patrons, in theme parks to ensure that tickets aren't transferred to other guests, and in corporate security systems, **biometric scanners** measure human characteristics such as fingerprints and eye retinas. Some notebook computers and smartphones use a fingerprint scanner to authenticate a user (Figure 4.33).

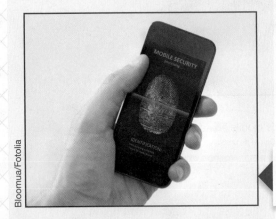

Bloomua/Fotolia

FIGURE 4.33 A fingerprint scanner built into a smartphone can be used for added security.

Microphones and Game Controllers

Common input devices include microphones, game controllers, and joysticks. **Microphones** convert sound into digital signals and are used to chat in real time, as part of voice-recognition applications, for playing video games, and for dictating text. They are often integrated into notebook computers and headsets or can be connected via USB or to the microphone port on a sound card.

Game controllers provide a way to interact with video games (Figure 4.34). Special game controllers include steering wheels, tennis rackets, guns, musical instruments, and pressure-sensitive mats. These controllers make the gameplay more realistic. A **joystick**, which is mounted on a base, consists of a stick, buttons, and sometimes a trigger. Typically used as a game controller, especially in flight-simulator games, a joystick also may be used for such tasks as controlling robotic machinery in a factory.

Production Perig/Fotolia

FIGURE 4.34 Game controllers and headsets are used to interact with video games.

Running Project

A mouse or touchpad and keyboard are standard input devices. Think about how you might use your computer in the future. What other input devices might you need? Pick at least one additional input device and research current models and costs. Which model would you choose, and why?

4 Things You Need To Know

- The mouse and keyboard are the most common input devices.
- Digital cameras and webcams input images and video.
- Scanners convert information into a digital format.
- Microphones are audio input devices.

Key Terms

biometric scanner	near field communication (NFC)
game controller	QR (Quick Response) code
input device	RFID tag
joystick	scanner
keyboard	stylus
keypad	touchpad
microphone	touchscreen
mouse	webcam

Viz Check—In MyITLab, take a quick quiz covering Objectives 1–4.

Wittybear/Fotolia

...Must Come Out

Objective 5

List and Describe Essential Video and Audio Output Devices

Processed information is returned to you through **output devices**. Computer output comes in two basic forms: tangible and intangible. In this article, we look at intangible outputs: video and audio. The output devices in this section enable you to listen to Beethoven or Lady Gaga and to view a Picasso painting or watch a guy fall off his skateboard on YouTube. Video and audio output has changed computers from simply being calculators of data to being an integral part of education and entertainment experiences.

Video Output Devices

What you see on your computer screen is video output. There are a variety of video output devices that provide visual output to the user. The most popular types of monitors and projectors come in many different sizes, technologies, and price ranges. Modern operating systems support multiple monitor configurations, enabling you to work on two or more screens at once.

Monkey Business/Fotolia

MONITORS

Similar to television screens, **monitors** work by lighting up **pixels**—short for picture elements—on the screen. Each pixel contains three colors: red, green, and blue (RGB). All colors can be created by varying the intensities of the three colors. Display **resolution** indicates the number of horizontal pixels by vertical pixels, such as 1280×1024 or 1920×1080. The higher the resolution, the sharper the image. The size of a monitor is measured diagonally across the screen.

Older **CRT monitors** and televisions use a cathode ray tube to excite phosphor particles coating the glass TV screen to light up the pixels. CRT monitors are big and use a lot of energy. As a result, they've been replaced by smaller and more energy-efficient flat-panel monitors (Figure 4.35). CRT monitors are considered **legacy technology**, which is old technology that's still used alongside its more modern replacement, typically because it still works and is cost-effective.

Most modern desktop and notebook computers have flat-panel monitors, which create bright, crisp images without using traditional picture tubes. Instead, such displays use LCD or plasma panels. Modern computers support the use of multiple monitors, allowing you to have the same content or different content displayed on each screen.

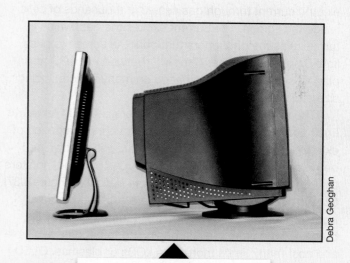

Debra Geoghan

FIGURE 4.35 An LCD monitor is much thinner than a CRT monitor of the same screen size.

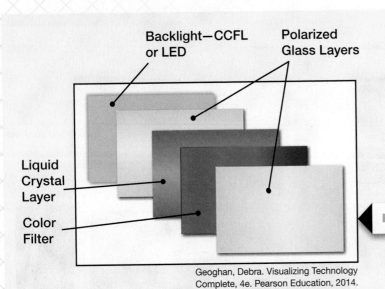

Backlight—CCFL or LED

Polarized Glass Layers

Liquid Crystal Layer

Color Filter

Geoghan, Debra. Visualizing Technology Complete, 4e. Pearson Education, 2014.

FIGURE 4.36 A Simplified Diagram of an LCD Panel

LCD (liquid crystal display) panels are found on most desktop and notebook computers. They consist of two layers of glass that are glued together with a layer of liquid crystals between them (Figure 4.36). When electricity is passed through the individual crystals, it causes them to pass or block light to create an image. LCDs do not give off any light, so they need to be backlit by a light source, typically CCFLs (cold cathode fluorescent lamps). Some LCD monitors are backlit by LEDs. The LED versions are generally thinner and more energy efficient, but they're also more expensive.

Available in larger screen sizes that you wouldn't use with a desktop computer, plasma screen monitors are typically included in media center systems or are used in conference rooms. **Plasma monitors** work by passing an electric current through gas sealed in thousands of cells inside the screen. The current excites the gas, which in turn excites the phosphors that coat the screen to pass light through an image. Choosing between an LCD and plasma screen monitor depends on many factors, including size and cost.

The newest technology in monitors is **OLED (organic light-emitting diode)**. These monitors are composed of extremely thin panels of organic molecules sandwiched between two electrodes. The prototypes of these monitors are less than 1 inch thick and are even bendable (Figure 4.37). OLEDs use very little energy and are expected to be at least 10 times more energy efficient than today's LCDs, but OLED monitors are just beginning to become available and cost many times more than LCDs or plasmas. OLED has a way to go before prices drop enough to make them practical for most consumers. AMOLED (active-matrix OLED) screens can be found in some mobile devices. AMOLED screens are sharper and have a wider viewing angle than LCDs, making them ideal for watching video and sports.

Frog/Fotolia

FIGURE 4.37 A Flexible OLED Tablet

PROJECTORS

When making a presentation or sharing media with a group in such places as classrooms, conference rooms, and home theaters, **projectors** are more practical than monitors because they produce larger output. They can be classified as video projectors, which are typically used in home media centers to display movies on a wall or screen, and data projectors, which are designed for presentations in a business or classroom setting. The two main types of projectors are DLP and LCD projectors.

DLP (digital light-processing) projectors have hundreds of thousands of tiny swiveling mirrors that are used to create an image. They produce high-contrast images with deep blacks but are limited by having weaker reds and yellows. The most portable projectors on the market today are DLP projectors, which weigh less than 3 pounds. DLPs also are very popular home theater projectors because of the higher contrast and deeper blacks that they produce.

LCD projectors pass light through a prism that divides the light into three beams—red, green, and blue—which are then passed through an LCD screen. These projectors display richer colors but produce poorer contrast and washed-out blacks. LCDs tend to have sharper images than DLPs and are better in bright rooms, making them ideal for presentations in conferences and classrooms (Figure 4.38).

FIGURE 4.38 A Projector Used to Give a Presentation to a Group of People

Contrastwerkstatt/Fotolia

Each technology has distinct advantages and disadvantages. The choice between them depends on many factors, including the primary use, the room the projector is in, whether it needs to be portable, and cost.

VIDEO CARDS

The data signal and connection for a monitor or projector are provided by an expansion card called a **video card**, graphic accelerator, or display adapter. Modern video cards contain their own memory, known as VRAM (video RAM), and a graphics-processing unit (GPU) in order to produce the best and fastest images. The **DVI (digital visual interface)** standard was released in 1999 to replace the analog VGA standard. It has been the standard video port found on video cards; but HDMI and DisplayPort have largely replaced it on newer systems. The DVI port provides a digital connection for flat-panel displays, data projectors, TVs, and DVD players. **VGA (video graphics array)** is a legacy analog standard used by CRT monitors and projectors (Figure 4.39). **HDMI (High-Definition Multimedia Interface)** is a digital port that can transmit both audio and video signals. It is the standard connection for high-definition TVs, video game consoles, and other media devices. **DisplayPort** is a digital video interface designed to replace DVI and VGA. It is sometimes implemented in the Mini DisplayPort format, which is ideal for smaller notebook bodies. A video card may also include input ports to connect a TV tuner or another video device to the system.

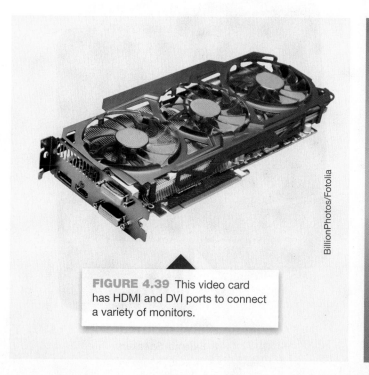

FIGURE 4.39 This video card has HDMI and DVI ports to connect a variety of monitors.

BillionPhotos/Fotolia

Audio Output Devices

Audio output can be anything from your favorite song to sound effects in a video game to an email alert chime. The sound can be heard through speakers or headphones.

Westend61 Premium/Shutterstock

SPEAKERS AND HEADPHONES

Speakers and **headphones** convert digital signals from a computer or media player into sound. Speakers may be integrated into notebook computers and monitors or connected via USB or to the speaker ports on a sound card. Typical desktop speaker systems include two or three speakers (Figure 4.40), but speaker systems designed for gaming or home theater uses include as many as eight speakers and can cost hundreds of dollars.

Headphones come in several different sizes and styles, ranging from tiny earbuds that fit inside your ear to full-size headphones that completely cover your outer ear. High-quality headphones can cost hundreds of dollars and incorporate up to eight speakers in the design. Noise-canceling headphones reduce the effect of ambient noise and are especially useful in noisy environments, such as airplanes. Headphones can plug into the headphone or speaker port of a computer or mobile device, the headphone port on a speaker, or a USB port, and they can connect wirelessly via Bluetooth. Headphones that also include a microphone are called headsets.

JackF/Fotolia

FIGURE 4.40 External Speakers

SOUND CARDS

A **sound card** provides audio connections for both input devices (microphones and synthesizers) and output devices (speakers and headphones), as shown in Figure 4.41. Sound cards can be integrated into the motherboard—onboard—or connected through expansion cards or external USB or FireWire ports. High-end sound cards support surround sound, have connections for up to eight speakers, and include a digital optical port for connecting to a home entertainment system.

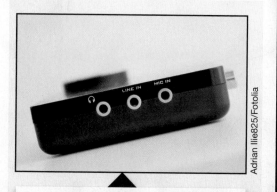

Adrian Ilie825/Fotolia

FIGURE 4.41 External Sound Card with Color-Coded Connections: Speakers or Headphones (Green), Line-in (Blue), and Microphone (Pink)

Running Project

If you were going to purchase a new desktop computer today, one decision you would have to make is what type and size of monitor to get. Think about the room you would put the system in and what you might use it for. Would you be watching movies on the screen? Is the room really bright? Does the screen need to be large enough for several people to view at once? Using the answers to these questions, determine the type and size of monitor(s) you would need. Use the Internet to compare several models and select the one that best fits your needs.

6 Things You Need To Know

- Most personal and notebook computers have LCD monitors.
- Large plasma monitors are commonly found in media centers and conference rooms.
- Resolution is the number of horizontal pixels by the number of vertical pixels on a screen.
- The two types of video projectors are DLP and LCD.
- Video cards connect monitors and projectors to a computer.
- Speakers and headphones are audio output devices that connect to a sound card.

Key Terms

CRT monitor	OLED (organic light-emitting diode)
DisplayPort	output device
DLP (digital light-processing) projector	pixel
DVI (digital visual interface)	plasma monitor
HDMI (High-Definition Multimedia Interface)	projector
headphones	resolution
LCD (liquid crystal display)	sound card
LCD projector	speakers
legacy technology	video card
monitor	VGA (video graphics array)

Maksym Dykha/Fotolia

Pick a printer

Objective

6

Compare Various Types of Printers

Hard copies of documents and photos are produced by printers. There are many different types of printers that generate everything from photos to blueprints to ID cards. In this article, we'll look at some of the most common types of printers used in homes and businesses.

Printers

Printers produce tangible output. The type of printer you choose depends on many things, including the type and size of output you need, cost, and size. Businesses might have several different types of printers on hand to meet all their needs. For a home user, a multifunction device might be the best choice. As the technology grows and the costs decrease, home users can make high-quality prints at home.

PHOTO PRINTERS: INKJETS AND DYE-SUBLIMATION PRINTERS

A **photo printer** is a printer designed to print high-quality photos on special photo paper. Photo printers can be inkjet printers that use special ink cartridges or dye-sublimation printers, which produce lab-quality prints. Some photo printers connect directly to a digital camera or read data from a memory card. Many newer cameras and cell phones connect to printers through Wi-Fi or Bluetooth Figure 4.42.

FIGURE 4.42 You can print directly from a digital camera or smartphone connected by Wi-Fi or USB cable to a compatible printer.

Naypong/Fotolia

FIGURE 4.43 CMYK (cyan, magenta, yellow, black) are the colors used by inkjet and dye-sublimation printers.

Guanta/Shutterstock

The most common personal printers are **inkjet printers**, which work by spraying droplets of ink onto paper. Some printers use one ink cartridge; others may use two, three, four, or even more. The standard ink colors are cyan, magenta, yellow, and key (black), abbreviated as **CMYK**. Printers mix these colors to form every color (Figure 4.43). Inkjets are inexpensive to purchase, but the cost of ink can quickly add up. When purchasing a printer, you should factor in the cost of ink, which is responsible for a large portion of the cost per page.

Dye-sublimation printers, or dye-sub printers, use heat to turn solid dye into a gas that's transferred to special paper. The dye comes on a three- or four-color ribbon that prints a single color at a time. After all colors have been printed, the print is then coated with a clear protective layer to produce high-quality photos that last longer than those printed on an inkjet printer. Dye-subs aren't general-purpose printers. They're limited to printing photos and some specialty items, such as ID badges and medical scans.

SPECIALIZED PRINTERS: THERMAL AND 3D PRINTERS

The receipts you receive from gas pumps, ATMs, and many cash registers are printed by **thermal printers**. They create an image by heating specially coated heat-sensitive paper, which changes color where the heat is applied. Because a thermal printed receipt will fade over time, you should scan it if you'll need the receipt later. Thermal printers can print in one or two colors and can also be used to print bar codes, postage, and labels (Figure 4.44).

Three-dimensional (3D) printers can create objects such as prototypes and models (Figure 4.45). A digital image can be created by scanning an object or can be designed using computer software. The 3D printer creates the model by building layers of material such as paper, polymers, resin, or even metal. 3D printing has many interesting uses, such as dental and medical imaging, paleontology, architecture, and creating sculptures and jewelry.

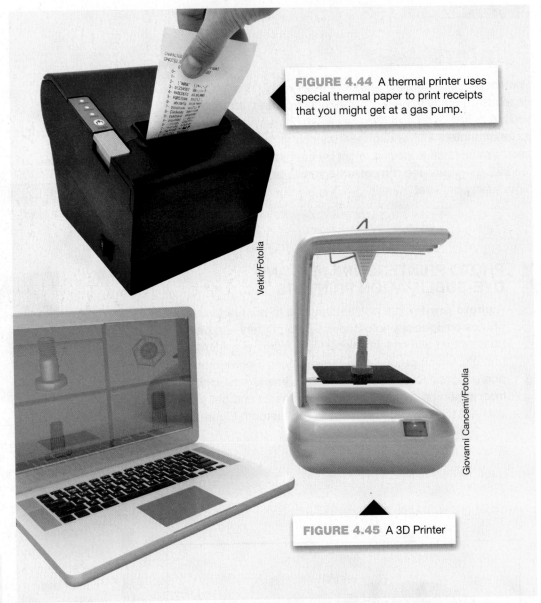

FIGURE 4.44 A thermal printer uses special thermal paper to print receipts that you might get at a gas pump.

Vetkit/Fotolia

Giovanni Cancemi/Fotolia

FIGURE 4.45 A 3D Printer

Toocan/Fotolia

LASER PRINTERS, PLOTTERS, AND MULTIFUNCTION DEVICES

The most common type of printers found in schools and businesses are **laser printers** (Figure 4.46). Laser printers produce the sharpest text at a much lower cost per page than inkjet printers. Although they initially cost more that inkjets, the lower cost per page makes them less expensive for high-volume printing. Laser printers use a laser beam to draw an image on a drum. The image is electrostatically charged and attracts a dry ink called toner. The drum is then rolled over paper, and the toner is deposited on the paper. Finally, the paper is heated and pressure is applied, bonding the ink to it.

FIGURE 4.46 Laser printers are commonly found in offices.

To produce very large printouts, such as blueprints, posters, and maps, **plotters** use one or more pens to draw an image on a roll of paper. Large inkjet and laser printers have mostly replaced pen plotters.

Also known as all-in-one printers, **multifunction devices** are laser or inkjet printers that have built-in scanners and sometimes fax capabilities. They can also be used as copy machines and eliminate the need for several different devices, saving both space and money. The disadvantage to using an all-in-one device is that if it needs to be repaired, all of its functions are unavailable.

Moreno Soppelsa/Fotolia

Running Project

What type of printer will you need? Think about the types of documents you'll print. Will you need to print mostly text? Do you print a lot of photos? Do you want to be able to connect your camera or memory card directly to the printer? Do you want to be able to scan and fax? Will your printouts get wet? Do they need to last a long time? Using the answers to these questions, decide which type of printer is right for you. Use the Internet to compare several models and select the one that best fits your needs.

4 Things You Need To Know

- The most common personal printer is an inkjet printer.
- The most common office printer is a laser printer.
- Dye-subs, thermal printers, and plotters are specialized printers.
- Three-dimensional (3D) printers can create objects such as prototypes and models.

Key Terms

CMYK

dye-sublimation printer

inkjet printer

laser printer

multifunction device

photo printer

plotter

thermal printer

three-dimensional (3D) printer

Reduce energy consumption using power settings

HOW TO VIDEO

Windows and OS X provide several ways to reduce the energy consumption of your computer. In this activity, you'll examine the power settings on your computer. From your student data files, open the file *vt_ch04_howto2_answersheet* and save the file as **lastname_firstname_ch04_howto2_answersheet**

1 Open File Explorer, click *This PC*, and, on the Computer tab, click *Open Settings*.

2 Click *System* and then click *Power & sleep*. Scroll down to the bottom of the window, and click *Additional power settings*. What power plans are available on your system? This may vary depending on your computer manufacturer.

Choose or customize a power plan

A power plan is a collection of hardware and system settings (like display brightness, sleep, etc.) that manages how your computer uses power. Tell me more about power plans

Plans shown on the battery meter

⦿ **Balanced (recommended)**   Change plan settings
Automatically balances performance with energy consumption on capable hardware.

◯ Power saver   Change plan settings
Saves energy by reducing your computer's performance where possible.

Show additional plans

Windows 10, Microsoft Corporation

3 Which power plan is your computer currently using? Click *Change plan settings* for the selected plan. What are the settings to turn off the display and put the computer to sleep? If this is a notebook computer, how do the settings differ when plugged in vs. on battery? Are these settings appropriate for the way you use your computer?

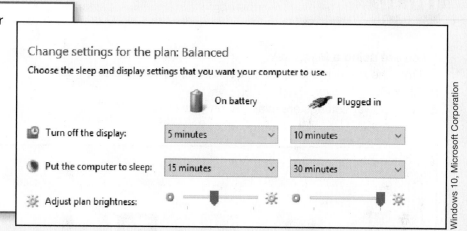

4 Click *Change advanced power settings*. Scroll down to and expand *Power buttons and lid*. What happens when you close the lid of your computer? When you press the Power button? When you press the Sleep button?

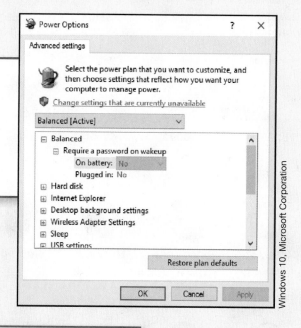

5 Use the Internet or Windows Help to learn about *sleep* and *hibernation*. What is the difference between the two, and what purpose do they serve? Type your answers in the answer sheet, save the file, and submit it as directed by your instructor.

If you are using a Mac:

1. From the Apple menu or dock, open *System Preferences*.
2. Click *Energy Saver*.
3. What power settings are available on your system?

Screen shot(s) reprinted with permission from Apple Inc.

4. What are your settings to put the computer and display to sleep? If this is a notebook computer, how do the settings differ when plugged in (Power Adapter) vs. on battery? Are these settings appropriate for the way you use your computer?
5. Click the Help button at the bottom right of the window—this opens the Help screen for Energy Saver preferences. Are there any settings in this list that are not available on your computer? What is Power Nap? Is it enabled on your system?
6. Use the Internet to learn about *Sleep*, *Safe Sleep*, and *Standby Mode*. What is the difference between them, and what purpose do they serve? Type your answers in the answer sheet, save the file, and submit it as directed by your instructor.

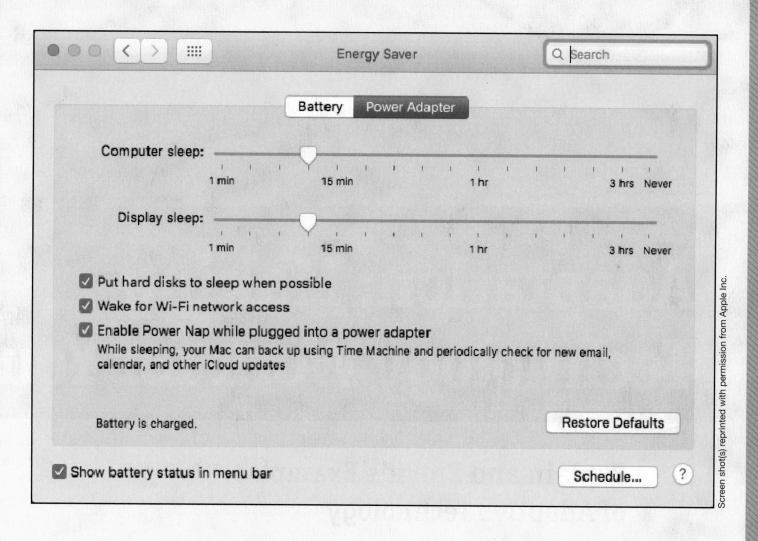

Screen shot(s) reprinted with permission from Apple Inc.

Elypse/Fotolia

Adaptation: Making Technology Work for You

7
Explain and Provide Examples of Adaptive Technology

The Americans with Disabilities Act (ADA) of 1990 requires employers with 15 or more employees "to make a reasonable accommodation to the known disability of a qualified applicant or employee if it would not impose an 'undue hardship' on the operation of the employer's business.

Reasonable accommodations are adjustments or modifications provided by an employer to enable people with disabilities to enjoy equal employment opportunities." As a result of the ADA, many hardware and software vendors have developed adaptive technology.

Also called assistive technology, **adaptive technology**, is used by individuals with disabilities to interact with technology—both hardware and software. In many cases, everyday input and output devices can be adapted to the user. For example, a computer monitor screen image can be enlarged for a visually impaired user, and a hearing-impaired user might have lights flash when an audio signal sounds. Modern operating systems include accessibility settings that can easily be changed.

Adaptive Input Devices

Alternate input devices include Braille-writing devices, eye-driven keyboards, and keyboards that have locator dots on commonly used keys or large-print key labels. Onscreen keyboards can be typed on using a pointing device or a touchscreen. Such devices are being used in many public locations, such as libraries, schools, and polling places (Figure 4.47). Trackballs, head wands, mouth sticks, and joysticks are all alternatives to the standard mouse.

Voice-recognition software enables you to verbally control a computer and dictate text. Dragon NaturallySpeaking and Dragon Dictate for Mac are two of the most popular voice-recognition programs, and Windows and OS X include built-in speech recognition. Software settings, such as Sticky Keys and Mouse Keys, adapt a standard keyboard for users with limited fine-motor control and enable the user to use arrow keys on the keyboard to move the pointer.

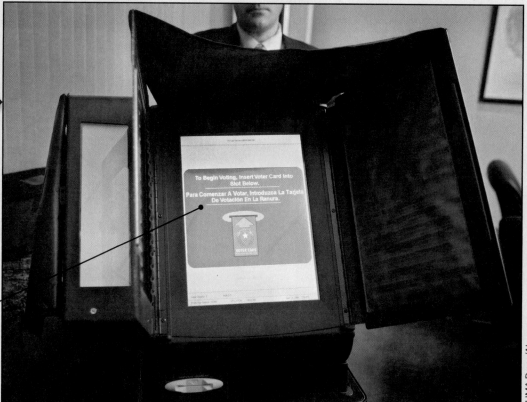

FIGURE 4.47 This touchscreen voting machine is wheelchair accessible and equipped for visual, auditory, and other disabilities.

Touchscreen

ZUMA Press/Alamy

Adaptive Output Devices

Standard monitors can be adapted by magnifying the screen (Figure 4.48) and adjusting color and contrast settings. Speech synthesis screen-reader software and audio alerts aid visually and learning-disabled users, while closed captions and visual notifications, such as flashing lights, aid those with auditory disabilities. Braille embossers are special printers that translate text to Braille. They're impact printers that create dots in special heavy paper that can be read by touch by visually impaired users. A Braille computer display (Figure 4.49) has movable pins that enable a blind person to read text output.

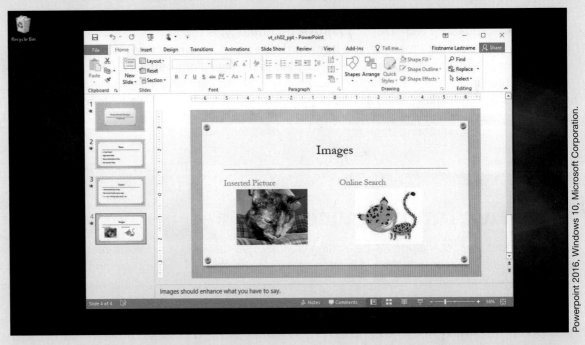

FIGURE 4.48 Windows includes Magnifier, a screen magnification program that can be used to enlarge portions of the screen, as it has in this PowerPoint presentation.

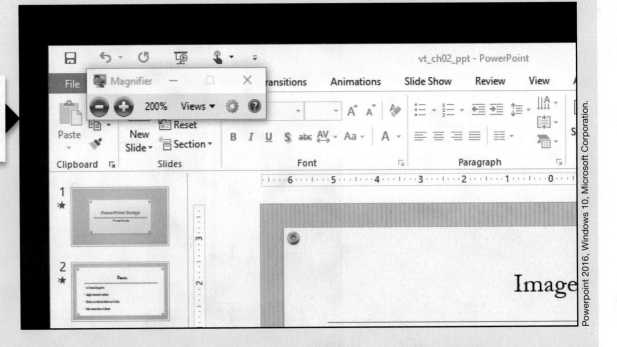

FIGURE 4.49
A blind person reads on a Braille display.

While adaptive technology can make technology more accessible for individuals with disabilities, it also benefits those without disabilities. Enlarging the screen, touch-sensitive surfaces, easy-to-read buttons, and other accommodations make accessing technology easier for everybody. Businesses benefit by gaining the skills and talents of employees with disabilities.

Running Project

If you were going to purchase a new desktop computer today, are there any adaptive technology devices that you would include to meet the current or future needs of any of the users of this computer?

3 Things You Need To Know

- Adaptive technology helps individuals with disabilities interact with technology.
- The Americans with Disabilities Act (ADA) requires employers to make reasonable accommodations for employees with disabilities.
- Adaptive technology includes both hardware and software.

Key Term

adaptive technology

Communicate, Communicate, Communicate

Discuss Communication Devices

Communication devices function as both input and output devices and enable you to connect to other devices on a network or to the Internet. These include network adapters, modems, and fax devices.

Network Adapters

Used to establish a connection with a network, a **network adapter**, also called a **network interface card (NIC)**, may be an onboard expansion card or USB device and may be wired or wireless. Wired cards are sometimes referred to as Ethernet cards and have a port that resembles a telephone jack, while wireless cards are used to connect to Wi-Fi networks at home and in hotspots in airports and cafes, as shown in Figure 4.50.

FIGURE 4.50 An Ethernet cable can plug into the onboard network adapter on a notebook computer.

Angellodeco/Fotolia

Modems and Fax Devices

Modems are used to connect computers to telephone lines and are most often used for dial-up Internet access. Modem is short for *mo*dulator-*dem*odulator. A modem modulates digital data into an analog signal that can be transmitted over a phone line and, on the receiving end, demodulates the analog signal back into digital data.

A cable modem is a special type of modem that connects to the cable system instead of a telephone line to provide fast Internet access. Digital subscriber line (DSL) modems, which are used to provide broadband services, aren't really modems at all because the DSL line is already digital, and there's no need to modulate the signal to analog.

A fax device (Figure 4.51) can be a stand-alone fax machine, part of a multifunction device, or built into a modem. A fax (or facsimile) device works by scanning a document and converting it into a digital format that can then be transmitted over telephone lines to a receiving fax device, which then outputs the document.

Communication devices enable you to connect your computers to other devices in your own home and to the world, providing you with access to resources that just a few short years ago were unimaginable.

Nerthuz/Fotolia

FIGURE 4.51 A fax machine can transmit and receive documents.

CAREER SPOTLIGHT

Ra2studio/Shutterstock

COMPUTER SALES—Computer sales is a good career choice for a person who has good communication and technical skills. Salespeople must be able to help customers find the right computer based on their needs and explain the features of a system in lay terms. Many companies offer their employees on-the-job training in this field, but a background in computers, including the CompTIA A+ certification, an industry certification for computer technicians, is helpful.

If you like helping people, have strong communication skills, and are good with computers, a computer technician position might be a good career for you. Companies such as Geek Squad send technicians out to homes and businesses to troubleshoot and repair computer systems. This is hands-on work that may involve travel and working nights and weekends. A+ certification is usually the minimum requirement at the entry-level positions in this field. Much of the training in this field takes place on the job.

Even if you're not looking for a technical career, understanding how computer hardware works and being able to make decisions about the hardware purchases you might make will help you be a better consumer and enable you to succeed in many different careers. For example, an office worker might need to make decisions about the type of printer to buy, or a teacher might need help choosing the type of projector to install in a classroom. Very few careers today don't involve the use of some computer technology.

GREEN COMPUTING
Shop Smart

The efficient and eco-friendly use of computers and other electronics is called green computing. Green computing is good for the environment, but it also saves money, making it a win–win proposition.

Choose Energy Star–rated devices. Energy Star (**energystar.gov**) is a rating system that's awarded to devices that use an average of 20–30 percent less energy than comparable devices. Saving energy saves money and reduces greenhouse gas emissions that contribute to global warming.

The Green Electronics Council has a program called the EPEAT (Electronic Product Environmental Assessment Tool; **epeat.net**) that can help you choose systems with environmentally friendly designs. The assessment is based on industry standards and ranks the devices as bronze, silver, or gold, depending on the number of environmental performance criteria they meet.

Running Project

If you were going to purchase a new desktop computer today, think about the location for this computer. What type of communication devices do you need to connect this system to the Internet? Will it connect to a network? Is it wired or wireless? Do you need fax capabilities?

Viz Check—In MyITLab, take a quick quiz covering Objectives 5–8.

3 Things You Need To Know

- A network adapter connects a computer to a network.
- A modem is used for dial-up Internet access.
- Digital signals carry more data and are less prone to interference than analog signals.

Key Terms

communication device

modem

network adapter

network interface card (NIC)

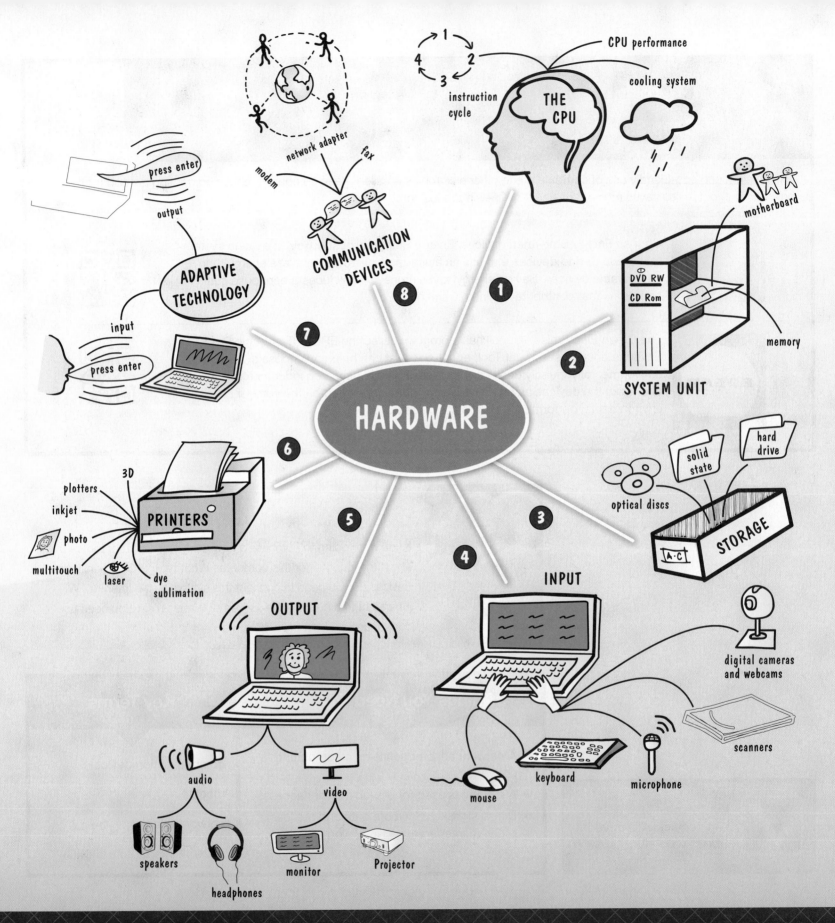

HARDWARE

THE CPU
- CPU performance
- cooling system
- instruction cycle

COMMUNICATION DEVICES
- modem
- network adapter
- fax

ADAPTIVE TECHNOLOGY
- output — press enter
- input — press enter

SYSTEM UNIT
- motherboard
- memory
- DVD RW
- CD Rom

STORAGE
- optical discs
- solid state
- hard drive
- A·C

PRINTERS
- plotters
- 3D
- inkjet
- photo
- multitouch
- laser
- dye sublimation

OUTPUT
- audio
  - speakers
  - headphones
- video
  - monitor
  - Projector

INPUT
- mouse
- keyboard
- microphone
- digital cameras and webcams
- scanners

1 2 3 4 5 6 7 8

Objectives Recap

1. Explain the Function of a CPU

2. Identify the Parts of a System Unit and Motherboard

3. Compare Storage Devices

4. List and Describe Common Input Devices

5. List and Describe Essential Video and Audio Output Devices

6. Compare Various Types of Printers

7. Explain and Provide Examples of Adaptive Technology

8. Discuss Communication Devices

Key Terms

adapter card **172**
adaptive technology **207**
AGP (Accelerated Graphics Port) **172**
arithmetic logic unit (ALU) **164**
biometric scanner **190**
BIOS (Basic Input Output System) **174**
Bluetooth **173**
Blu-ray disc (BD) **178**
booting **174**
cache memory **175**
CD (compact disc) **177**
central processing unit (CPU) **164**
clock speed **166**

CMOS (complementary metal oxide semiconductor) **174**
CMYK **199**
communication device **210**
control unit **164**
CRT monitor **193**
data bus **172**
DisplayPort **195**
DLP (digital light-processing projector) **195**
drive controller **171**
DVD (digital video disc/digital versatile disc) **177**
DVI (digital visual interface) **195**
dye-sublimation printer **199**

EIDE (Enhanced Integrated Drive Electronics) **171**
expansion card **172**
expansion slot **172**
FireWire **173**
flash drive **178**
flash memory **178**
game controller **191**
gigahertz (GHz) **166**
GPU (Graphics-Processing Unit) **166**
hard drive **179**
hardware **163**
HDMI (High-Definition Multimedia Interface) **195**
headphones **196**
heat sink **168**
hot-swappable **172**
IEEE 1394 **173**
inkjet printer **199**
input device **184**
instruction cycle **165**
joystick **191**
keyboard **185**
keypad **186**
laser printer **200**
LCD (liquid crystal display) **194**
LCD projector **195**
legacy technology **193**
memory **174**
memory card **179**
microphone **191**
modem **211**
monitor **193**
motherboard **171**
mouse **187**
multi-core processor **166**
multifunction device **201**
near field communication (NFC) **190**
network adapter **211**
network interface card (NIC) **211**
nonvolatile **174**
OLED (organic light-emitting diode) **194**

optical disc **177**
overclock **169**
output device **192**
parallel processing **167**
PCI (Peripheral Component Interconnect) **172**
PCIe (PCI Express) **172**
peripheral device **163**
photo printer **199**
pipelining **167**
pixel **193**
plasma monitor **194**
plotter **201**
port **172**
processor **164**
projector **195**
PS/2 port **172**
QR (Quick Response) code **189**
RAM (random access memory) **174**
resolution **193**
RFID tag **190**
ROM (read-only memory) **174**
SATA (Serial Advanced Technology Attachment) **171**
scanner **188**
serial and parallel ports **172**
solid-state drive (SSD) **178**
solid-state storage **178**
sound card **197**
speakers **196**
stylus **188**
system unit **170**
thermal printer **200**
three-dimensional (3D) printer **200**
Thunderbolt **173**
touchpad **187**
touchscreen **188**
USB (Universal Serial Bus) **172**
USB hub **172**
video card **195**
VGA (video graphics array) **195**
volatile **174**
webcam **188**

Summary

1. Explain the Function of a CPU

The CPU is the brain of the computer and consists of the control unit and arithmetic logic unit. It processes data through the instruction cycle: fetch, decode, execute, and store. Features such as parallel processing, pipelining, and multi-core processing increase the CPU's ability to process multiple instructions at the same time.

2. Identify the Parts of a System Unit and Motherboard

The system unit is the case that houses the power supply, motherboard, processor (CPU), heat sink and cooling fan, and memory of a computer. It also has drive bays to hold the storage devices and openings for peripheral devices to connect to expansion cards on the motherboard. The motherboard is the main circuit board of a computer. In addition to housing the CPU, it contains drive controllers and interfaces, expansion slots, data buses, ports and connectors, BIOS, and memory. A motherboard may also include integrated peripherals, such as video, sound, and network cards.

3. Compare Storage Devices

Optical discs are removable and include CDs, DVDs, and Blu-ray discs. They range in capacity from 700 MB to 50 GB and are used to distribute music, programs, and movies as well as to archive data. Flash memory is a non-mechanical form of storage found in solid-state drives (SSDs), flash drives, memory cards, personal media players, and netbooks. Hard disks are a form of magnetic storage and can be mounted in the system unit or connected via USB or FireWire cable. They have the largest capacities of any current storage device and hold the operating systems, programs, and data on the computer.

4. List and Describe Common Input Devices

Input devices include keyboards and keypads for entering text; pointing devices, such as the mouse, touchpad, stylus, and touch-sensitive screens that move the cursor on the screen; cameras and webcams for video input; optical scanners, RFID scanners, magnetic strip readers, and biometric scanners that read data and convert it into digital form; near field communication (NFC) devices that can share data among devices by bringing them near each other; microphones that convert sound into digital signals; and video game controllers and joysticks to interact with games and other software programs.

5. List and Describe Essential Video and Audio Output Devices

The most common output devices are monitors and projectors attached to video cards that produce video output; printers that produce hard copies; and speakers and headphones attached to sound cards that produce audio output.

6. Compare Various Types of Printers

The most common personal printer is the inkjet, which works by spraying droplets of ink onto paper. Dye-sublimation printers use heat to turn solid dye into a gas that's then transferred to special paper to primarily produce photos. Photo printers can be either inkjet or dye-sublimation printers. Thermal printers use special heat-sensitive paper to produce receipts, postage, and bar code labels. Three-dimensional (3D) printers can create objects such as prototypes and models. Plotters produce very large printouts, such as blueprints, posters, and maps. Laser printers produce the sharpest text at a much lower cost per page than inkjet printers. A multifunction device combines a printer with a scanner and sometimes a fax machine.

7. Explain and Provide Examples of Adaptive Technology

Adaptive technology enables users with a variety of disabilities to access technology through special hardware and software. Input devices include head wands, mouth sticks, voice-recognition software, and onscreen keyboards. Output devices include Braille embossers, screen readers, and enlarged screens.

8. Discuss Communication Devices

Communication devices serve as both input and output devices and include network adapters, modems, and fax devices. A network adapter connects a computer to a network. A modem connects a computer to a telephone line for dial-up Internet access. The cable and DSL modems are special modems that enable access to high-speed Internet. Fax devices, which can be stand-alone fax machines, part of a multifunction device, or built into a modem, scan and convert a document into a digital form that can be transmitted over telephone lines.

Multiple Choice

Answer the multiple-choice questions below for more practice with key terms and concepts from this chapter.

1. The _____ is part of the processor that manages the movement of data through the CPU.

   a. arithmetic logic unit

   b. control unit

   c. data bus

   d. peripheral device

2. A(n) _____ consists of two or more processors that are integrated on a single chip.

   a. arithmetic logic unit (ALU)

   b. CMOS

   c. GPU (Graphics-Processing Unit)

   d. multi-core processor

3. A(n) _____ is an interface on the motherboard that expansion cards plug in to.

   a. adapter card

   b. data bus

   c. expansion slot

   d. USB hub

4. Which type of memory is a volatile form of memory that holds the operating system, programs, and data the computer is currently using?

   a. Cache

   b. CMOS

   c. RAM

   d. ROM

5. Data is stored on _____ using a laser to either melt the disc material or change the color of embedded dye.

   a. flash drives

   b. hard drives

   c. optical discs

   d. SSDs

6. A(n) _____ is an input device that may include one or more buttons and a scroll wheel and works by moving across a smooth surface to signal movement of the pointer.

   a. joystick

   b. mouse

   c. scroll wheel

   d. touchpad

7. _____ measure human characteristics such as fingerprints and eye retinas.

   a. Biometric scanners

   b. Near field communications

   c. Optical scanners

   d. QR codes

8. What type of monitor is composed of extremely thin panels of organic molecules sandwiched between two electrodes?

   a. CRT

   b. LCD

   c. OLED

   d. Plasma

9. What type of printer produces the highest quality text?

   a. Laser

   b. Dye-sublimation

   c. Inkjet

   d. Thermal

10. _____ are used to connect a computer to a telephone line for dial-up Internet access.

    a. Analog signals

    b. Modems

    c. Network interface cards

    d. Wi-Fi adapters

True or False

Answer the following questions with T for true or F for false for more practice with key terms and concepts from this chapter.

_____ 1. Pipelining requires multiple processors or cores.

_____ 2. The terms *CPU* and *system unit* mean the same thing.

_____ 3. Bluetooth is a short-range, wireless technology used to connect peripheral devices to a computer.

_____ 4. Random access memory (RAM) loses the information stored in it when power is turned off.

_____ 5. SSDs store data optically.

_____ 6. Hard drives store data magnetically on metal platters.

_____ 7. QWERTY keyboards were designed to improve ergonomics.

_____ 8. LCD monitors consist of two layers of glass that are glued together with a layer of liquid crystals between them.

_____ 9. Adaptive technology includes the hardware and software used by individuals with disabilities to interact with technology.

_____ 10. Analog signals are superior to digital signals because they don't have to be converted for use by computers and other digital devices.

Fill in the Blank

Fill in the blanks with key terms from this chapter.

1. A computer's clock speed is measured in _____.

2. The _____ performs arithmetic (addition and subtraction) and logic (AND, OR, and NOT) calculations, and the _____ manages the movement of data through the CPU.

3. To keep the processor from overheating, a(n) _____ and cooling fan are installed above the processor to dissipate the heat the processor produces.

4. The _____ is the main circuit board of a computer that houses the processor (CPU) and contains drive controllers and interfaces, expansion slots, data buses, ports and connectors, the BIOS, and memory.

5. A device that can be plugged and unplugged without turning off the computer is known as _____.

6. The _____ is a program stored on a chip on the motherboard that is used to start up the computer.

7. _____ technology enables devices to share data with each other by touching them together or bringing them within a few centimeters of each other.

8. A(n) _____ monitor is composed of extremely thin panels of organic molecules sandwiched between two electrodes.

9. _____ printers create objects such as prototypes and models.

10. A(n) _____ is used to connect a computer to a computer network.

Running Project . . .

. . . The Finish Line

Use your answers to the previous sections of the Running Project to determine what you would need in a desktop system. Look at computer ads on some current retail websites and select a computer system that meets your needs. Pick a system in the $300–600 price range. Does it include everything you need? What's missing? What additional features does it have that you will find useful? Does it have extras that you could do without? Is it fairly priced? What features would you get if you spent more money? What would you lose if you spent less? Justify why the system you chose is a good choice for you.

Write a report describing your selection and responding to the questions raised. Save your file as **lastname_firstname_ch04_project** and submit it to your instructor as directed.

Do It Yourself 1

Color calibration helps you set your monitor to display colors as accurately as possible. You may need to supply an administrator password to complete some steps in this exercise. If you can't adjust the settings, read each screen for information only. From your student data files, open the file *vt_ch04_DIY1_answersheet* and save the file as **lastname_firstname_ch04_DIY1_answersheet**

1. From the Windows 10 Search bar or Windows 8 Start screen, type **calibrate** and click *Calibrate display color* from the search results. What is display color calibration? How does it work? Follow the directions on the next several screens to adjust your color.

   If you are using a Mac:

1. From the dock, open *System Preferences*, click *Displays*, click the *Color* tab, and then click *Calibrate*.

2. Use the information on each screen or search the Internet to answer the following questions. What is gamma? What does brightness adjustment control? What is contrast? How does color balance work? Type your answers in the answer sheet, save the file, and submit it as directed by your instructor.

Do It Yourself 2

Windows and OS X provide several ways to adjust accessibility settings of your computer. In this activity, you'll examine these settings on your computer. From your student data files, open the file *vt_ch04_DIY2_answersheet* and save the file as **lastname_firstname_ch04_DIY2_answersheet**

1. Open File Explorer, in the Navigation pane, click *This PC*, and on the Computer tab, click *Open Settings* (Windows 8, open the Control Panel). Click *Ease of Access*.

2. Click each tab and read the description and settings for each. What is the Narrator? Click *Keyboard*. What are Sticky Keys, Toggle Keys, and Filter Keys? Click *Mouse*. What are Mouse keys?

   If you are using a Mac:

1. From the Apple menu or dock, open *System Preferences* and click *Accessibility* to examine the settings.

2. Click each tab and read the description and settings for each. What is the VoiceOver? Click *Keyboard*. What are Sticky Keys and Slow Keys? Click *Mouse* (or *Mouse and Trackpad*). What are Mouse Keys?

3. Type your answers in the answer sheet, save the file, and submit it as directed by your instructor.

File Management

Windows and OS X include a Downloads folder for each user. From your student data files, open the file *vt_ch04_FM_answersheet* and save the file as **lastname_firstname_ch04_FM_answersheet**

1. Open File Explorer or Finder and click *Downloads*. Are there any files in this folder? If so, what types of files are they? Search Windows Help or Spotlight or use the Internet to learn about the Downloads folder. What is the purpose of the Downloads folder? Type up your answers, save the file, and submit the assignment as directed by your instructor.

Critical Thinking

You are a member of a student club on campus that is in need of a new computer to keep records, produce newsletters etc. It needs to run Microsoft Office 2016 and needs wireless network access. Because you're the computer expert in the group, you have been given the job of choosing a computer that meets the club's needs. Determine other requirements based upon the type of club (your choice). You have $700 to spend. From your student data files, open the file *vt_ch04_CT_answersheet* and save the file as **lastname_firstname_ch04_CT_answersheet**

1. Evaluate three computer choices from current newspaper ads or websites and compare them with respect to the club's requirements. Complete the following table, comparing the features of each computer. Explain your recommendation in a two- to three-paragraph summary. Which computer should the club buy and why? What other peripherals and software will they need to purchase? Also recommend necessary peripherals, including a monitor and printer. Remember your budget is fixed, so you can't exceed $700. Save your file, and submit both your table and summary as directed by your instructor.

	Computer 1	Computer 2	Computer 3
Website or store			
Brand			
Model			
Price			
Processor type			
Processor speed			
Memory type			
Memory amount			
Hard drive capacity			
Additional equipment/ features			
Additional purchases required/ recommended			

Ethical Dilemma

The Americans with Disabilities Act (**ada.gov**) requires businesses with 15 or more employees to provide reasonable accommodation for all employees who have—or who have a record of having—a disability. A disability is any condition that limits one or more major life activities. From your student data files, open the file *vt_ch04_ethics_answersheet* and save the file as **lastname_firstname_ch04_ethics_answersheet**

Should small businesses be required to provide adaptive technology to all employees, regardless of cost? Should they have to provide the technology the employee wants? Or can they choose other methods of addressing the issue of concern? What if the disability becomes so great that it causes the business financial hardship? Is the business then legally required to provide accommodation? What is the moral responsibility? Type up your answers, save the file, and submit it as directed by your instructor.

On the Web

The EPEAT website provides information to help you "evaluate, compare and select electronic products based on their environmental attributes." From your student data files, open the file *vt_ch04_web_answersheet* and save the file as **lastname_firstname_ch04_web_answersheet** and visit the site **www.epeat.net** to answer the following questions:

1. What manufacturers participate in the program? How is it funded? Is there any conflict of interest?

2. What types of devices are included in the system? How are they placed into the registry?

3. What testing do they undergo? What are the environmental performance criteria the devices must meet?

Type up your answers, save the file, and submit it as directed by your instructor.

Collaboration

Instructors: Divide the class into small groups, and assign each group one topic for this project. The topics include motherboards, processors, storage devices, input devices, and output devices.

The Project: As a team, prepare a multimedia presentation for your assigned topic. The presentation should explain your hardware category and compare different types of devices in that category. Use at least three references, only one of which may be this textbook. Use Google Docs or Microsoft Office to plan the presentation, and provide documentation that all team members have contributed to the project.

Outcome: Prepare a multimedia presentation on your assigned topic in PowerPoint or another tool approved by your instructor, and present it to your class. The presentation may be no longer than 3 minutes and should contain five to seven slides. On the first slide, be sure to include the name of your presentation and a list of all team members. Turn in a final version of your presentation named **teamname_ch04_presentation** and your file showing your collaboration named **teamname_ch04_collab** and submit your presentation to your instructor as directed.

Application Project

my**it**lab grader

Office 2016 Application Projects
Word 2016: Ergonomics

Project Description: *You have been asked to write an article on ergonomics. You will need to change alignment, line and paragraph spacing, margins, and lists and edit the header and footer. You will also find and replace text, create and modify a footnote, and use the Format Painter. If necessary, download the student data files from.* **pearsonhighered.com/viztech**.

Ergonomics

January 2, 2016

Welcome back to a new year. I am excited to get started. We have a lot of work to do this year and some exciting new projects underway. One important task we have to do this year is evaluating our safety practices. To that end, we have compiled this informative tip sheet on ergonomics. Please take a few moments to review the important safety tips included in this tip sheet.

SAVE YOUR EYESIGHT

How many hours a day do you spend in front of your computer? Don't forget to include the hours at home! The average person spends at least several hours a day in front of a video screen. This can cause eyestrain- in fact there is a name for it—video terminal syndrome or VTS. So what can you do about it?

- ✓ Proper monitor placement
- ✓ Good lighting
- ✓ Prescription eyewear if needed[1]
- ✓ Take a break—at least 5 minutes for every hour
- ✓ Exercise your eyes

BACK AND NECK PAIN

Sitting at a desk all day can literally be a pain in the neck. Setting up your workstation properly can help you avoid painful neck and back pain. Here are some recommendations for avoiding neck and back pain.

- ✓ Set monitor height so you are looking straight ahead or slightly up—not down
- ✓ Adjust chair height so feet are flat or slightly elevated—not dangling
- ✓ Sit up straight- your mom had it right, proper posture is important
- ✓ Take frequent breaks—get up and move around

WRISTS AND HANDS

If you spend a lot of time using the keyboard and mouse, you could be bothered by repetitive stress injuries. To avoid these painful conditions, follow these suggestions.

---

[1] May be covered under your health insurance benefits.

2

- ✓ Make sure keyboard and mouse are set at a proper height—if necessary get an adjustable drawer or shelf
- ✓ Use an ergonomic keyboard
- ✓ Grip mouse loosely
- ✓ Use gel wrist rests
- ✓ Rest elbows on chair arms

As you can see, with proper ergonomics you can avoid many discomforts. Here's to a healthy and productive new year!

 Sally Mosley—CEO

lastname_firstname_ch04_word

Step	Instructions
1	Start Word. From your student data files, open the Word file *vt_ch04_word*. Save the file as **lastname_firstname_ch04_word**
2	Change the left and right margins of the document to 1.0".
3	Center the first two paragraphs (title and date).
4	Change the line spacing of the entire document to 1.5 lines. Change the paragraph spacing of the entire document to 6 pt after.
5	Center the heading *Save Your Eyesight*.
6	Using the Format Painter, apply the formatting from the heading *Save Your Eyesight* to the headings *Back and Neck Pain* and *Wrists and Hands*.
7	Use the Find and Replace dialog box to search for and replace all instances of the word *report* with **tip sheet** There should be two replacements.
8	In the *Save Your Eyesight* section, format the list beginning *Proper monitor placement* and ending *Exercise your eyes* as a bulleted list using check mark bullets.
9	In the *Back and Neck Pain* section, format the list beginning *Set monitor height* and ending *Take frequent breaks* as a bulleted list using check mark bullets.
10	In the *Wrists and Hands* section, format the list beginning *Make sure keyboard and mouse are set a proper height* and ending *Rest elbows on chair arms* as a bulleted list using check mark bullets.
11	In the document header, add a page number using the Plain Number 2 style at the Top of Page. In the footer, add the File Name field using the default format. Ensure the header and footer are not displayed on the first page.
12	In the *Save Your Eyesight* section, in the bulleted list, insert a footnote immediately following the text *Prescription eyewear if needed* reading **May be covered under your health insurance benefits.** (include the period).
13	Use the Spelling and Grammar dialog box to correct the misspelling of the word *importatn* to *important*. Ignore all other spelling and grammar suggestions.
14	Place the insertion point at the beginning of the last line of the document— before Sally. Insert the picture *vt_ch04_image1.* Change text wrapping to Square.
15	Save the file and close Word. Submit the document as directed.

Application Project

myitlab grader

Office 2016 Application Projects
PowerPoint 2016: Comparing Printers

Project Description: *In this project, you will create a presentation about printers. In creating this presentation you will apply design, font, and color themes. You will also change font colors, bullet symbols, and slide layout. If necessary, download the student data files from* **pearsonhighered.com/viztech**

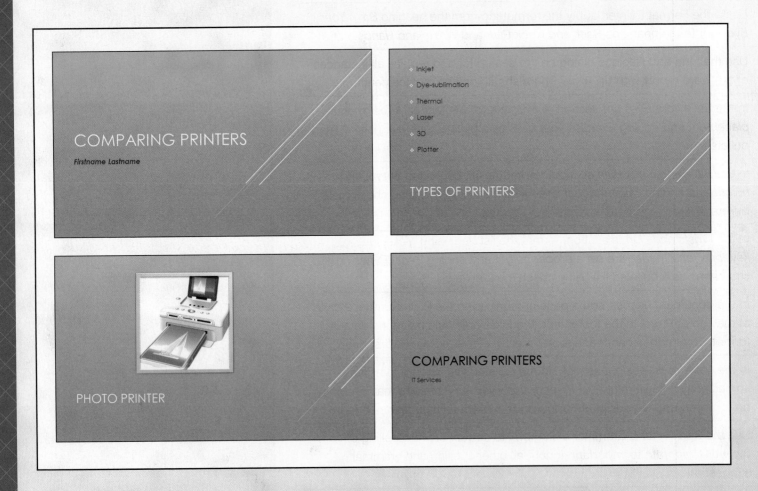

Step	Instructions
1	Start PowerPoint. From your student data files, open the file *vt_ch04_ppt*. Save the presentation as **lastname_firstname_ch04_ppt**
2	Apply the Slice theme to the presentation. From the Variant gallery, apply the orange variant to the presentation.
3	On Slide 1, using your own name, type **Firstname Lastname** in the subtitle placeholder. Apply bold and italic formatting to the subtitle text.
4	On Slide 2, type **Types of Printers** in the title placeholder.
5	On Slide 2, change the bullets to Star Bullets and change the line spacing of the bullets to 1.5.
6	On Slide 3, insert the image *vt_ch04_image2* in the content placeholder. Apply the Metal Frame picture style to the image.
7	On Slide 1, copy the title text, *Comparing Printers*. On Slide 4, paste the copied text into the title placeholder using the destination theme.
8	Change the layout of Slide 4 to Section Header.
9	On Slide 4, type **IT Services** in the content placeholder. Change the font color of the title text, *Comparing Printers*, to Black, Background 1 (under Theme Colors).
10	Insert the page number and the footer **Firstname Lastname** on the notes and handouts pages for all slides in the presentation. View the presentation in Slide Show view from beginning to end, and then return to Normal view.
11	Save the presentation and close PowerPoint. Submit the presentation as directed.

System Software

In This Chapter

VIZ INTRO

A computer is a programmable machine that converts raw data into useful information. Programming is what makes a computer different from a toaster. In this chapter, we look at the system software used to make computers run smoothly and securely. When you have finished this chapter you will be able to recognize and use the features of various operating systems.

Chapter Objectives

1 Explain What an Operating System Does

2 Compare Desktop Operating Systems

3 Configure a Desktop Operating System

4 Compare Specialized Operating Systems

5 Compare the Most Common Network Operating Systems

6 List and Explain Important Utility Software

Running Project

In this chapter, you'll learn about different kinds of system software. Look for instructions as you complete each article. For most, there's a series of questions for you to research. At the conclusion of the chapter, you'll submit your responses to the questions raised.

THE BOSS

Who's the Boss?

Explain What an Operating System Does

Application software is software that performs a useful task for the user. Software that makes the computer run is **system software**. The **operating system (OS)** is the most important type of system software because it provides the user with the interface to communicate with the hardware and other software on the computer and manages system resources. Without an operating system, a personal computer is useless.

VIZ CLIP

Installing Hardware Device Drivers

Provides User Interface

The **user interface** is the part of the operating system that you see and interact with. Modern operating systems, such as Microsoft Windows, Linux, and MAC OS X, have a **graphical user interface (GUI)** . A GUI enables you to point to and click on graphic objects such as icons and buttons to initiate commands. Older operating systems used a command-line interface, which required you to type out all commands. If you look at the interface on most personal computers, you'll see that they have a lot in common. Figure 5.1 shows how the interface has changed from command-line to GUI in Microsoft operating systems. This change made PCs more user friendly, which helped them increase in popularity. A similar evolution occurred in the Apple systems. In fact, in 1988, Apple sued Microsoft for copyright infringement, but the case was later dismissed.

FIGURE 5.1 The user interface of the Microsoft operating system has evolved from the MS-DOS command-line (bottom right), to the Windows 10 GUI (top).

WINDOWS 10

WINDOWS 8.1

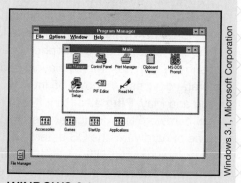

WINDOWS 7

WINDOWS XP

WINDOWS 98

WINDOWS 3.1

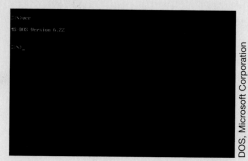

MS-DOS

All user interfaces serve the same basic function: to allow the user to control the computer. If you want to play a game, for example, you navigate to the icon for the game and click on it to begin. The clicking tells the computer to open the file—in this case, to run the game. The procedure to open a Word document is the same. These tasks require the OS user interface. GUIs use icons, menus, dialog boxes, and windows, and often there are multiple ways to perform the same task.

Manages Resources and Controls Hardware

The resources on your system include the processor and the memory. The operating system has the important job of managing how these resources are allocated to both hardware and software. The OS makes sure that each process is allocated its own memory and manages the instructions that are sent to the processor. Modern operating systems support **multitasking**, which is the ability to do more than one task at a time. A single processor can't actually do more than one thing at a time but switches between the tasks so quickly that it's transparent to the user. Each running application is assigned its own area of memory and is prevented from accessing the memory area of other programs. This prevents a program crash from affecting other processes running in other areas of memory.

The OS manages and controls the hardware. Early PCs were simple devices that had limited hardware: a keyboard, a monochrome monitor, a disk drive, and not much else. Today, there is a wide variety of peripheral devices, including printers, scanners, cameras, media players, video and sound cards, and storage devices. Windows 95 introduced a feature known as Plug and Play. **Plug and Play (PnP)** allows you to easily add new hardware to a computer system. When you plug in a new piece of hardware, the OS detects it and helps you set it up. An OS communicates with hardware by means of a device driver. A **device driver** acts as a translator, enhancing the capabilities of the operating system by enabling it to communicate with hardware. It's what allows you to expand your computer with new hardware. If it were not for device drivers, there would be no

way for you to install new hardware on your system. When you first connect the hardware, Windows detects it and informs you that it's installing the device driver software. If Windows cannot locate the device driver, it asks you for permission to search the web or instructs you to insert the manufacturer's disc. The message *Device driver software installed successfully* indicates your new hardware is now ready to use. In Figure 5.2, Windows has installed the driver and now asks the user to choose how the device is configured.

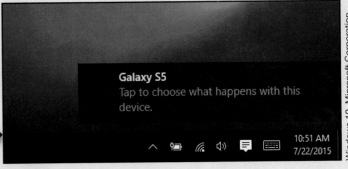

Galaxy S5
Tap to choose what happens with this device.

10:51 AM
7/22/2015

Windows 10, Microsoft Corporation

Jannoon/Shutterstock

FIGURE 5.2 After the operating system installs a device such as this phone, it notifies you of the status of the device or asks you to choose what happens next.

Interacts With Software

When you look at the system requirements to install software, you'll see a list of supported operating systems. The OS on a computer interacts directly with the software you install, giving the software access to resources it needs to run. This happens through the use of an **application programming interface (API)**, which allows the application to request services—such as printing or saving a file—from the operating system. An API lets a computer programmer write a program that will run on computers with different hardware configurations by sending such service requests to the OS to handle. Figure 5.3 shows Microsoft Word using the API to request save services from Windows. Different applications use a common Windows dialog box to save files.

An operating system manages interactions between the user, the software, and the hardware of a computer. These critical functions make the computer more user-friendly, flexible, and expandable. The OS is the most important software on the computer because without it the computer won't run at all.

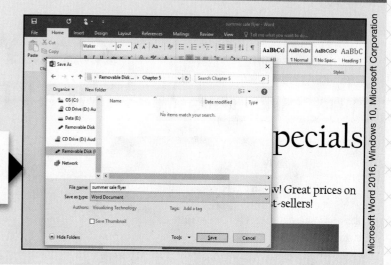

FIGURE 5.3 Programs use the application programming interface (API) to save files.

Running Project

What operating system is on your computer? To check on a Windows computer, open File Explorer, if necessary click *This PC*, and on the ribbon, click *System Properties*. To check a Mac, open the About This Mac window from the Apple menu. Is your OS the latest version? If you have not upgraded yet, why not? If you could change the OS, would you? Which OS would you use instead?

4 Things You Need to Know

- A GUI allows you to point and click to control your computer.
- The OS manages the system resources: processing and memory.
- PnP allows you to add new hardware easily.
- Application software communicates with the OS through an API.

Key Terms

application programming interface (API)

device driver

graphical user interface (GUI)

multitasking

operating system (OS)

Plug and Play (PnP)

system software

user interface

How To?

Keep Your Desktop OS Up to Date

HOW TO VIDEO

One of the most important things you can do to protect your system is to keep your software up to date. Some programs will check automatically and prompt you when a new version or update is available. In this activity you will examine your update settings. It's important to set the utility up correctly and monitor it to be sure that your updates are being installed. (Note: the IT department at your school may have disabled these settings through group policies.) Complete each step, and compare your screen to the figures that accompany each step. If necessary, download student data files from **pearsonhighered.com/viztech**. From your student data files, open the *vt_ch05_howto1_answersheet* file and save the file as **lastname_firstname_ch05_howto1_answersheet**

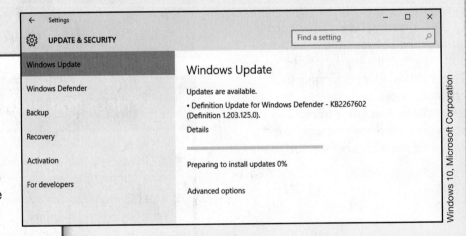

1 On a Windows 10 computer, click the Start button and click *Settings*. Click *Update & security*. (For Windows 8, open the Settings charm, click *Change PC settings*, and then click *Update and recovery*.) Take a screenshot of the Windows Update screen and paste it in your document. If necessary, click *Check for updates*. How many updates are available on your system? When was the most recent check for updates?

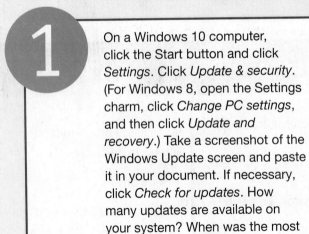

Windows 10, Microsoft Corporation

2 On a Windows 10 computer, click *Advanced options* (for Windows 8, click *Choose how updates get installed*) to verify that you're getting the updates you need. How is your computer configured to handle updates? What types of updates are included? Click the checkboxes for the other options you want. Microsoft Update will also get you updates for other Microsoft products, such as Office. (On a Windows 8 computer, click the back arrow to return to the Windows Update window.)

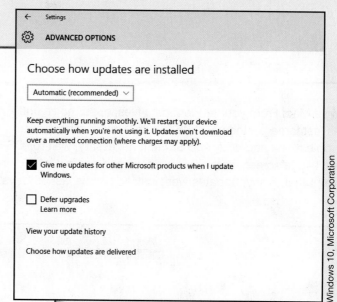

Windows 10, Microsoft Corporation

3 Click *View your update history.* Take a screenshot of this window and paste it into your answer sheet. Close the Settings window, save your file, and submit it as directed by your instructor.

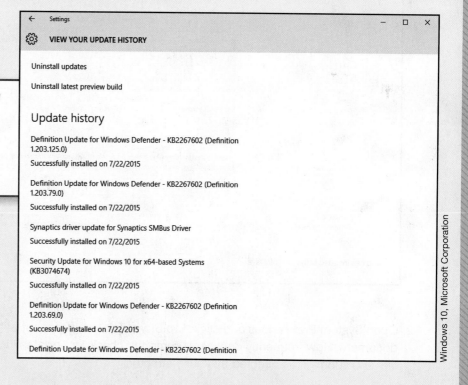

Windows 10, Microsoft Corporation

MAC

If you are using a Mac: From your student data files, open the *vt_ch05_howto1_answersheet_mac* file and save the file as lastname_firstname_ch05_howto1_answersheet_mac

1. Open the Apple menu and click *App Store.* If necessary, wait for OS X to check for updates. Click the *Updates* tab, take a screenshot of this window, and paste it into your document. How many updates are available? What, if any, updates were installed in the last 30 days? Close the App Store window.

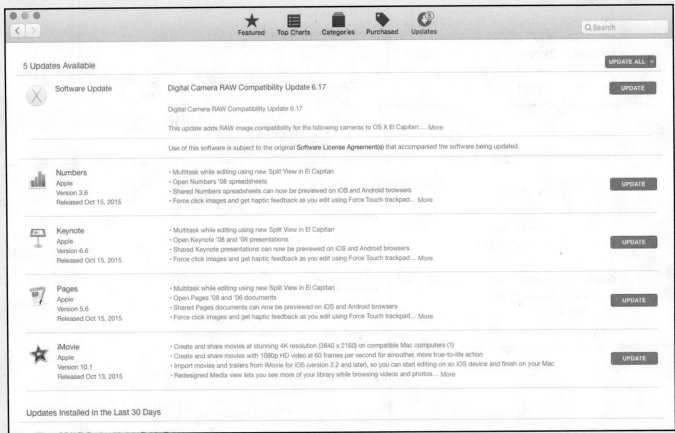

2. Open System Preferences and click *App Store*. Take a screenshot of this window and paste it into your document. How frequently does your computer check for updates? When was the last check? Save your file, and submit it as directed by your instructor.

GREEN COMPUTING
Power Management

Did you know that you could cut the energy used by your computer in half, saving between $25 and $75 a year in energy costs, by using its power management features? That would save more than lowering your home thermostat by 2 degrees or replacing six regular light bulbs with compact fluorescents (CFLs). Putting your computer into a low-power mode can save on home cooling costs and even prolong the life of your notebook battery.

Energy Star power management features are standard in both Windows and OS X operating systems. Activating these settings is easy and saves both money and resources. The EPA recommends setting computers to sleep or hibernate after 30 to 60 minutes of inactivity. To save even more, set monitors to sleep after 5 to 20 minutes of inactivity. And don't use screensavers—they actually increase energy use.

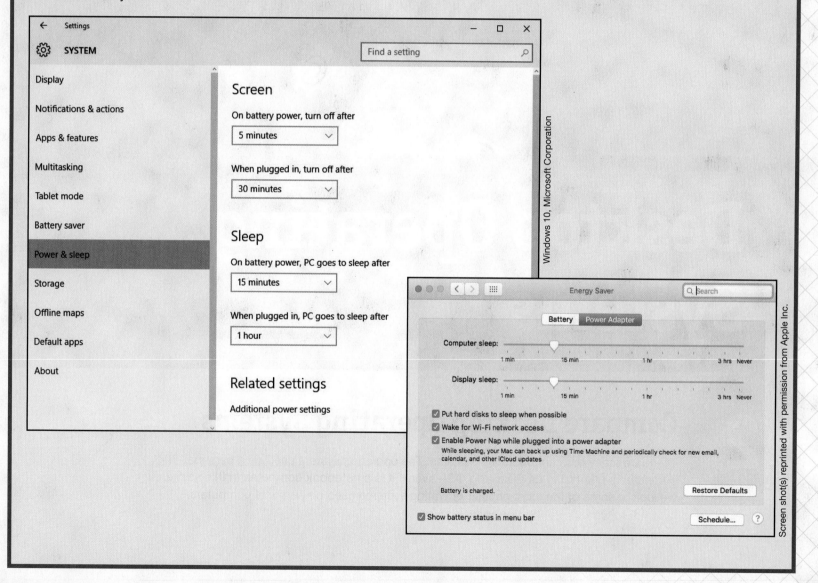

Ahmetov Ruslan/Shutterstock

Desktop Operating Systems

Objective

2

Compare Desktop Operating Systems

There are many different operating systems. The operating system used on a personal computer is referred to as a desktop OS—even if it is a notebook computer. In this article, we look at some of the most popular operating systems used on personal computers.

Windows

The most common desktop operating system is **Microsoft Windows**. Figure 5.4 shows a timeline of the release of successive versions of Windows desktop operating systems. At the time of this writing, the current version is Windows 10, although you'll still find many computers running previous versions of Windows, notably Windows 7 or 8.1. About 90 percent of personal computers are running a version of Windows. Windows XP was released in 2001 and was still the most widely used operating system in the world in 2010. Sales of Windows XP ended in 2008, and Microsoft support for Windows XP ended in 2014, leaving older systems without patches or updates for any newly discovered problems. Windows Vista was released in 2006 but was met with much resistance from both the public and business customers. The hardware requirements to install Vista were much more stringent than those for XP, so it would not run on many older systems. In addition, software and device driver compatibility were problematic when Vista was first released, adding to the cost of upgrading. Windows 7 was greeted much more favorably, and both home and business users who were still using XP began to upgrade to it. In 2013, nearly half of all PCs were running Windows 7. In 2012, Microsoft released Windows 8, updated to Windows 8.1 in 2013. Windows 10 was released in 2015 as a free upgrade for Windows 7 and 8 systems.

Each release of Windows added new features and security measures and was designed to be easier to use, more secure, and able to incorporate new technologies. Moving from one version of Windows to the next usually requires a fairly small learning curve, and users adapt quickly to the changes.

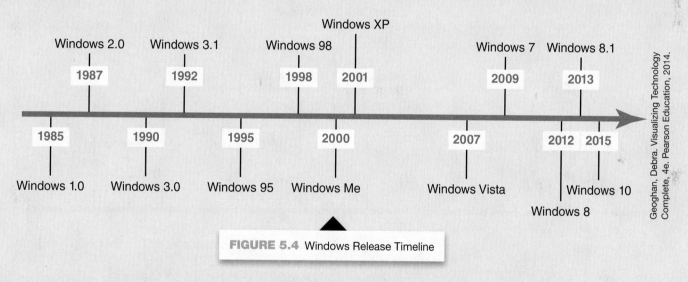

FIGURE 5.4 Windows Release Timeline

Geoghan, Debra. Visualizing Technology Complete, 4e. Pearson Education, 2014.

- Windows 95 introduced Plug and Play (PnP), enhanced support for CD-ROMs, and the right mouse click.
- Windows 98 included Internet Explorer, better PnP support, and more multimedia features.
- Windows XP introduced a new interface, automatic updates, easier networking and Internet connectivity, and increased reliability.
- Windows Vista introduced a new interface, gadgets, enhanced networking, entertainment, and accessibility features.
- Windows 7 included a redesigned taskbar, new ways to manipulate windows, Remote Media Streaming, and Windows Touch multi-touch technology.
- Windows 8 introduced a totally new interface, which uses a Start Screen with Live Tiles instead of a Start menu to access applications.
- Windows 10 restores the Start button that users missed with Windows 8, while keeping the Live Tiles from the Start screen. A new browser, Edge, replaces the tired Internet Explorer. A virtual assistant—Cortana—a feature on Windows phones, is now part of the desktop OS. Screenshots in this book use Windows 10.

MAC OS X

In 1984, Apple introduced its first Macintosh computer, which had a GUI interface. The OS at the time was called Mac System Software. New versions and updates that improved stability and hardware support were released between 1984 and 1991. Figure 5.5 shows a timeline of Mac releases.

- System 7 was released in 1991 with an updated GUI, multitasking support, built-in networking, better hardware and memory management, and new applications. Beginning with version 7.6, the name was changed to Mac OS.
- Mac OS 8 was released in 1997 and included a new interface, a better file system, searching, and Internet browsing.
- Mac OS 9 had improved wireless networking support, a better search tool, and the ability to be updated over the Internet. Mac OS 9 is referred to today as Mac Classic.

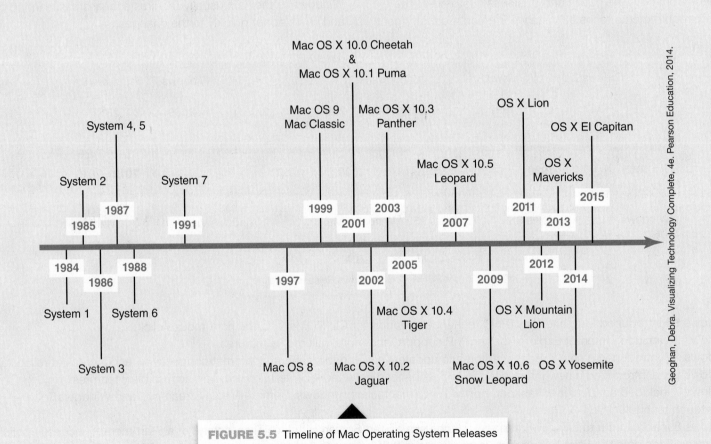

FIGURE 5.5 Timeline of Mac Operating System Releases

Geoghan, Debra. Visualizing Technology Complete, 4e. Pearson Education, 2014.

The **OS X** operating system was first released in 2001 as Mac OS X 10.0, also called Cheetah. This OS wasn't an updated version of the classic Mac OS but an entirely new operating system based on UNIX. Early versions of OS X included a Mac OS 9 emulation to run older applications. Cheetah introduced iMovie and iTunes; Puma added iDVD. Each new version included more integrated applications for email, chat, Internet, and multimedia. Screenshots in this book use OS X El Capitan (Figure 5.6).

ETHICS

Early versions of Mac OS only ran on Mac hardware with PowerPC processors, but modern Macs now use Intel processors just like many PCs. With a bit of tweaking, it's possible to get the Mac OS to run on a non-Mac PC. *Hackintosh* is the name given to a PC that's been modified so OS X can be run on it. The question is, is it legal? Is it ethical? What are the restrictions on the OS X EULA? Why do people do it? Would you?

FIGURE 5.6 OS X El Capitan

Linux

Unlike Windows and Mac, Linux doesn't refer to a single operating system but rather many different versions or distributions that use the same kernel, or core OS: Linux. **Linux** was first developed in 1991 by Linus Torvalds, then a graduate student at the University of Helsinki. It was designed to be similar to **UNIX**—a multiuser OS developed in the 1970s that is still used on servers and some specialized workstations. Unlike UNIX, however, Linux is **open source**. The code is publicly available, and developers around the world have created hundreds of Linux distributions (distros) with all kinds of features. Distros include the OS, various utilities, and software applications, such as web browsers, games, entertainment software, and an office suite. One popular personal version of Linux is Fedora (Figure 5.7). Most Linux distros come with a GUI that's similar to Windows or OS X, and users can easily navigate through the system.

FIGURE 5.7 The Fedora desktop features a GUI that's easy to navigate for most users.

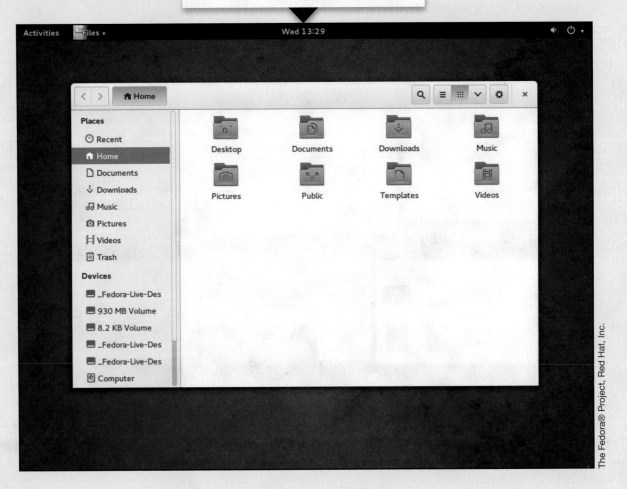

The Fedora® Project, Red Hat, Inc.

Linux desktops make up a very small percentage of personal computers, but the number is growing. Linux has found a niche in the netbook market. On machines with limited memory and processing power, Linux shines. In 2011, several manufacturers began shipping Chromebooks—notebooks that run the Chrome OS, a Linux distro released by Google. These notebooks are designed to work best when connected to the Internet and rely on web apps and cloud storage rather than traditional software. In businesses, Linux has a less than 2 percent market share of desktop computers, but it has a larger share of the server market. Red Hat Enterprise Linux is the world's leading open source application platform.

PSL Images/Alamy

Beta Software

When new software is being developed, it is often released in preview or beta versions. A **beta version** of a program is a pre-release version that is provided to some users and developers to preview and test before the final version is released. Beta and other early releases of software should only be used for testing, as they are often incomplete, unstable, and buggy.

Running Project

Microsoft Windows is the primary desktop operating system installed on new personal computers, but not every consumer is happy with that choice. Some manufacturers sell Linux computers such as Chromebooks. Use the Internet to research the versions of Linux currently available preinstalled on new computers. Write a two- to three-paragraph essay summarizing your findings, which applications are included, the cost, and any other details you deem important.

4 Things You Need to Know	Key Terms
• Microsoft Windows is the primary OS installed on PCs.	beta version
• OS X is the proprietary Mac OS.	Linux
• Linux is an open source kernel OS that's distributed as part of many versions or distros.	Microsoft Windows
	open source
• UNIX is a multiuser OS developed in the 1970s that is still used on servers and some specialized workstations.	OS X
	UNIX

Ollyy/Shutterstock

Make Your OS Work for You

Objective

3

Configure a Desktop Operating System

A desktop operating system has features that you can configure to make your system more secure, more efficient, and more personalized. In this article we'll look at some of the settings that you can change on your system. On a Windows 10 computer, the settings can be changed through the Settings app or the Control Panel. On a Windows 8.1 computer, the settings can be changed through PC settings, the Control Panel, or the Settings charm. In OS X, most settings are changed through System Preferences.

Configuring Your OS

The Windows 10 **Settings window** enables you to change many common settings on your system (Figure 5.8). It helps you to configure user accounts, privacy settings, and accessibility settings. You can add and remove hardware devices and customize time and date and language settings.

- System: configure displays and power and sleep settings; get more information about your PC
- Devices: configure Bluetooth settings, mouse and keyboard settings, and printers
- Network & Internet: change network, Wi-Fi, and workplace VPN settings
- Personalization: configure how Windows looks (Figure 5.9)
- Accounts: configure, add, and remove user accounts
- Time & language: set time and language settings
- Ease of Access: set accessibility settings
- Privacy: change privacy and location settings
- Update & security: configure Windows Update, backup, and recovery options

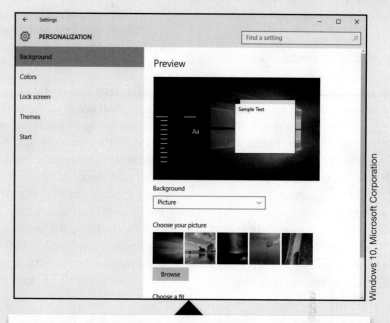

FIGURE 5.8 The Windows 10 Settings window has nine categories.

Windows 10, Microsoft Corporation

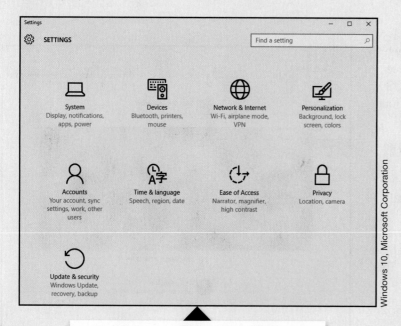

FIGURE 5.9 Personalization Settings enable you to customize how your system looks.

Windows 10, Microsoft Corporation

The **Control Panel** gives you access to even more options to configure, monitor, or troubleshoot settings, hardware, and software (Figure 5.10). To access Control Panel, right-click the Start button or use Windows search. There is a control panel in every recent version of Windows. Most of the settings in the Settings window are also accessible in Control Panel; however, Control Panel includes many more advanced settings. The programs that make up Control Panel are sometimes called **control panel applets**. Some third-party programs and computer manufacturers may add items to the Control Panel. If you are not sure which tool to use to change a setting, type a keyword or phrase into the Search on the taskbar or Control Panel window. The default view of Control Panel is by

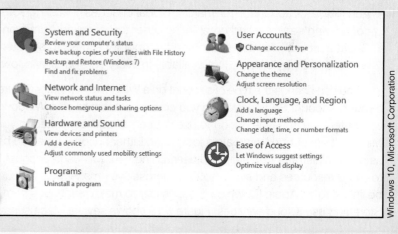

FIGURE 5.10 Control Panel

Windows 10, Microsoft Corporation

category, which groups the applets into the following categories:

- System and Security: computer status, backups, troubleshooting applets
- Network and Internet: network, sharing, and Internet settings
- Hardware and Sound: devices and printers, and other hardware settings
- Programs: install, uninstall, and configure software
- User Accounts: add, remove, and configure user accounts and set up parental controls
- Appearance and Personalization: change desktop and display settings
- Clock, Language, and Region: change language and input settings, set date and time
- Ease of Access: set accessibility settings

System Preferences in OS X are grouped into rows (Figure 5.11). You can configure hardware settings, manage user accounts, and customize the way your computer looks and responds. Some third-party applications may install items in the System Preferences that can be used to configure the settings for that application. The System Preferences are accessed through the Apple menu or by clicking the icon on the dock.

FIGURE 5.11 OS X System Preferences

User Accounts

Create a separate **user account** for each person that shares a device, which grants each user access to the system and enables you to keep your files private and set restrictions on what other users can do. Windows and OS X user accounts have several layers of security built into them. There are four types of user accounts:

- Standard account—for everyday computing; can modify settings that affect the user account only.
- Child account—a Windows standard account that has Family Safety turned on by default. On a Mac this is called Managed with Parental Controls. Not available in every version of Windows.
- Administrator account—for making global changes, installing software, configuring settings, and completing other tasks; called Admin on a Mac.
- Guest account—for users who need temporary access to a system. This account is off by default. Not available in every version of Windows.

You can change the type of account on a Windows computer (Figure 5.12) through Account Settings. When you create an account on a Windows computer, you have the option to use your email address linked to your Microsoft account or to create a local user. Either account type can be set up as an administrator or a standard user. Using your Microsoft account links you to cloud resources and syncs settings across systems. A Mac account can be linked to an Apple ID, which is necessary to make purchases from the App Store and use iCloud services. Figure 5.13 shows several Mac user accounts.

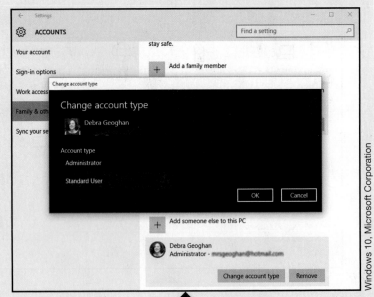

FIGURE 5.12 Change a Windows Account Type

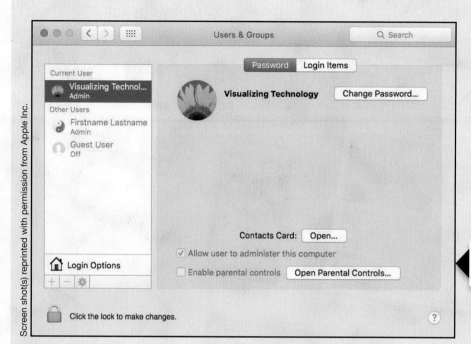

It's good practice to create a standard user account for your day-to-day tasks and use the administrator account only when necessary. Tasks that require administrator-level permission, such as installing a new program, will prompt you for administrator credentials. In a business, only the IT staff should have administrator rights to a computer. Computer settings can be controlled by the IT staff through the use of group policies, which can be configured for a local computer or through a network domain.

FIGURE 5.13 A Mac with Admin, Managed, Standard, and Guest Accounts

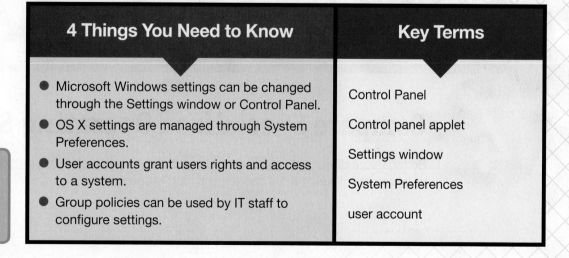

Running Project

Use the Internet to research group policies on a Windows computer. What types of settings can be controlled? What is the advantage of using group policies over allowing users to modify their own settings?

Viz Check—In MyITLab, take a quick quiz covering Objectives 1–3.

4 Things You Need to Know

- Microsoft Windows settings can be changed through the Settings window or Control Panel.
- OS X settings are managed through System Preferences.
- User accounts grant users rights and access to a system.
- Group policies can be used by IT staff to configure settings.

Key Terms

Control Panel

Control panel applet

Settings window

System Preferences

user account

Oleksiy Mark/Shutterstock

Something Special for You

Compare Specialized Operating Systems

So far, we've discussed operating systems that run on personal computers.
In this article, we look at embedded and mobile operating systems.

Embedded Operating Systems

Devices such as ATM machines, GPS devices, video game consoles, ultrasound machines, and communication and entertainment systems in automobiles run **embedded operating systems** (Figure 5.14). Because they have very specialized and limited functions, embedded operating systems can be very small and are able to run on simple hardware.

The Windows Embedded OS has been around since 1996. It can be found on many devices from set-top cable boxes and GPS devices to complex industrial automation controllers and medical devices. The advantage to using an embedded version of Windows is that users recognize the familiar interface.

Mobile devices such as smartphones and tablets run embedded **mobile operating systems**. These are more full-featured than the versions on devices such as GPS and cable boxes. Windows Phone can be found on many smartphones. The iPhone, iPad, and iPod Touch run **iOS**, a scaled-down version of Mac OS X that uses direct manipulation and multi-gesture touch such as swipe, tap, and pinch to control it. **Android** is an embedded version of Linux that runs on many phones and tablets. BlackBerry OS runs on BlackBerry smartphones. These small operating systems have familiar interfaces and features, including touch-screen support, email, and web browsers. As people have become more dependent upon mobile devices, these mobile OSs have become more full-featured and easier to use. The newer versions of desktop operating systems have even begun to look more like their mobile cousins.

Maksym Yemelyanov/Fotolia

FIGURE 5.14 A GPS unit runs an embedded OS.

The most popular mobile operating systems are illustrated in Figure 5.15. The market changes quite rapidly as new technologies are released. As technology becomes more mobile, smaller, faster, and less tethered to the desk, alternative operating systems become an important way to interface with your files and applications. Developers know this and strive to create the best interfaces—ones you can learn to use easily and quickly come to depend upon.

FIGURE 5.15 Smartphone Operating Systems

OS Version	Features	
Apple iOS	Proprietary; found only on Apple devices such as iPad, iPod Touch, Apple TV, and this iPhone 6.	 Jacek Lasa/Alamy
Google Android	Linux kernel, found on devices from many companies including this Samsung Galaxy S5.	 Jacek Lasa/Alamy
Microsoft Windows	Windows mobile version, found on devices from many companies including this Nokia Lumia 900.	 Stanca Sanda/Alamy

CAREER SPOTLIGHT

HELPDESK—An entry-level IT job that requires good OS skills is a computer support specialist working at a helpdesk. Helpdesk specialists are the folks you speak with when you call, chat, or email for tech support. Computer support specialists assist people with computer problems—both hardware and software related. As you can imagine, a good foundation in operating systems is a must. Helpdesk technicians typically have an associate's degree or certifications such as CompTIA A+. According to the U.S. Bureau of Labor Statistics, by 2022, the demand for helpdesk jobs will increase by 17 percent.

Andy Dean/Fotolia

Running Project

What's the mobile OS on your favorite handheld device? What are some of the features that you like about it? Are there any features that are missing? What features do you use the most? Did you select your device because of the OS?

2 Things You Need to Know

- Embedded OSs are small and specialized for devices such as GPS and ATMs.
- Mobile operating systems are embedded OSs on smartphones and tablets.

Key Terms

Android

embedded operating system

iOS

mobile operating system

Kovaleff/Fotolia

The NOS Knows

Compare the Most Common Network Operating Systems

In a business or school environment, a network server centralizes resources, storage, and security in a **client–server network**, a network that has at least one server at its center. Users log in to the network instead of their local computers and are granted access to resources based on that login. Servers run a specialized operating system called a network operating system.

SIMULATION **System Software**

What is an NOS?

A **network operating system (NOS)** is a multiuser operating system that controls the software and hardware running on a network. The NOS allows multiple computers—**clients**—to communicate with the server and each other to share resources, run applications, and send messages. The NOS provides services such as file and print services, communication services, Internet and email services, and backup and database services to the client computers. Table 5.1 details the most common network operating systems.

TABLE 5.1 Comparing Modern Network Operating Systems

Network (NOS)	Current Version	Comments
Windows Server: First released as Windows NT in 1993	Windows Server 2012 R2—at the time of this writing Windows Server 2016 was in beta release.	Scalable; found on many corporate networks; available in versions from Small Business edition to Enterprise and Datacenter editions.
Linux: Linux kernel is part of many different distros	Some of the most popular server versions used in business are Red Hat Enterprise Linux and Novell SUSE.	It's impossible to know how many Linux servers are currently installed because many versions can be downloaded and installed for free and without registration.
UNIX: The oldest NOS	UNIX itself is not an OS but a set of standards that are used to create a UNIX OS.	Found on servers from HP, IBM, and Sun.
Apache Web Server	Apache Web Server is the most widely used NOS found on web servers.	Apache can run on UNIX, Linux, or Windows servers.
Novell	Novell Open Enterprise Server 11	Novell was a leader in business servers throughout the 1980s and 1990s with its Netware products but has moved to open source products.

Geoghan, Debra. Visualizing Technology Complete, 4e. Pearson Education, 2014.

Your school network is most likely a client–server network. When you log in to the network, you're given access to certain resources, such as printers and file storage. Figure 5.16 shows the Windows login screen from a Windows computer for the VIZTECH network. When the user name and password is entered correctly, the user is granted access to network resources on the VIZTECH network.

firstname lastname

VIZTECH\firstname_lastname

Password →

firstname lastname
VIZTECH\firstname_l

Windows 8.1, Microsoft Corporation

FIGURE 5.16 Windows Login Screen for the VIZTECH Client–Server Network

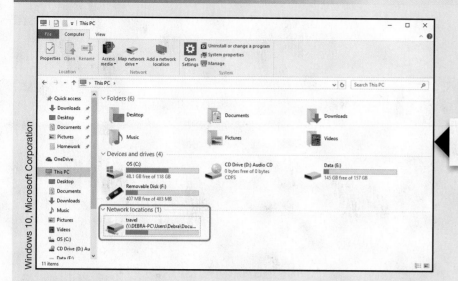

FIGURE 5.17 This Windows client has access to a drive on another computer in the network.

Centralized resources and security make a network operating system indispensable in a business setting. When a client logs in to a network, the appropriate resources appear in the client's environment. In Figure 5.17, you can see a network drive that appears in the File Explorer window of a Windows client.

At home, the network you set up is a **peer-to-peer network (P2P)** that doesn't require an NOS. Although your personal operating system has networking features, the files and services that are shared between your devices aren't centralized. An NOS provides important security and resource management in a business environment. Without an NOS, businesses would have to rely on P2P networks, which are not practical for more than a few computers.

Running Project

The one area of NOS usage that can be easily monitored is activity on web servers. These are the servers that serve up web pages when you go to a URL, such as **amazon.com**. Netcraft does a monthly survey of web servers. Go to **news.netcraft.com/archives/category/web-server-survey/** and look at the most recent month. What are the three most popular web servers for this month? How much has it changed in the past month? Are there any servers not mentioned in this chapter?

3 Things You Need to Know

- An NOS controls the software and hardware running on a client-server network.
- The most common NOSs are Windows Server, UNIX, and Linux.
- An NOS isn't needed on a peer-to-peer network.

Key Terms

client

client–server network

network operating system (NOS)

peer-to-peer network (P2P)

server

Maxx-Studio/Shutterstock

Utilities You Should Use

List and Explain Important Utility Software

VIZ CLIP

System software isn't just the operating system. **Utility software** helps you maintain your computer and is also considered system software. In this article, we look at some important utilities.

Using Disk Utility Software

Why Use Disk Utilities?

It's important to keep your disks healthy to keep your system running efficiently and to protect the files stored on them. **Formatting** a disk prepares it to store files by dividing it into tracks and sectors and setting up the file system. When a hard disk is first formatted, a set of concentric circles called tracks are created. The disk is then divided up like a pie into sectors (Figure 5.18). The files you save to your disk are stored in **clusters**, which consist of one or more sectors. This physical, low-level formatting occurs when the disk is manufactured. Think of this like a library full of empty bookshelves. The second part of formatting a disk is called high-level formatting. High-level formatting sets up the **file system** of the disk. You can think of it like a library catalog. When you save files to your disk, the file system keeps track of what you saved and where you saved it. The file system used on hard disks in Windows is the NTFS file system. External disks or those from older versions of Windows may be formatted with the FAT file system. The OS X file system is HFS+.

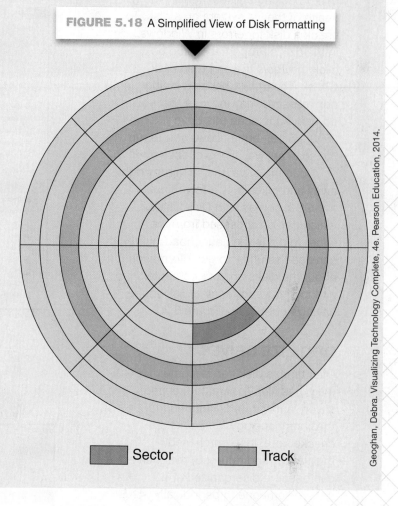

FIGURE 5.18 A Simplified View of Disk Formatting

Sector   Track

Geoghan, Debra. Visualizing Technology Complete, 4e. Pearson Education, 2014.

Utilities For Disk Health

Windows includes several disk utilities to help you maintain your disks: Check Disk, Optimize Drives, and Disk Cleanup. To open these tools, open the File Explorer, This PC window, and then right-click the disk you want to work with. Click *Properties* to open the Properties dialog box for the disk.

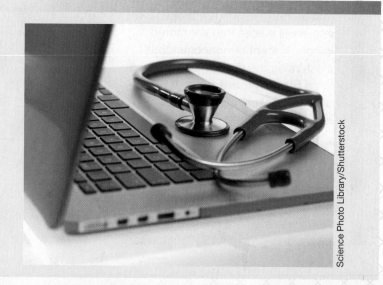

Science Photo Library/Shutterstock

DISK CHECKING

Disk-checking utilities monitor the health of the file system on a disk. To check a disk for errors in Windows, in the disk's Properties dialog box, click the *Tools* tab and then click *Check*. The Error Checking dialog box message may indicate that you don't need to scan this drive (Figure 5.19), but it allows you to run the scan anyway if you choose to. If you scan the drive, the scan runs right away and takes only a few minutes.

OS X comes with Disk Utility, which can be accessed from the *Other* folder in the Launchpad. You can use this utility to get information about the disks on your computer and to verify and repair a disk you're having trouble with (Figure 5.20).

OPTIMIZE DRIVES

Over time, a disk can become messy as files are created, edited, saved, and deleted. Returning to the library analogy, as books are checked out, lost, purchased, misplaced, and returned, the shelves can become disorganized and require someone to periodically go through and clean them up. In addition to being unorganized, files that are fragmented are broken into small pieces that are stored in nonadjacent or noncontiguous clusters on the disk. This is referred to as **file fragmentation**. A disk **defragmenter** is a utility that rearranges the fragmented files on your disk to improve efficiency. You should not run a defragmenter on a solid-state disk (SSD) as it will shorten the life of the disk, and because the files are not stored on SSDs in the same way they are on mechanical disks, defragmenting isn't necessary.

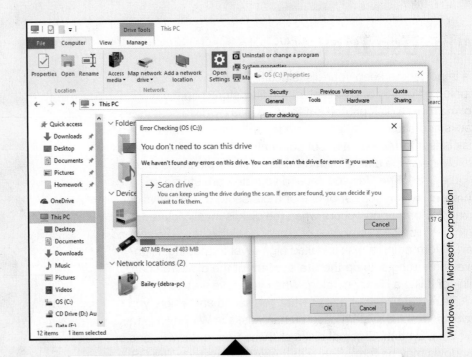

FIGURE 5.19 The Windows Check Disk utility can check both the file system and the physical health of the disk.

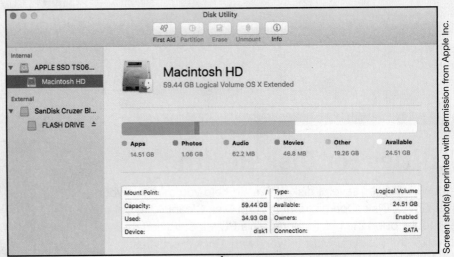

FIGURE 5.20 The OS X Disk Utility

The Windows Optimize Drives utility optimizes and defragments hard drives and runs automatically on a weekly basis. You can also run it manually if you need to. Microsoft recommends that you defragment a drive that's more than 10 percent fragmented. Figure 5.21 shows the Optimize Drives utility. Like the Disk Check utility, the Optimize Drives utility can be accessed from the Tools tab of the disk's Properties dialog box.

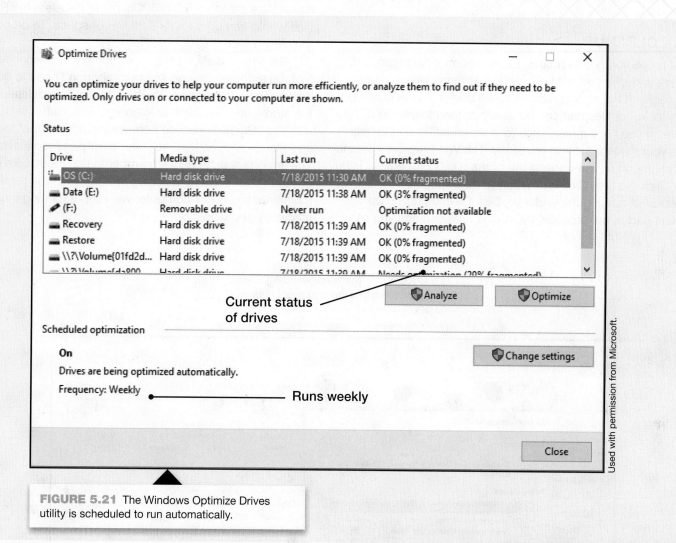

FIGURE 5.21 The Windows Optimize Drives utility is scheduled to run automatically.

FIND OUT MORE

Is defragmenting a hard disk really necessary? Some people say no. Use the Internet to research the controversy. Do you agree with the contention? Why or why not? What webpages did you find supporting this argument? What credentials does the author have that makes you trust the information you found? Make sure you're using recent information.

Mac OS X's HFS+ file system has some safeguards against fragmentation, and Macs rarely need to be defragmented. OS X does not include a defragmenter utility, although there are third-party tools you can use.

DISK CLEANUP

Back to the library—over time, books become damaged, old, outdated, duplicated, and obsolete. A librarian will go through the stacks of books and remove those books. A disk cleanup utility looks for files that can be safely deleted to free up disk space so you have more space to store your files and to help keep your system running efficiently. The Windows Disk Cleanup utility is found on the General tab of the disk's Properties dialog box. Click the *Disk Cleanup* button to begin. Figure 5.22 shows the result of running the Windows Disk Cleanup utility. During the first part of the process, the disk is analyzed and you can review the results. When you click on any of the file types listed, a description displays to help you decide which files you can safely delete. Several types of files are checked by default, and in this example, the total amount of disk space that would be gained is a meager 95.2 MB. Choosing to delete the Recycle bin files would free up another 7.22 MB of space. To proceed with the cleanup, click OK.

Macs have daily, weekly, and monthly maintenance routines that run automatically, so you normally don't need to do any other disk cleanup of your own. You should regularly delete unneeded files and empty the Trash to keep your disk clutter free.

The utilities discussed here are included with Windows and Mac; however, there are also third-party tools available. The important thing is to remember to use them. Like changing the oil in your car and checking the tire pressure, regular maintenance of your computer will keep it running more efficiently and help it last longer.

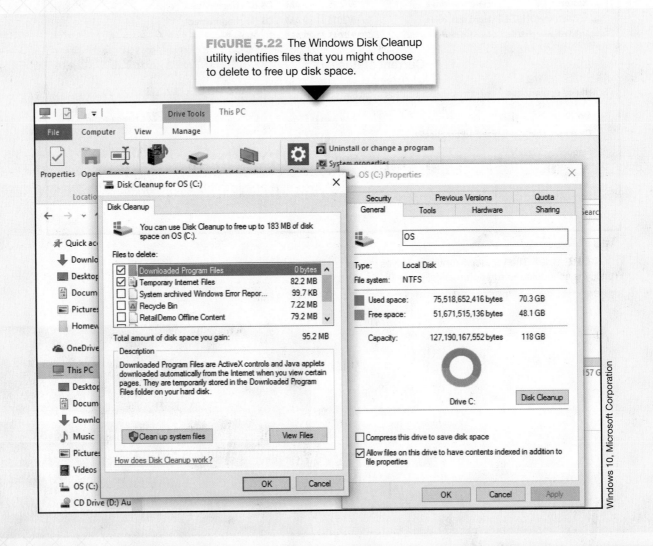

FIGURE 5.22 The Windows Disk Cleanup utility identifies files that you might choose to delete to free up disk space.

Windows 10, Microsoft Corporation

Security Software

Security software such as firewalls, antivirus software, and antispyware software, is also considered utility software. **Firewall** software blocks unauthorized access to a computer. Both Windows and OS X include a software firewall, although you have to manually enable it on a Mac.

Malware is a computer program that's designed to be harmful or malicious, such as a virus, worm or spyware. An **antivirus program** protects against viruses, Trojan horses, worms, and spyware. **Antispyware software** prevents adware and spyware infections. Windows includes Windows Defender to protect against viruses and spyware (Figure 5.23).

A security suite is a package of security software that includes a combination of features such as antivirus, firewall, and privacy protection. If you connect your computer to the outside world, it is important to protect it with good security software. Malicious attacks are common and difficult to avoid without using good security software and practicing smart computing.

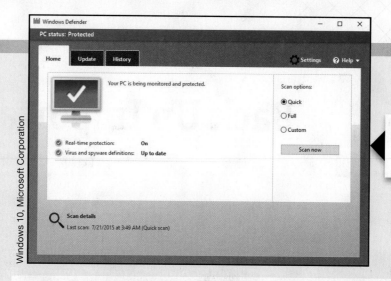

Windows 10, Microsoft Corporation

FIGURE 5.23 Windows Defender scans your system for malware.

Running Project

Open the disk properties for your primary hard drive (C). What's the disk file system? What is the capacity of the drive, and how much disk space is used? If you are using a Windows computer, on the Tools tab, click *Optimize* to start the Optimize Drives utility. When was the disk last defragmented? What percentage of the disk is currently fragmented?

4 Things You Need to Know

- Utility software helps you maintain your computer.
- You format a disk to prepare it to hold data.
- Files that are broken up and stored in noncontiguous clusters are considered to be fragmented.
- NTFS is the file system used on Windows-formatted hard drives. HFS+ is the file system used on Macs.

Key Terms

antispyware software

antivirus program

cluster

defragmenter

file fragmentation

file system

firewall

formatting

malware

utility software

Viz Check—In MyITLab, take a quick quiz covering Objectives 4–6.

How To?

Essential Job Skill

Back Up Important Files

HOW TO VIDEO

Backing up your important files allows you to recover them if something happens to your system. You can use a third-party tool or the built-in tools in your operating system to do this. In this activity, you will use File History or Time Machine to back up your files. You will need a flash drive or access to another external or network drive to complete this activity. (Note: Security settings may prevent you from performing these steps in the lab.) If necessary, download student data files from **pearsonhighered.com/viztech**. From your student data files, open the *vt_ch05_howto2_answersheet* file and save the file as **lastname_firstname_ch05_howto2_answersheet**

1 Insert your flash drive into your system. Right-click the *Start* button and click *Control Panel*. If necessary, click the *View by* arrow, and then click *Category*. Under System and Security, click *Save backup copies of your files with File History*. In the File History window, what files are listed as *Copy files from*? What location is listed under *Copy files to*? Is File History turned on? If it is off, click *Turn on*. Paste a screenshot of this window in your answer sheet.

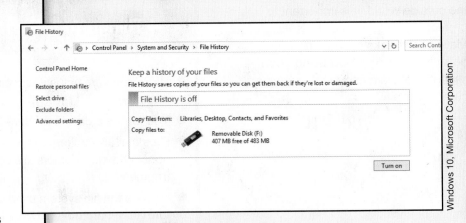

Windows 10, Microsoft Corporation

2 In the Navigation pane, click *Select drive*. What options are listed on your system? Paste a screenshot of this window in your answer sheet.

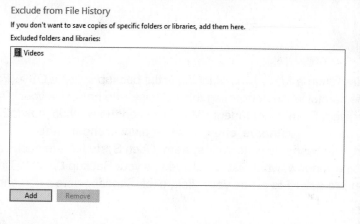

Select a File History drive

Choose a drive from the following list, or enter a network location.

Available drives	Free space	Total space
Removable Disk (F:)	152 KB	483 MB

Add network location

Show all network locations

Windows 10, Microsoft Corporation

3 In the Navigation pane, click *Exclude folders*. Are there any items listed? Click *Add*. In the Select Folder window, click *Videos*, and then click *Select Folder*. This excludes the Video library from your File History. Paste a screenshot of this window in your answer sheet. Click *Cancel*.

Exclude from File History

If you don't want to save copies of specific folders or libraries, add them here.

Excluded folders and libraries:

Videos

Add   Remove

Windows 10, Microsoft Corporation

4 In the Navigation pane, click *Advanced settings*. How often are files saved? How long are they kept? Change the Save copies of files setting to *Every 10 minutes* and the Keep saved versions to *Until space is needed*. Take a screenshot of this window and paste into your answer sheet. Click *Cancel*.

Advanced settings

Choose how often you want to save copies of your files, and how long to keep saved versions.

Versions

Save copies of files: Every 10 minutes

Keep saved versions: Until space is needed

Clean up versions

HomeGroup

If this PC is part of a homegroup, you can recommend this drive to other homegroup members.
Create or join a homegroup

Event logs

Open File History event logs to view recent events or errors

Windows 10, Microsoft Corporation

5 If File History was off when you began this exercise, click *Turn off* to restore that setting. If necessary, remove your flash drive from the system. Save your answer sheet and submit as directed.

If you are using a Mac: Time Machine is the backup utility in OS X. For this activity, you will need a flash drive. Be careful when performing this exercise—do not erase your disk when prompted unless it can be safely erased. From your student data files, open the *vt_ch05_howto2_answersheet_mac* file and save the file as **lastname_firstname_ch05_howto2_answersheet_mac**

1. Insert your flash drive into your system. Open System Preferences and click *Time Machine.* In the Time Machine window, what disk is selected as your Backup Disk? Is Time Machine on? If it is off, click ON. **If you are asked to erase your disk, click** *Cancel.* Paste a screenshot of this window in your answer sheet.

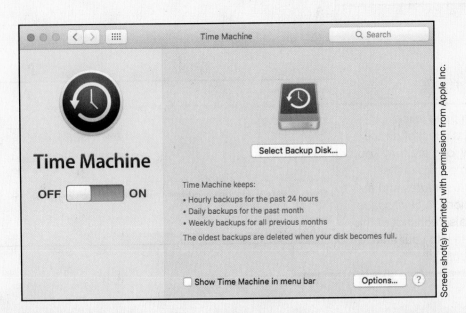

Screen shot(s) reprinted with permission from Apple Inc.

2. Click *Select Backup Disk*. What options are listed on your system? Paste a screenshot of this window in your answer sheet. Click *Cancel*.

3. Click *Options*. Are there any items listed? Click **+**. In the Documents window, in the Sidebar, click your user name, click *Movies*, and then click *Exclude*. This excludes the Movies folder from your Time Machine. If you do not see the Movies folder, select another folder for this exercise. Paste a screenshot of this window in your answer sheet. Click *Cancel*.

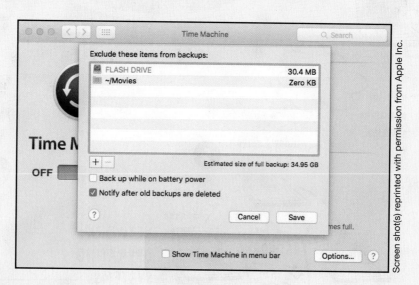

4. How frequently does Time Machine back up your files? How long does it keep the backup copies? If Time Machine was off when you began this exercise, click *OFF* to restore that setting. If necessary, remove your flash drive from the system. Save your answer sheet and submit as directed.

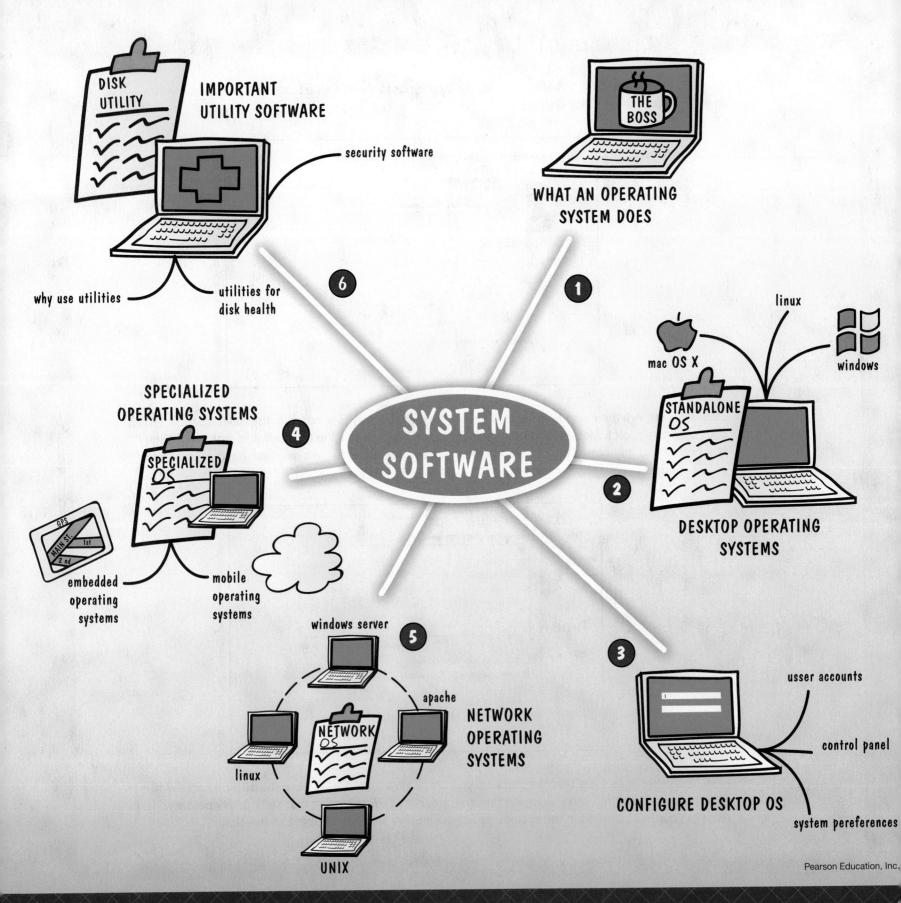

IMPORTANT UTILITY SOFTWARE

DISK UTILITY

security software

why use utilities

utilities for disk health

WHAT AN OPERATING SYSTEM DOES

THE BOSS

6

1

linux

mac OS X

windows

STANDALONE OS

SPECIALIZED OPERATING SYSTEMS

SPECIALIZED OS

4

SYSTEM SOFTWARE

2

DESKTOP OPERATING SYSTEMS

GPS
MAIN ST.
1st
2nd

embedded operating systems

mobile operating systems

5

3

windows server

apache

NETWORK OPERATING SYSTEMS

NETWORK OS

usser accounts

control panel

linux

CONFIGURE DESKTOP OS

system pereferences

UNIX

Objectives Recap

1. Explain What an Operating System Does
2. Compare Desktop Operating Systems
3. Configure a Desktop Operating System
4. Compare Specialized Operating Systems
5. Compare the Most Common Network Operating Systems
6. List and Explain Important Utility Software

Key Terms

Summary

1. **Explain What an Operating System Does**

   The operating system (OS) is the most important type of system software because it provides the user with the interface to communicate with the hardware and other software on the computer. The OS also manages the allocation of memory and processing resources to both hardware and software, manages and controls hardware using Plug and Play and device drivers, and provides services to applications through the use of an application programming interface (API).

2. **Compare Desktop Operating Systems**

   The three most common desktop operating systems are Microsoft Windows, Mac OS X, and Linux. Windows has been around since 1985 and is installed on over 90 percent of personal computers. The Mac OS has been around since the first Mac computer was released in 1984. Linux was first released in 1991 and is the OS kernel for hundreds of different distributions (distros) that come bundled with utilities and applications.

3. **Configure a Desktop Operating System**

   Windows settings can be configured through the Settings window and Control Panel. OS X settings are configured through System Preferences. A user account grants users access and rights to a system and keeps each user's files private.

4. **Compare Specialized Operating Systems**

   Embedded operating systems run on devices such as ATM machines, GPS devices, video game consoles, ultrasound machines, and communication and entertainment systems. Because they have specialized and limited functions, these operating systems can be very small and run on simpler hardware.

   A mobile operating system such as Windows Phone, iOS, or Android runs on devices such as smartphones and tablets and is more full-featured than other embedded OSs.

5. **Compare the Most Common Network Operating Systems**

   A network operating system (NOS) is a multiuser operating system that controls the software and hardware running on a network. It allows multiple client computers to communicate with the server and each other as well as to share resources, run applications, and send messages. An NOS centralizes resources and security and provides services such as file and print services, communication services, Internet and email services, and backup and database services. Most servers run some version of Windows server, Linux, or UNIX. Apache Web Server is the most widely used NOS found on web servers.

Summary continues on the next page

Summary *continued*

6. List and Explain Important Utility Software

Windows includes several disk utilities to help you maintain your disks: Check Disk, Optimize Drives, and Disk Cleanup. Disk-checking utilities monitor the health of the file system on a disk. OS X includes Disk Utility to verify and repair disk problems. A defragmenter is a utility that rearranges fragmented files on your disk to improve efficiency. Security software such as firewalls, antivirus software, and antispyware software is also considered utility software.

Multiple Choice

Answer the multiple-choice questions below for more practice with key terms and concepts from this chapter.

1. Which is a function of an operating system?
   a. Browse the Internet
   b. Edit images
   c. Protect against malware
   d. Provide a user interface

2. What OS feature enables an application to request services from the operating system, such as a request to print or save a file?
   a. Application programming interface
   b. Device driver
   c. Graphical user interface
   d. Plug and Play

3. _____ enables you to easily add new hardware to a computer system.
   a. Graphical user interface
   b. Multitasking
   c. NOS
   d. Plug and Play

4. Which operating system is an open source distribution?
   a. Microsoft Windows
   b. Mac OS X
   c. Linux
   d. NOS

5. A limitation of Mac OS X is that it _____
   a. can't be updated over the Internet.
   b. can't be used in a home network.
   c. does not have a GUI.
   d. only runs on Mac computers.

6. Which Windows feature allows you to change, configure, monitor, or troubleshoot most system settings, hardware, and software?
   a. Application programming interface (API)
   b. Control Panel
   c. Settings Charm
   d. System Preferences

7. Which mobile operating system is found on iPods, iPhones, and iPads?
   a. Android
   b. BlackBerry OS
   c. iOS
   d. Windows Phone

8. Which is the most popular NOS found on web servers?
   a. Apache
   b. Novell Linux Enterprise
   c. Red Hat Enterprise
   d. Windows NT

9. _____ is the process of preparing a disk to store files by dividing it into tracks and sectors.
   a. Defragmenting
   b. Disk cleanup
   c. File system
   d. Formatting

10. Which Windows utility should you use to reorganize the files on your disk to improve efficiency?
    a. Disk Checker
    b. Disk Cleanup
    c. Disk Properties
    d. Optimize Drives

True or False

Answer the following questions with T for true or F for false for more practice with key terms and concepts from this chapter.

_____ **1.** You can use a computer without an operating system installed.

_____ **2.** he user interacts with the operating system through the use of a GUI.

_____ **3.** The OS communicates with software applications via device drivers.

_____ **4.** A popular version of Linux is iOS.

_____ **5.** You should use a guest account for everyday computing.

_____ **6.** Android is a mobile Linux operating system found on many smartphones and tablets.

_____ **7.** An NOS centralizes resources and security and provides services such as file and print services to clients.

_____ **8.** The file system used on hard disks in Windows is the NTFS file system.

_____ **9.** Malware is a computer program that's designed to be harmful.

_____ **10.** Disk-checking utilities monitor the health of the file system on a disk.

Fill in the Blank

Fill in the blanks with key terms from this chapter.

1. A(n) _____ acts as a translator, enhancing the capabilities of the operating system by enabling it to communicate with hardware.

2. _____ is the ability to do more than one task at a time.

3. Yosemite is a version of _____.

4. Chrome and Fedora are popular distros of _____.

5. _____ software has its source code published and available to the public, enabling anyone to copy, modify, and redistribute it without paying fees.

6. The programs that make up the _____ are sometimes called applets.

7. The OS in a smartphone or tablet is referred to as a(n) _____.

8. A(n) _____ is a multiuser operating system that controls the software and hardware running on a network.

9. A(n) _____ keeps track of what files are saved and where they're stored on the disk.

10. A software _____ blocks unauthorized access to an individual computer.

Running Project...

...The Finish Line

Use your answers from the previous sections of the running project. Assume that you just got a new computer with no software on it. What operating system and version would you install? Select one utility that you consider indispensable. Which program did you pick and why?

Write a report describing your selections and responding to the questions raised. Save your file as **lastname_firstname_ch05_project** and submit it to your instructor as directed.

Do It Yourself 1

Utility software is important to protect and maintain your computer. In this activity, you'll examine your computer to determine what type of utility software is installed on it and if it's properly protected. From your student data files, open the file *vt_ch05_DIY1_answersheet* and save the file as **lastname_firstname_ch05_DIY1_answersheet**

Open the Control Panel, click *System and Security*, and then click *Security and Maintenance* (Windows 8, click *Action Center*). If necessary, click the arrow to open the Security section. What is your status for each category? Are there any important notices? What software is reported for virus protection and spyware? If necessary, click the arrow to open the Maintenance section. What is your status for each category? Are there any important notices? Take a screenshot of the Security and Maintenance window and paste it into your answer sheet. Type up your answers, save your file, and submit your work as directed by your instructor.

If you are using a Mac:

Open the *Other* folder from the Launchpad. Take a screenshot of the Other folder and paste it into your answer sheet. Explore the Activity Monitor, AirPort Utility, and System Information utilities. Use Help to look up each of these utilities. What is the purpose of each of these? Type up your answers, save your file, and submit your work as directed by your instructor.

Do It Yourself 2

In this exercise, you'll perform a disk check on your flash drive. From your student data files, open the file *vt_ch05_DIY2_answersheet* and save the file as **lastname_firstname_ch05_DIY2_answersheet**

1. Insert your flash drive into the computer. If necessary, wait until Windows finishes installing drivers. Close any windows that open automatically. Open File Explorer. Right-click on your flash drive, and choose *Properties*. What file system is on the disk? What is the capacity, and how much free space is on the disk? Take a screenshot of the Properties dialog box, and paste it into your answer sheet.

2. Click the *Tools* tab and click *Check*. When the scan is finished, take a screenshot of the results and paste it into your answer sheet. Type up your answers, save the file, and submit your work as directed by your instructor.

If you are using a Mac:

1. Insert the flash drive into the computer. Open the Disk Utility from Launchpad, Other folder. Select the flash drive from the left pane of the Disk Utility. What file system is on the disk? What's the capacity, and how much free space is on the disk? Take a screenshot and paste it into your answer sheet.

2. If necessary, click the *First Aid* tab and click *Verify Disk*. Make sure *Show details* is checked. When the scan is finished, take a screenshot of the results and paste it into your answer sheet. Type up your answers, save the file, and submit your work as directed by your instructor.

File Management

Utility software such as disk defragmenters and cleanup utilities help you keep your computer running efficiently. In this activity, you'll use the Windows Disk Cleanup utility to examine some of the files on your computer. From your student data files, open the file *vt_ch05_FM_answersheet* and save the file as **lastname_firstname_ch05_FM_answersheet**

1. Open File Explorer, and if necessary, click *This PC*. What items are listed under Devices and drives? Right-click the C: drive, and click *Properties*. What is the capacity of the disk? How much free space is currently available?

2. Click the *Disk Cleanup* button. Allow the Disk Cleanup utility to analyze your system. When it's finished, take a screenshot of this dialog box and paste it into your answer sheet. Note: This process may take several minutes to complete.

3. Click on each of the categories of files listed, and read the descriptions in the bottom of the dialog box. What types of files are included in Downloaded Program Files and Temporary Internet Files? What are Temporary Files, and is it safe to delete them? What other categories of files are listed? Which ones have check marks next to them? How much space could you free up if you cleaned up all the files found? Type up your answers, including the screenshot from step 2. Save your file and submit it as directed by your instructor.

If you are using a Mac:

There is no disk cleaning utility in OS X. For this exercise, you will learn how to manually clean up your disk. On the Finder menu bar, click *Help*, and then search for *increase disk space*. What are the recommended methods for cleaning up your disk? Open the section *Delete files, folders, or apps*. What options are listed? How do you delete items in Mail? Type up your answers, save your file, and submit it as directed by your instructor.

Critical Thinking

Your school is still running Windows 8.1 in the computer lab. It's considering upgrading to Windows 10. As a user of the computer lab, you've been asked to give some input into the decision process. From your student data files, open the file *vt_ch05_CT_answersheet* and save the file as **lastname_firstname_ch05_CT_answersheet**

Use the Internet to research the improvements in Windows 10 over Windows 8.1. What are the improvements you feel are the most important? Do they require any special hardware or software to be installed? Do you recommend the school upgrade the computer lab? Give two reasons supporting your recommendation. Type up your answers, save the file, and submit your assignment as directed by your instructor.

Ethical Dilemma

Miriam works at a small company and was just passed over for a promotion, which was given to a new employee, Bill, because he has a certification. Bill let it slip that he easily passed the test because he paid $50 for a study guide that had all the test answers in it. From your student data files, open the file *vt_ch05_ethics_answersheet* and save the file as **lastname_firstname_ch05_ethics_answersheet**

Miriam is frustrated. She has experience with the company, but Bill got the job because he has the certification. What should she do? Should she report Bill to her employer? To the certification testing center? Borrow the questions and take the exam herself? What would you do? Because this has been a common issue in the past, the certification tests have become stricter and more difficult to cheat on, but it still happens. Use the Internet to find out the penalty for cheating on one of the current IT industry exams. Type up your answers to the questions above. Save the file and submit it as directed by your instructor.

On the Web

In this activity, you'll compare the hardware requirements for different versions of Windows. From your student data files, open the file *vt_ch05_web_answersheet* and save the file as **lastname_firstname_ch05_web_answersheet**

Use the Internet to research the hardware requirements for each of the following versions of Windows:

- Windows XP
- Windows Vista
- Windows 7
- Windows 8
- Windows 10

Choose the original release and the Home (or Home Premium) version, and complete the table below. What websites did you use to locate this information? Save the file and submit your work as directed by your instructor.

Windows Version	Year Released	Minimum Processor	Minimum Memory	Minimum Free Disk Space	Optical Disc Type	Other Requirements
Windows XP						
Windows Vista						
Windows 7						
Windows 8						
Windows 10						

Collaboration

Instructors: Divide the class into groups of three to five members, and assign each group one topic for this project. The topics include Windows 10, OS X El Capitan, and Fedora (Linux). For larger classes, assign multiple groups the same operating system.

The Project: As a team, prepare a commercial that includes an explanation of your assigned operating system and special features that aren't included in this book. Use at least three references. Use Google Drive or Microsoft Office to prepare your presentation and provide documentation that all team members have contributed to the project.

Outcome: Prepare a commercial on your assigned topic. The presentation may be no longer than 2 minutes. You may record it or perform it live for your class. On the first page of your written outline, be sure to include the name of your commercial and a list of all team members. Turn in a final version of your outline and script named **teamname_ch05_collab** and submit your project to your instructor as directed.

Application Project

Office 2016 Application Projects

PowerPoint 2016: Should You Upgrade Your OS?

Project Description: In this project, you will create a presentation about upgrading your operating system. In creating this presentation you will apply design, font, and color themes. You will also change font colors, bullet symbols, and slide layout. If necessary, download student data files from **pearsonhighered.com/viztech**.

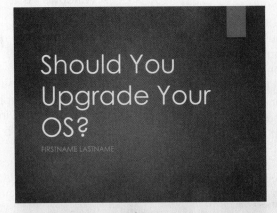

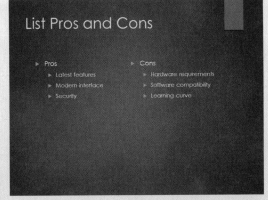

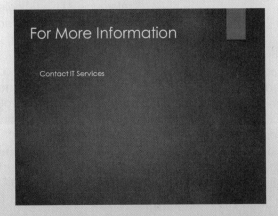

Step	Instructions
1	Start PowerPoint. From your student data files, open the PowerPoint file *vt_ch05_ppt*. Save the presentation as **lastname_firstname_ch05_ppt**
2	Apply the Ion theme, purple variant, to the presentation.
3	On Slide 1, using your name, type **Firstname Lastname** in the subtitle placeholder.
4	On Slide 2, type **Will it Run?** in the title placeholder. On Slide 2, change the bullet style to Arrow Bullets, and change the line spacing of the bullets to double.
5	On Slide 3, change the title to **Check Hardware and Software**
6	On Slide 3, insert the image *vt_ch05_image1* in the content placeholder. Apply the Reflected Perspective Right picture style to the image and change the picture height to 4".
7	Change the layout of Slide 4 to Two Content.
8	On Slide 4, in the left pane, type the following four list items. **Pros**, **Latest features**, **Modern interface**, **Security**
9	On Slide 4, in the right pane, type the following four list items. **Cons**, **Hardware requirements**, **Software compatibility**, **Learning curve**
10	On Slide 4, select the last three items in each list, and use the Increase List level button to indent them.
11	Insert a new Title and Content slide after Slide 4.
12	On Slide 5, in the title placeholder, type **For More Information** In the content placeholder, type **Contact IT Services** and change the bullet to None.
13	Insert the page number and the footer **Firstname Lastname** on the notes and handouts pages for all slides in the presentation.
14	Apply the Cover slide transition to all slides, with a duration of 2.00. View the presentation in Slide Show view from beginning to end, and then return to Normal view.
15	Save the presentation and close PowerPoint. Submit the presentation as directed.

Application Project

Office 2016 Application Projects

Excel 2016: Worldwide Smartphone Sales

Project Description: Data is collected every year comparing worldwide shipments of computers and mobile devices. In this project, using the data for 2014, you will format cells and use functions and an absolute cell reference in a formula. You will also create and format a pie chart. If necessary, download student data files from **pearsonhighered.com/viztech**.

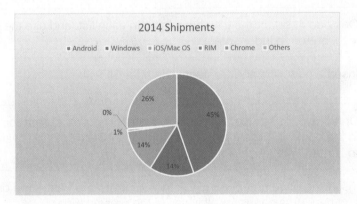

Step	Instructions
1	Start Excel. From your student data files, open the Excel file *vt_ch05_excel*. Save the workbook as **lastname_firstname_ch05_excel**
2	Set the width of columns A, B, and C to **20**. Set the height of row 1 to **40**
3	Merge and center the text in cell A1 over columns A:C. Apply the cell style Heading 1. Merge and center the text in A2 over columns A:C. Apply the cell style Heading 2.
4	Select the range A3:C3 and center and middle align the text in the selected range.
5	In cell A10, type **Total** In cell B10, use the SUM function to calculate the 2014 shipments.
6	In cell C4, create a formula using an absolute cell reference to calculate the Market Share of Android. Copy the formula in cell C4 down to C5:C9. Apply the Percent number format. Display 1 decimal place.
7	Select the range A10:C10 and apply the Total cell style.
8	Select the range A4:B9 and insert the Recommended pie chart. Move the chart so that its upper left corner aligns with the upper left corner of cell A13.
9	Change the layout of the chart to Layout 2. Change the chart title to **2014 Shipments**
10	Format the chart area with the default gradient fill.
11	Insert a header with the Sheet name in the center cell. Insert a footer with the file name in the left cell. Return to Normal View.
12	Change the orientation of Sheet 1 to Portrait. Center the worksheet horizontally and vertically on the page.
13	Rename Sheet 1 as **2014**
14	Ensure that the worksheets are correctly named and placed in the following order in the workbook: 2014, Source. Save the workbook and close Excel. Submit the workbook as directed.

Maksym Yemelyanov/Fotolia

Digital Devices and Multimedia

In This Chapter

Digital devices, such as digital cameras, smartphones, and tablets, have become essential tools. **Multimedia**, which is the integration of text, graphics, video, animation, and sound, describes the type of content you view and create with these devices. In this chapter, we discuss digital devices and multimedia content and how we use them every day. After completing this chapter you will be able to recognize different types of media and select and use various hardware and software to create and play multimedia files.

Objectives

1 Explain the Features of Digital Cameras

2 Compare Methods for Transferring Images from a Digital Camera

3 Identify Several Ways to Edit and Print Photos

4 Recognize Important Audio File Types

5 Describe Several Ways to Create Videos

6 Compare Portable Media Players, Tablets, and Smartphones

Running Project

In this chapter, you'll explore how to select and use digital devices and share multimedia content that you create. Look for instructions as you complete each article. For most articles, there is a series of questions for you to research. At the conclusion of the chapter, you'll submit your responses to the questions raised.

Bedrin/Fotolia

Digital Camera Basics

Objective

1

Explain the Features of Digital Cameras

Digital cameras have become more popular as they've dropped in price and become easier to use. You don't even need to have a computer to use a digital camera. In this article we look at the different types of digital cameras on the market, the features that distinguish them, and how to use them to capture memories.

VIZ CLIP

Photo and Print Resolution

Key Features

Choosing a digital camera can be bewildering with all of the choices available. Three important features that can help you sort it all out are resolution, storage type, and lenses.

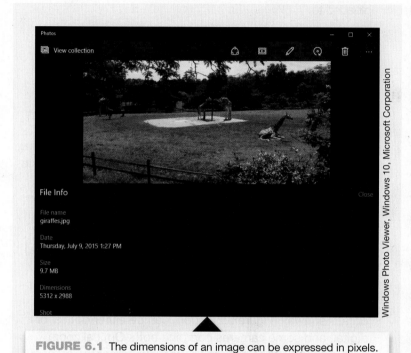

FIGURE 6.1 The dimensions of an image can be expressed in pixels.

Windows Photo Viewer, Windows 10, Microsoft Corporation

Pearson Education, Inc.

RESOLUTION

The quality of the images that a camera can take is determined by the resolution. **Resolution** is the measure of the number of pixels in an image and is expressed in megapixels. When you view a picture file in File Explorer or Finder, the picture dimension is listed in pixels. The resolution can be calculated by multiplying the length by the width of the image in pixels. The image in Figure 6.1 has the dimensions 5,312 × 2,988 pixels, so it has a resolution of 15,872,256 pixels, or about 16 megapixels. Another way to measure resolution is in dots per inch (dpi). An image that is 300 pixels wide will have 300 dots (pixels) across, whether the screen or print is 3 inches or 30 inches wide. If the image dimension is large but the dpi is small, the pixels become visible.

The higher the resolution, the more detail in the image and the larger the prints you can make before the image quality suffers. Table 6.1 lists the best resolutions to use for various photo print sizes. Images that will only be viewed on a computer screen can be taken at a lower resolution than those intended for photo-quality prints. This is important because resolution also affects file size: The higher the resolution, the larger the file. A very-high-resolution image is not appropriate for use on a webpage because larger files take longer to load onto the screen. File size also impacts storage. An image file taken with a digital camera on its highest setting can yield a file of more than 25 MB in size, while the lower quality setting yields a file of 1 to 2 MB. Many cameras enable you to select the image quality before you take a picture. Setting the camera to take lower-resolution pictures will allow you to fit more pictures on your camera or memory card.

Table 6.1 Image Resolution for Photo-Quality Prints

Resolution	Photo-Quality Print Size (in inches)
1–2 megapixels	Up to 4 × 6
2–3 megapixels	Up to 5 × 7
4–5 megapixels	Up to 8 × 10
6–7 megapixels	Up to 11 × 14
8 megapixels	Up to 16 × 20
10 megapixels	Up to 20 × 30

STORAGE

Digital cameras can store images internally or on removable memory cards. The internal memory on most cameras is relatively small compared to the capacity of removable media. The type of card you choose depends on the camera. Flash memory cards come in capacities up to 2 TB in size, depending on the type of card. Memory cards are relatively inexpensive, so you might want to carry multiple cards with your camera. The advantage to carrying these cards is that they can be read by most computers and photo printers that can read memory cards, or you can bypass your computer and simply bring the memory cards to a local store to have the pictures printed. Once the images have been printed, saved to your computer, or uploaded to the web, the memory card can be erased and reused.

Debra Geoghan

FIGURE 6.2 These images illustrate how zoom can make the subject appear closer.

LENSES

To focus a camera, you adjust the **focal length**—the distance at which subjects in front of the lens are in sharp focus—by changing or moving the lens. Some cameras are **autofocusing**. When you point the camera at a subject, the camera adjusts the focal length by using a small motor to move the lens in or out. If you snap the shutter too quickly, the camera may not have time to properly focus the image, resulting in a blurry photo. **Fixed-focus** cameras—meaning the lens does not move—have a lens with a preset focal length that focuses well on objects within a specific distance.

Most digital cameras have the ability to **zoom** in or out before you take a picture, making objects appear closer or farther away (Figure 6.2). Zoom can be either optical or digital, and some cameras combine both. Optical zoom uses a zoom lens to change the focal length of the camera. Low-end digital cameras have an optical zoom of 3×–5×, while more advanced cameras may have 20×–24× zoom or more. Cameras may have a macro setting, or close focus, for taking pictures of objects that are very close. A **telephoto lens** enables you to zoom in on an object. A **wide-angle lens** gives you a wider view, which makes the objects appear farther away, much like taking a step backward does. A wide-angle lens is useful for shooting images such as panoramas or landscapes.

Digital zoom crops the image and enlarges a portion of it, resulting in a zoomed image of lower quality because the dpi of the image doesn't change. Total zoom on a camera is determined by multiplying its optical zoom by its digital zoom. A camera with a 3× optical zoom and a 10× digital zoom has a total zoom of 300×. Because digital zoom lowers the image quality, it's better to rely on optical zoom when taking a picture. You can always use software to crop and enlarge the image later.

Types of Digital Cameras

Digital cameras range from disposable cameras you can buy in a drugstore for a few dollars to high-performance **digital single-lens reflex (DSLR) cameras** that use interchangeable lenses, can be manually focused, and can cost thousands of dollars. Most fall somewhere in between the two. Your smartphone has the advantage of always being in your pocket, and many smartphones have high-quality digital cameras built in, but taking lots of pictures can quickly use up your battery. Choosing the camera that is right for you will depend on a number of factors, including the types of pictures you plan to take, ease of use, and cost.

POINT-AND-SHOOT

Point-and-shoot cameras are the simplest, least expensive type of digital camera, and they have the fewest features. You can purchase one for as little as $20 or spend hundreds of dollars for more sophisticated cameras. The most basic cameras have fixed focus, may not have a flash, and may suffer from noticeable **shutter lag**—the time between pressing the button and the camera snapping the picture. When your subject is smiling and waiting for the flash to go off, several seconds can seem like a long time, and shutter lag can cause you to miss that action shot.

Single-use disposable cameras are basic point-and-shoot cameras that can be purchased in many retail stores and at tourist spots such as monuments, theme parks, and hotels. These are great to carry on trips, send to school with your kids, and put out on tables at weddings and other celebrations for the guests to take pictures.

Advanced point-and-shoot cameras are moderate in price and features. Although still easy to use, they include better zoom, macro functions, viewfinders, auto focus, and other special effects. Most also include the ability to capture video and may have special features like **image stabilization**, which compensates for camera shake to take sharper images, and **burst mode**, which enables you to take several pictures in quick succession by holding down the shutter button. They may also include some more professional features, such as the ability to adjust speed and exposure settings. Table 6.2 compares features of different types of point-and-shoot cameras.

Massimhokuto/Fotolia

Table 6.2 Comparison of Point-and-Shoot Digital Cameras

	Basic Point-and-Shoot	Advanced Point-and-Shoot
General	Small size, inexpensive, easy to use Good for snapshots, especially outdoors and web/email	Produces better pictures, provides more control, zoom, and features, but still lets you point and shoot Good for snapshots, portraits, enlargements, and web/email
Resolution	1–16 megapixels	18–24 megapixels and up
Price	$20–200	$50–600
Features	Low-resolution video, may be used as a webcam, may not have a flash or viewfinder	May capture short video clips and include macro and other special effects, manually controlled settings, image stabilization, burst mode, little or no shutter lag
Lens	Usually has little optical zoom, fixed focus	Up to 24× optical and additional digital zoom, autofocus

Pearson Education, Inc.

Most point-and-shoot cameras don't have a viewfinder to help you frame your image. They rely instead on an LCD screen (Figure 6.3). Most of the time an LCD screen works fine, but a true viewfinder does a better job of framing a shot.

MIRRORLESS COMPACT SYSTEM CAMERAS

Also known as superzooms, **compact system cameras (CSC)** are advanced point-and-shoot cameras that have interchangeable lenses (Figure 6.4), some manual controls, 10× to 26× optical zoom lenses, and the ability to capture HD video. CSCs are also known as mirrorless cameras, because unlike DSLRs, they do not use a mirror to bounce light up from the lens to a viewfinder. This is one of the key differences between CSCs and DSLRs and makes CSCs smaller and lighter than DSLRs. CSCs can produce better images than point-and-shoots. Other features include hot-shoe and accessory ports to attach an external flash, microphone, or viewfinder. Priced from about $300 to $2,000, these cameras are more expensive than most point-and-shoot cameras, but they're less expensive than most DSLRs.

FIGURE 6.3 Point-and-shoot cameras use an LCD screen to frame a shot.

FIGURE 6.4 A Compact System Camera with Interchangeable Lenses

lofoto/Shutterstock

Lourens Smak/Alamy

DIGITAL SINGLE-LENS REFLEX (DSLR) CAMERAS

If you really want control and a more traditional type of camera, then you'll want a DSLR camera. With DSLRs, you can change the lens, which can cost hundreds or even thousands of dollars, to get the exact zoom you need. You can attach a hot-shoe flash, and you can manually adjust focus and exposure. DSLRs use a mirror that enables you to see the image you're about to shoot through a viewfinder, allowing you to create artistic images that autofocusing point-and-shoots can't. Most DSLRs also include an LCD that you can use to review your images as soon as you shoot them. There is almost no shutter lag, so DSLRs are the best type of digital camera for shooting action shots. Most DSLRs can shoot HD video. All this comes at a steep cost—from $600 to $5,000, plus hundreds or thousands of dollars for additional lenses (Figure 6.5).

Sergio Martinez/Fotolia

FIGURE 6.5 A DSLR Camera with Various Lenses and Hot-Shoe Flash

Running Project

Use the Internet to research digital cameras. What is the highest resolution available today in point-and-shoot cameras? CSCs? DSLRs? Choose one point-and-shoot, one CSC, and one DSLR camera with the same resolution. How do they compare in terms of price, features, and reviews? What other factors affect the price?

5 Things You Need To Know

- Resolution determines the quality of the print you can make and the size of the image file.
- Optical zoom is better than digital zoom for increased image quality.
- Point-and-shoot cameras are the easiest to use.
- CSCs blend the ease of use of point-and-shoot with some of the control and quality of a DSLR.
- DSLRs take the best pictures and cost the most.

Key Terms

autofocus

burst mode

compact system camera (CSC)

digital single-lens reflex (DSLR) camera

fixed-focus

focal length

image stabilization

multimedia

point-and-shoot camera

resolution

shutter lag

telephoto lens

wide-angle lens

zoom

Expressiovisual/Fotolia

Bridging The Gap: Transferring Photos

2 Compare Methods for Transferring Images from a Digital Camera

You take photos for many reasons—to remember a special occasion, a vacation, friends and family members, and pets—and for more practical reasons, such as documenting an accident or how to take apart (and put back together) a car engine. Once the pictures have been transferred to your computer or the cloud, they can be saved, edited, printed, and shared.

Memory Cards

If your camera uses a memory card to store images, you can take the card out of the camera and put it in a card reader attached to your computer. Many computers have a card reader built in, or you can purchase a removable card reader that plugs into a USB port. When you put the memory card into the reader, Windows will detect it, and it will appear in the File Explorer window under Devices and drives (Figure 6.6). You can copy, move, and delete the pictures just as you would any other type of file, and you can add and edit some file properties, such as tags. **Tagging** images or files with keywords makes it easier to organize and search for them. If you are using a Mac, the memory card will appear as a disk on your desktop, and you can simply open it and copy the images over to your computer (Figure 6.7), or the Photos app may open and give you the option to import the images.

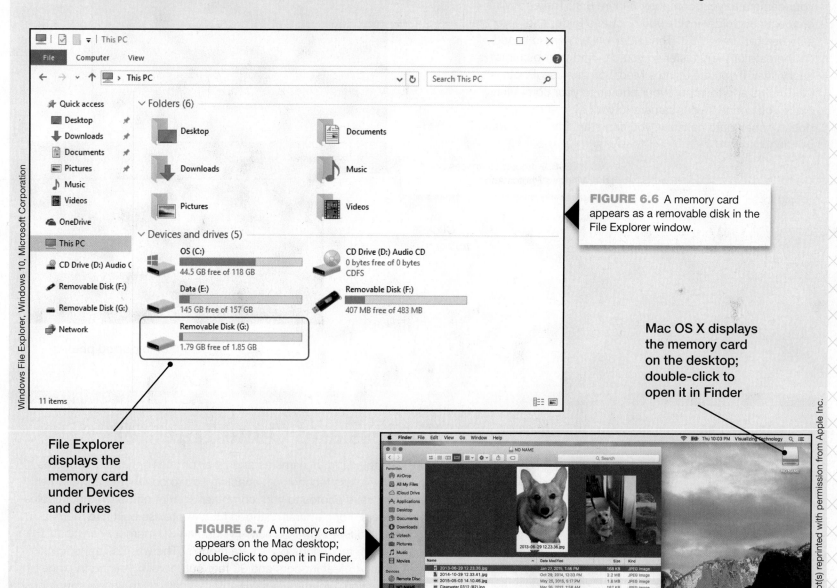

FIGURE 6.6 A memory card appears as a removable disk in the File Explorer window.

File Explorer displays the memory card under Devices and drives

Mac OS X displays the memory card on the desktop; double-click to open it in Finder

FIGURE 6.7 A memory card appears on the Mac desktop; double-click to open it in Finder.

Windows File Explorer, Windows 10, Microsoft Corporation

Screen shot(s) reprinted with permission from Apple Inc.

USB or Firewire Cable

Digital cameras have a USB or, less commonly, a FireWire connection that can be used to connect a camera directly to a computer. This requires device drivers in order for the computer to be able to talk to the camera. The driver may be installed through software that comes with your camera or through the operating system itself. Using the Windows Photos app, you can import your pictures directly from your camera to your computer (Figure 6.8). The app will create a new folder inside your Pictures folder and copy the selected pictures into it. The folder will be named based on the date of the transfer so you can find your pictures easily later. If you are using a Mac, you can use iPhoto or the Photos app to import your photos to your computer. Once you connect your camera to your Mac, if the app doesn't open automatically, you can start it from the dock or Launchpad.

1. Connect your camera and select the device that contains your pictures

FIGURE 6.8 Importing Images Using the Windows Photos App

2. Click *Import*

3. Imported photos

Windows Photo App, Windows 10, Microsoft Corporation

Wireless and Cloud Transfer

Wireless-enabled digital cameras and smartphones can transfer photos using Wi-Fi wireless technology, enabling you to connect to a computer network and save photos to your computer or print photos without cables or card readers. For cameras that don't have wireless built into them, a company called Eye-Fi makes a Wi-Fi-enabled SD memory card that is compatible with thousands of camera models. The wireless transmission range is about 45 feet indoors and 90 feet outdoors. If you are in range of the stored network, your images will automatically fly to your computer or mobile device.

leonardo2011/Fotolia

Screen shot(s) reprinted with permission from Apple Inc.

FIGURE 6.9 From an iPad you can email, message, tweet a photo, or use iCloud to sync a photo to all your devices.

Cameras built into smartphones and tablets can use either 4G or Wi-Fi to wirelessly transfer photos. Many mobile apps enable you to configure this to happen automatically, sending your pictures to the cloud so they are accessible on all of your devices. There is even a wedding app that guests can use to share all the photos they take with the happy couple.

Instagram, Dropbox, Photobucket, Facebook, OneDrive, and Google Photos are commonly used apps that work on multiple platforms. **iOS devices** (iPad, iPhone, iPod) use iCloud (Figure 6.9), which can sync your data among multiple devices—even a Mac or Windows PC.

Running Project

Do any of the cameras you researched in the last section include wireless capabilities? If so, how fast can they transfer images? What are the limitations? If the cameras didn't include wireless, look up the current Eye-Fi card. Is your camera compatible with the card? How much will it cost to purchase the card? Find a similar-model camera that includes wireless. How does the price compare to adding the Eye-Fi card instead?

3 Things You Need To Know

- Memory cards can be transported from camera to computer.
- USB and FireWire cables connect a camera directly to a computer.
- Wireless transfer uses a Wi-Fi or cellular network to transfer photos to your computer or the cloud.

Key Terms

iOS device

tagging

Artur Marciniec/Fotolia

A Picture is Worth a Thousand Words

3 Identify Several Ways to Edit and Print Photos

The beauty of digital photography is what you can do with the images after you transfer them from your camera. With film photography, unless you invest in expensive darkroom equipment, you are limited to choosing the size and finish of your prints and maybe ordering double prints to share with someone else; cropping a photo means taking a pair of scissors to it. Today, anyone can create amazing-looking photos by using a home computer and free or inexpensive software.

Editing Photos

One of the biggest advantages of digital photography over film is the ability to edit images. This can mean doing something as simple as cropping out unwanted parts of the image or removing red-eye, as advanced as using sophisticated software to create works of art, or anything in between. You can add a variety of special effects to photographic images, as well as remove blemishes, adjust colors, and save images in a variety of file formats.

EDITING SOFTWARE

Photo editing software is available in simple, free programs, such as Picasa from Google, up to very sophisticated and expensive professional programs, such as Adobe Photoshop. Older versions of Windows include the ability to edit your pictures using the Windows Photo Gallery, but Windows no longer includes this feature. The Windows Photos app gives you some limited ability to edit photos. Macs include Photos (Figure 6.10). These programs also integrate online photo sharing.

ONLINE EDITING

Many online photo services, such as Google Photos (Figure 6.11), Shutterfly, and Flickr, include basic editing tools with options such as cropping, resizing, and red-eye removal. Editing options also often include special effects like making the picture look black-and-white and adding special borders.

FIGURE 6.10 Photos app is free on Mac computers.

Screen shot(s) reprinted with permission from Apple Inc.

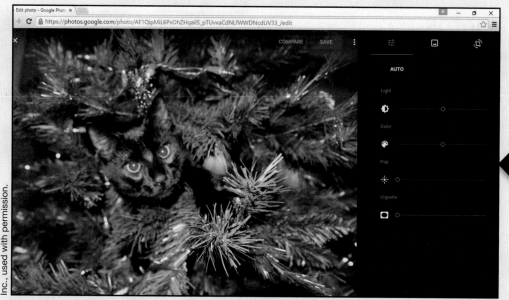

Google and the Google logo are registered trademarks of Google Inc., used with permission.

FIGURE 6.11 Online photo editing tools enable you to edit your images without installing software on your computer.

IMAGE FILE FORMATS AND COMPRESSION

Several different file formats are used for digital photos. Point-and-shoot cameras normally take JPEG images, but higher-end cameras may also be able to take higher-quality images using TIFF or other formats. Table 6.3 lists some common graphic file formats.

Lossless compression takes advantage of the fact that files contain a lot of redundant information, and it creates an encoded file by removing redundant information. When a file is decompressed, all the information from the original file is restored. A TIFF image compressed with lossless compression can be decompressed with no loss of data. A JPG/JPEG image is compressed using lossy compression. The **lossy compression** algorithm removes information that humans can't normally detect. It's possible to compress an image after it's been taken, but once the file is compressed using lossy compression, it can't be fully restored to the original format.

TABLE 6.3 Important Image File Types

Format	File Extension	Description
Joint Photographic Experts Group	JPEG or JPG	• Can store up to 16.7 million colors • Uses lossy compression to reduce file size
Windows Bitmap	BMP	• A standard graphic format originally developed for Microsoft Windows • Compression is optional, resulting in large file size
Tagged Image File Format	TIFF or TIF	• A lossless graphic format, often with no compression applied, resulting in large file size
RAW	Camera manufacturers have proprietary file formats, such as NEF (Nikon) or CRW/CR2 (Canon)	• Raw images are not processed by the camera and must be processed by software in order to be used

Pearson Education, Inc.

Printing and Sharing Photos

The cost of creating prints of your photos varies depending on the paper, ink, and type of printer you use. Photo printers can be inkjet printers that use special ink cartridges or dye-sublimation printers, which produce lab-quality prints. Less expensive prints using regular ink and paper have a lower quality and shorter lifespan. At home, printing can cost 50 to 70 cents per print (Figure 6.12).

FIGURE 6.12 A Camera and Photo Printer, No Computer Needed

Naypong/Fotolia

PICTBRIDGE

PictBridge is an industry standard that enables a camera to connect directly to a printer, usually via a USB connection or special dock. Cameras that are compatible with this system don't require connecting to a computer to handle the transfer of data. You can use a small, portable printer to print photos on the spot. You may also be able to do some limited editing on either the camera or printer before you print. PictBridge is a legacy technology that is no longer supported in newer printers, which instead read directly from memory cards.

KIOSKS

Photo kiosks in retail stores have built-in editing capabilities and are very easy to use. These kiosks enable you to print only the pictures you want and fine-tune your images without needing to use your own computer. You can connect your camera via USB or FireWire, or you can insert a memory card into the kiosk. Kiosks can even print photos you have stored in the cloud or on websites like Facebook. These prints typically cost between 15 and 59 cents per print.

ONLINE PRINTING AND SHARING

Websites like Shutterfly are personal image-sharing sites. Their main goal is to get you to buy prints and other merchandise they offer. The advantage to using these sites is that you can share your photos with your friends and family members, who can order the items they want. The prints can be mailed or picked up at local retail partners. Companies like Walgreens and Walmart enable you to upload your pictures at home and pick up the prints in a store. Standard prints from these sites cost about 15 cents each.

Flickr is an online photo-sharing community owned by Yahoo. Flickr has millions of users and millions of images in its vast repository. When you upload images to Flickr, you are able to tag them with keywords that you define. The tags link your images to other Flickr images with the same tags, and though you can choose to keep your pictures private, the majority of the images on Flickr are publicly available. Another feature is **geotagging** (Figure 6.13), which allows you to add location information to your digital photos.

FIGURE 6.13
Geotagging Images on Flickr

Flickr also allows you to control how other people can legally use your pictures by applying **Creative Commons (CC) licensing**. According to the Creative Commons website, Creative Commons "tools give everyone from individual creators to large companies and institutions a simple, standardized way to grant copyright permissions to their creative work. The Creative Commons licenses enable people to easily change their copyright terms from the default of 'all rights reserved' to 'some rights reserved.'"* You can visit the Creative Commons website to learn more about how it works. You can search Flickr for images that have CC licensing applied. Another feature of Flickr is The Commons. There are dozens of institutions participating in The Commons, a project that is designed to make publicly held photography collections accessible to everyone. This is a great resource to use when you need an image for a school project. Images in The Commons have no known copyright.

Creative Commons (**creativecommons.org**) is a project that has been developed as a way to increase sharing and collaboration by specifying how images and other materials can be used. One of the first institutions to embrace this idea was the Smithsonian Institution, which made hundreds of images available on Flickr under Creative Commons. Visit **flickr.com/photos/smithsonian** to see them (Figure 6.14).

*Creative Commons - https://creativecommons.org/about

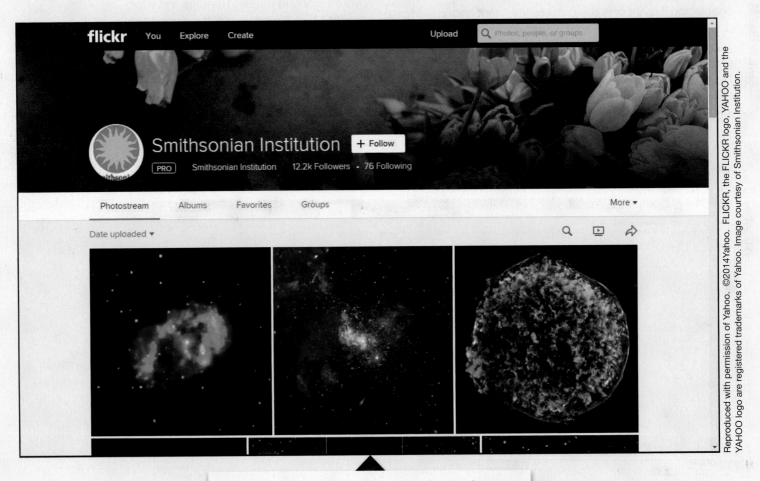

FIGURE 6.14 Smithsonian Photos from Creative Commons

George Dolgikh/Fotolia

For years, whenever I celebrated a special occasion with family and friends, I would take my film to the store to be developed—always ordering a second set of prints so I could share them. It was expensive, it would take at least a day or two to get back, and often there were several (okay, many) prints that were just awful, and I would throw them away. There was no way to decide ahead of time which prints I wanted; I had to pay for them all. Not anymore—now, if I take a lousy picture, I can review it right on my camera, and if needed, delete it and reshoot. When I get home, I download the pictures to my computer, crop and enhance them, upload them to Facebook or Google Photos, and share away. That process is so much easier and faster—and much less expensive—because I do not print all the pictures and instead view and share them online.

 Viz Check—In MyITLab, take a quick quiz covering Objectives 1–3.

Running Project

Use the Internet to compare the cost and quality of photo prints from several home photo printers, online services, and local retailers in your area. Create a chart comparing them. Include the following information: cost per print, sizes, finish types, expected lifespan of prints, water resistance, and any other details you think might be important. When might you choose to use each of these methods for prints?

4 Things You Need To Know

- Photo editing software can be used to enhance and fix your photos.
- Printing photos at home is easy but can be expensive.
- Kiosks in stores enable you to edit and print better-quality photos less expensively than you could print them at home.
- Online printing and sharing sites enable you to edit and share your photos easily, and using them is the least expensive way to print quality photos.

Key Terms

Creative Commons (CC) licensing

geotagging

lossless compression

lossy compression

PictBridge

How To? Digital Literacy Skill

Edit a Photo Using the Windows Photos or OS X Photos App

HOW TO VIDEO

In this exercise you will perform some basic editing on a photo using the Windows Photos app or the OS X Photos app. If you do not have this app, use another program such as Windows Photo Gallery or iPhoto. If necessary, download the student data files from **pearsonhighered.com/viztech**.

1

Open File Explorer. Locate the student data files for this chapter. Right-click the file *vt_ch06_kids* and click *Copy*. Navigate to the folder where you save your work and then on the Home tab of the ribbon, click *Paste*. Right-click the file, click *Rename*, type **lastname_firstname_ch06_howto1** and press Enter. Right-click the new file, point to *Open with*, and then click *Photos*.

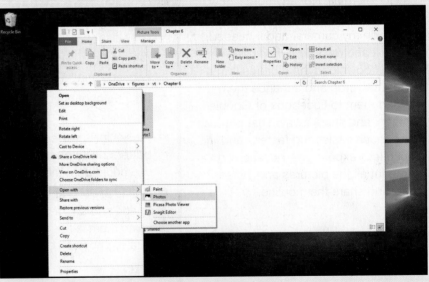

Windows 10, Microsoft Corporation

2 Click the *Edit* button on the menu bar. With *Basic fixes* selected on the left, click *Enhance* on the right. (Windows 8: Right-click to display the menu bar, click *Edit*. With *Auto fix* selected on the left, click the third option on the right. Click *Basic fixes*.) Click the *Red eye* tool and click each eye to clean up the eyes.

3 Click *Crop*. On the menu bar, click the *Aspect ratio* button, and then click *5:7*. Drag and resize the grid to crop the image so that the boys make up most of the image. Drag the image to the center of the grid and then click *Apply*.

4 On the left, click *Color*, and then on the right, click *Temperature*. Use the arrow keys on your keyboard to adjust the temperature to *15*.

Windows 10, Microsoft Corporation

5 On the left, click *Light*, and then on the right, click *Contrast*. Use the arrow keys on your keyboard to adjust the contrast to *25*. Click *Shadows*. Use the arrow keys on your keyboard to adjust the shadows to *-25*. Click *Save*. Close Photos and submit your image as directed by your instructor.

Windows 10, Microsoft Corporation

If you are using Photos on a Mac:

1. Open Finder. Locate the student data files for this chapter. Press `Ctrl` + click the file *vt_ch06_kids* and click *Copy "vt_ch06_kids.jpg"*. Navigate to the folder where you save your work and then press `Command ⌘`+`V`. Click the file one time, press `Return`, type **lastname_firstname_ch06_howto1** and press `Return`. Open Photos. From the File menu, click *Import*. Browse to the location of your files for this chapter, click the image *lastname_firstname_ch06_howto1*, and then click *Review for Import*. Double-click the image and then click *Edit*.

2. In the right pane, click *Enhance*. Click the *Red eye* tool and click each eye to clean up the eyes.

3. Click *Crop*, click *Aspect*, and click *5:7*. Drag and resize the grid to crop the image so that the boys make up most of the image. Drag the image to the center of the grid and then press Return.

4. Click *Adjust*. To the right of *Color*, click the *Auto* arrow. Adjust the *Cast* slider to 0.15.
5. To the right of *Light*, click the *Auto* arrow. Adjust the *Contrast* slider to 0.25. Adjust the Shadows slider to -0.25.

Screen shot(s) reprinted with permission from Apple Inc.

6. Click *File*, point to *Export*, and then click *Export 1 Photo*. In the dialog box, click *Export*. Close Photos and submit your image as directed by your instructor.

Kentoh/Fotolia

Making Sense of Sound

4

Recognize Important Audio File Types

From listening to songs on a mobile device, to using speech to control computers and video games, to receiving alerts about new email and text messages, sound plays an important role in the multimedia experience. In this article we'll examine the differences between several audio file types and compare various media player programs and speech-recognition programs.

Audio File Types

When multimedia files are stored on your computer, they can take up large amounts of storage space. To use the space on your hard drive efficiently and improve file transfer speeds over the Internet, multimedia software reduces file size by using codecs, short for compression/decompression. **Codecs** are compression algorithms that reduce the size of digital media files. Without the use of codecs, downloads would take much longer than they do now because the files would be significantly larger. There are hundreds of codecs, but you probably use only a few of them on a regular basis. Common audio codecs include MP3 and AAC.

Sound files contain digitized data in the form of recorded live sounds or music, which are saved in one of several standardized sound formats. These formats specify how sounds should be digitally represented and commonly include some type of data compression. A common music file format is **MP3 (MPEG-1 Audio Layer 3)**. The MP3 codec creates files that are compressed, enabling them to maintain excellent quality while being reasonably small. When you rip a CD, you transfer your music files to your computer and convert them to a compressed format such as MP3 or AAC. The files on an audio CD are very large, which is why there are usually only 10–12 songs per disc. An MP3 file is about one-tenth the size of a CD audio file. There is, however, a trade-off between file size and quality: The smaller MP3 files are not the same quality as the original audio files. MP3 files have the file extension .mp3.

The default file type used by Apple's iTunes software is **AAC (advanced audio coding)**, which compresses a file in a manner similar to MP3. The AAC codec creates files that are somewhat higher quality than MP3 files, and support for it is growing on other devices, such as the Sony PlayStation 4, Nintendo Wii, and many smartphones and media players.

There are several other common audio file types, including Windows Media Audio (WMA) files and MIDI files, which are synthesized digital media files you might hear as a soundtrack to a video game.

Ra2 studio/Fotolia

Digital rights management (DRM)
is a technology that is applied to digital media files, such as music, eBooks, and videos, to impose restrictions on the use of these files. This may mean that you cannot transfer the file from one device to another or make a backup copy, or that your access to the file will expire in a specific amount of time. The companies that apply DRM to media files argue that it is necessary to protect the copyright holder. The Digital Millennium Copyright Act (DMCA) made it illegal to remove DRM from protected files. Opponents of DRM argue that it not only prevents copyright infringement but also restricts other lawful uses of the media.

ETHICS

Cameron purchased an eBook to use for his physics course at school. He downloaded the book to his desktop computer, intending to transfer it to his tablet to take it to class with him. To his surprise, the DRM protection on the file prevented him from reading it on any device other than the computer he originally downloaded the file to. Because he can't bring his computer to class, Cameron sees no way to bring the eBook to school. His friend Abbie has a solution—a free program that can strip the DRM from the file, making a new copy that Cameron can easily transfer to his tablet. Cameron takes her advice, makes a copy of the book, and brings it to class with him. Cameron feels that this is okay because he paid for the book and should be able to read it on any device he owns.

Was stripping the DRM rights from the book legal? Was it ethical? Was Cameron justified in what he did? Did he have any other alternatives?

Screen shot(s) reprinted with permission from Apple Inc.

FIGURE 6.15 White House Press Briefings Podcasts in iTunes

Media Software

Media software is used to organize and play multimedia files such as music, videos, and podcasts. You can rip your music CDs to your computer; organize your songs into playlists for working out, driving, or dancing; and find new music that you might like by using the online store feature. You can watch a movie trailer, a professor's lecture, or a music video. The content available to you grows daily.

iTunes is a program from Apple that you can use to organize your music, videos, and other media files. If you have an iOS device, then you use iTunes to transfer music and other media files from your computer to your device. You can use iTunes to shop for new music, find podcasts to subscribe to, rip your music CDs to your computer, and watch movies. **Podcasts** are prerecorded radio- and TV-like shows you can download and listen to or watch any time. There are thousands of podcasts you can subscribe to. Your instructors may even have podcasts of their class lectures. Figure 6.15 shows the iTunes podcasts page for White House briefings. With iCloud, items purchased using iTunes will automatically sync to all your registered devices and computers.

Windows Media Player is included with Windows, and like iTunes, it can be used to organize and play all your media files, find media on the web to purchase and download, rip CDs, and transfer your media files to your media player (unless it's an iOS device). Windows Media Player has the ability to stream media files to computers and other devices on your home network. You can also use it to burn CDs of your music.

Connecting your music to the cloud enables you to listen to your favorite songs on any device that has an Internet connection. There are a lot of music services out there—some that incorporate your own tracks and others that don't. Many radio stations stream live over the Internet. In fact, some radio stations broadcast exclusively over the Internet.

With a Pandora account, you can listen on a game console, Blu-ray player, computer, Internet-enabled TV, set-top box, or mobile device. You create stations by selecting songs or artists that you like. Pandora has a massive collection of music that has been analyzed and classified by musician-analysts. You can refine the results you get by giving each track a thumbs up or thumbs down. Pandora also displays the lyrics for many songs, so you can sing along to your favorite tunes.

Spotify (Figure 6.16) uses both the music on your devices and millions of tracks stored in the cloud. It enables you to share playlists and recommend tracks to your friends. Spotify has a radio feature that can automatically create stations for you based on both your music collection and your most frequently played tracks.

There are other services such as Amazon Prime, Google Play, and Apple Music. Most services have free, ad-supported plans and premium subscriptions that eliminate ads and include more features. Connections to Facebook, Twitter, and other services make sharing and listening to music a social experience. Using one of these services allows you some control over the songs you listen to—unlike with a normal radio broadcast. If you like to create and share your own music or listen to tracks from independent musicians, check out SoundCloud.

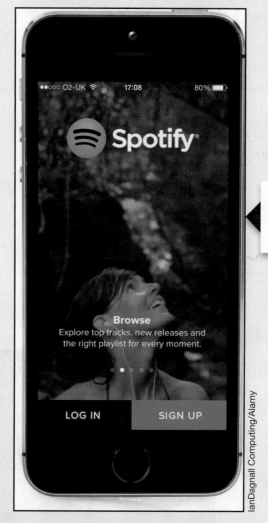

FIGURE 6.16 Spotify uses both your local music files as well as those shared online by others.

IanDagnall Computing/Alamy

FIND OUT MORE

Use the Internet to find a list of Internet radio stations. How many did you find? Which of them have you used? Are any of your favorite local stations broadcasting over the Internet? Do you listen to them online?

Speech Recognition

Speech recognition, also known as voice recognition, is a feature that enables you to use a device by speaking commands. It can be used to automatically provide customer service through a call center, dial a cell phone, dictate a term paper, or control your vehicle navigation system. Speech recognition enables you to use a computer or mobile device without a keyboard. Windows, OS X, iOS, and Android all have built-in speech recognition, and there are also third-party speech-recognition programs and apps.

Apple iPhones include Siri, an intelligent personal assistant app that enables you to speak using natural language to send messages, make phone calls, and ask questions. Siri uses information from your contacts, music library, calendars, and reminders to make recommendations and perform other actions. It works with built-in apps and some third-party apps, like Facebook and Twitter. Over time, Siri learns your speech patterns and gets even better at understanding you. Android devices have a built-in assistant system called Google Now that can be controlled with voice commands, which is also available as a download for other platforms. Google Now presents information in cards that reflect information from your contacts, searches, and email messages. The personal digital assistant on Windows phones and in Windows 10 is called Cortana.

Sound is an important component of multimedia content. Speech recognition enables you to interact with your systems by using voice commands, making for easy access and increasing safety. The use of compression enables you to convert your music collection into digital files that are small enough to enable you to carry thousands of songs on a media player or smartphone while still maintaining high-quality sound. Media player software gives you control over how and what you listen to. How many songs do you have on your playlist?

WavebreakMediaMicro/Fotolia

GREEN COMPUTING

Sharon Day/Shutterstock

E-WASTE—The amount of **e-waste** (electronic waste) generated every year is staggering. Old computers, cell phones, TVs, and other electronic devices make up e-waste, some of which is considered hazardous. A CRT monitor can contain more than 8 pounds of lead, and by Environmental Protection Agency (EPA) regulations cannot be disposed of in a landfill. eCycling, or recycling electronics, is one way to reduce the amount of e-waste and hazardous materials that end up in landfills, as well as to cut down the cost of hauling it away. The EPA provides information on its website about eCycling in your community (**epa.gov/epawaste/ conserve/materials/ecycling**).

You can also dispose of e-waste in an altruistic manner by donating working electronics to worthwhile charities. Your donations of working electronics not only help reduce e-waste but also benefit the recipients.

Running Project

Use Windows Help and Support or the Mac Help Center to research speech recognition. What are three ways you can use speech recognition on your computer? What advantages can you see to using this feature? What disadvantages? Think about your interactions with technology every day and give an example of speech recognition that you use.

5 Things You Need To Know

- MP3 and AAC are the most common music file types.
- Digital rights management imposes restrictions on the use of DRM-protected media files.
- Media programs organize and play multimedia files.
- Streaming media services allow you to listen to music on any Internet-connected device.
- Speech recognition allows you to interact with your systems by using voice commands.

Key Terms

AAC (advanced audio coding)

codec

digital rights management (DRM)

MP3 (MPEG-1 Audio Layer 3)

podcast

speech recognition

Lights, Camera, Action

5

Describe Several Ways to Create Videos

It's estimated that more than one-third of all Internet traffic is video, and that number continues to rise. Creating, viewing, and sharing video is not very different from handling any other media, except that video files tend to be larger and require more storage and bandwidth. To ensure the best accessibility for your videos, they should contain **captions** that display the text of the audio in a video. A caption file is a specially formatted text file that includes the captions and the timing of the captions in the video.

VIZ CLIP

Watching TV on Your Own Terms

Videoconferencing, Webcasting, and Streaming Video

Webcams are specialized video cameras that provide visual input for online communication. They can be used in live video chat sessions through an app such as FaceTime or Skype, or through more sophisticated videoconferencing software (Figure 6.17). Webcams enable you to have virtual meetings with people miles away, connect classrooms on different campuses, collaborate on projects with others in real time, or say goodnight to your family when you are far away. Such two-way interactions require both ends to have webcams and software setups that allow them to communicate with each other. Webcams are relatively inexpensive and come built in to most tablets and notebook computers.

Broadcasting on the web, or **webcasting**, can be used to monitor a child in daycare, stream a live performance or lecture, check out the waves on your favorite surfing beach, or watch a live feed from the International Space Station (Figure 6.18). Webcasting is not interactive—it's a one-way process. The broadcast, known as a video stream, can be live or prerecorded. **Streaming** media begins to play immediately as it is being received and does not require the whole file to be downloaded to your device first.

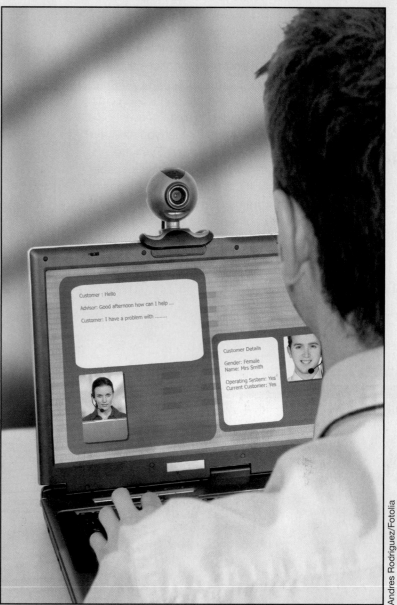

FIGURE 6.17 Online customer support is one application of live video chat.

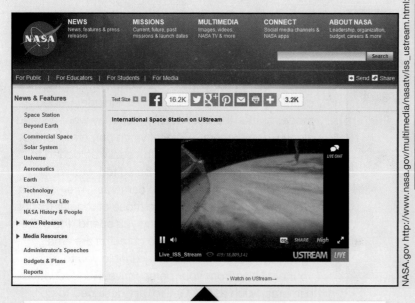

NASA.gov http://www.nasa.gov/multimedia/nasatv/iss_ustream.html>

FIGURE 6.18 Live video from the International Space Station can be viewed at **www.nasa.gov/multimedia/nasatv/iss_ustream.html**.

Streaming video services such as Amazon Prime, Netflix, Hulu, and VuDu, as well as many television networks, stream commercial television and movie content. Some content is available for free, some requires a subscription, and some services allow you to pay for individual shows. Streaming video services allow you to time- and place-shift—deciding when and where to watch your favorite shows and movies—and include apps that let you stream content to your game consoles, smart TVs, and mobile devices (Figure 6.19). These services enable you to binge-watch multiple episodes or seasons of current and older programs. They also have some original content that can't be seen anywhere else. Each service has different content, and choosing the right service depends on the types of programming you prefer.

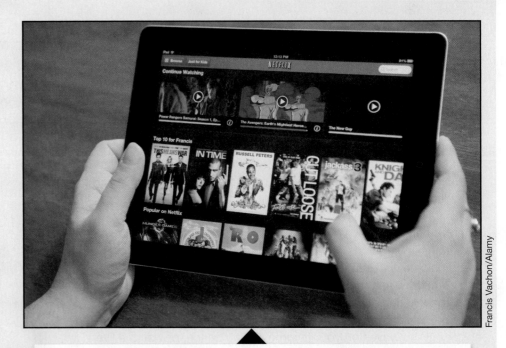

Francis Vachon/Alamy

FIGURE 6.19 Netflix streaming video service lets you take the show on the road.

Aquapix/Shutterstock

FIGURE 6.20 A video camera can record the action anywhere it occurs.

Video Cameras

You can use a webcam to record video, but if you want to record something that is not right in front of your computer, you need a video camera. Most digital cameras and smartphones include a video mode, but for the best quality, you may want a stand-alone video camera. A digital video camera enables you to record video that can be easily uploaded to your computer, where it can be edited, stored, and shared. The features of video cameras—megapixels, storage, zoom—are similar to those of regular digital cameras, and the more money you spend, the more features you get. Some video cameras are small, lightweight, and durable. They enable you to record your activities from your perspective. Rugged video cameras, such as the GoPro, are designed to go anywhere, even under water (Figure 6.20)!

An important thing to consider when buying a digital video camera is the media it uses. Some video cameras have a built-in hard drive or flash memory and do not use any removable media. Although this is convenient, it also means that once the internal drive is full, you'll need a computer nearby to upload the video to before you can record any more. Another option is a camera that uses flash memory cards. Memory cards come in large capacities, are relatively inexpensive, and can be easily reused. In addition, it is easy to carry several with you. Cost, convenience, and the amount of storage you need will all affect your decision.

Screen Capture

There are several ways to create videos. **Screen capture** software tools enable you to create a video of what happens on your computer screen. This is a handy way to create a how-to video or to capture a video of a problem you are having. You don't need a camera to do it. Some programs, such as Screenr and Screencast-O-Matic, are web based and enable you to share the video online without installing the software on your machine. **Machinima**, the art of creating videos using screens captured from video games, is one creative use of screen capture software. Windows 10 includes a built-in tool called the Game Bar, which is part of the Game DVR feature in the Xbox app. The tool is designed to record your PC game play, but can also be used to record other screen activities.

Sharing Video

As with photos, many people create videos intending to share them. This can mean using an online service or burning the video onto a DVD or Blu-ray disc. Regardless of how you decide to share your video, you may want to do some editing before you share it.

VIDEO EDITING

Video editing software, like photo editing software, comes in a variety of forms. Video editing software ranges from free online services such as YouTube, to free programs including Windows Movie Maker and Apple iMovie, to very expensive professional-quality programs such as Adobe Premiere and Sony Vegas. All video editing software will capture, edit, and export video. Most programs allow you to add features like captions, credits and titles, fades between scenes, and music. The software enables you to share your video by burning it to a DVD or uploading it to the web.

If you want more than the free programs offer but don't want to spend hundreds of dollars for professional software, programs in the $50 to $200 range, such as Adobe Premiere Elements or Corel VideoStudio, may have all the features you need.

DVD authoring is a feature of most video editing software. Basic programs have design templates you can use to create attractive titles and menus and enable you to burn your creation to a DVD that can be played in any DVD player.

CAREER SPOTLIGHT
Healthcare

The use of technology has become commonplace in many healthcare careers. Many medical schools and nursing programs now require their students to learn to use handheld devices, which give them instant access to vast amounts of clinical information in one small mobile device. These devices can be loaded with drug and diagnostics manuals, calculators, and other medical reference materials. They can also be used for patient tracking, ordering laboratory tests, and even billing. Handheld devices and other computing technology have changed the way healthcare providers practice medicine. Using digital technologies is a critical skill for practitioners to have.

Nyul/Fotolia

YOUTUBE

YouTube (Figure 6.21) is the most popular video-sharing site on the Internet. Some photo sites and social media sites—including Facebook, allow you to upload video, too. According to YouTube, 48 hours of video are uploaded every minute, resulting in nearly 8 years of content uploaded every day. The quality ranges from awful cell phone videos to professionally created music videos, movie trailers, and full-length programs. You can upload your videos to YouTube and other video-sharing sites and share them with friends and family—or the world. You can create channels to group and share videos about a similar topic. I have created a YouTube channel for each of the classes I teach, and I subscribe to channels other people have created with videos that I am interested in.

In 1888, Thomas Edison filed a caveat with the U.S. Patent Office describing his plan to invent a motion picture camera that would "do for the eye what the phonograph does for the ear*." In 1892, he opened a motion picture production studio to create motion pictures. One of the first motion pictures made there was called "Fred Ott's Sneeze," a recording of an Edison employee sneezing for the camera. You can watch the clip on YouTube today. Little could Edison have imagined the impact that video would have on society a century later.

*Thomas Edison - caveat to U.S. Patent Office, 1888

Video permission granted by the author, Debra Geoghan.

Google and the Google logo are registered trademarks of Google Inc., used with permission.

FIGURE 6.21
YouTube Video of the Author

Running Project

Use the Internet to research digital video cameras. Select a model in the same price range as the point-and-shoot camera you researched earlier. Compare the video capabilities of the two cameras. What features does a dedicated video camera have that the point-and-shoot camera does not? Is the video camera capable of taking still images? How do still images taken with a video camera compare to those taken with a point-and-shoot camera? Do you think it is worth the money to purchase both types of camera? Explain your answer.

4 Things You Need To Know	Key Terms
● Screen capture software records what happens on your computer screen. ● Webcams allow you to videoconference with others. ● Webcasting is broadcasting on the web. ● YouTube is the most popular video-sharing site on the web.	caption machinima screen capture streaming webcam webcasting

Create a Screen Capture Video Using Screencast-O-Matic

HOW TO VIDEO

In this activity, you will use the web tool Screencast-O-Matic (S-O-M) to create a screen capture video. Screencast-O-Matic requires your browser to have the Java plugin to run. You may need to use a different browser if your chosen browser will not allow the plugin to run. Another option is to download and install the S-O-M app on your system. You can create a free account using your email address, or log in using your Facebook account. If necessary, download the student data files from **pearsonhighered.com/viztech**. From your student data files, open the *vt_ch06_howto2_answersheet* file and save the file as **lastname_firstname_ch06_howto2_answersheet**

1 Navigate to the student data files for this chapter and then open the PowerPoint file *vt_ch06_presentation*. Leave the presentation open and open your browser.

2 Go to **screencast-o-matic.com** and click *login*. Create a new Screencast-O-Matic account using your email address, agree to the Terms of Service, and then click *Register*.

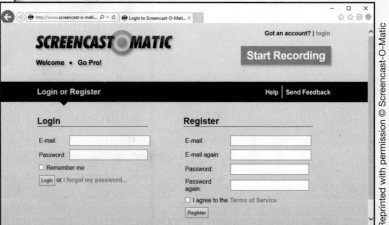

3 Click *Start Recording*. Click *Record Screencast*. If you are prompted to download the recorder launcher, click the link to use the old Recorded v1.0 instead. Follow any steps necessary to configure your system to run S-O-M. Minimize the browser window so that you can see the S-O-M frame over PowerPoint.

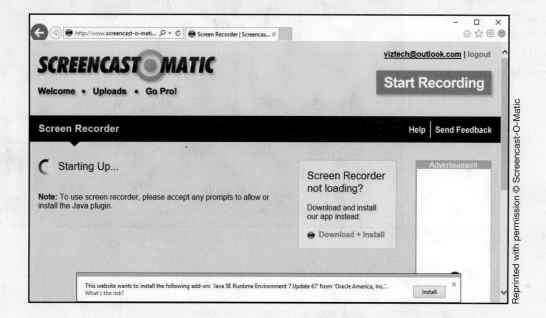

If you are unable to run the browser-based version of Screencast-o-matic because of browser security, you can download and install the SOM app instead.

4

On the S-O-M toolbar, click the size button and select *Fullscreen*. Start the PowerPoint slideshow. Click the red record button on the S-O-M toolbar to begin recording.

5

If you are using a microphone, you will record your voice-over for this presentation. If you do not have a mic, you can still read the voice-over prompts out loud to practice.

Read and record the following script, keeping in mind that the slides will automatically advance after 8 seconds:

Title slide (JMG Landscaping): We are JMG Landscaping, family owned and operated since 1985.

Slide 2: Beautiful patio furniture and gazebos to make your outdoor spaces as inviting as your indoor rooms.

Slide 3: Decks in wood or newer high-tech materials last a lifetime.

Slide 4: Cedar fences age with grace.

Slide 5: Hardscaping with stone and other materials create walls, gardens, pathways, and more.

6 Press [Alt] to pause the recording and then click *Done*. Click *Upload to Screencast-o-matic*.

7 Change the title to **Firstname Lastname VT Project** and in the description, type **JMG promo** Click Captions, click *Add New*. Click *Choose Text File*, navigate to the student data files, and upload the *vt_ch06_caption* file.

8 Click the Play button to preview your video in the S-O-M window. Take a screenshot of this page and paste it into your answer sheet. Click *Publish*. Click *Copy Link*, paste it into your answer sheet, and submit to your instructor as directed. Click *Done* and close your browser.

You have created a video that can be shared on popular video hosting websites, embedded in your own website, or shared via other media. Purchasing a premium subscription to the S-O-M service will enable you to create longer videos and includes editing features that will help you make your video more professional— for example, editing out any mistakes you made when reading the script.

Rawpixel/Fotolia

Technology on The Move

6 Compare Portable Media Players, Tablets, and Smartphones

Digital mobile devices enable you to take technology everywhere you go. These mobile devices range from small, inexpensive MP3 players to multifunction smartphones and tablets costing hundreds of dollars. Apple's release of the iPod in 2001 changed the way we listen to music forever, and smartphones and tablets are changing how we watch videos, share photos, and much more.

Digital Devices and Multimedia

Analog Vs. Digital

The terms *analog* and *digital* are used throughout this book. The difference is in the way the data is encoded and transmitted (Figure 6.22). Analog devices convert data signals into continuous electronic waves or pulses; analog devices, such as telephones and legacy CRT monitors, translate the electronic pulses back into audio and video signals. In **digital devices**, the audio or video data is represented by a series of 0s and 1s. Digital signals can carry more data and are less prone to interference than analog signals.

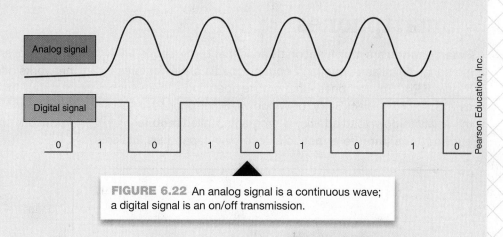

Analog signal

Digital signal

0 1 0 1 0 1 0 1 0

Pearson Education, Inc.

FIGURE 6.22 An analog signal is a continuous wave; a digital signal is an on/off transmission.

Portable Media Players

Today **MP3 players**, or **portable media players**, allow you to carry thousands of songs and podcasts, and perhaps photos, videos, and games, with you, so you can access them wherever you are. You can plug portable media players into your computer, your home stereo, and even your car. Tablets and smartphones have built-in media players, and many people choose not to have a separate media device at all. But there are times when you might find it convenient to have a media player—for example, on a plane, in the gym, or by the pool. Playing music and videos on your phone can use a lot of battery life, so using a separate device can help you stay connected longer.

The simplest MP3 players, like the iPod Shuffle and SanDisk Sansa Clip Zip, have flash memory capacities from less than 2 GB to 8 GB, start at under $20, and have limited features. Midrange flash media players, with capacities ranging from 8 GB to 32 GB, can hold up to two days' worth of music and may have more features, such as video and photo support. Because they use flash memory, they have no moving parts, which makes them ideal for high-impact activities like jogging (Figure 6.23). Higher-end media players, such as the iPod Touch and iPod classic, can hold many days' worth of music, video, and photos on flash memory up to 64 GB or hard drives up to 160 GB in size. These players also have other features like built-in games and Internet access.

Juice Images/Alamy

FIGURE 6.23 Portable media players are great for listening to music on the move.

Smartphones

Smartphones are multifunction devices that blend phone, PDA (personal digital assistant), and portable media player features (Figure 6.24). Smartphones run a mobile operating system such as iOS, Android, BlackBerry, or Windows. Smartphones have the ability to download additional programs, called **mobile applications (mobile apps)**, to extend their capabilities, making them convergence devices. The 4G—or fourth generation—cellular networks offered by major carriers have data transfer speeds that rival those of home connections. Such improved connection speeds enable you to watch TV, video chat, and play online games from your phone.

FIGURE 6.24 Mobile devices have the ability to download apps to extend their capabilities.

Boris Lehner/Alamy

Tablets

A **tablet** falls somewhere between a notebook computer and a smartphone. These handheld devices can be multifunctional devices or dedicated e-readers and cost from under $100 to nearly $1,000. Many tablets run a mobile operating system: iOS, Android, or Windows. Other tablets run a full version of Windows. Tablets have an LCD screen, a fairly long battery life, built-in Wi-Fi, and

possibly 3G or 4G cellular connectivity, making them great for travel. Tablets come with a variety of mobile apps preinstalled. Out of the box, you can surf the web, send and receive email, watch videos, and much more. The coolest part is the vast collection of apps that you can download to your device—many for free or very little cost. At the time of this writing, the iOS App Store (Figure 6.25) and the Google Play Store (Android) each had more than 1 million apps.

FIGURE 6.25 Apple's iOS App Store has more than 1 million apps.

IanDagnall Computing/Alamy

E-READERS

E-readers are a special class of tablets that are designed specifically for reading books, magazines, and other publications. Dedicated e-readers are lightweight, inexpensive devices that can hold thousands of books (Figure 6.26). Through a wireless connection, users can browse an electronic bookstore and download a new book in seconds. Some libraries also lend eBooks, and many textbooks come in eBook form that can be read on a computer or e-reader.

Some e-readers use e-ink, including the Kindle Paperwhite and Nook Simple Touch. E-ink technology creates a screen that is most like the experience of reading an actual book and extends battery life for as long as two months. The screen can easily be read, even in the brightest conditions—like on the beach—but as with a paper book, you need a book light to read in bed at night because e-ink readers are not backlit. Some e-ink readers have a built-in book light. Other e-readers have an LCD screen. An LCD screen is backlit, and the brightness can be adjusted so you can read in bed at night—but the glossy screen is subject to glare and is harder to read in a brightly lit location, and battery life is shortened.

FIGURE 6.26 With an e-reader, you can hold thousands of books in the palm of your hand.

Dmitry Lobanov/Fotolia

The two main e-reader tablets available are the Amazon Kindle and the Barnes & Noble Nook. Both come in several versions and cost anywhere from $79 to $379, depending on the features you choose. The Kindle Fire HD and the Nook HD are full-fledged tablet computers. As prices have come down, the lines have blurred between the devices, but for someone who really just wants a lightweight, inexpensive device to read and store a library collection, a dedicated e-reader is still a smart choice.

For many people, mobile devices have become a part of everyday life. Even the simplest cell phone is likely to have a built-in camera, the ability to send and receive text messages via Short Message Service (SMS) and multimedia text messages via Multimedia Messaging Service (MMS), and perhaps a game or two. Many people find that they are so plugged in that they can never really relax. Sometimes it makes sense to just turn off your mobile devices. Hey, leave a message. Beep.

FIND OUT MORE

There are lots of places on the web to find free eBooks. Some notable resources include the Google Books Library Project, Project Gutenberg, and the Online Computer Library Center. Choose one of these resources to research. When and why was it established? What types of books and other materials are included? Are there any partner institutions or projects? How can you access the materials? Where did you find this information?

Running Project

Use the Internet to research the newest smartphones. Select two models you would like to purchase. Create a table comparing their features. Include the following information: cost, carrier, contract length, camera type, media player, video, games, Internet, email, mobile operating system, and any other information you think is important. How do the devices stack up? Write up a summary explaining which one you would buy and why.

4 Things You Need To Know

- Portable media players can carry music, videos, photos, and games.
- Flash-based media players have small capacities—up to 32 GB.
- Hard drive media players have larger capacities—up to 160 GB.
- Multifunction devices like tablets and smartphones combine the features of different devices.

Key Terms

digital device

e-reader

mobile application (mobile app)

MP3 player

portable media player

smartphone

tablet

 Viz Check—In MyITLab, take a quick quiz covering Objectives 4–6.

features

zoom lens 2x

zoom lens 4x

smartphones

portable media devices

types

DIGITAL CAMERAS

point-and-shoot

compact system

DSLR

TRANSFERRING PHOTOS TO YOUR COMPUTER

memory cards

4 GB

tablets

e-readers

DIGITAL MOBILE DEVICES

1

2

USB & firewire

6

DIGITAL MEDIA DEVICES

5

cloud

wireless

YouTube

VIDEO

3

video camera

4

EDITING, PRINTING AND SHARING PHOTOS

editing

screen capture

webcam

AUDIO

file types .mp3 .acc

speech

media & software

recognition

online

Learn It Online

- Visit **pearsonhighered.com/viztech** for student data files

- Find simulations, VizClips, and additional study materials in MyITLab

- Be sure to check out the **Tech Bytes** weekly news feed for current topics to review and discuss

Objectives Recap

1. Explain the Features of Digital Cameras
2. Compare Methods for Transferring Images from a Digital Camera
3. Identify Several Ways to Edit and Print Photos
4. Recognize Important Audio File Types
5. Describe Several Ways to Create Videos
6. Compare Portable Media Players, Tablets, and Smartphones

Key Terms

AAC (advanced audio coding) 299
autofocus 278
burst mode 279
caption 304
codec 299
compact system camera (CSC) 280
Creative Commons (CC) licensing 290
digital device 315
digital rights management (DRM) 300
digital single-lens reflex (DSLR) camera 279
e-reader 317
e-waste 303
fixed-focus 278
focal length 278
geotagging 289
image stabilization 279
iOS device 285
lossless compression 288
lossy compression 288

machinima 307
mobile application (mobile app) 316
MP3 (MPEG-1 Audio Layer 3) 299
MP3 player 314
multimedia 275
PictBridge 289
podcast 300
point-and-shoot camera 279
portable media player 315
resolution 277
screen capture 307
shutter lag 279
smartphone 316
speech recognition 302
streaming 305
tablet 316
tagging 283
telephoto lens 278
webcam 305
webcasting 305
wide-angle lens 278
zoom 278

Summary

1. **Explain the Features of Digital Cameras**

The main types of digital cameras are: point-and-shoot, compact system, and DSLR. Each type is progressively more expensive and complex. Resolution is the measure of pixels in an image, and higher-resolution cameras can take higher-quality pictures. Storage includes internal camera storage as well as flash memory cards. Zoom and lenses are important features that can make an object appear closer or farther away.

2. **Compare Methods for Transferring Images from a Digital Camera**

Flash memory cards can be removed from a camera and plugged directly into a card reader in a computer or a kiosk in a store. Most cameras can also be connected to a computer via USB or FireWire cable. Some cameras include Wi-Fi or can use a Wi-Fi-enabled SD card. The images can be copied to a disc, the cloud, or a computer or made into prints.

3. **Identify Several Ways to Edit and Print Photos**

At home, you can print photos by first transferring the images to a computer or by directly connecting a printer and camera. In-store kiosks can read most memory card types or access images on the Internet, and online services allow you to upload images to be printed that can be mailed home or picked up at a local retailer.

4. **Recognize Important Audio File Types**

Codecs are compression algorithms that reduce the size of digital media files. The most common audio codecs include MP3, which is the most common format for music files, and AAC, which is primarily used by Apple iTunes. Another common audio file is a MIDI file, which is often used for synthesized music in video games.

5. **Describe Several Ways to Create Videos**

Screen capture software is used to create a video of what is happening on a computer screen, but video cameras are needed to record action away from the screen. You can use a webcam to stream a live feed or to have a real-time video conference.

6. **Compare Portable Media Players, Tablets, and Smartphones**

Portable media players are small, handheld devices that play music, video, and photos and may also have games, Internet access, and other features. Tablet devices are multifunction devices that fall somewhere between notebook computers and smartphones and include built-in apps as well as the ability to download others. Smartphones are cell phones with PDA functions and portable media players built in. Smartphones can extend their capabilities with mobile apps and are true convergence devices.

Multiple Choice

Answer the multiple-choice questions below for more practice with key terms and concepts from this chapter.

1. What is the measure of the number of pixels in an image?
   a. Codec
   b. PictBridge
   c. Resolution
   d. Zoom

2. What type of cameras have a lens with a preset focal length that focuses well on objects within a specific distance?
   a. Autofocusing
   b. Fixed-focus
   c. Macro
   d. Optical zoom

3. Which type of lens would be best for shooting a beach scene?
   a. Digital zoom
   b. Macro
   c. Telephoto
   d. Wide-angle

4. What type of camera has the most options and give you the most control?
   a. Compact system camera (CSC)
   b. Digital single-lens reflex (DSLR)
   c. Point-and-shoot
   d. Smartphone

5. What enables a computer and camera to talk to each other?
   a. Device drivers
   b. Memory cards
   c. PictBridge
   d. Tagging

6. Which file format results in the smallest file size?
   a. BMP
   b. JPG
   c. RAW
   d. TIF

7. Which codec is the default audio file type used by Apple iTunes?
   a. AAC
   b. MIDI
   c. MP3
   d. WMA

8. Which tool enables you to create a video of what happens on your computer screen?
   a. Machinima
   b. Screen capture software
   c. Streaming
   d. Webcam

9. Why might you carry a tablet instead of a notebook?
   a. Longer battery life
   b. To listen to music
   c. To take pictures
   d. All of the above

10. What e-reader technology makes a screen that is easy to read and extends battery life?
    a. Backlight
    b. E-ink
    c. HD
    d. LCD

True or False

Answer the true–false questions below for more practice with key terms and concepts from this chapter.

_____ 1. Multimedia is the integration of text, graphics, video, animation, and sound.

_____ 2. Resolution is the distance at which subjects in front of the lens are in sharp focus.

_____ 3. Autofocus cameras automatically adjust the focal length by using a small motor to move the lens in or out.

_____ 4. Zoom can be either optical or digital, but not both.

_____ 5. Point-and-shoot cameras use interchangeable lenses and can cost thousands of dollars.

_____ 6. Tagging images or files with keywords makes it easier to organize and search for them.

_____ 7. Once an image is compressed using a lossless compression it can't be fully restored to the original format.

_____ 8. Geotagging allows you to add location information to your digital photos.

_____ 9. The AAC codec creates files that are higher quality than MP3 files.

_____10. A podcast is a prerecorded radio- and TV-like show that you can download and listen to or watch any time.

Fill in the Blank

Fill in the blanks using the words from the key terms.

1. _____ is the measure of the number of pixels in an image and is expressed in megapixels.

2. The _____ is the distance at which subjects in front of the lens are in sharp focus.

3. _____ is a feature found on some digital cameras that enables you to take several pictures in quick succession by holding down the shutter button.

4. _____ use a mirror that enables you to see the image you're about to shoot through a view finder.

5. An iPad, iPhone, or iPod is an example of a(n) _____.

6. An industry standard that enables a camera to connect directly to a printer is _____.

7. You can change copyright terms on your work by applying _____.

8. _____ is a technology that is applied to digital media files, such as music, eBooks, and videos, to impose restrictions on the use of these files.

9. Broadcasting on the web, or _____, can be used to stream a live performance or lecture.

10. A(n) _____ can be downloaded to extend the functionality of a mobile device.

Running Project . . .

. . . The Finish Line

In this chapter you researched a number of digital devices. Think about the career you are planning to pursue. What is one such device that would be important in your career? Using your answers to the previous sections of the Running Project, write a report describing your selections and responding to the questions raised. Save your file as **lastname_firstname_ch06_project** and submit it to your instructor as directed.

Do It Yourself 1

Purchasing a smartphone can be a difficult task, as there are many different models to choose from. In this exercise, you will research several smartphones and determine which is right for you. For this exercise, the cellular provider should not be a factor that you consider. From your student data files, open the file *vt_ch06_DIY1_answersheet* and save the file as **lastname_firstname_ch06_DIY1_answersheet**

Use the Internet to research three smartphones. Complete the following chart. Write up a summary of your findings. Which device is the best choice for you and why? If you had more money, would your choice change? Save your file and submit your work as directed by your instructor.

	Phone 1	Phone 2	Phone 3	Comments
Smartphone model				
Price				
Mobile operating system				
Wireless connectivity				
Memory capacity				
Expandability				
Included apps				
Additional app availability				
Special features				
Website where you found your information				

Do It Yourself 2

In this activity, you will use iTunes to locate podcasts. From your student data files, open the file *vt_ch06_DIY2_answersheet* and save the file as **lastname_firstname_ch06_DIY2_answersheet**

1. Open iTunes. Click *Go to the iTunes Store*. (*Note*: Your college may have disabled the iTunes store on your campus.) On the menu bar, click the *Podcasts* arrow. List three categories where you would you find shows to help you with this course.

2. Click the *Technology* link. Scroll down to What's Hot and then click *See All*. Browse through some of the featured shows. Select one that interests you and watch it. What show did you pick and why? Is there a Subscribe button on the show page? If so, what options are listed for subscribing to the show? Take a screenshot to capture the page and paste it into your answer sheet. Type your answers and include the screenshot. Save the file and submit your work as directed by your instructor.

File Management

Files stored on your computer have properties attached to them that make searching for and organizing files easier. In this exercise, you will examine and modify the properties of an image file. From your student data files, open the file *vt_ch06_FM_answersheet* and save the file as **lastname_firstname_ch06_FM_answersheet**

1. Use File Explorer to locate the data files for this chapter. Open the image file *vt_ch06_tags* and save a copy to the folder where you save your work for this class as **lastname_firstname_ch06_tags**

2. In File Explorer, navigate to the folder where you save your work for this class. Select, but do not open, the file *lastname_firstname_ch06_tags*. Click the *View* tab, and then, if necessary, click the *Details* pane. Click *Add a tag* in the Details pane and type **logo** and then click *Save*. Take a screenshot of this window and paste it into your answer sheet.

3. On the Home tab of the ribbon, in the Open group, click *Properties*. Click the *Details* tab and compare the properties visible to those in the Details pane of File Explorer. Point to each property in the dialog box. Which properties can you change?

4. Add your name as the author and **VT Chapter 6** as the title. Take a screenshot and paste it into your answer sheet. Save your image file and answer sheet and submit both as directed by your instructor.

Critical Thinking

You are excited about the idea of using the cloud to stream your entertainment, but before you begin, you need to do some homework to decide what the best option is for you. From your student data files, open the file *vt_ch06_CT_answersheet* and save the file as **lastname_firstname_ch06_CT_answersheet**

Use the Internet to research three video-streaming services, such as Netflix, Amazon Instant Video, M-GO, VuDu, or Hulu Plus. If you are a TV subscriber, be sure to include your TV provider as one of the services to compare. What are the basic features of each? Do they require any special hardware or software to be installed? What is the difference between their free, ad-supported service and premium paid subscription? Is it worth the price? Examine your own computer. Does it have all of the hardware you will need? If not, what will you need to purchase? What about your mobile devices?

Write up a summary that includes the answers to these questions. Save the file and submit your assignment as directed by your instructor.

Ethical Dilemma

Anna received some music CDs of her favorite band for her birthday. She likes to listen to her music on her smartphone, so she ripped the music to her computer and transferred the songs to her phone. Because she no longer needs the CDs to listen to her music, her roommate Monica suggested that she sell them on eBay. This would free up some space in their cramped apartment and generate some much needed cash. From your student data files, open the file *vt_ch06_ethics_answersheet* and save the file as **lastname_firstname_ch06_ethics_answersheet**

Anna wonders if this is ok. Is it ethical to sell the CDs and still keep the music? Is it legal? Because Anna and Monica share a computer, is it ok for both of them to transfer the music files to their smartphones? Write up a one-page summary that includes the answers to the questions above. Save the file and submit it as directed by your instructor.

On the Web

Webcams have become common tools for scientists to use to monitor animals, weather conditions, and even volcanoes. From your student data files, open the file *vt_ch06_web_answersheet* and save the file as **lastname_firstname_ch06_web_answersheet**

Search the web for a webcam that is streaming a live feed of a place you would like to visit. Choose a webcam that is sponsored by a reputable organization. Visit the site, take a screenshot of the webcam feed, and paste it into your answer sheet. Are there any other webcam feeds on the same site? What is the address of the webcam you chose? What location is being observed? What organization sponsors the webcam? How did you locate it?

Type your answers, save the file, and submit your file as directed by your instructor.

Collaboration

In this project you will create your own video podcast. You'll need a video camera and video editing software such as Windows Movie Maker or iMovie to complete this project.

Instructors: Divide the class into small groups of two to four students. The topic for each group is a smartphone or tablet that is used by a member of the group.

The Project: As a team, prepare a video podcast that includes an explanation of your chosen device, favorite features, and a demonstration of how to send and receive email using the device. Write a script for a two- to five-minute presentation. Choose a format that best suits your group. For example, it can be a news magazine, talk show, game show, or any other format you'd like to use. Use at least three references. Use Google Drive or Microsoft Office to prepare the presentation and provide documentation that all team members have contributed to the project.

Outcome: Prepare a video podcast on your assigned topic. Submit a copy of the script. Save the file as **teamname_ch06_collab** and be sure to include the name of your podcast and a listing of all team members on the first page. The podcast will be two to five minutes in length and uploaded to YouTube. It requires participation from everyone in the group. Save the final project as **teamname_ch06_podcast** and submit it as directed by your instructor.

Application Project

Office 2016 Application Projects

Excel 2016: Worldwide Digital Camera Sales

Project Description: *In this project, you will analyze the global digital camera sales from 2007 to 2013. You will format cells and use a function, and you will create and format a column and a pie chart. If necessary, download the student data files from* **pearsonhighered.com/viztech**.

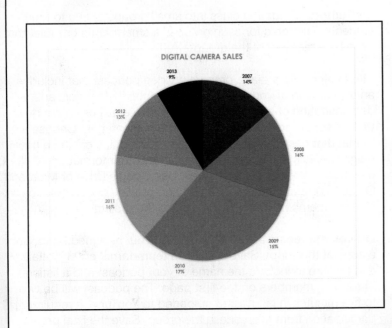

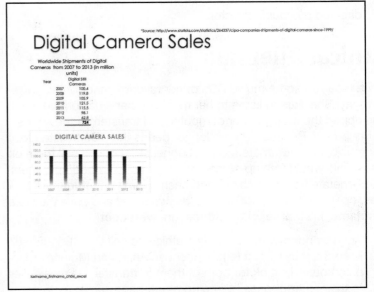

Step	Instructions
1	Start Excel. From your student data files, open the Excel file *vt_ch06_excel* Save the workbook as **lastname_firstname_ch06_excel**
2	Apply the Slice theme to the workbook.
3	Merge and center the text in cell A7 over columns A:C. Increase the font size to 14 pt. Wrap text, center and middle align the text, and change the row height to 65.
4	Select the range A8:C8 and set the text to wrap in the cells. Center and middle align the text in the selected range.
5	In cell B16, use the SUM function to calculate the digital still camera sales from 2007 to 2013.
6	Change the cell style of the B16 to Comma [0] and Total. Apply the Comma cell style to the range B9:B15. Decrease the decimals displayed to 1.
7	Select the range A8:B15 and insert the Recommended Clustered Column chart. Move the chart so that its upper left corner aligns with the upper left corner of cell A18.
8	Format the column chart with Chart Style 10. Change the chart title to **Digital Camera Sales**
9	Select the range A8:B15 and insert the Recommended Pie chart. Move the chart to a new sheet named **Sales Chart**
10	Change the layout of the pie chart to Layout 1. Change the title to **Digital Camera Sales** Format the chart with the chart Style 9.
11	On the 2007–2013 sheet, insert the text **Digital Camera Sales** as WordArt using the Fill – Dark Blue, Accent 1, Shadow. Move the WordArt so that its upper left corner aligns with the upper left corner of cell A1.
12	Change the scaling of the 2007–2013 worksheet so the width will fit to one page. Center the 2007–2013 worksheet horizontally on the page. Change the orientation to Landscape.
13	Ensure that the worksheets are correctly named and placed in the following order in the workbook: Sales Chart, 2007–2013. Save the workbook and close Excel. Submit the workbook as directed.

Application Project

Office 2016 Application Projects

Word 2016: Making the Most of Your Cellphone Camera

Project Description: *You have been asked to write an article on digital cameras. You will need to change alignment, line and paragraph spacing, margins, and lists and edit the header and footer. You will also find and replace text, create and modify a footnote, and use the Format Painter. If necessary, download the student data files from* **pearsonhighered.com/viztech.**

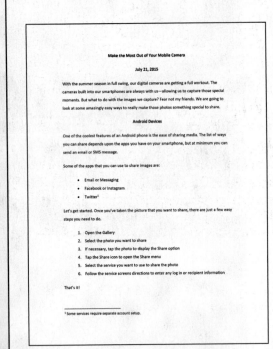

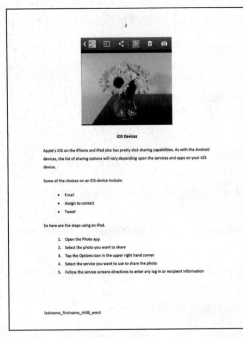

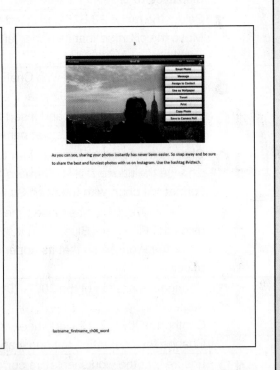

Step	Instructions
1	Start Word. From your student data files, open the Word file *vt_ch06_word*. Save the file as **lastname_firstname_ch06_word**
2	Change the left and right margins of the document to 1.25". Change the line spacing of the entire document to 1.5 lines. Change the paragraph spacing (before and after) of the entire document to Auto.
3	Center the heading *Android Devices*. Using the Format Painter, apply the formatting from the heading *Android Devices* to the heading *iOS Devices*.
4	Use the Find and Replace dialog box to search for and replace all instances of the word *cellphone* with **smartphone** There should be two replacements.
5	In the Android Devices section, format the list beginning *Email* and ending *Twitter* as a bulleted list using solid round bullets. Increase the left indent of the bulleted list to 0.5".
6	In the Android Devices section, format the list beginning *Open the Gallery* and ending *Follow the service screens* as a numbered list using the 1., 2., 3. format. Increase the left indent of the numbered list to 0.5".
7	In the iOS Devices section, format the list beginning *Email* and ending *Tweet* as a bulleted list using solid round bullets. Increase the left indent of the bulleted list to 0.5".
8	In the iOS Devices section, format the list beginning *Open the Photo app* and ending *Follow the service screens* as a numbered list using the 1., 2., 3. format. Increase the left indent of the numbered list to 0.5".
9	In the document header, add a page number using the Plain Number 2 style at the Top of Page. In the footer, add the FileName field using the default format. Ensure the header and footer are not displayed on the first page.
10	In the Android Devices section, in the bulleted list, insert a footnote immediately following the text *Twitter* reading **Some services require separate account setup.** (Include the period).
11	Use the Spelling and Grammar dialog box to correct the misspelling of the word *lsit* to *list*. Ignore all other spelling and grammar suggestions.
12	Place the insertion point after the last line of the Android Devices section (That's it!). Press Enter and insert the picture *vt_ch06_image1*. Center align the image and change the image height to 3 inches.
13	Place the insertion point at the beginning of the last paragraph ("As you can see …"). Press Enter, move the insertion point up to the new blank line, and insert the picture *vt_ch06_image2*. Center align the image and change the image height to 3 inches.
14	Save the file and close Word. Submit the document as directed.

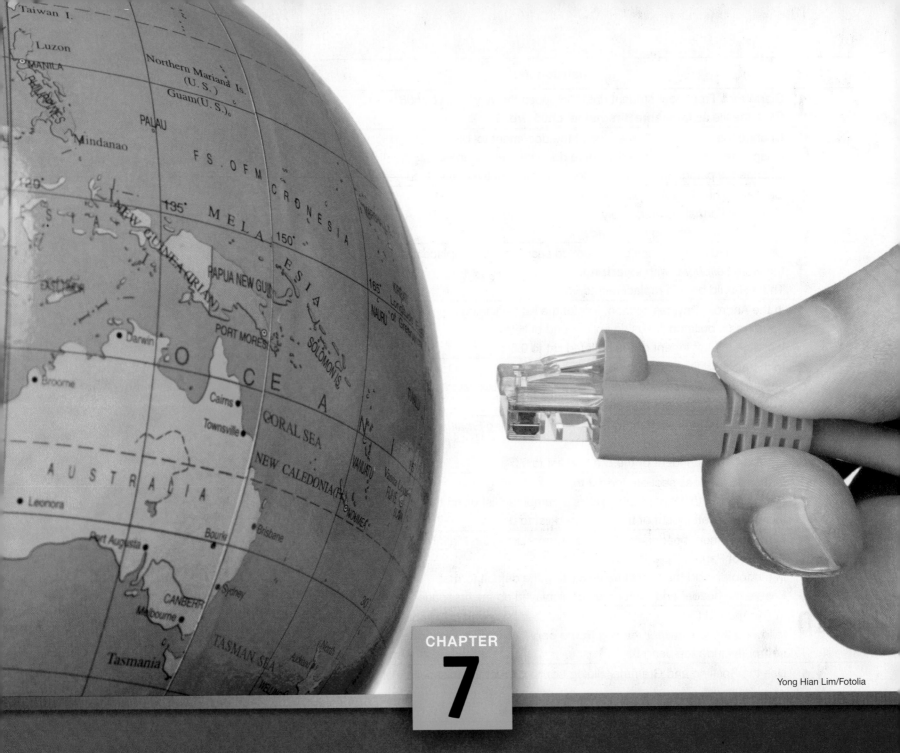
Yong Hian Lim/Fotolia

The Internet

In This Chapter

VIZ INTRO

The Internet is such an integral part of our everyday lives that you may already know a lot about it. But there's so much to know that most people only scratch the surface. After reading this chapter you'll understand the wide variety of tools and information at your fingertips and why you need to be fluent in the tools and language of the Internet in order to be an educated consumer, a better student, and a valuable employee.

Objectives

1 Recognize the Importance of the Internet

2 Compare Types of Internet Connections

3 Compare Popular Web Browsers

4 Demonstrate How to Navigate the Web

5 Discuss How to Evaluate the Credibility of Information Found on the Web

Running Project

In this chapter, you'll learn about the Internet. Look for project instructions as you complete each article. For most articles, there's a series of questions for you to research. At the conclusion of the chapter, you'll submit your responses to the questions raised.

BillionPhotos.com/Fotolia

Internet Timeline

1

Recognize the Importance of the Internet

There is an urban myth that Al Gore invented the Internet. Al Gore didn't invent the Internet, but early on, he recognized its potential and, as a congressman and vice president, promoted its development through legislation. In 2005, he received a Webby Lifetime Achievement Award for his contributions (webbyawards.com). He was one of the first politicians to see the potential of the Internet, but it actually started much earlier.

How it All Got Started

In 1957, the Soviet Union launched the first space satellite, *Sputnik*. The United States and the Soviet Union were, at the time, engaged in a political conflict—called the Cold War—and the launch of *Sputnik*

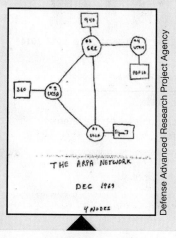

Defense Advanced Research Project Agency

FIGURE 7.1 This original drawing of ARPANET shows the first four sites at UCLA, SRI, UCSB, and the University of Utah.

led to fears that the United States was falling behind in the technology race. In 1958, President Eisenhower created the Advanced Research Projects Agency (ARPA) to jumpstart U.S. technology for the military. One of ARPA's early projects was to create a "Galactic Network" that would connect smaller networks around the world.

The Internet started as a U.S. Department of Defense ARPA project in the 1960s to design a communications system that had multiple pathways through which information could travel so that losing one part of the system (for example, in a nuclear strike) wouldn't cripple the whole thing. It took about 10 years to develop the technology. The original system, called **ARPANET**, connected four sites (Figure 7.1): The University of California—Los Angeles (UCLA), the Stanford Research Institute (SRI), the University of California—Santa Barbara (UCSB), and the University of Utah.

In 1979, the National Science Foundation (NSF) created CSNET—the Computer Science Network—to connect the computer science departments at universities using the ARPANET technology. In the mid-1980s, the NSF created NSFNET, giving other academic disciplines access to supercomputing centers and connecting smaller networks together. By the late 1980s, NSFNET was the primary **Internet backbone**—the high-speed connection between networks. In 1995, NSF decommissioned the NSF backbone, the Internet backbone was privatized, and the first five large **Network Access Points (NAPs)** that made up the new backbone were established in Chicago, New Jersey, San Francisco, San Jose, and Washington, D.C. Today, the backbone of the Internet is composed of numerous **Internet Exchange Points** around the world.

World Wide Web

Many people use the terms *Internet* and *World Wide Web* interchangeably, but they are two different things. The **Internet**, or just *net*, is the physical entity—a network of computer networks. The **World Wide Web**, or just *web*, is just one way that information moves on the Internet. Email, instant messaging, file sharing, and making calls via **VoIP (Voice over IP)** are other ways that you might use the Internet.

In 1991, Tim Berners-Lee and CERN (European Organization for Nuclear

Research) released the hypertext system known as the World Wide Web. The web is made up of **hypertext**, which is text that contains links to other text or objects such as images. Hypertext enables you to navigate through pieces of information by clicking the links, or **hyperlinks**, that connect them. The milestone of having a million Internet nodes—networks or web servers—was reached in 1992, and commercial sites, such as Pizza Hut, began to appear. The first White House website was launched in 1994.

In 1993, a group of graduate students led by Marc Andreessen released the Mosaic point-and-click graphical browser for the web, which later became Netscape Navigator—the dominant web browser in the 1990s. These events helped create a user-friendly Internet. A couple years later, Microsoft released Windows 95 and Internet Explorer, which made personal computers easier to use and more popular. Around that time, existing online service companies such as AOL and CompuServe began offering Internet access to subscribers. As personal computers dropped in price and became more powerful, the Internet grew at an incredible rate, and it had almost 3 billion users by 2014. Figure 7.2 shows the global growth of Internet use from 2005 to 2014. Over the past several years, the widespread use of mobile devices such as tablets and smartphones has put Internet access in the hands of even more people.

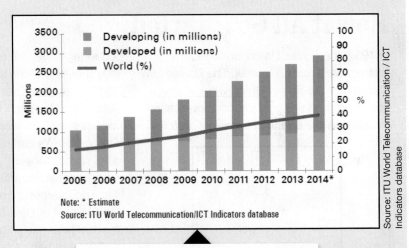

Note: * Estimate
Source: ITU World Telecommunication/ICT Indicators database

Source: ITU World Telecommunication / ICT Indicators database

FIGURE 7.2 Individuals Using the Internet per 100 Inhabitants, 2005–2014

Internet2

The original uses of the Internet—research and education—have been overtaken by commercial and social uses. Even as bandwidth and the Internet infrastructure have increased, educational and research institutions have been unable to access the speed and resources they need, and so the Internet2 project was born. **Internet2** is a second Internet, designed for education, research, and collaboration, very much like the original Internet—only faster. In 1995, when NSFNET was decommissioned, a small part of it was retained just for research. Called the Very High Speed Backbone Network Service (vBNS), it later evolved into the Internet2 project. Although the Internet is composed of a mix of older telephone cables and newer fiber optics, the Internet2 backbone is all fiber. The data travels much faster and is less prone to corruption.

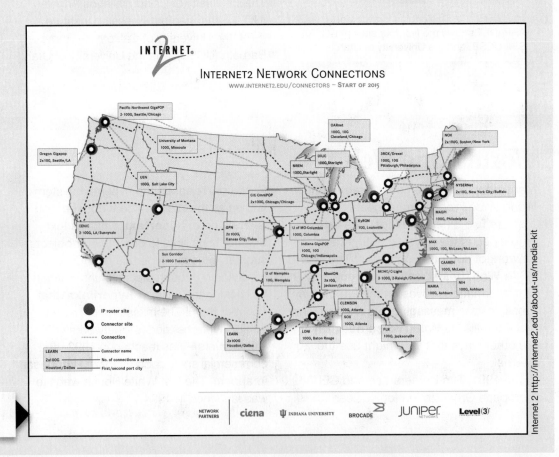

Internet 2 http://internet2.edu/about-us/media-kit

FIGURE 7.3 Institutions around the country are connected to Internet2.

Membership in Internet2 is limited to colleges, universities, other educational institutions, museums and art galleries, libraries, hospitals, and other organizations that work with them. It's a pretty small group, and that's one of the reasons it's so fast. Collaboration, streaming video, and web conferencing are just some of the applications that benefit from the faster speed. Figure 7.3 shows the Internet2 Connectors map. A connector site provides an Internet2 connection and other network services to regional participant institutions.

From its inception, the Internet was designed to be a place for collaboration and information sharing. Today, it's an integral part of education, business, and communication. Even if you don't spend a lot of time surfing the web, it's hard to deny the impact it has on your life.

Running Project

Does your school participate in the Internet2 project? Ask your librarian or instructor. If yes, what features does your school use? Where is your Internet2 connector? If your college does not use Internet2, find out why not.

4 Things You Need To Know

- ARPANET was the original Internet.
- The Internet is the physical network; the web is just one way data moves on the Internet.
- Hypertext is used to navigate the World Wide Web by using hyperlinks.
- Internet2 is a second Internet, designed for education, research, and collaboration.

Key Terms

ARPANET

hyperlink

hypertext

Internet

Internet backbone

Internet Exchange Point

Internet2

Network Access Point (NAP)

VoIP (Voice over IP)

World Wide Web

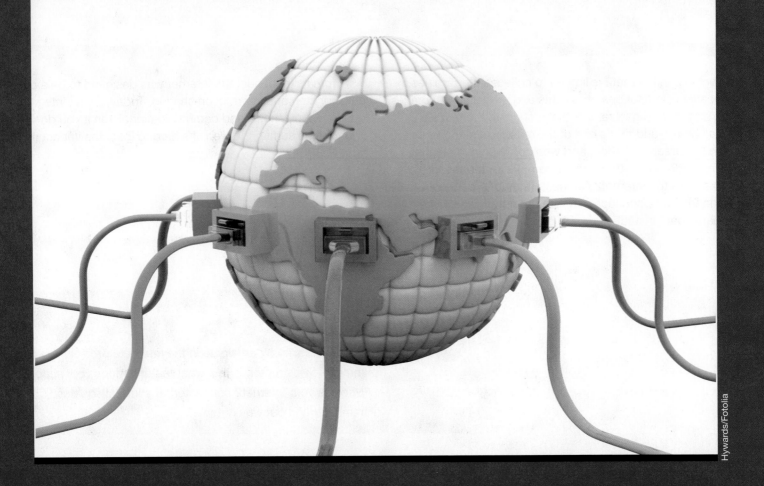

Get Connected

Compare Types of Internet Connections

There are many different ways to get on the Internet. **Internet service providers (ISPs)** are companies that offer Internet access. The options available to you depend on where you live and how much you have to spend.

The
Internet

How Do You Get Connected?

A good place to find local ISPs is by searching the web. If you don't have access at home, most schools and libraries offer free access. Search for a list of ISPs that offer service in your area; there are many websites that compare services and prices for you. Before you begin your search, read the rest of this article to learn about the questions you should ask when comparing packages.

Ask yourself what you need, based on how you use the Internet. Do you just check email and look up recipes? If so, a slower connection might work for you. If you work from home, play games, share photos, or watch videos, you'll need a faster connection. **Bandwidth** is the data transfer rate of a network and is measured in kilobits per second (Kbps), megabits per second (Mbps), or gigabits per second (Gbps). Advertised rates are maximum download speeds, but the actual rate can fluctuate and may often be much lower. Most types of Internet access deliver lower upload speeds. Table 7.1 compares the bandwidths of various types of Internet connections.

TABLE 7.1 Comparing Bandwidth of Internet Connections

Type	Residential Download Speeds	Business-Class Speeds
Dial-up	56 Kbps	
DSL	384 Kbps to 20 Mbps	
Cable	1 Mbps to 150 Mbps	400 Mbps
Fiber	15 Mbps to 1 Gbps	1 Gbps
Satellite	512 Kbps to 15 Mbps	

Pearson Education, Inc.

DIAL-UP

The least expensive type of connection is usually **dial-up**. With a dial-up connection, you use your regular phone lines to connect to the Internet. Plans range from about $10 to $30 per month. This might be a good back-up plan to have in case your normal connection becomes unavailable. You might set this up on your notebook for when you travel, in case there's no other access where you are. For some people, a dial-up connection may be the only option available. Dial-up maxes out at 56 Kbps, and it can be very slow, especially if you're trying to download a file or watch a video. Another drawback is that the connection ties up your phone line while you're online. Aging phone lines were not designed to carry data, so they do a poor job of it.

Blackday/Fotolia

BROADBAND

To get more speed than with dial-up, you have several options: cable, DSL, fiber-optic, and wireless technologies. The Federal Communications Commission (FCC) defines **broadband** as anything over 10 Mbps, and in 2015 raised its benchmarks for measuring advanced broadband to 25 Mbps. Availability, speed, and costs vary depending on where you live. You'll have to do some research to get the best price and service. You can use the National Broadband Map at **broadbandmap.gov** to find out what types of broadband options are available where you live (Figure 7.4).

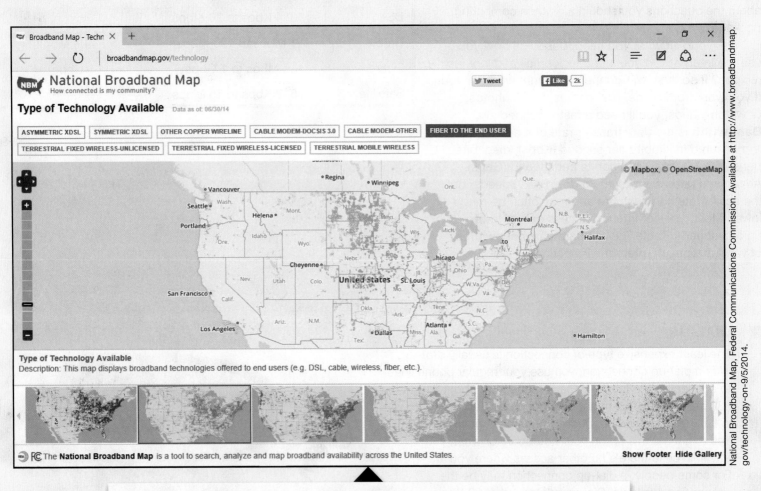

FIGURE 7.4 This version of the National Broadband Map shows the availability of DSL technologies.

Cable Internet access is offered by your cable TV provider and uses the same wires to carry both signals. Some cable companies also offer digital phone service. This requires older cable systems to be upgraded, so it's not available everywhere. Residential cable speeds range from 1–150 Mbps but are typically 16–50 Mbps. Business-class connections can reach 400 Mbps. One drawback to using cable Internet access is that you share the cable, and therefore bandwidth, with your neighbors. This could potentially negatively impact your Internet speed if many neighbors are online at the same time.

DSL (digital subscriber line) technologies use telephone lines to carry digital signals. Unlike your normal phone line that's designed to carry analog signals (sound), DSL lines are designed to carry digital signals and are much faster than ordinary telephone lines. DSL averages speeds of 384 Kbps to 20 Mbps, which is slower than cable; however, it's generally less expensive. One of the biggest problems with DSL is its distance limitations. You must be within 3 miles of the DSL service provider's facilities. The further away you are, the slower your connection will be. Aging phone lines can also significantly slow down DSL.

Fiber-to-the-home (FTTH), also known as fiber-to-the-premises, is the fastest of the broadband alternatives, with top speeds of 300–500 Mbps—although most companies offer rates only of up to 150 Mbps. FTTH can carry Internet, TV, and phone calls to your home over fiber-optic cable and is available in limited areas—those where the fiber-optic cable has been installed. In the United States, the primary FTTH service is Verizon **FiOS (Fiber Optic Service)**. Google Fiber, which is currently available in limited markets, offers speeds of 1 Gbps (1,000 Mbps). Unlike cable and DSL lines, which many people already have, FTTH requires a contractor to lay a fiber-optic conduit directly to the home, which can be costly and can involve digging up your lawn.

WIRELESS

What if you live in a rural or remote area without cable, DSL, or fiber access? What about if you're on the road? There are several wireless alternatives available, too. These options include mobile cellular access, Wi-Fi, and satellite.

Mobile Internet access enables you to connect to the Internet using the cellular network standards 3G (third generation) and 4G (fourth generation). 4G is faster and includes **WiMAX Mobile Internet** and **LTE (Long-Term Evolution)** technologies. The signals are transmitted by a series of cellular towers; thus, coverage can be spotty in some places (Figure 7.5). Coverage maps that are available on the providers' websites allow you to verify whether coverage exists where you need it before you make a commitment.

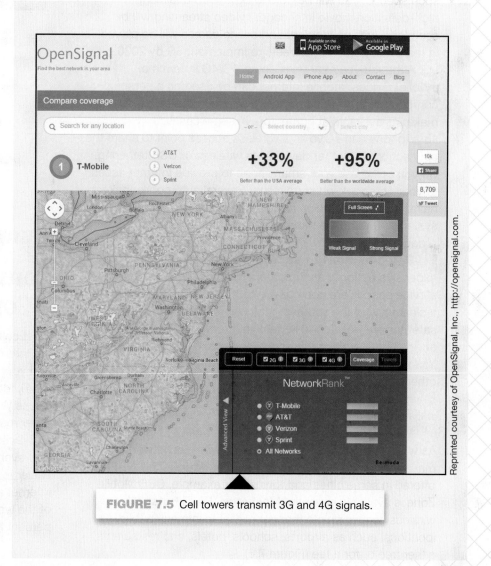

Reprinted courtesy of OpenSignal, Inc., http://opensignal.com.

FIGURE 7.5 Cell towers transmit 3G and 4G signals.

Oleksii Akhrimenko/Fotolia

Samsung Electronics and other companies are developing mobile technologies for fifth-generation networks that will provide data transmission up to several hundred times faster than the current 4G technology. The new 5G networks will transmit data up to 1 Gbps, which exceeds the wired broadband speeds currently available to most consumers. The 5G networks will transmit large amounts of data over long distances, using a wide band of frequencies. With such speeds, you will be able to download a full-length high-definition movie in seconds; video streaming will be seamless, with no lagging; and online games will be played in real time. Samsung expects to implement 5G by 2020.

Although you may think about 3G/4G in terms of mobile devices, mobile Internet can be used on a personal computer with a special network adapter. Special modems make 4G available at home, too. In some cases, a smartphone can serve as a wireless access point to share the connection with other devices via wireless or USB tethering. So you could use your smartphone to provide Internet access to your notebook when traveling. Several automobile makers have incorporated 4G into their entertainment and navigation systems. Top mobile Internet speeds are considered broadband and rival wired broadband service.

Satellite Internet access is a more global and more expensive option than the others mentioned so far. Satellite service speeds are comparable to those of DSL. You need a clear view of the southern sky, where the communication satellites are positioned in geosynchronous orbit 22,000 miles above Earth, and weather conditions can affect your service. You would probably consider satellite only if there were no other options available where you live. In the next few years, several new satellites are scheduled to be launched, which will increase the availability and speed of satellite Internet.

Wi-Fi uses radio waves to provide wireless high-speed network connections. It is the type of wireless networking you may have set up in your home or office. **Municipal Wi-Fi** is offered in some cities and towns. For example, CBS Mobile Zone is available in central Manhattan. Wi-Fi **hotspots** are wireless access points that are available in many public locations, such as airports, schools, hotels, and restaurants, either free or for a fee (Figure 7.6).

Labalajadia/Fotolia

FIGURE 7.6 You can find Wi-Fi hotspots in many public spaces.

Connecting Without a Computer

Most cell phones offer at least a limited ability to connect to the Internet. Smartphones, tablets, video game consoles, and your media player may be able to connect via cellular or Wi-Fi, too. Some e-readers include free 3G Internet access or use Wi-Fi to shop for and download books and to access other resources. These devices generally have small screens and limited keyboards, which can make using them difficult. However, mobile devices are becoming more powerful and easier to use, and many people rely on them as their primary Internet access devices. Although only about 25 percent of the world's population has personal computers, over 60 percent has cell phones.

Satellite phones connect to satellites instead of cellular towers, making them useful in places where cell service is lacking, such as remote locations. They need a clear view of the sky and don't work well indoors. Satellite phones and satellite phone services are very expensive.

According to the Pew Research Center, in 2015, 85 percent of adults in the United States were Internet users, and 70 percent of adults had home broadband access. For those who don't have broadband at home, cost and inaccessibility are often cited as the reasons. The 2015 Broadband Progress Report concluded that 17 percent of the U.S. population lack access to advanced broadband—broadband exceeding 25 Mbps download service. Of course, some people just aren't interested—they don't find any need to have Internet access at home. But for the rest of us, not having a good Internet connection just isn't an option.

FIND OUT MORE

The Open Internet Transparency Rule is an ambitious plan to ensure that all Americans have access to fast, affordable Internet access. Go to fcc.gov to find out why the U.S. government considers this so important. Explain the Open Internet Transparency Rule.

Federal Communications Commission

Running Project

Use the Internet to research the current state of satellite Internet access. Have the newest satellites been deployed? What services and speeds are available, and what do they cost? Is satellite Internet access a viable option where you live?

3 Things You Need To Know

- Dial-up is the slowest type of Internet access.
- Broadband Internet access includes cable, DSL, FTTH, satellite, and cellular 3G/4G.
- The type of Internet access you choose largely depends on where you live.

Key Terms

bandwidth

broadband

cable Internet access

dial-up

DSL (digital subscriber line)

fiber-to-the-home (FTTH)

FiOS (Fiber Optic Service)

hotspot

Internet service provider (ISP)

LTE (Long-Term Evolution)

municipal Wi-Fi

satellite Internet access

Wi-Fi

WiMAX Mobile Internet

Surf's Up

Objective 3

Compare Popular Web Browsers

Some people use the Internet strictly for email, others for schoolwork, and still others for watching videos. Some folks visit specific websites regularly, while others like to surf and explore. Regardless of how you use the web, you need the right tools to access it and enjoy the content.

VIZ CLIP

HTML

Browsers

Most information on the web is in the form of basic **webpages**, which are written in **HTML (Hypertext Markup Language)**. HTML is the authoring language that defines the structure of a webpage. Mosaic, released in 1993, was the first **web browser**—a program that interprets HTML to display webpages. Mosaic eventually became Netscape Navigator, which dominated the market until Microsoft got in the game. Microsoft Internet Explorer, Microsoft Edge, Mozilla Firefox, Google Chrome, and

Apple Safari are the most widely used browsers for personal computers today, but there are numerous alternatives. Many people simply use the browser that comes preinstalled on their device, but using an alternate browser, or even multiple browsers, allows you to use the best browser for each application. Some websites, tools, and technologies are optimized or better supported by specific browsers, so you may find it helpful to have more than one browser installed on your system.

INTERNET EXPLORER AND MICROSOFT EDGE

First released in 1995, Internet Explorer (IE) is included with Windows, so there's no special download needed. Windows 8.1 includes two versions of IE: a full-screen app and a desktop version. Windows 10 includes the desktop version of IE 11, and a new browser—Microsoft Edge—which has replaced IE as the default browser. Figure 7.7 shows the NASA website (**nasa.gov**) displayed in Edge, and Figure 7.8 shows the National Weather Service site (**weather.gov**) displayed in Internet Explorer 11.

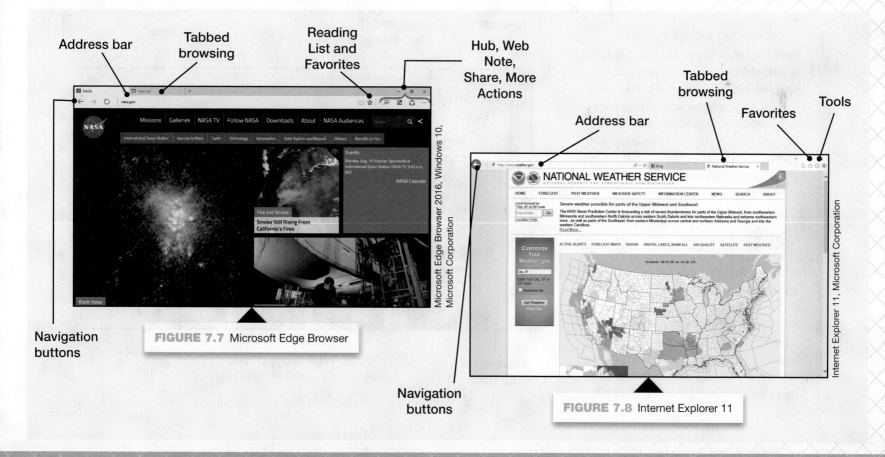

FIGURE 7.7 Microsoft Edge Browser

FIGURE 7.8 Internet Explorer 11

Some important features of Edge and Internet Explorer are:

- **Navigation buttons:** Provide a means to navigate back and forward through browsed webpages.
- **Address bar:** Contains the web address of the current webpage. You can also search the web from the address bar without having to go to a search provider's website first.
- **Favorites:** Enables you to save web addresses, giving you easy access to your favorite websites. Favorites are sometimes called bookmarks.
- **Tabbed browsing:** Enables you to have multiple webpages open in tabs.

FIREFOX

You can download and install Mozilla Firefox for free. Firefox, first released in 2004, is available across platforms and enables you to sync your bookmarks and settings across your computers automatically. Figure 7.9 shows the FBI (**fbi.gov**) website in Firefox. If you compare the Firefox image with the Edge and IE images, you'll see that they're very similar.

CHROME

Google Chrome was released in 2008. Chrome's main focus is on speed, and it loads webpages faster than other browsers. Figure 7.10 shows the Smithsonian website (**www.si.edu**) in Chrome. You can see that although it has a streamlined interface, it is very similar to Edge, IE, and Firefox.

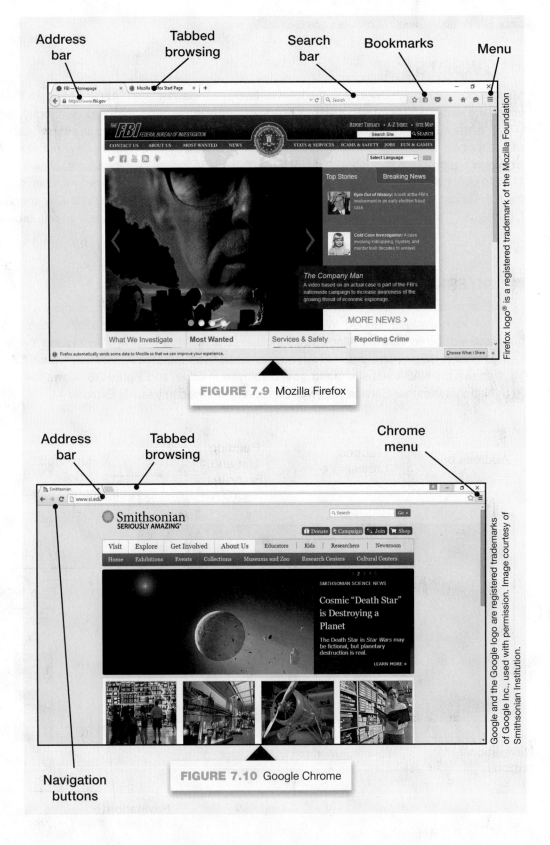

Address bar · Tabbed browsing · Search bar · Bookmarks · Menu

FIGURE 7.9 Mozilla Firefox

Firefox logo® is a registered trademark of the Mozilla Foundation

Address bar · Tabbed browsing · Chrome menu

Navigation buttons

FIGURE 7.10 Google Chrome

Google and the Google logo are registered trademarks of Google Inc., used with permission. Image courtesy of Smithsonian Institution.

SAFARI

Safari is the most popular web browser for Macs. It comes bundled with Mac OS X. The mobile version of Safari—the default on iOS devices—has almost 60 percent of the mobile browser market. Figure 7.11 shows the National Science Foundation website (nsf.gov) displayed in Safari.

MOBILE BROWSERS

Small-screen devices, such as tablets, e-readers, and smartphones, use **mobile browsers**, which are sometimes called **microbrowsers**. Mobile browsers are optimized for small screens. IE, Firefox, Chrome, Safari, and Opera all come in mobile versions. Other mobile browsers are proprietary—such as the Kindle and Android browsers. Most websites today can be accessed with a mobile browser, and many websites offer alternative pages that are optimized to be viewed with a mobile browser. Figure 7.12 shows the Library of Congress website (**loc.gov**) displayed in the iPad version of Safari.

Sidebar button

Menu bar

Search and address bar

Navigation buttons

FIGURE 7.11 Safari

Address bar

Navigation buttons

FIGURE 7.12 Mobile browsers such as Safari for iPad are optimized for small screens.

Screen shot(s) reprinted with permission from Apple Inc.

Configuring Your Web Browser

The first time you open any browser, it will be set to the default settings, such as the home page and search provider. You can customize it for your own use.

SETTING THE HOME PAGE

The term **home page** has several meanings. It can mean the first page of a website or the webpage that appears when you first open your browser. The default home page for IE is **bing.com** or **msn.com**. You can set any page you want as your home page. In fact, because most browsers support tabbed browsing, you can set multiple home pages. Think about the things you do as soon as you open your browser. Do you check Facebook? Web mail? Weather? Stock prices? Traffic? Knowing where you most commonly go online will help you choose your home page(s). Microsoft Edge does not use a home page by default but rather a news feed that you can customize. In the settings for Edge, you can change what page(s) open in Edge (Figure 7.13).

SETTING THE SEARCH PROVIDERS

When you type a search term in the address bar or search box of your browser, what search provider is used? By default, the search provider will probably be either Microsoft Bing or Google—the provider that your browser, computer manufacturer, or ISP chose. But as with your home page, you can modify this to your own preferences. In IE, click the arrow next to the magnifying glass in the address bar, and you'll see what search providers are already set up. You can choose any one of them during a search by clicking the name from the list, but if your favorite is missing, click *Add*. This will take you to a webpage with numerous search providers that you can choose from. Microsoft Edge defaults to Bing, but you can add other search engines from the settings menu, under *Advanced settings* (Figure 7.14). Safari does not allow you to add search providers.

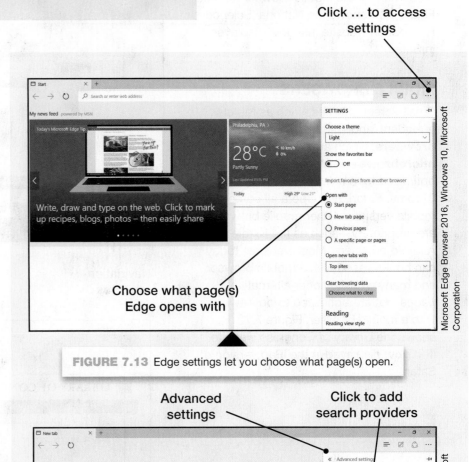

Click ... to access settings

Choose what page(s) Edge opens with

Microsoft Edge Browser 2016, Windows 10, Microsoft Corporation

FIGURE 7.13 Edge settings let you choose what page(s) open.

Advanced settings

Click to add search providers

Microsoft Edge Browser 2016, Windows 10, Microsoft Corporation

FIGURE 7.14 You can easily modify the search provider in most browsers.

Add-Ons, Plug-Ins, and Toolbars

You can extend the functionality of your web browser by installing extensions—add-ons, plug-ins, and toolbars. The distinction between the terms *add-on* and *plug-in* varies by browser. A **plug-in** is a third-party program, such as Adobe Reader. An **add-on** is created for a specific browser to add features to it. Some popular add-ons capture video from the web, block ads, and connect to maps and shopping. Adding a toolbar to your browser gives you quick access to the features of the application that installed it—but be wary of toolbars that come bundled with software you install. Toolbars can be a source of malware and may slow down your browsing.

Plug-in software, such as Adobe Flash Player, Microsoft Silverlight, and Sun Java, helps your browser display the multimedia-rich, interactive, dynamic content that's increasingly common on the Internet. You don't need a plug-in to view a static webpage of text, such as a Wikipedia page; but dynamic content, videos, games, and even flashy ads all rely on plug-ins. If your school uses an online learning management system or other tools, you might need to install specific plug-ins on your computer. You can quickly install plug-ins for free. Modern browsers may restrict some plug-ins from running, and you may find you can't access certain websites with your browser of choice. Many common plug-ins are becoming replaced with newer, safer options such as HTML5.

Figure 7.15 shows the Add-ons Manager in the Firefox browser. From this window, you can discover new add-ons and disable those that you don't want. Add-ons and plug-ins need to be updated regularly, as they can present security risks when they're not properly patched.

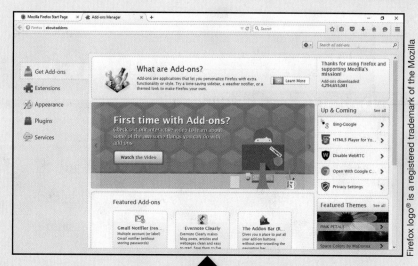

FIGURE 7.15 Managing Firefox Add-ons

Running Project

Research the versions and market shares of the top five web browsers. What is the market share of each desktop version? What about mobile versions? Are there any browsers in the current list that are not mentioned in this text?

4 Things You Need To Know

- The most popular web browsers are Internet Explorer, Microsoft Edge, Mozilla Firefox, Google Chrome, and Apple Safari.
- Mobile browsers are optimized for the small screens of mobile devices.
- You can customize the home page and other settings in most browsers.
- Add-ons and plug-ins extend the functionality of web browsers.

Key Terms

add-on

home page

HTML (Hypertext Markup Language)

microbrowser

mobile browser

plug-in

web browser

webpage

Viz Check—In MyITLab, take a quick quiz covering Objectives 1–3.

Use Google Drive

Digital Literacy Skill

HOW TO VIDEO

Google provides free online storage, called Google Drive, and applications that you can use to create and share many types of documents. If you do not have a Google account, on the Google

home page, click *Sign in*, click *Create an account*, and create a new account for this exercise. You can delete it when you have finished the exercise, or you can keep it as an extra account.

Using Google Drive is an easy way to create and share documents with others. There is no software to purchase or install; the Google

Docs applications run right from your browser. Google Docs is an example of SaaS (software-as-a-service). It doesn't matter if you have a PC and your friend has a Mac. Collaboration with Google Docs is easy, and you can work on files together even if you are not in the same location.

1 Go to **Google.com** and sign in to your Google account. Click the *Apps* menu icon at the top of the screen and then click *Drive*.

Google and the Google logo are registered trademarks of Google Inc., used with permission.

2

On the Google Drive page, you can see the files you have created and shared, and you can see files others have shared with you. To create a new file, click the *NEW* button and choose the type of file you want to create. Click *Google Docs*.

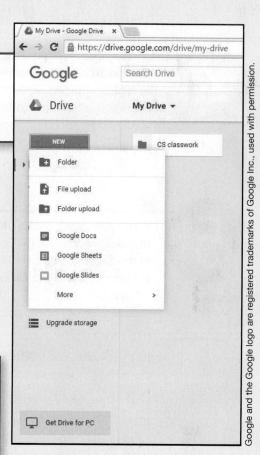

3

The word processing tool includes standard formatting options and is easy to use. Enter the following text in the document, pressing Enter after each sentence.

A simple Google document can be shared and used as an easy collaboration tool, no installation required!
The toolbar includes standard formatting options, including font styles and alignment.
You can add elements such as links, images, and lists.
There is a built-in spell checker.
You can share your file with others by clicking the blue Share button.

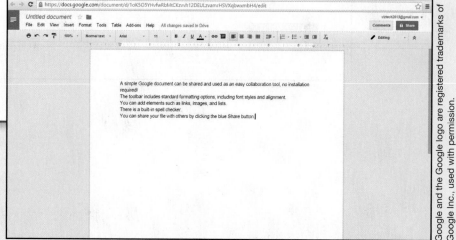

4 Google automatically saves your file as *Untitled document*, so you need to rename the file. Above the menu bar, click *Untitled document* and then change the file name to **lastname_firstname_ch07_howto1**

5 If possible, work with a classmate on this part of the activity. Click the *Share* button and, in the *Share with others* box, enter an email address to share the file with your classmate. Click *Send*.

Share with others   Get shareable link

People

Enter names or email addresses...   ✏ Can edit ▾

Done   Advanced

6 Close the browser tab to close the file and return to Google Drive. Take a screenshot of the file list and then open the shared file. If you are working with a classmate, you should both open the same shared file. If you are working alone, open the file you created for this exercise. Paste the screenshot at the end of the document.

From the File menu, choose *See revision history* to see each revision of the document. You can collaborate in real time. A list of people working on the document displays in the upper right corner, and you can see their edits in real time. Open the list to view and chat with collaborators in the current session. At the end of the document, each collaborator should type a sentence about the topic and include his or her own name.

You can download the file into many popular formats, such as a Microsoft Office format, by clicking *Download as* on the File menu. Submit as directed by your instructor.

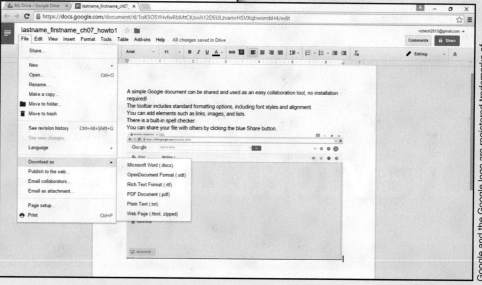

Navigating The Net

Nerthuz/Fotolia

Objective

4

Demonstrate How to Navigate the Web

Congratulations—you're connected. Now what? There's so much information out there, it can be overwhelming. How do you know where to start? How do you find what you're looking for?

VIZ CLIP

Smart Searching

Web Addresses

There are two ways to move around the web. First, you can type in the **URL (uniform resource locator)** or address of the website you want to visit—such as **http://www.google.com**—or you can follow hyperlinks embedded in webpages from one place to the next. A **website** consists of one or more webpages, all located in the same place. The home page of a website is the main, or starting, page. It's the page you see when you type in the web address for a site. A URL consists of several parts, including the protocol, domain name, and top-level domain.

http://www.google.com

http is the protocol that tells your computer what type of page you're looking at. This is almost always http (a webpage) but can be other such as https (a secure webpage) or ftp (file transfer protocol). It is so likely to be http that you can leave out this part of the address when you type it.

http://www.google.com

The *www* represents the computer on the *google* domain and is called the third-level domain, or subdomain. It is common to name the computer *www*, so this part of the URL is also often omitted. In this book, the *http://www* part of a URL is generally omitted.

http://www.google.com

The **domain name**, also called the second-level domain, represents a company or product name and makes the address easy to remember. In this example, *google* is the domain name.

http://www.google.com

.com is the **top-level domain (TLD)** and represents the type of website you're visiting. Generic TLDs, or gTLDs, can be sponsored (sTLD), meaning they are restricted to specific purposes defined by the sponsor organization, such as .edu (educational institutions) and .gov (government). Common unsponsored gTLDs, which do not have restrictions, are .com, .org, and .net, as well as many newer ones, such as .biz and .tv. Websites outside the United States have a country code TLD, or ccTLD, such as .ca (Canada) or .uk (United Kingdom).

When you visit other pages on a website, the URL will have an additional part after the TLD that indicates the location of the webpage on the web server. For example, to view the webpage about this book, you can type **pearsonhighered.com/viztech**.

ICANN (Internet Corporation for Assigned Names and Numbers) coordinates the Internet naming system. Computers on the Internet are assigned **IP (Internet Protocol) addresses**. An IP address is a unique numeric address assigned to each node on a network.

FIND OUT MORE

Wondering what your favorite website used to look like? The Internet Archive Wayback Machine can show you. Go to archive.org and enter the address of the website you want to see. The archives go back only to 1996, so you can't see the original Pizza Hut or White House site, but you can see the 1996 versions. Type in the address of your school's website and click *Take Me Back*. Click on several available dates to see how the site has changed over time. Try a few other sites that you visit regularly.

IANA

IP addresses are composed of numbers, which can be hard for a person to remember, so the DNS system was developed. **DNS (Domain Name System)** enables you to use a friendly name like **google.com** instead of an IP address like 74.125.224.72 to contact a website. DNS works like a telephone directory. When you enter a URL in your browser, your computer requests the IP address of the computer. Your DNS server, which is probably provided by your ISP, locates the IP address information and sends it back to your computer, which then uses it to address your request (Figure 7.16).

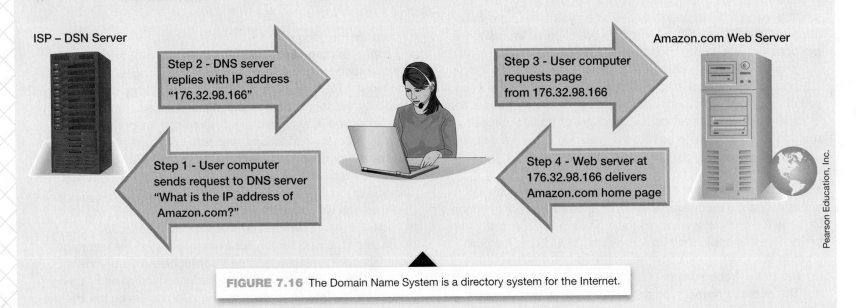

ISP – DSN Server

Step 2 - DNS server replies with IP address "176.32.98.166"

Step 1 - User computer sends request to DNS server "What is the IP address of Amazon.com?"

Amazon.com Web Server

Step 3 - User computer requests page from 176.32.98.166

Step 4 - Web server at 176.32.98.166 delivers Amazon.com home page

Pearson Education, Inc.

FIGURE 7.16 The Domain Name System is a directory system for the Internet.

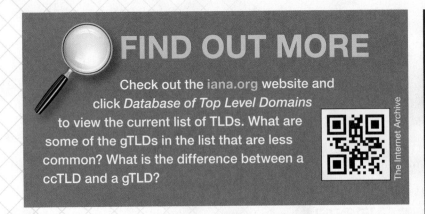

FIND OUT MORE

Check out the iana.org website and click *Database of Top Level Domains* to view the current list of TLDs. What are some of the gTLDs in the list that are less common? What is the difference between a ccTLD and a gTLD?

The Internet Archive

ETHICS

In the early days of the web, it was common practice to buy up domain names to resell them. Speculators would buy domain names that they anticipated would be worth a lot of money. This practice is known as *cybersquatting*. Intentionally buying a domain name that's the same as a trademark another company owns (for example, Avon or Hertz, which were both victims) for the purpose of selling it to the trademark owner at a profit is a trademark infringement, but what about something that's not trademarked but still recognizable—like a catchphrase or a person's name?

Smart Searching

When did *google* become a verb? The verb *google*—to use the Google search engine to obtain information about (as a person) on the World Wide Web—was added to the Merriam-Webster Dictionary in 2006. With billions of webpages on the Internet, how do you begin to find what you're looking for, and when you do find it, how can you trust it? Searching for information on the Internet is a crucial skill in today's world. Although it may seem that everything you want to know is on Google, Google covers only part of the Internet. Also, when you type the words *dog care* in a search page such as Google, you'll get millions of results, or hits. So, the first part of the puzzle is knowing how to ask the right question.

Suppose you want to learn about the eagle you saw nesting in a building on the news. You go to **google.com** and type the word *eagles* in the search box. Performing that search on Google displayed 130 million hits on the day of this writing. Because the web is constantly changing, if you perform the same search today, your numbers will be different. Also, if your browser or device is using location services, your results might be location specific. Because the search was performed from a computer in Philadelphia, the Philadelphia Eagles football team is near the top of the results. If you live in Denver, the results might be different (unless it happens to be football season).

So where do you start? A good approach is to look at the first few hits and see if what you want is there. If not, think about a better way to ask the question. To narrow down the results, you can add some more keywords to the search. The first few hits using the word *eagles* got the football team and the rock band. You need to be more specific in your query if you're really interested in the kind of eagles that fly! You can do this by adding more terms to your search, such as *birds*, *raptors*, or *bald*. To get narrower search results, you can use the advanced search tool to filter the results. You can add or exclude terms as well as specify a language and date, among other things. The advanced search options are fairly common among search sites. Using Google, click the *Options* button (Figure 7.17) to access the Advanced search screen.

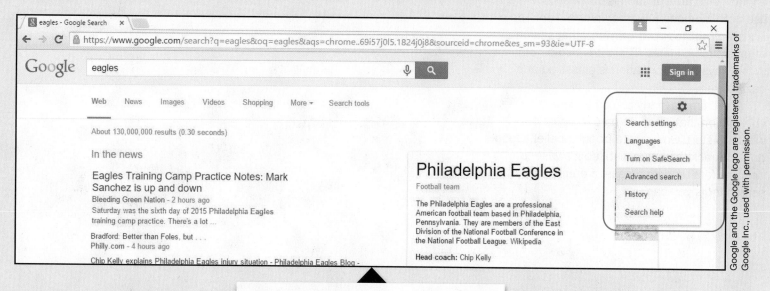

FIGURE 7.17 Starting Google Advanced Search

You can use **Boolean operators** to refine your search. A Boolean operator defines the relationship between words or groups of words and is used to create a search filter. There are three Boolean operators: AND, OR, NOT. Using AND to join two words results in pages that include both words—so the number of hits is lower. Joining two words with an OR means that either word can be present—so the number of hits is much larger. Using NOT is exclusive, which means the results must include the first word but cannot include the second word. Table 7.2 shows the eagles search using various Boolean operators.

What's the difference between search tools? **Search engines** are huge databases. They send out software called spiders, or bots, to crawl the web and gather information, which is then indexed. Because the web is dynamic and constantly changing, this method helps the search engine stay up to date. Some search engines also accept submissions, and others use both methods to gather information. There are even **metasearch engines** that search other search engines. There are also differences in the ways the information is classified and categorized.

There are so many places to search for information that it can be hard to figure out where to start. Contrary to popular belief, Google doesn't track the entire web, so it's wise to become familiar with at least a couple other search tools you can use.

TABLE 7.2 Using Search Filters in Google

Search Term	Search Filter/ Boolean Operator	Number of Results
eagles		130,000,000
eagles AND birds	AND	21,200,000
eagles OR birds	OR	628,000,000
eagles NOT football	NOT	57,500,000

Pearson Education, Inc.

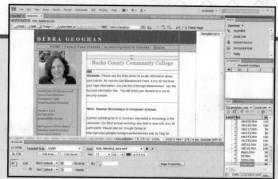

CAREER SPOTLIGHT

WEB DESIGNER—A person who decides how a website will look is called a web designer. For a simple website, the web designer may also be the person who creates the website. If you have ever created your own webpage, then you were the designer.

Today, it's pretty easy to create a basic website. There are software programs, templates, and websites such as Squarespace and Wix that can help you make something quickly and easily. A professional web designer, however, goes beyond the basics and creates designs that are customized and branded for a business. A web designer needs to have a good understanding of the capabilities of the web to design an interesting, dynamic, and professional site. Some web designers are self-taught; others have degrees in graphic arts, computer science, e-business, or marketing.

Running Project

Think Google, Bing, and Yahoo! are the only search engines around? Try googling *search engine* to see how many you get. How many of them have you used in the past? Select two that look interesting and search for the name of your local sports team on each. Did you get the same results? How were the results different? Read the About section of the search tool to determine how content is added. You can usually find this link at the bottom of a webpage. What are some of the unique features of each?

5 Things You Need To Know

- A web address is also known as a URL.
- gTLDs include .com, .edu, .gov, and so on. ccTLDs are country codes.
- DNS enables you to use URLs instead of IP addresses to access websites.
- Every node on the Internet has a unique IP address.
- Search engines are databases that index the web.

Key Terms

Boolean operator

DNS (Domain Name System)

domain name

IP (Internet Protocol) address

metasearch engine

search engine

top-level domain (TLD)

URL (uniform resource locator)

website

Create a Website Using Wix

A small business or organization can use free or low-cost services to create a professional-looking website that provides customers with important information. In this project, you will use Wix to create a free website for JMG Landscaping.

One advantage to using a website tool like Wix is the availability of premade templates that provide you with a professional layout and look without requiring you to build something from scratch. To use Wix, you can log in with your Facebook or Google account, or you can create a new Wix account using your email address. Note: The figures in this activity were taken using Google Chrome. If you use a different browser, your screens may differ slightly.

If necessary, download the student data files from pearsonhighered.com/viztech. From your student data files, open the *vt_howto2_answersheet* file and save the file as **lastname_firstname_howto2 _answersheet**

1 Go to **wix.com**, click *Sign In*, and log in or create a new Wix account. On the *Welcome to Wix!* page, below the category list, click the link to view *all templates*. On the *Pick the website template you love* page in the search box, type **landscaping**

2 Point to the *Landscape Gardener* template and click *Edit*. (Note: If this template is not available, select an appropriate template to use instead).

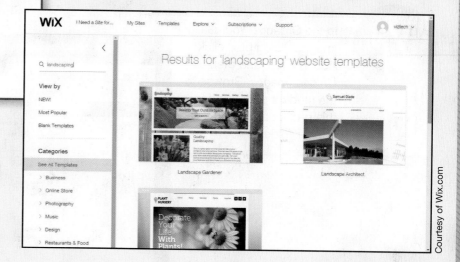

Courtesy of Wix.com

3 If an introductory video displays, watch and then close the video. On the menu bar at the top of the page, click *Save*. Name your site **jmglandscapes** and click *Save and continue*. Click *Done*. On the Home page, click the top picture, and then on the menu bar that displays above the image, click *Change Images*.

Courtesy of Wix.com

4 In the Organize Your Gallery Images dialog box, click *Add Images*, and then click *Upload Images*. Browse to the student data files for this project and open the *banner* folder.

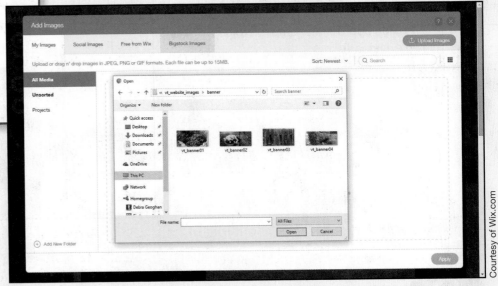

Courtesy of Wix.com

5 In the Open dialog box, drag to select all four images in the folder and then click *Open*. When the images have finished uploading, in the Add Images window, select all four images and then click *Apply*.

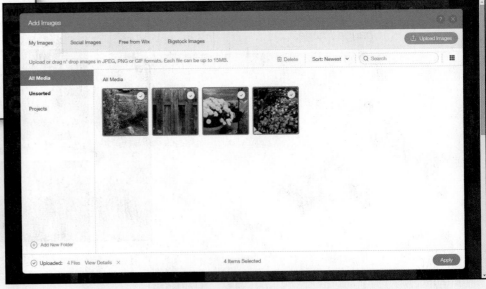

Courtesy of Wix.com

6

In the Organize Your Gallery Images window, click the yellow flower image *vt_banner02.jpg* and then drag the yellow flower image *vt_banner02.jpg* to position 1. On the right side of the window, change the title of the image to **Fall Mums**

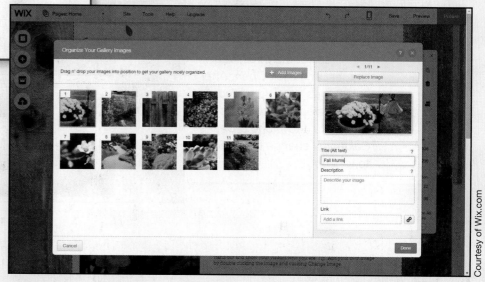

Courtesy of Wix.com

Alt text is the term for text that displays in a ToolTip when you hover over an image, which makes the website more accessible for visitors who use screen readers to read the content.

7

Click the second picture of the shrubs and rock, and change the title of the image from *vt_banner04.jpg* to **Rock Garden** Change the next two image titles: *vt_banner03.jpg* to **Cedar Fence** and *vt_banner01.jpg* to **Fall Color** and then click Done.

8 Scroll down and, in the *Quality Landscaping* section, click the flower image and then click *Change Image*. In the *Choose an Image* dialog box, click *Upload Images*. Browse to the *vt_website_images* folder, select the three web images, and click *Open*. After the images have uploaded, click *vt_web01* and then click *Apply*. Next to *Stone & Deck Solutions*, change the image to *vt_web02*.

Courtesy of Wix.com

9 Scroll up to *Quality Landscaping*. Read the text in the box, click anywhere in the text box, and then click *Edit Text*.

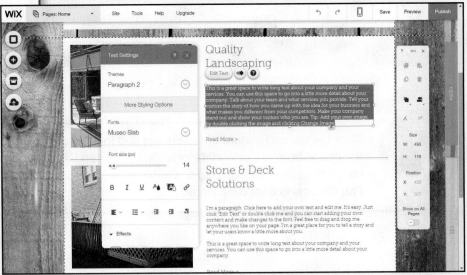

Courtesy of Wix.com

10 Select all of the text and press Delete. In the blank box, type **We are JMG Landscaping, family-owned and operated since 1985.** (include the period). Drag to select the text *JMG Landscaping* and click the *B* button in the Text Settings pane, and change the font size to 24 px. Replace the text in the textbox under *Stone, Deck & Solutions* with **Making beautiful outdoor spaces.** (include the period). Select all of the text and change the font size to 30 px. Close the Text Settings pane. Click outside the textbox to deselect it, take a screenshot and paste it into your answer sheet.

Courtesy of Wix.com

These text boxes should contain important keywords and phrases that customers would use when searching for you.

11 Scroll to the bottom of the page. In the footer, click any of the social network icons to select the *Social Bar*, and then click Set Social Links. Click the Facebook icon, click in the textbox that contains the link, and change the URL to **http://www.facebook.com/ visualizingtechnology** click *Done*, and then click *Done*.

Courtesy of Wix.com

12 Scroll to the top of the page. Click the *Pages menu* at the top of the page, click *Services*. The banner at the top of the page does not change, but the content below the banner changes to the Services page. Close the Pages menu. Scroll down to display *Our Services* at the top of the screen. Change the image in the *Landscaping* section to *vt_web03* and change the paragraph text to **Fences, stonework, gardens, and more.** (include the period). Close the Text Settings pane.

Courtesy of Wix.com

13 At the top of the page, click *Save*, click *Done*, and then click *Preview*. Test that everything is working correctly, click *Back to Editor*, and edit if necessary. Save your site and then click *Publish*. In the *Congratulations* pop-up, click View Site. From the address bar, copy the URL of your website, paste it into your answer sheet, and submit to your instructor as directed.

Your URL is your brand name. Using the default URL from WiX is fine for building and testing your page, but a real business or organization should register a domain name, such as **jmglandscaping.net**. To register a domain name, you can upgrade your Wix account or use a website hosting service or a domain name registrar, such as **GoDaddy.com** or **register.com**. Your registered domain name URL belongs to you, not the service that you use to register it. You can create and host your website on any hosting site, or even your own web server, and link your site to your domain URL.

Brian Jackson/Fotolia

Would I Lie to You?

5

Discuss How to Evaluate the Credibility of Information Found on the Web

So, now that you have millions of hits, how do you know what to believe? The Internet is full of **user-generated content**—content that has been written by everyday users. Although there's a lot of wonderful content out there, anyone can say almost anything on the Internet. You need to be able to evaluate the information you find. There are many clues to look for when deciding whether a website is one that you can trust. Here are just a few.

Who Wrote It?

Do you believe everything you hear? Or everything you read? Do you evaluate the credentials of the people that you take advice from? How do con artists scam so many people into investing their money with them? They are convincing, and nobody questions the results until it is too late—even if what is promised is too good to be true. Be a skeptic when evaluating information you find on the Internet.

Look at the URL. Ask yourself: Is it an sTLD like .edu or .gov, or a general one like .com? Take a look at **fda.gov** and **fda.com** and compare them. The .com version isn't the Food and Drug Administration website. On the fda.com website, at the top of the page in small type you will see, "Food and Drug Assistance; Resources for Industry and Consumers." Because most people are in the habit of typing *.com* rather than *.gov*, it's easy to end up at

a site you didn't intend to visit. Some organizations go so far as to own both domains so you can't make that mistake—for example, you can reach the U.S. Postal Service website by typing either **www.usps.com** or **www.usps.gov**. When you enter the .gov URL you are automatically redirected to the .com site (Figure 7.18). A restricted TLD such as .edu or .gov gives some authority to a site, but even that's not a guarantee that the author is credible.

For more information, read the home page and About Us page, and look for the credentials of the author or organization. Check out the Contact page. Is there contact information? Ask yourself if there are any conflicts of interest or obvious biases. How up to date is the website? You can usually find this information at the bottom of the home page. Not being able to find any of this information should raise a red flag.

FIGURE 7.18
The United States Post Office owns both the usps.gov and usps.com domains.

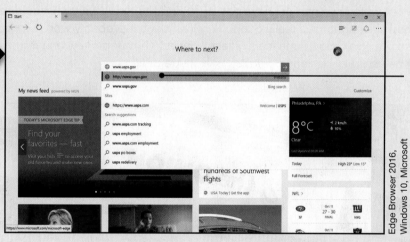

www.usps.gov
entered in browser

Edge Browser 2016, Windows 10, Microsoft Corporation

Redirected to
www.usps.com

USPS.Gov

Stick to well-known sources for important information. For example, if you're looking up health advice, try websites of trustworthy authorities, such as WebMD and the American Cancer Society. On the other hand, **skipyourselfhealthy.info** may not be trustworthy. Then again, it might, but you'll need to do a bit of research before you can be sure. Take a look at other sites. Does the information you've found match what you can find on other sites that cover the same topics? Does it make sense? This is really key: If it's too good to be true, it probably is.

A good search tool to use when doing scholarly research is Google Scholar (**scholar.google.com**) to search for articles, theses, books, abstracts, and court opinions. Also check with your school library to see which databases and resources you have access to as a student.

What About The Design?

Look at the design of the site, including its sophistication, grammar, and spelling. What impression do you get from the site? Don't be fooled: A well-designed and well-executed site can still have bad information, and a poorly designed site might have really good information. Pop culture websites like The Onion, America's Finest News Source (Figure 7.19), may be very well designed but are certainly not valid news sources.

Critically evaluating the information you find on a website is a skill that takes time to master. It may not be a big deal if you believe a website that says you should eat tofu to make your hair grow (although it probably won't work), but if you follow online advice to invest all your money, and it turns out to be a scam, then it will be a huge deal.

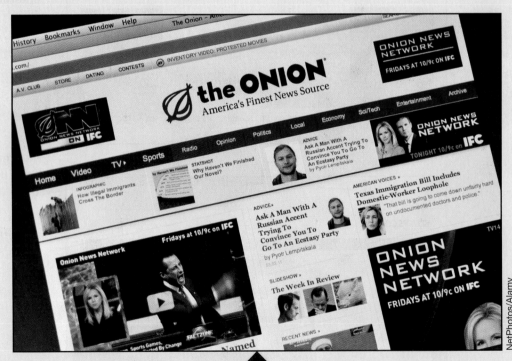

FIGURE 7.19 **theonion.com** Website

GREEN COMPUTING
Telecommuting To Save

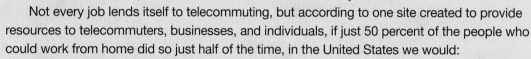

As I write this, I'm sitting in my home office in my sweat pants. I'm one of the millions of Americans who telecommute at least part-time. I go to campus a few days a week to teach classes, but I also teach many online classes, especially in the summer, which allows me to work from home. Although there are lots of arguments for and against telecommuting, there's no denying the positive impact it can have on the environment. It saves me a few days' worth of gas, which at today's prices really adds up. It's better for the environment to keep my car off the road, and it's better for my wallet, too.

Alamy

Not every job lends itself to telecommuting, but according to one site created to provide resources to telecommuters, businesses, and individuals, if just 50 percent of the people who could work from home did so just half of the time, in the United States we would:

Save over $650 billion a year

Reduce greenhouse gas emission by the equivalent of taking 9 million cars off the road

Reduce oil imports by 37 percent

Businesses that encourage telecommuting can also save on real estate expenses. Having fewer employees onsite means smaller office space requirements and lower utility bills.

Sun Microsystems has a large telecommuting program that saves over 5,000 kilowatt-hours per year for each person who works from home just two days a week.

Running Project

Compare these two websites: **choosemyplate.gov** and **foodpyramid.com**. Use the guidelines discussed in this article to evaluate and compare the two. Pay special attention to the About Us section on each site.

Viz Check—In MyITLab, take a quick quiz covering Objectives 4–5.

4 Things You Need to Know

- User-generated content means anybody can create content on the web.
- Use the home page, contact information, and About pages of a website to look for credentials of the author or organization.
- Sponsored TLDs are restricted and include .gov and .edu. They add some credibility to the content.
- Good website design doesn't guarantee credible website content.

Key Term

user-generated content

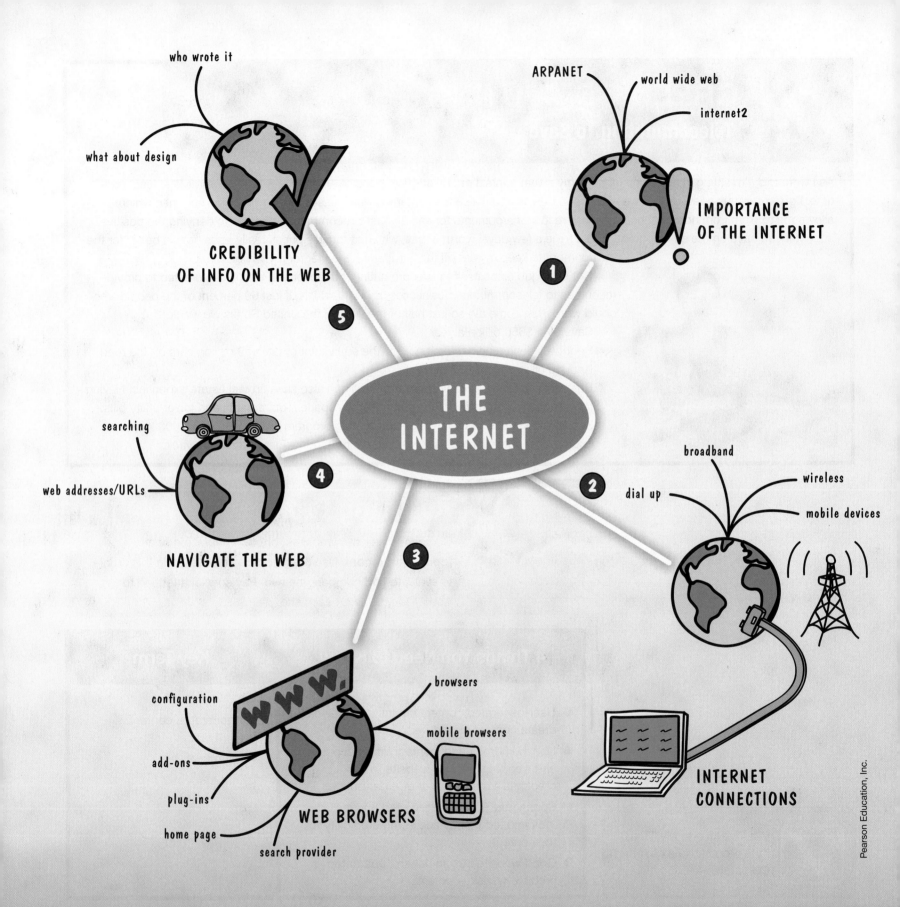

who wrote it

what about design

**CREDIBILITY
OF INFO ON THE WEB**

ARPANET

world wide web

internet2

**IMPORTANCE
OF THE INTERNET**

①

⑤

**THE
INTERNET**

searching

web addresses/URLs

NAVIGATE THE WEB

④

③

②

broadband

dial up

wireless

mobile devices

**INTERNET
CONNECTIONS**

configuration

browsers

mobile browsers

add-ons

plug-ins

home page

WEB BROWSERS

search provider

Pearson Education, Inc.

Objectives Recap

1. Recognize the Importance of the Internet
2. Compare Types of Internet Connections
3. Compare Popular Web Browsers
4. Demonstrate How to Navigate the Web
5. Discuss How to Evaluate the Credibility of Information Found on the Web

Key Terms

add-on **347**
ARPANET **333**
bandwidth **337**
Boolean operator **356**
broadband **338**
cable Internet access **339**
dial-up **337**
DNS (Domain Name System) **354**
domain name **353**
DSL (digital subscriber line) **359**
fiber-to-the-home (FTTH) **339**
FiOS (Fiber Optic Service) **339**
home page **346**
hotspot **340**
HTML (hypertext markup language) **343**
hyperlink **333**
hypertext **333**
Internet **333**
Internet backbone **333**
Internet Exchange Points **333**
Internet service provider (ISP) **336**

Internet2 **334**
IP (Internet protocol) address **353**
LTE (Long Term Evolution) **339**
metasearch engine **356**
microbrowser **345**
mobile browser **345**
municipal Wi-Fi **340**
Network Access Point (NAP) **333**
plug-in **347**
satellite Internet access **340**
search engine **356**
top-level domain (TLD) **353**
URL (uniform resource locator) **353**
user-generated content **366**
VoIP (Voice over IP) **333**
web browser **343**
webpage **343**
website **353**
Wi-Fi **340**
WiMAX Mobile Internet **339**
World Wide Web **333**

Summary

1. Recognize the Importance of the Internet

Since its invention in 1969, the Internet has grown to almost 3 billion users. It's now an integral part of research, education, commerce, and communication for people around the world. The Internet2 project is a second Internet that's limited to educational and research institutions.

2. Compare Types of Internet Connections

Dial-up Internet uses regular telephone lines to access the Internet and is very slow. Broadband connections provide speeds at least four times faster than dial-up and include cable, DSL, and fiber. Cable is provided by the same company that provides you with cable TV and uses the same lines for both services. DSL (digital subscriber line) uses digital telephone lines to provide Internet access. DSL is slower than cable and is affected by the distance from the telephone company switch. Fiber-to-the-home (FTTH) delivers Internet access over fiber-optic cable. FTTH is the fastest option. Wireless Internet access includes municipal Wi-Fi, satellite, and 3G/4G cellular service.

3. Compare Popular Web Browsers

The most popular web browsers are Internet Explorer, Microsoft Edge, Mozilla Firefox, Google Chrome, and Apple Safari. Mobile browsers are optimized for small-screen devices, such as smartphones and tablets.

4. Demonstrate How to Navigate the Web

A web address or URL (uniform resource locator) can be broken down into four parts: protocol, TLD (top-level domain), domain name, and subdomain. URLs can be typed in or embedded into a webpage as a hyperlink that you can click on. When you type a URL in your browser, your computer sends a DNS (Domain Name System) request to find the IP (Internet protocol) address of the website. You can search for information using search engines—huge databases that index webpages.

5. Discuss How to Evaluate the Credibility of Information Found on the Web

Be skeptical. Look at the URL for restricted TLDs such as .gov and .edu. Read the About Us page and other website information to view the author's credentials. Look for professional design and writing style. Finally, verify information using other sources.

Multiple Choice

Answer the multiple-choice questions below for more practice with key terms and concepts from this chapter.

1. The original Internet was called:
   a. ARPANET
   b. CSNET
   c. NSFNET
   d. Sputnik

2. The web is made up of _____, which links text or other objects such as images.
   a. Connectors
   b. Internet Exchange Points
   c. Hypertext
   d. VoIP

3. _____ is the data transfer rate of a network: measured in kilobits per second (Kbps), megabits per second (Mbps), or gigabits per second (Gbps).
   a. Bandwidth
   b. Broadband
   c. LTE
   d. WiMAX

4. Which technology uses telephone lines to carry digital signals?
   a. Cable
   b. DSL
   c. Fiber Optic Service
   d. Wi-Fi

5. You can view multiple webpages in most browsers using:
   a. Add-ons
   b. Extensions
   c. Plug-ins
   d. Tabs

6. A(n) _____ is optimized for a small-screen device.
   a. add-on
   b. extension
   c. mobile browser
   d. tab

7. Examples of restricted TLDs (top-level domains) are:
   a. .gov and .edu
   b. .org and .net
   c. .tv and .biz
   d. .ca and .af

8. The _____ enables you to type a URL in your browser instead of an IP address.
   a. DNS (Domain Name System)
   b. Hypertext
   c. ICANN
   d. TLD (top-level domain)

9. A _____ is a search engine that searches other search engines.
   a. Boolean operator
   b. bot
   c. metasearch
   d. spider

10. Check the _____ on a website for the credentials of the author or organization.
    a. About Us page
    b. Contact page
    c. Home page
    d. All the above

True or False

Answer the following questions with T for true or F for false for more practice with key terms and concepts from this chapter.

_____ **1.** The web was developed in 1991 by the Advanced Research Projects Agency (ARPA).

_____ **2.** The Internet is just one way that information moves on the web.

_____ **3.** You can access the Internet2 through your home ISP.

_____ **4.** Internet service providers (ISPs) are companies that offer Internet access.

_____ **5.** With a dial-up connection, you use your regular phone lines to connect to the Internet.

_____ **6.** Most information on the web is in the form of basic HTML webpages.

_____ **7.** Microsoft Silverlight is a popular web browser.

_____ **8.** It's necessary to type **http://** when entering a URL in your browser.

_____ **9.** Every device on the Internet must have a unique IP address.

_____ **10.** Much of the Internet consists of user-generated content that should be critically evaluated.

Fill in the Blank

Fill in the blanks with key terms from this chapter.

1. The backbone of the Internet is composed of numerous _IEPs _____ around the world.

2. The _____ is the part of the Internet that uses hypertext to connect pieces of information.

3. VoIP _____ is making calls over the Internet instead of standard telephone lines.

4. The _____ is a network designed for education, research, and collaboration.

5. Internet access that exceeds 10 Mbps is considered _____.

6. _____ uses radio waves to provide wireless high-speed network connections.

7. A(n) _____ is a program that interprets HTML to display webpages.

8. A(n) _____ is a third-party program that extends the functionality of a browser.

9. A(n) _____, or web address, consists of three main parts: the protocol, domain name, and top-level domain.

10. A(n) _____ is a unique numeric address assigned to each node on a network.

Running Project . . .

. . . The Finish Line

Use your answers to the previous sections of the project to answer the following questions. Why is the Internet important to you, and why is it important to be knowledgeable about it? Write a report describing how you use the Internet in your daily life and respond to the questions raised. Save your file as **lastname_firstname_ch07 project** and submit it to your instructor as directed.

Do It Yourself 1

The actual Internet access speed that you get is rarely as high as your ISP advertises. In this activity, you'll use an online speed test to measure your speed. From your student data files, open the file *vt_ch07_DIY1_answersheet* and save the file as **lastname_firstname_ch07_DIY1_answersheet**

Close anything that uses Internet access, such as your email or instant messaging programs. Open your browser and search for **broadband speed test** using your favorite search engine. From your search results, run three speed tests on your connection using three different test services. Because results can fluctuate, run your test at least twice on each service. Is there a significant difference? Take a screenshot of the results screen for each of your tests (six total) and paste them into your answer sheet. What type of Internet connection do you have? How do the results compare to your expected speeds? Save your answer sheet and submit it as directed by your instructor.

Do It Yourself 2

In this activity, you will perform a search using Google and refine your search using advanced options. From your student data files, open the file *vt_ch07_DIY2_answersheet* and save the file as **lastname_firstname_ch07_DIY2_answersheet**

1. Open your browser and go to **google.com**. In the search box, type **rose** and press Enter. Take a screenshot of this page and paste it into your answer sheet. How many results did you get? What type of information is displayed in the first page of results?

2. Add the word **red** before rose and press Enter. How does this affect the results?

3. Click the *Options* icon at the top right of the screen, and then click *Advanced search*. In the *none of these words* box, type **king** to exclude it from the search. Press Enter. How are the results affected? Take a screenshot of the results, and paste it into your answer sheet. Type up your answers, save the file, and submit it as directed by your instructor.

File Management

Saving information from the web can be tricky. In this exercise you will save a webpage in various formats and compare them using Internet Explorer or Safari. From your student data files, open the file *vt_ch07_FM_answersheet* and save the file as **lastname_firstname_ch07_FM_answersheet**

1. Open Internet Explorer or Safari and go to your school's home page. Click the *Tools* icon, point to File, and then click *Save as*. Safari users, click *File*, and then click *Save As*. What is the default Save as type/format? Save the page as **Home1** using the default file format.

2. Repeat the procedure and save the page using each of the other Save as file types, changing the name each time to reflect the change. What other file types are available?

3. Close your browser and open the folder that contains the saved files. Open each file by double-clicking it. What application opens each format? Compare how the page appears. Which format do you think is the best way to save this file and why?

4. Type up your answers, save the file, and submit as directed by your instructor.

Critical Thinking

In this exercise you will consider the Internet options available where you live. From your student data files, open the file *vt_ch07_CT_answersheet* and save the file as **lastname_firstname_ch07_CT_answersheet**

Use the Internet to determine which broadband services are available where you live. Create a chart comparing prices and features. What questions should you ask to help you choose? Write up a summary of the services available and the questions you would ask each company. Save the file and submit it as directed by your instructor.

Ethical Dilemma

Use the Internet to research laws regarding parking and selling unused URLs. From your student data files, open the file *vt_ch07_ethics_answersheet* and save the file as **lastname_firstname_ch07_ethics_answersheet**

Is it legal to grab up domains and park them? Is it ethical? What about changing the TLD of a well-known website (nasa.com, for example)? With new TLDs being implemented, such as .biz, .bargain, and .tv, should all related domain names be protected? Suppose you purchase a domain name for your own use, and it turns out that a company wants to buy it from you? Is it legal to sell it to them? At a profit? Type up your answers, save the file, and submit it as directed by your instructor.

On the Web

Many websites will allow you to personalize the content that you see. Choose one of the following websites: NetVibes, My Yahoo!, igHome, uStart, or ProtoPage. In this exercise you will create a personalized web portal page that brings information from various sources together onto one page. From your student data files, open the file *vt_ch07_web_answersheet* and save the file as **lastname_firstname_ch07_web_answersheet**

If necessary, create an account on your chosen website and log in. (This might be a good time to use a secondary email account created just for such purposes.) What personalization and customizations are available to you? Create your personal page on the site. What items did you choose to modify, add, or delete? Type up your answers, take a screenshot of your customized page, and paste it in your answer sheet. Save the file and submit it as directed by your instructor.

Collaboration

Instructors: Divide the class into five groups, and assign each group one browser for this project. The topics include Internet Explorer, Edge, Firefox, Chrome, and Safari.

The Project: As a team, prepare a multimedia commercial for your assigned browser. The presentation should be designed to convince a consumer to use the browser. Use at least three references. Use Google Drive or Microsoft Office to prepare your presentation and provide documentation that all team members have contributed to the project.

Outcome: Prepare a multimedia presentation or video on your assigned topic and present it to your class. The presentation should be 2–3 minutes long. Be sure to include the name of your presentation and a list of all team members. Turn in a final version of your presentation named **teamname_ch07_presentation** and your file showing your collaboration named **teamname_ch07_collab** and submit your presentation to your instructor as directed.

Application Project

my**it**lab grader

Office 2016 Application Projects
Word 2016: Cellular Internet Service

Project Description: You have been asked to write an article on cellular Internet service. You will need to change alignment, line and paragraph spacing, margins, and lists and edit the header and footer. You will also find and replace text, create and modify a footnote, and use the Format Painter. If necessary, download student data files from **pearsonhighered.com/viztech**.

Cellular Internet

First-generation, or 1G, cellular telephone technology was analog. It was introduced in the 1980s and was replaced by the digital 2G or second-generation in the early 90s. 2G not only carried voice signals, but also data such as text messages and email.

Third-generation, or 3G, access was launched in 2001 and was the first cellular technology that offered reasonably fast data transfer speeds.[1] Smartphones became increasingly popular and more websites began to support mobile access.

The first 4G networks began appearing in 2009 and offer even faster data rates.

- **1G** - introduced 1979- Speed 28- 56 kbps
- **2G** - introduced 1991- Speed 56-384 kbps
- **3G** - introduced 2001- Speed At least 200 kbps
- **4G** - introduced 2009- Speed 1 Gbps for stationary and 100 Mbps for mobile operation

[1] Some earlier technologies were referred to as 2.5G and 2.75G.

lastname_firstname_ch07_word

Step	Instructions
1	Start Word. Download and open the Word file named *vt_ch07_word* Save the file as **lastname_firstname_ch07_word**
2	Change the left and right margins of the document to 1.25".
3	Change the line spacing of the entire document to 2.0 lines. Change the paragraph spacing (before and after) of the entire document to 6.0 points.
4	Apply the Title style and center the heading *Cellular Internet*.
5	Use the Find and Replace dialog box to search for and replace all instances of the word *wireless* with **cellular** There should be two replacements.
6	In the paragraph that begins *1G,* apply bold and underline formatting to the text *1G.* Using the Format Painter, apply the formatting from the text *1G* to the text *2G, 3G,* and *4G* in the three lines that follow.
7	Select the last four lines and format as a bulleted list using solid square bullets.
8	In the paragraph that begins *Third-generation*, insert a footnote immediately following the period following the text *data transfer speeds,* reading **Some earlier technologies were referred to as 2.5G and 2.75G.** (include the period).
9	Move the insertion point to the end of the document, press Enter twice, and insert the picture *vt_ch07_image1*
10	Resize the image to a height of 2.5". Position in Bottom Center with Square Text Wrapping. Apply the Double Frame, Black Picture Style.
11	Use the Spelling and Grammar dialog box to correct the misspelling of the word *genaration* to *generation*. Ignore any other spelling and grammar suggestions.
12	In the document footer, add the FileName field using the default format.
13	Save the file and close Word. Submit the document as directed.

Application Project

my**it**lab grader

Office 2016 Application Projects
PowerPoint 2016: Internet Services

Project Description: *In* this project, you will create a presentation about Internet services. In this presentation you will apply design, font, and color themes. You will also change font colors, bullet symbols, and slide layout. If necessary, download student data files from ***pearsonhighered.com/viztech***.

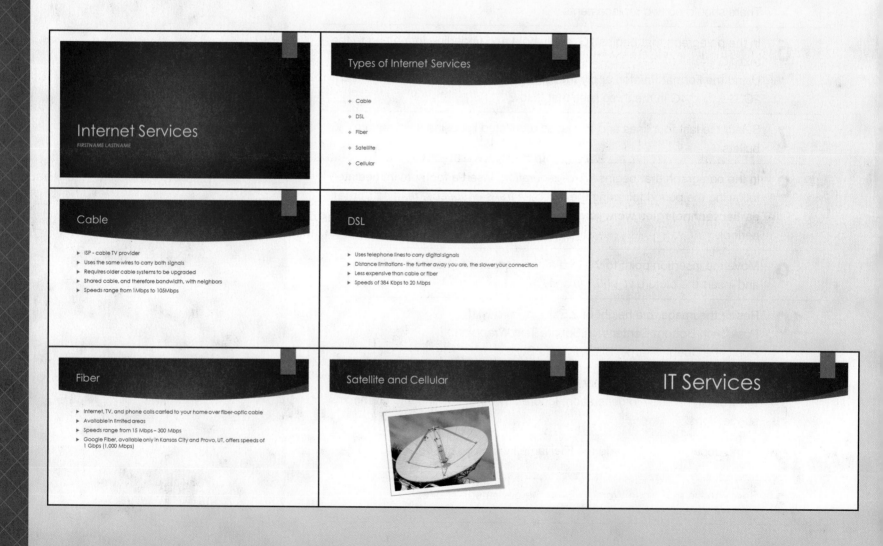

Step	Instructions
1	Start PowerPoint. Download and open the file named *vt_ch07_ppt* Save the presentation as **lastname_firstname_ch07_ppt**
2	Apply the Ion Boardroom theme, green variant, to the presentation.
3	On Slide 1, in the subtitle placeholder, using your name, type **Firstname Lastname** Apply bold and italic formatting to the subtitle text.
4	On Slide 2, in the title placeholder, type **Types of Internet Services** In the content placeholder, enter the following five bullet points: **Cable DSL Fiber Satellite Cellular**
5	On Slide 2, change the bullet style to Star bullets and set the line spacing to 2.0.
6	On Slide 3, in the title placeholder, type **Cable** On Slide 4, in the title placeholder, type **DSL** On Slide 5, in the title placeholder, type **Fiber**
7	Insert two new slides after Slide 5. On Slide 6, in the title placeholder, type **Satellite and Cellular**
8	On Slide 6, in the content placeholder, insert the downloaded *vt_ch07_image2* Apply the Rotated White picture style to the image.
9	Change the layout of Slide 7 to Title Only.
10	On Slide 7, in the title placeholder, type **IT Services** Center the title and change the font size to 72.
11	Apply the Split transition to all slides with a duration of 2.00.
12	Insert the page number and the footer **Firstname Lastname** on the notes and handouts pages for all slides in the presentation. View the presentation in Slide Show view from beginning to end, and then return to Normal view.
13	Save the presentation and close PowerPoint. Submit the presentation as directed.

CHAPTER
8

Communicating and Sharing: The Social Web

In This Chapter

The first thing I do every morning is check my email and the notifications on my smartphone. Then, when I come downstairs, I open the browser on my computer. I have multiple home page tabs, which include my email, calendar, social media feeds, and RSS feeds from my favorite blogs and news and sports websites. In just a few minutes, I can find out everything I need to start my day. Online communication is an integral part of my life—and probably yours, too. When you have finished this chapter, you'll have an understanding of the world of online communication and the impact it has on society.

Objectives

1 Compare Different Forms of Synchronous Online Communication

2 Compare Different Forms of Asynchronous Online Communication

3 Discuss the Impact of Social Media in Society

4 Locate User-Generated Content in the Form of a Blog or Podcast

5 Discuss How Wikis and Other Social Media Sites Rely on the Wisdom of the Crowd

6 Explain the Influence of Social Media on E-commerce

7 Develop a Brand Marketing Strategy Using Social Media and Other Online Technologies

Running Project

In this project, you'll explore online communication. Look for instructions as you complete each article. For most articles, there's a series of questions for you to research. At the conclusion of the chapter, you'll submit your responses to the questions raised.

Talk To Me

Objective

1

Compare Different Forms of Synchronous Online Communication

Want to talk to someone right now? That's what chat and instant messaging allow you to do. The term **synchronous online communication** means communication that happens in real time, with two or more people online at the same time. Face-to-face conversations and telephone calls are examples of synchronous communication. Online synchronous communication tools let you communicate in real time on the web.

Installing
Hardware
Device Drivers

Chat and IM

Online **chat** allows you to talk to multiple people at the same time in a chat room. **Instant messaging (IM)** allows you to talk to one person at a time, although most IM software also supports group chats. The line between chat and IM has blurred over the years. For example, by this definition, Facebook chat is really a form of IM.

You can find chat rooms that are geared toward common interests, such as travel or cooking, or more general chats for people who just want to talk. Some chats are moderated, which means a moderator screens all content; others are not moderated, and anything goes. Many chat rooms are adult in nature, and, unfortunately, sexual predators often find their victims in such chat rooms. It's important to put safety first when using chat rooms—or any other form of online communication, for that matter.

Traditional chat rooms are text-based and persistent, and users come and go, often not knowing each other. To access client-based chats, you need to install client software. Some IM programs allow you to create group chats. Social media sites such as Facebook (Figure 8.1) and Google hangouts also enable you to chat with others. Using chat is perfect for a class discussion or getting a group of family members together to plan a reunion. And if you're on the go, you can use mobile versions of these tools—so you can start a chat while you're in front of your computer and then continue the conversation from your smartphone or tablet when you're not.

FIGURE 8.1 Facebook Messages

Dolphfyn/Alamy

Instant messaging sessions can be web-based, but many popular IM services, such as Skype, iMessage and AIM, use client software that must be installed on your computer or mobile device. Many businesses find IM and chat to be useful tools for holding meetings and providing customer support (Figure 8.2).

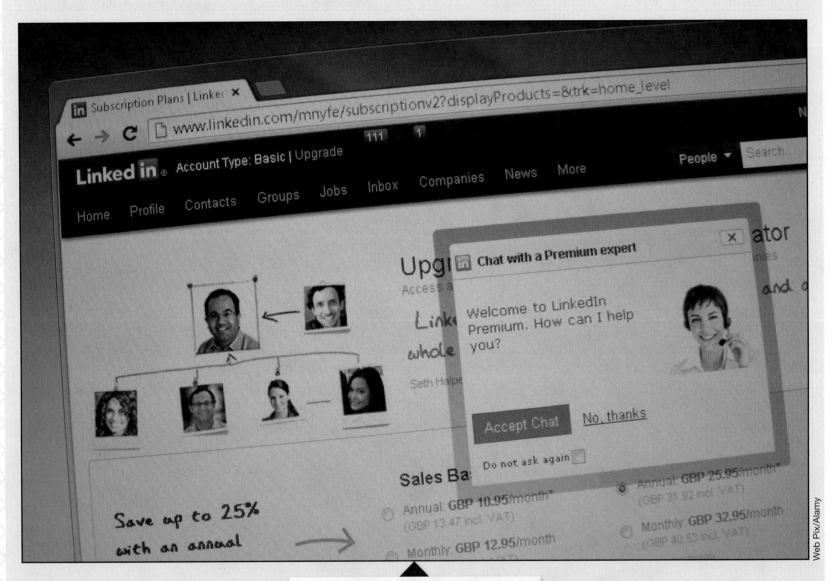

FIGURE 8.2 LinkedIn offers support via chat.

VOIP

You can make voice and video calls (Figure 8.3) using **VoIP (Voice over IP)**, which enables calls to be transmitted over the Internet instead of via traditional phone lines or cellular towers. You can make calls from your computer or mobile device from anywhere you have Internet access, even if you don't have phone service. If you have broadband Internet access, your Internet service provider may offer VoIP phone service. Apple FaceTime, which is built into OS X and iOS, enables you to make video calls to other FaceTime users. Skype, which is available across platforms and devices, enables you to place calls to other Skype users for free or to regular phones for a small fee. Using FaceTime or Skype to talk to friends and family members who are in other countries can save a lot of money over traditional telephone calls. My cousin, who lives in Australia, talks regularly with his family here in the United States, and his children are able to keep in touch with their faraway grandparents.

FIGURE 8.3 VoIP helps people keep in touch using the Internet.

Straight 8 Photography/Shutterstock

Running Project

Use the Internet to research chat and IM safety rules for kids. Create a list of five rules you consider most important when it comes to keeping kids safe.

3 Things You Need To Know

- Multiple people can be in a chat room at one time.
- IM occurs between two people at a time.
- VoIP uses the Internet, rather than landlines or cellular towers, to make phone calls.

Key Terms

chat

instant messaging (IM)

synchronous online communication

VoIP (Voice over IP)

Leave A Message

Objective

2 Compare Different Forms of Asynchronous Online Communication

Asynchronous forms of communication don't require the participants to be online at the same time. Like leaving a voicemail or sending a letter, **asynchronous online communication** technology lets you send a message that the receiver can access later.

SIMULATION **Communicating and Sharing**

How do You Read and Send Email?

The Internet was designed for communicating and sharing. One of the first applications was email, which quickly became the most widely used Internet application. **Email** is a system of sending electronic messages using store-and-forward technology. That means an email server holds your messages until you request them. So someone can send you an email message even if you're not online at the time. Even if you prefer other forms of communication for your personal contacts, using email to communicate is an essential business skill.

There are two ways to access email: using an email client on a device or reading it online through a webmail interface. When you use an email client, such as Outlook or Thunderbird, the email server sends you a copy of the message. The client then makes the message available to read even after you disconnect from the Internet. If you configure your client to leave a copy of the message on the email server, then you will still be able to access the messages from a webmail interface as well. The advantage to using a webmail interface is that your email is available to you from anywhere—home, school, vacation, or work—whenever you're online (Figure 8.4).

It makes sense to have multiple email accounts, which enable you to keep your private, work, and school communication separate. Think about the impression you'd make if you sent a job inquiry from cutiepie_cupcake@hotmail.com. You might have one account just for shopping websites, another for friends and family, and yet another at school. Your ISP will provide you with at least one email account. Your employer or school may provide you with another. There are also many places for free email accounts, such as Yahoo!, Google, and Outlook. com. The advantage to using an email account not tied to your ISP is that you will not lose your email account if you change your ISP.

Figure 8.5 shows how easy it is to create a free email account on Outlook.com. The hardest part of the process is getting the letters of the captcha right. A **captcha (Completely Automated Public Turing Test to Tell Computers and Humans Apart)** is a series of letters and numbers that are distorted in some way so that they are difficult for automated software to read but relatively easy for humans to read. Captchas are used to prevent automated software from creating online accounts. Free email accounts are often linked to other services, such as online storage.

FIGURE 8.4 You can access email on any Internet-connected device.

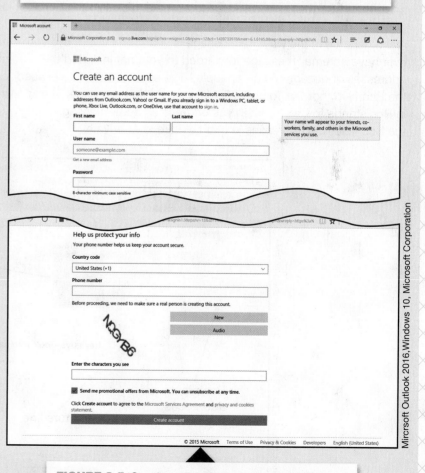

FIGURE 8.5 Creating a Free Outlook.com Email Account

One very important thing to remember about email is that it's not secure. As it travels from your computer over the Internet, it can be read by hackers along the way. Copies of the message exist on servers and routers it crosses on its journey, and those copies can be retrieved long after you've deleted the message from your inbox. Your email provider might scan your messages to deliver you targeted advertising, and your employer or school network administrator might also read your email. A good analogy is to think of email as a postcard, not a letter in a sealed envelope.

Parts of An Email Message

Figure 8.6 shows some of the important parts of a new email message. The most important part of the message is the address. If you don't address it correctly, the message will not reach its recipient. There are three address fields that you can use: To, Cc, and Bcc. To is the field you normally use when sending an email to someone. Cc, which stands for *carbon copy*, is the field you use to send a copy to someone who's not the main addressee—so he or she knows about a conversation, for example. It's like an FYI and generally means that a reply isn't expected. Functionally, there's no real difference in the way the message is sent or received. Did you ever have an email message forwarded to you that included the addresses of dozens of other people? The sender should have used the Bcc field, not the To or Cc fields, to send that message. The B in Bcc stands for *blind*. When you address an email message using the Bcc field, the addresses in that field are kept private.

The subject line of an email message gives the recipient some idea of the content of the email. The body of the message should contain the rest of the information. The body of the message in Figure 8.6 includes some formatted text and an image. Most email programs let you format text or include images, but to view those elements you need to use an email program that's configured to read HTML email messages. An email program that's configured to view only text email messages will only display the text in a message.

An email signature is a block of text that's automatically put at the end of a message you compose. It can be a very simple message that just includes your name, or it can contain more contact information and perhaps a privacy statement. You need to create a signature and enable it in your email settings for the signature to appear on your email messages.

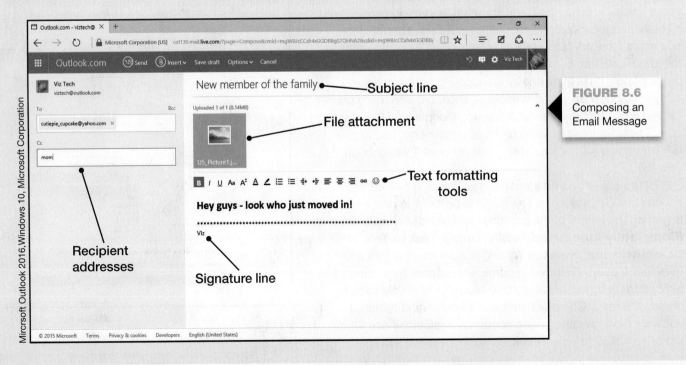

FIGURE 8.6
Composing an Email Message

Mircrosoft Outlook 2016,Windows 10, Microsoft Corporation

When you receive an email message, you can reply to the message or forward it to someone else (Figure 8.7). When you choose Reply, your response is sent back to the original sender. When you choose Reply all (or Reply to All), the response is sent to all the addressees in the To and Cc lines of the original message as well as the original sender. Think carefully before you use this option. Do you really want everyone to receive your reply? The subject line for a reply will include Re: before the original subject. If you want to send the message to someone else, then you should use the Forward option, which allows you to select new addresses and puts Fw: before the subject.

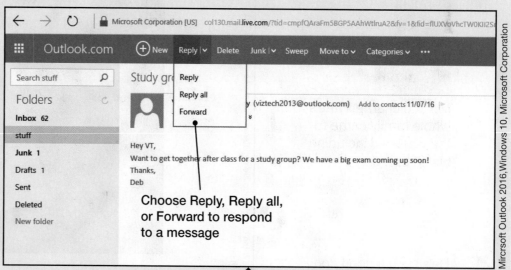

Choose Reply, Reply all, or Forward to respond to a message

FIGURE 8.7 Replying to an Email Message

Mircrsoft Outlook 2016;Windows 10, Microsoft Corporation

Text and Multimedia Messaging

A popular form of asynchronous communication is **text messaging**. Using the Short Message Service (SMS), you can send brief electronic messages between mobile devices. Messages that include multimedia such as images or videos use the Multimedia Messaging Service (MMS). Most mobile devices include a built-in messaging app (Figure 8.8). Snapchat—a multimedia messaging app that you can download to your mobile device—allows you to send a photo or short video message to specific recipients (Figure 8.9). Once the message is opened, it is viewable for a brief amount of time (1–10 seconds) that the sender specifies and then disappears from the recipient's device. Snapchat stories allow you to string together multiple snaps you have posted in a 24-hour period to create a video that persists for up to 24 hours. You can share your Snapchat stories with specific people or with everyone.

FIGURE 8.8 Using the Android Messaging App

Google and the Google logo are registered trademarks of Google Inc., used with permission.

FIGURE 8.9 Snapchat App on a Tablet

Jeffrey Blackler/Alamy

Forums and Discussion Boards

Forums, also known as discussion boards or message boards, were one of the first forms of social media. They're conversations much like chat but not in real time. There are forums for people with common interests, such as sports, pets, video games, or travel (Figure 8.10). Many technology and product websites include forums, which may be used as a support system. Some websites refer to a forum as a community.

Participants post comments and questions, usually about a particular topic or problem, and other participants respond. Each conversation is called a thread, and the responses are called posts. Forums are great places to get help with problems, ask for advice, or just communicate with folks with similar interests. Threads can be searched and read long after the initial conversation has ended. Most forums are moderated and require you to create an account before you're allowed to post.

The advantage to using email or a forum over chat or IM is that the conversations have a longer life span. You can save email messages indefinitely, as long as you have the storage space, and forums can persist for years after a thread is started. These tools have become critical ways to communicate in all types of businesses.

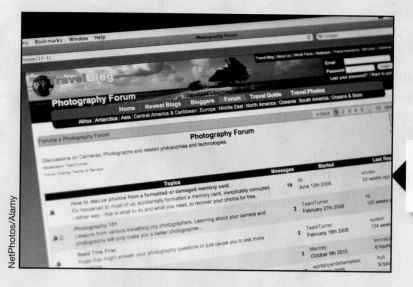

NetPhotos/Alamy

FIGURE 8.10 Users with common interests share ideas in online forums.

Running Project

Visit tripadvisor.com/forum. Select a destination that you have visited in the past. Read some of the threads. Select a thread that you would like to reply to. Do you agree with the replies posted? Would you find them helpful if you were deciding to visit this location?

5 Things You Need To Know

- Email is a store-and-forward technology, so you don't need to be online when someone sends a message to you.
- Email is not necessarily private.
- A captcha ensures that a person and not a machine is creating an account.
- Text messaging and multimedia messaging send electronic messages between mobile devices.
- Forums are online discussion boards.

Key Terms

asynchronous online communication

captcha (Completely Automated Public Turing Test to Tell Computers and Humans Apart)

email

forum

text messaging

Niroworld/Fotolia

There's A Place For Everyone ...

Objective

3 Discuss the Impact of Social Media in Society

There are many ways to connect with people! Forums and email are old technologies, having been around almost as long as the Internet itself. Newer communication tools, sometimes called **Web 2.0**, are changing the way people communicate and collaborate on the web. Web 2.0 tools enable you to be a creator, not just a consumer, of content.

VIZ CLIP

Facebook Security

Collectively, the websites that use these tools—which enable you to create content, connect, network, and share—are called **social media**. As ordinary users create more content, what's important, interesting, or relevant is no longer decided by a few experts or journalists sitting around a table but by the crowd of participants. The concept of the **second screen**, using a computer or mobile device while watching television to interact with other viewers or view enhanced content, has changed TV watching from a passive experience to an active, social experience. It's really important to think about your **digital footprint**. Your digital footprint is all the information that someone could find out about you by searching the web, including social media sites. Remember that once something has been posted on the web, it's almost impossible to completely get rid of it. Suppose you were a prospective employer. Would you hire someone who had compromising pictures on Facebook? You need to develop your own brand and make sure that anything that's publicly viewable fits into that brand.

Simeonvd/Fotolia

Social Network Sites

Facebook and LinkedIn are **social networks**—online communities that combine many of the features of other online communication tools, enabling people with common interests to communicate and share content with each other. Social networks allow you to chat in real time, post messages for many people to see, or send personal messages similar to emails. There are hundreds of social networking sites. Some focus on business, others are language- or location-specific, and still others are available where anything goes. Social networking allows you to keep in touch with old friends and make new ones.

I have accounts on several different social websites and use different accounts for my personal and professional communication. I have different friends on each and post different information.

For example, on my professional profile, I might post a link to an interesting tech article and join a group related to technology or education. Because my personal profile is private, only my friends can see what I post there. I play games, post pictures, and chat with friends on my private profile. I belong to several groups that match my interests, including corgis, sports, and the neighborhood where I grew up. My privacy settings are very high, and I carefully choose the friend requests I send and accept.

If you have friends who tag you in their photos, even if your profile is private, you may be sharing more than you meant to. Be sure to use the security and privacy settings to keep your private life private and consider creating a second public profile on a professional social network such as LinkedIn.

FACEBOOK

The first social network sites began in the late 1990s. Facebook was launched in 2004 for Harvard students and in 2006 for everyone else. Today, Facebook has hundreds of millions of users worldwide. A user creates a profile that includes some personal information, pictures, and interests and then can connect with other users or friends (Figure 8.11). For some people, using a social network is all about the number of "Friends"; for others, it is a way to stay in touch with people. You can Like the pages of organizations, businesses, celebrities, news outlets, and places, to keep up with the latest information.

Courtesy of Facebook, Inc.

FIGURE 8.11 A Facebook profile has posts and information shared with friends and family.

BUSINESS SOCIAL NETWORKS

Many employers will expect you to be technically literate and use social networking tools, so not having a profile at such a site could be a negative. You may receive friend requests from people who have interviewed you for jobs and internships and from bosses at work; these are the types of people who should be in your professional social network. Facebook is great for making connections with friends and family, but for a more business-centered social network, consider using a site such as LinkedIn, which is designed for business connections (Figure 8.12). There are no games or silly applications, no place to post photos (except a profile image), and no chat. You have connections instead of friends. LinkedIn—or other business social networks that relate to your field of interest—should be part of your personal brand.

Petrroudny/Fotolia

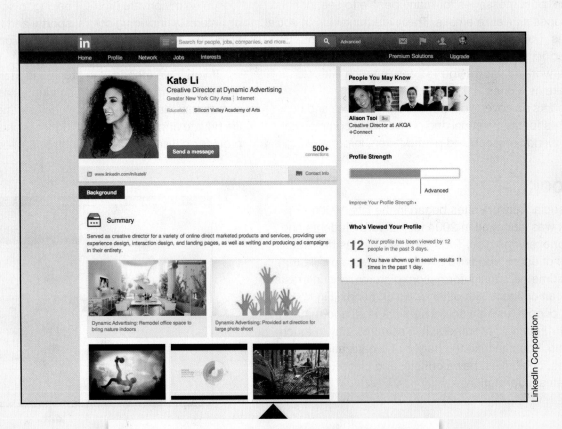

FIGURE 8.12 LinkedIn is a business-oriented social network.

LinkedIn Corporation.

VIRTUAL WORLDS

Virtual communities, such as Second Life and Webkinz, and **massively multiplayer online role-playing games (MMORPG)**, such as World of Warcraft and Elder Scrolls, enable you to interact online with people in real time using an **avatar**, or virtual body (Figure 8.13). Some schools even offer virtual classes in Second Life. Second Life and multiplayer games have pretty high system requirements and require fairly new and powerful systems.

FIND OUT MORE

Some colleges have a virtual presence on Second Life. Go to http://secondlife.com/destinations and click Education & Nonprofits to find out which institutions are using it and why.

Macrovector/Shutterstock

FIGURE 8.13 Avatars interact in a virtual world.

Social Video, Image, and Music Sites

Social sharing sites, such as YouTube, Flickr, and SoundCloud, enable anyone to create and share media. These sites are outside social networks like Facebook, although you can often share content between the networks. One of the key features of these sites is the ability to tag items. Tagging makes the sharing even more social, as users tag not just their own creations but also those of others.

VIDEO

You probably know about YouTube; it's the largest online video-hosting site in the world. It's also social in the sense that you can subscribe to other users' channels, send messages, and recommend videos. A **viral video** (Figure 8.14) is a video that becomes extremely popular because of recommendations and social sharing. There are other video-sharing sites, including CollegeHumor, Vimeo, TeacherTube, and even Facebook and Flickr. Streaming sites like Hulu and Netflix don't host user-created content but are still social in that they keep track of the popularity of videos and have users review and discuss the videos.

Web Pix/Alamy

FIGURE 8.14 "Charlie bit my finger—again!" has been viewed millions of times.

IMAGES

Flickr is the largest image-sharing site (Figure 8.15). With a free account, you can post up to 1 terabyte of images—that's more than 500,000 images. You can mark your pictures as private or make them public. You can adjust the copyright to allow others to use your images legally, and tag them so that people can search for things that interest them. Other popular photo-sharing sites include Facebook and Google. Instagram and other mobile apps allow you to take and edit photos on your mobile device and upload them to the web automatically. You can also comment on and share images that you like and add location information to them.

FIGURE 8.15 My Flickr Photostream

MUSIC

What is more social than music? There are lots of places on the web to find music, but if you want a social experience, you can create an account on a site such as Last.fm or Pandora (Figure 8.16). These sites recommend music to you based on what you listen to and what your friends are listening to. You can add tags and comments, and mark tracks you like, which will help you get recommendations. The more you listen to and mark tracks, the more recommendations you will get. On the Last.fm site, you can browse users with similar music tastes and discover what they're listening to.

If you like to make and share your own music, you can use a website like SoundCloud (soundcloud.com). Using a browser or mobile app, you can upload sound files that you have created and share them with the community. Users can follow their favorites and comment and share new finds. Artists can communicate directly with their fans, and musicians can collaborate with each other, even if they are many miles apart.

FIGURE 8.16 Pandora app on a smartphone.

Richard Levine/Alamy

GREEN COMPUTING
Raising Social Awareness

How much paper mail do you receive every week? And how much of it do you actually read? The cost of a direct-mail campaign is huge, and many people simply toss into the trash what they see as junk mail anyway, so the costs are also large in terms of the environment. SMM isn't just for businesses; it can also be used to raise awareness of important issues.

Debra Geoghan

Not long ago, thousands of people began posting videos of themselves dumping ice water over their heads and challenging others to do the same. The ALS Ice Bucket Challenge went viral and, as a result, the ALS foundation received millions of dollars in donations—and many people who had known nothing about ALS before learned about the disease. So a simple act of social networking resulted in raising money and also raising social awareness without printing a single piece of paper.

Running Project

Imagine that you're a job applicant. Search the web and major social networks to see what your prospective employers would find. Log out of your social networking sites to see how an outsider would view you. How is your brand? Would you hire yourself? Was it easy to find things that you would rather keep private?

4 Things You Need To Know

- Social networks are online communities where people connect with each other.
- Video-, image-, and music-sharing sites allow users to post their creations on the web for others to see and use.
- Tagging creates a way to search for content on social websites.
- You should be very careful about your digital footprint.

Key Terms

avatar

digital footprint

massively multiplayer online role-playing game (MMORPG)

second screen

social media

social network

viral video

Web 2.0

Viz Check—In MyITLab, take a quick quiz covering Objectives 1–3.

Create a LinkedIn Profile

In this exercise, you will create an account on LinkedIn. Many companies now use LinkedIn as a recruiting tool. Because this is a business network, you should use a professional email address, not a cute nickname. If you don't have an appropriate email address to use, this would be a good time to create one. You will be required to confirm your email address before you can successfully complete your LinkedIn sign-up. If necessary, download the student data files from **pearsonhighered.com/viztech**. From your student data files, open the *vt_ch08_howto1_answersheet* file and save the file as **lastname_firstname_ch08_howto1_answersheet**

1 Open your browser and go to **linkedin.com** On the home page, type your name and email address and create a password. Click *Join now*.

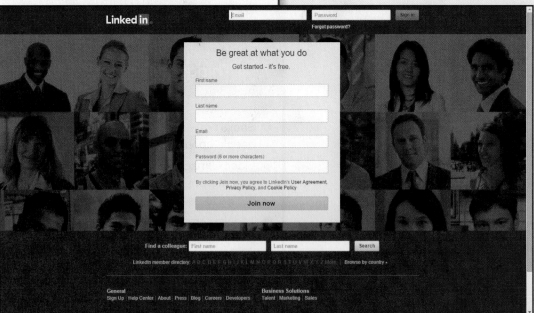

2 Create your professional profile by completing the information on the next screen. Select *Student* and complete your school and dates attended information, and then click *Create your profile*.

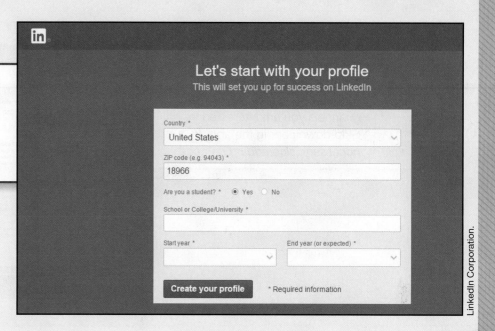

Let's start with your profile
This will set you up for success on LinkedIn

Country *
United States

ZIP code (e.g. 94043) *
18966

Are you a student? * ● Yes ○ No

School or College/University *

Start year *   End year (or expected) *

Create your profile   * Required information

LinkedIn Corporation.

3 For the sign-up Step 2, click *Not sure yet. I'm open.* Skip adding your email contacts (you can do this later if you choose). Open your email program and click the link in the confirmation email to confirm your email address and activate your LinkedIn account.

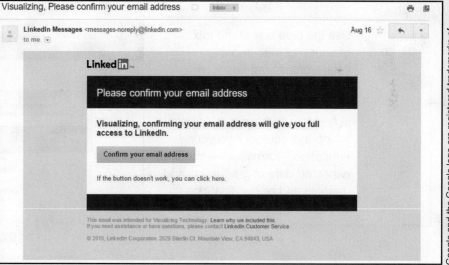

Visualizing, Please confirm your email address   Inbox   x

LinkedIn Messages <messages-noreply@linkedin.com>   Aug 16
to me

Linked in™

Please confirm your email address

Visualizing, confirming your email address will give you full access to LinkedIn.

Confirm your email address

If the button doesn't work, you can click here.

This email was intended for Visualizing Technology. Learn why we included this.
If you need assistance or have questions, please contact LinkedIn Customer Service
© 2015, LinkedIn Corporation, 2029 Stierlin Ct. Mountain View, CA 94043, USA

4

Select a few businesses to follow and select a few channels you are interested in. Skip downloading the app. *If necessary, skip adding contacts.*

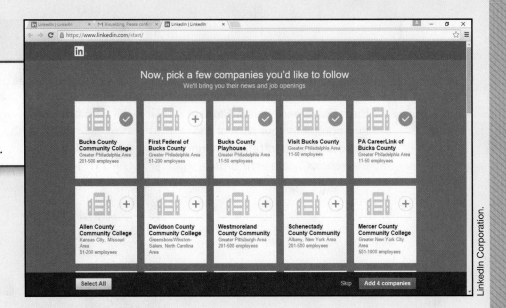

LinkedIn Corporation.

5

Use the blue box at the top of your profile to improve your profile by adding work experience and industry. Add a few items under *Skills*, including skills that you have gained from taking this course. Add your education information—including expected date of graduation and degrees and or certifications earned.

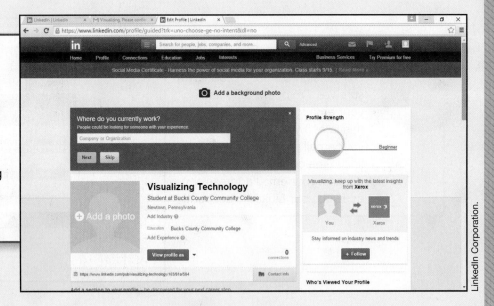

LinkedIn Corporation.

6 Make sure to add current contact information and a photo. Remember that potential employers may view this profile, so make it professional and appealing. When you are finished entering your profile information, click *Done editing.* Take a screenshot of your finished profile and paste it into your answer sheet. Include your LinkedIn profile name. Save your file and submit it as directed by your instructor.

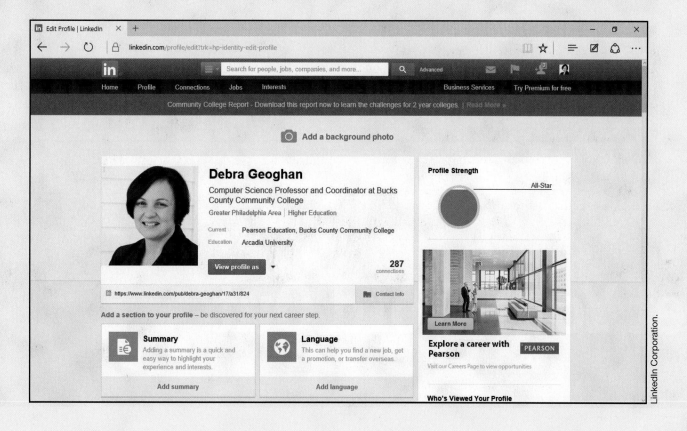

Get Your Word Out

Locate User-Generated Content in the Form of a Blog or Podcast

User-generated content is content created not by professional writers and photographers but by ordinary people. It includes videos and photos posted online, as well as things that are written and said.

During national disasters and major weather events, social media is often the fastest way to receive information. Every award season, major sporting event, election, and breaking news story sets the social media world abuzz.

VIZ CLIP

Microblogging with Twitter

Blogs

A **blog**, or weblog, is an online journal that anyone can set up using simple blog tools and write about whatever they like. Vlogs, or video blogs, are video journals. Blogs are a running commentary—with posts coming frequently (or not so frequently). The difference between just creating a webpage and writing a blog is that a blog can be interactive—your readers can post comments about your blog posts.

There are many prolific bloggers, and some even earn a living by blogging. Some organizations have multi-author blogs, in which multiple authors blog at a common site, rather than have each blogger use his or her own address. Many bloggers link to other related blogs. There are millions of blogs in the **blogosphere**—all the blogs on the web and the connections among them. Two of the most popular blog sites are WordPress (Figure 8.17) and Blogger. Both of these sites allow you to create an account and blog for free.

A more social form of blogging in which posts are typically limited to a relatively small number of characters and users post updates frequently is called **microblogging**. Twitter and Tumblr are the most popular microblogging sites.

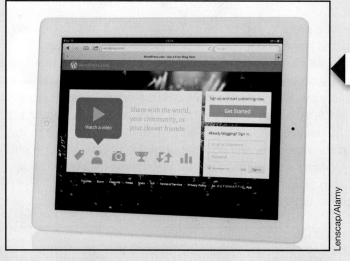

FIGURE 8.17 Wordpress.com

Twitter posts, which are called tweets, are limited to 140 characters each (Figure 8.18). Instead of friends, Twitter users have followers. You can link your Twitter account to your Facebook account, so your tweets will also appear in your Facebook feed. Unlike with most other social networks, you don't have to ask for permission to follow someone on Twitter or Tumblr—although they can block you or create restricted accounts.

With Tumblr, you can post anything from photos, text, and links to videos and music. You can even link your Tumblr account to your Twitter account so that your posts appear on both sites.

FIGURE 8.18 Twitter tweets are limited to 140 characters each.

Podcasts

A **podcast** is a digital media file of a prerecorded radio- or TV-like show that's distributed over the web to be downloaded and played on a computer or portable media player. Podcasts allow both time shifting (listening on your own schedule) and location shifting (taking it with you).

You can find and play podcasts by using a **podcast client** or media player program, such as iTunes, and download single episodes or subscribe to a podcast that's part of a series. There are hundreds of thousands of podcasts available. A few places to search for podcasts are YouTube, iTunes, **podcasts.com**, and **stitcher.com**. Many U.S. government agencies, such as the National Oceanic and Atmospheric Administration (NOAA), produce regular podcasts that you can listen to using a podcast client or directly from their websites, using your browser (Figure 8.19).

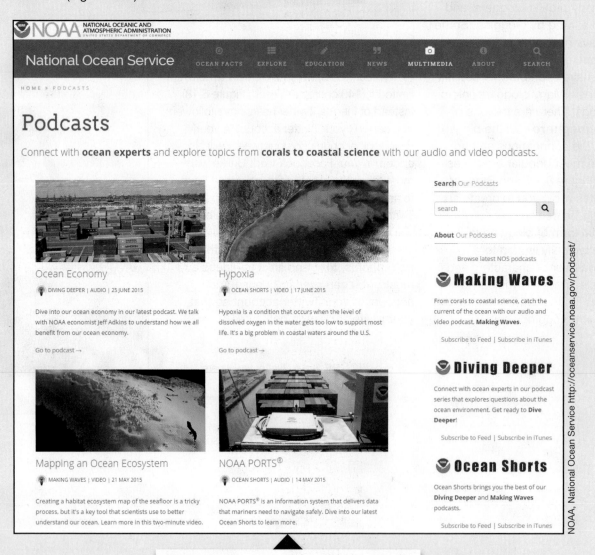

FIGURE 8.19 National Ocean Service Podcasts

RSS

So, how do you keep up with all your favorite websites? **RSS (Really Simple Syndication)** is a format used for distributing web feeds that change frequently—for example, blogs, podcasts, and news. RSS saves you time by sending you updates on the sites you subscribe to. Subscribing to the RSS feeds of your favorite blogs, podcasts, and other websites brings the information right to you. You need a feed reader, such as feedly or Flipboard (Figure 8.20). To subscribe to an RSS feed, you just click the orange RSS icon at the top of the page.

Slaved/Fotolia

Consumer Trends/Alamy

FIGURE 8.20 Flipboard App on an iPad

Running Project

Search for a podcast at podcasts.com about a topic that interests you. Find out as much as you can about the podcast and its creators. Listen to or watch an episode and write a short summary of the contents. Did you enjoy it? Would you subscribe to it? Would you recommend it to a friend? Do you feel this is a good way to get this information? Explain your answers.

Crowdfunding

A social way to get investors for your start-up project or to fund social and charitable projects is **crowdfunding**, which raises money from multiple small investors rather than a few large investors. It also replaces the need to take out a traditional loan. On websites such as **gofundme.com**, **kickstarter.com**, and **indiegogo.com** you can set up campaigns to seek out investors for your project. Or, you can search for interesting projects to support. Often, the investors receive something in return, such as early access to a game or movie, a discounted price for a product, or a t-shirt.

5 Things You Need To Know

- Anybody can create a blog to talk about almost anything.
- A microblog site restricts posts to a limited number of characters.
- Podcasts are radio- or TV-like shows that you can download and listen to or watch anytime.
- You can subscribe to the RSS feeds of blogs, podcasts, and other sites to be notified of new content.
- Crowdfunding raises money from many small investors to fund a project.

Key Terms

blog (weblog)

blogosphere

crowdfunding

microblogging

podcast

podcast client

RSS (Really Simple Syndication)

user-generated content

Create a Blog with Blogger

HOW TO VIDEO

A blog is an online journal that you can easily set up using simple blog tools. In it you can talk about whatever you like. Blogs can be interactive, allowing readers to post comments about blog posts. One website for creating free blogs is **Blogger.com**. To use Blogger, you need to have a Google account. If necessary, download the student data files from pearsonhighered.com/viztech. From your student data files, open the *vt_ch08_howto2_answersheet* file and save the file as **lastname_firstname_ch08_howto2_answersheet**

1 Go to Blogger.com. Use your Google account to log in to Blogger. If necessary, confirm your profile and then click *Continue to Blogger*. Click *New Blog*.

2 On the Create a new blog screen, enter a blog title and address and choose a template. Try to select something that is easy to remember (and spell). You want it to be easy for people to find your blog. Choose a template that visually complements the style and content of your blog. Don't worry—you can change or customize it later. Take a screenshot of this window and paste it into your answer sheet. Click *Create blog!* If necessary, on the Google Domains dialog box, click *No thanks*.

3 You now have a blog. Click the orange *New post* button to begin. The Post screen is where you compose and format your blog postings. Use the formatting toolbar to format your text. Include a title using the Heading Style, center align, and insert an image or video clip in your post.

4 Under Post settings, click *Labels* and type at least one label (tag) to help your readers find posts that are related, and then click *Done*. Click *Options* and allow comments (the default), and then click *Done*.

5 Click *Preview* to view your blog post. Close the Preview tab. Make any edits, and then when you are satisfied with your post, click *Publish*. Share on Google+ if you so choose.

6 Click the *View blog* button to view your finished product. Explain the steps you took to create your blog and include the URL of your blog and a screenshot of the finished blog in your answer sheet. Save the file and submit it as directed by your instructor.

Kurhan/Fotolia

The Wisdom of The Crowd

5 Discuss How Wikis and Other Social Media Sites Rely on the Wisdom of the Crowd

One of the most interesting aspects of the social uses of the web is the reliance on the wisdom of the crowd, or **crowdsourcing**—obtaining the collective opinion of a crowd of people rather than the individual opinion of an expert.

Sites such as Digg, reddit, and Slashdot allow users to share content and webpages they find interesting. **Wikis** are websites that allow users to edit content, even if it was written by someone else. Review sites such as Yelp and TripAdvisor give you both a voice and a place to get advice and recommendations from other folks. Relying on the wisdom of the crowd is much like asking your friends, family, and coworkers for advice. Did you enjoy the movie? Where should I go for the best ice cream? How do you change the oil in your car? Everybody's an expert in something, and the web makes it easier for us to find and share that expertise with each other. But just a word of caution: With anything you read on the web, you should be critical in your evaluation of the credibility and reliability of its author.

Soloviova Liudmyla/Fotolia

Wikis

Wikis differ from blogs and podcasts in that they're designed for collaboration—not just posting responses to another post but actually editing the content. The most well-known wiki is Wikipedia (Figure 8.21), which is a massive free encyclopedia that is written by—anyone. What? How can you trust something that anyone can edit? Well, that's part of the design. The idea is that if many people are involved in a wiki, then the person who knows the right information will (eventually) be the one to write or edit it. There are people that deliberately vandalize Wikipedia articles with incorrect information, so always verify the information you read. In less than 15 years, Wikipedia grew to over 5 million articles in English alone. Wikipedia is a great place to start but is generally frowned upon for use as a source in academic research.

Wikipedia is the most well-known wiki, but it's not the only one. Wikis abound and are often used as a way for communities to develop instructions. For example, wikiHow (Figure 8.22) is a website that contains how-to articles on thousands of topics. You can read, write, or edit an existing wikiHow article or request that someone else write one if you can't find what you're looking for.

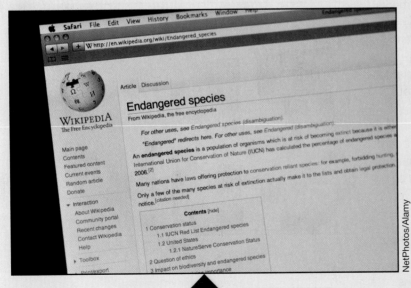

NetPhotos/Alamy

FIGURE 8.21 Wikipedia Online Encyclopedia

NetPhotos/Alamy

FIGURE 8.22 wikiHow has thousands of articles.

Social Review Sites

Social review sites such as TripAdvisor and epinions let users review hotels, movies, games, books, and other products and services. Yelp allows users to review local businesses and places with physical addresses such as parks. Figure 8.23 shows a Yelp map of Times Square restaurants on the iPad app. The reviews are from regular people, not expert food critics, and can help you decide where to eat. You can use the Yelp app on a mobile device to get information when you are right in the area.

FIGURE 8.23 Searching for a Place to Eat in Times Square Using the Yelp App on an iPad

Social Bookmarking and News Sites

Social bookmarking sites allow you to save and share your bookmarks or favorites online. Delicious allows you to not only save and share your bookmarks online but also search the bookmarks of others. It's a great way to quickly find out what other people find interesting and important right now. The links are organized into topics, or tags, to make it easier for you to find links. You can click the *Follow* button if you have a Delicious account, but you don't need an account to browse Delicious.

Pinterest allows you to create virtual cork boards around topics of interest and pin webpages to them (Figure 8.24). You can share your boards with others, and you can follow other people to see what they have pinned. StumbleUpon discovers websites based on your interests. When you sign up, you indicate topics that interest you. Then, as you visit websites, you can click the *StumbleUpon* button to be taken to a similar site. You can click *I like this* to improve the selection of pages you stumble onto.

Social news sites are different from traditional mass media news sites in that at least some of the content is submitted by users. Social news is interactive in a way that traditional media isn't. It's like having millions of friends sharing their finds with you. Content that's submitted more frequently or gets the most votes is promoted to the front page.

FIGURE 8.24 Pinterest

Blaize Pascall/Alamy

Three of the most popular social news sites are reddit, Digg, and Slashdot. Digg doesn't publish content but allows the community to submit content they discover on the web and puts it in one place for everyone to see and to discuss. reddit (Figure 8.25) allows community members to submit content and to vote that content up or down, as well as discuss it. reddit is organized into categories called subreddits. Celebrities often participate in AMA— ask me anything—interviews on reddit. Slashdot, which focuses primarily on technology topics, produces some content but also accepts submissions from its readers. Whatever your interests, there's probably a social news site for you.

FIGURE 8.25 reddit

Ian Dagnall Computing/Alamy

ETHICS

Some people create multiple accounts on social bookmarking and news sites so they can promote their own content. For example, a blogger might create several accounts on Digg and use each one to Digg a blog post, artificially raising its popularity on Digg and driving more traffic to it. This violates the Digg terms of use. But what if the blogger had all his friends and family members create accounts and Digg his post? Is it ethical? Does it violate the terms of use? Is it fair to other bloggers?

Running Project

Go to the Wikipedia article "Reliability of Wikipedia" at wikipedia.org/wiki/Reliability_of_Wikipedia. How does Wikipedia ensure that the content is correct? What procedures are in place to remove or correct mistakes? How does Wikipedia compare to other online sources of information?

3 Things You Need To Know

- Social media relies on the wisdom of the crowd rather than that of an expert.
- Anybody can edit a wiki.
- Social bookmarking and news sites help users find content that others recommend.

Key Terms

crowdsourcing

social bookmarking site

social news site

social review site

wiki

Vladislav Kochelaevs/Fotolia

E-Commerce

6 Explain the Influence of Social Media on E-commerce

Businesses use social media sites to provide support and interaction to customers.
Social media marketing (SMM) is the practice of using social media sites to sell products and services.

Types of E-Commerce

E-commerce is doing business on the web and consists of three categories—B2B, B2C, and C2C—where *B* stands for *business* and *C* stands for *consumer*.

B2B, or business-to-business, services are those that one business provides another, for example, website hosting, website design, and payment services such as PayPal and Google Checkout. B2B services allow smaller companies to have a web presence or store without needing to have the in-house expertise or expense. A small business is able to have a professional-looking website and a sophisticated shopping cart system because of B2B services it purchases from other companies (Figure 8.26).

B2C, or business-to-consumer, is the most familiar form of e-commerce. Amazon.com, Overstock.com, and most other retailers sell their goods and services online. Many small businesses sell exclusively online, eliminating the overhead of running a brick-and-mortar store and increasing their reach to customers outside the area (Figure 8.27). This form of e-commerce has grown exponentially since Pizza Hut began offering pizza ordering on its website in 1994. B2C companies leverage social media to help customers find out about their products.

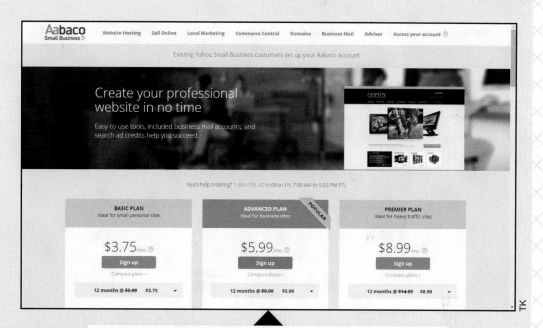

FIGURE 8.26 Aabaco provides B2B services for small companies that want a web presence.

FIGURE 8.27 A small business can use the web to reach customers.

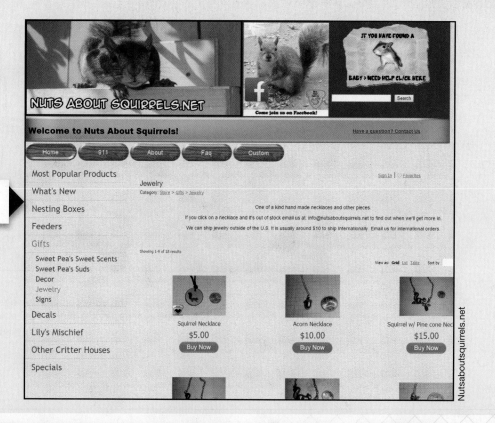

The third form of e-commerce is C2C, or consumer-to-consumer. Websites such as eBay and Craig's List have created a global yard sale, where you can find, sell, or trade virtually anything. eBay (Figure 8.28) has a seller rating system that helps ensure honest transactions and a community that includes discussion boards, groups, and chats. An unscrupulous seller will quickly get a bad reputation, and a top-rated seller will see more sales as a result.

FIGURE 8.28 The eBay community adds social media to the world's largest C2C site.

Vicki Beaver/Alamy

How Safe is My Credit Card?

E-commerce on the web requires you to hand over some sensitive information. So is it okay to shop online? Yes, but just as you wouldn't leave your doors unlocked, you need to be sure that you're shopping wisely. Shop at well-known sites or use third-party payment sites such as Google Checkout or PayPal to protect credit card information. Make sure you're on a secure website when completing transactions. Look at your browser's address bar. If the URL begins with *https*, then the site is using **Secure Sockets Layer (SSL)** security—a protocol that encrypts information before it is sent across the Internet. You'll also notice a padlock icon that indicates a secure site. Clicking on the padlock will open a security report about the website. And don't forget to regularly monitor all credit card transactions to look out for fraud.

JackF/Fotolia

Running Project

Visit Amazon.com. What are two ways that Amazon uses social media marketing? Can you find any other ways? How is this experience different from shopping in a store?

2 Things You Need To Know

- E-commerce is business on the web.
- Social media marketing (SMM) uses social media sites to sell products and services.

Key Terms

e-commerce

Secure Sockets Layer (SSL)

social media marketing (SMM)

Aey/Fotolia

Build A Brand

Develop a Brand Marketing Strategy Using Social Media and Other Online Technologies

When customers go looking for a company or service, they turn to the web. A successful organization in today's digital world needs to have an online presence that includes both a traditional website and social media. There are dozens of social media sites that you could use to promote your business or organization. In this article we'll look at just a few of them.

Facebook Pages

Unlike a Facebook profile, which is linked to a person, a Facebook Page is used to promote an organization, a product, or a service (Figure 8.29). A Facebook Page can have more than one administrator, so you can share the responsibilities among several people or departments. The Facebook Page for this textbook can be found at **facebook.com/visualizingtechnology**. A Page is public, so it can be viewed by anyone, even those who are not logged in to Facebook.

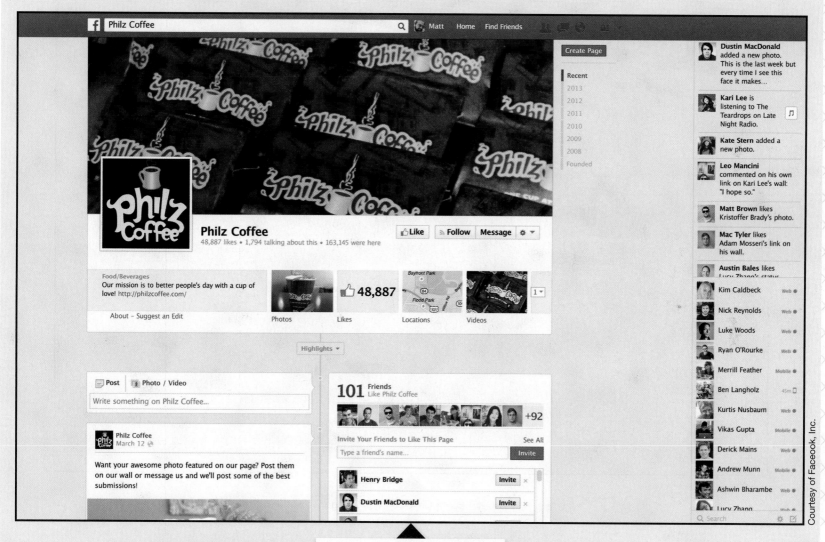

FIGURE 8.29 A Facebook Page

To create a Facebook Page, you need a personal Facebook account. Facebook's Terms of Service permit you to have only one personal Facebook account, but you can create multiple Facebook Pages. So, for example, a college representative might create a page for each department, club, or office. Once you are logged in to your personal account, the option *Create Page* can be found in the menu options. You can choose from several page categories (Figure 8.30). A page for a business or an organization will have different features than a page for a person or cause. When you create a page, read the Facebook Pages terms carefully. Customize your page with a profile picture and header image that represents your brand.

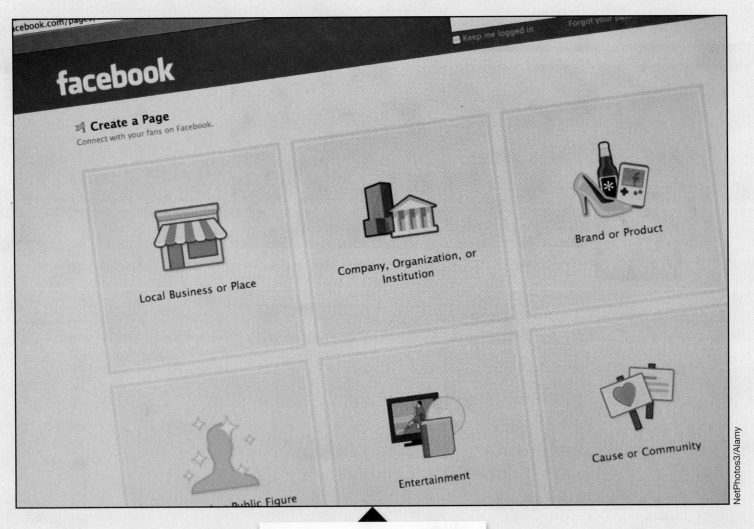

FIGURE 8.30 Create a Page Categories

NetPhotos3/Alamy

A Facebook Page has an Insights section that allows you to view page activity and engagement (Figure 8.31). You can also pay for ads to promote your Facebook Page or website. The key to successful use of any social media tool is to keep it up to date and relevant to your customers. A Facebook Page shouldn't just be a static webpage. Use it to interact with and engage your customers and use it to post interesting updates, specials, and links to relevant information. Check out what other companies are doing on their pages. Try typing **facebook.com/** followed by a brand, an organization, or a company name.

Twitter

Unlike Facebook, Twitter has only one type of account, and you do not have to create a personal account first. So you can use Twitter to engage your customers and members even if you don't use Twitter personally. Visit **business.twitter.com** for information about ways that businesses use Twitter and tools and advice to help you target and engage followers. You can use Twitter to advertise specials, reward loyal customers with discounts, and share your mission and achievements. Share positive messages and include links, images, and videos. Use hashtags—a **hashtag** is a word or phrase preceded by a # symbol—to organize and make your tweets searchable, and respond to customers when they tweet you or retweet your messages. You can set up a Twitter ad campaign, which helps you target your tweets to drive traffic to your website and gain new customers. You pay a fee when users follow your account or retweet, favorite, reply, or click on your promoted tweet.

Customize your profile with a photo, header, bio, and website link and start tweeting. Figure 8.32 shows a Twitter account created for this book, **twitter.com/VizTech4**, with a profile photo, header image, and #myfirsttweet. I used the same images from the book's Facebook Page to keep the brand consistent. You can link your Twitter feed to other accounts like Facebook, and you can embed your feed in your website or blog, so the content you post on Twitter also displays in the other media as well.

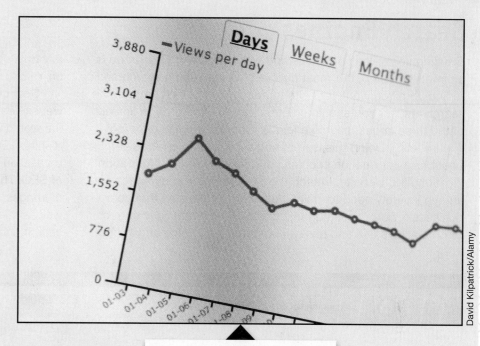

FIGURE 8.31 Facebook Insights

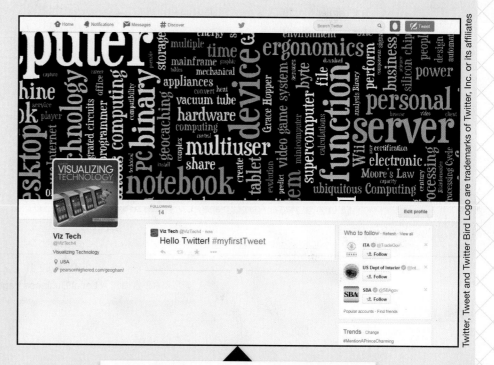

FIGURE 8.32 Customize Your Twitter Profile Page

Search Engines

Creating social media profiles and websites using your brand is an important step, but most people start by using a search engine to find you. You want your site to appear on the first page of the search results. You should create a local business page on each of the three largest search engines: Google, Bing, and Yahoo! (Figure 8.33). Doing this is free, and such a page enables you to post basic information such as your hours, contact information, location, and website. In fact, the page might already exist, and you simply need to claim it as yours. Make sure that your business is correctly categorized and that everything is correct. Google allows users to review businesses, but Bing and Yahoo! rely on Yelp reviews—so you might also want to list your business on Yelp.

Search engine optimization (SEO) is used to make a website easier to find by both people and software that indexes the web and to increase the webpage ranking in search engine results. SEO is most often associated with using keywords and key phrases in the webpage content and code, but this is only one part of SEO. The quality and quantity of content on a site; the number of images, videos, and external links; the social media presence; as well as the number of visitors that click on the link to a site in the search engine results all factor into search engine rankings.

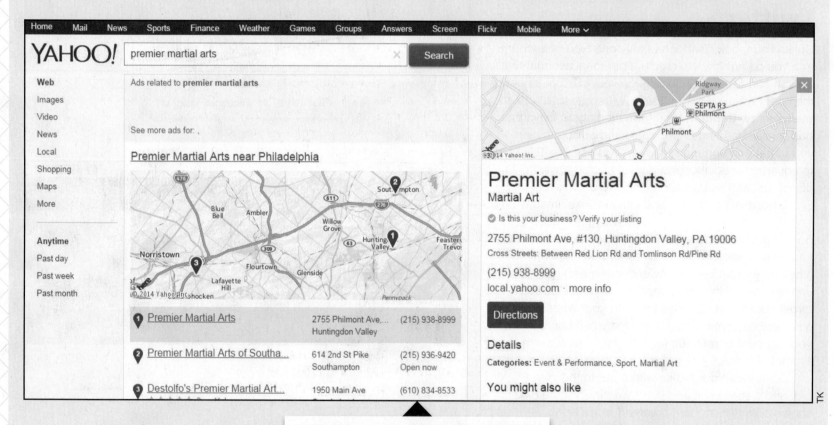

FIGURE 8.33 A Local Business Page on Yahoo!

BLOGGER—Although many blogs are personal in nature and earn the writer no compensation, some lucky folks are professional bloggers. These bloggers may be paid by a company to blog about a product or provide news or reviews, and their blogs are usually part of a bigger website. Some professional bloggers use their blogs to drive customers to their other products. Successful bloggers monetize the content on their sites in several ways, including placing ads and links to other sites. A professional blog may earn money by using Google AdSense to place ads and links on it. It takes a lot of time and work to write a good blog and even more to make money doing it.

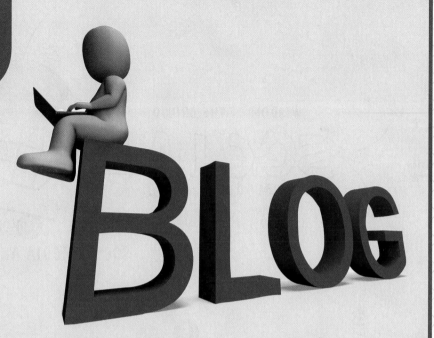

Stuart Miles/Fotolia

Running Project

Select a local business that you regularly patronize or are interested in learning about, and search the web for evidence of online brand marketing. Does this business have a social media presence on Facebook, Google, Yahoo!, Twitter? How easy is it for a potential customer to locate information about the business? What advice would you give to this business to improve its online presence?

Viz Check—In MyITLab, take a quick quiz covering Objectives 4–7.

2 Things You Need To Know

- Organizations should maintain an online presence that includes both a traditional website and social media.
- Successful search engine optimization (SEO) makes a website easier to find.

Key Terms

hashtag

search engine optimization (SEO)

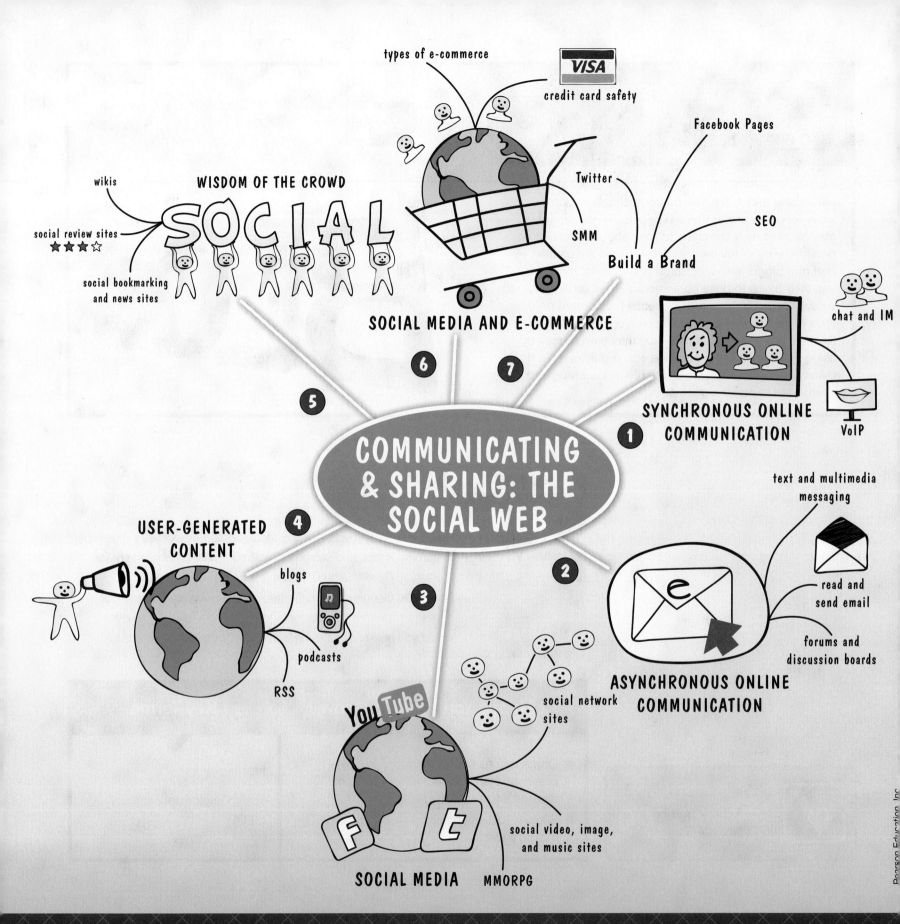

WISDOM OF THE CROWD

wikis

social review sites ★★★☆

social bookmarking and news sites

SOCIAL

types of e-commerce

VISA

credit card safety

Facebook Pages

Twitter

SEO

SMM

Build a Brand

SOCIAL MEDIA AND E-COMMERCE

chat and IM

VoIP

SYNCHRONOUS ONLINE COMMUNICATION

⑥ ⑦

⑤

①

COMMUNICATING & SHARING: THE SOCIAL WEB

USER-GENERATED CONTENT

④

blogs

podcasts

RSS

text and multimedia messaging

read and send email

②

forums and discussion boards

ASYNCHRONOUS ONLINE COMMUNICATION

③

YouTube

social network sites

social video, image, and music sites

SOCIAL MEDIA   MMORPG

Objectives Recap

1. Compare Different Forms of Synchronous Online Communication
2. Compare Different Forms of Asynchronous Online Communication
3. Discuss the Impact of Social Media in Society
4. Locate User-Generated Content in the Form of a Blog or Podcast
5. Discuss How Wikis and Other Social Media Sites Rely on the Wisdom of the Crowd
6. Explain the Influence of Social Media on E-commerce
7. Develop a Brand Marketing Strategy Using Social Media and Other Online Technologies

Key Terms

asynchronous online communication **386**
avatar **395**
blog (weblog) **405**
blogosphere **405**
captcha (Completely Automated Public Turing Test to Tell Computers and Humans Apart) **387**
chat **383**
crowdfunding **407**
crowdsourcing **412**
digital footprint **393**
e-commerce **417**
email **387**
forum **391**
hashtag **423**
instant messaging (IM) **383**
massively multiplayer online role-playing game (MMORPG) **395**
microblogging **405**
podcast **406**

podcast client **406**
RSS (Really Simple Syndication) **407**
search engine optimization (SEO) **424**
second screen **393**
Secure Sockets Layer (SSL) **419**
social bookmarking site **414**
social media **393**
social media marketing (SMM) **416**
social network **393**
social news site **414**
social review site **414**
synchronous online communication **382**
text messaging **390**
user-generated content **404**
viral video **396**
VoIP (Voice over IP) **385**
Web 2.0 **392**
wiki **413**

Summary

1. **Compare Different Forms of Synchronous Online Communication**

   Synchronous communication happens in real time. Chat usually involves more than two people having a conversation in a chat room and is usually text based. Instant messaging is similar to chat, but the conversation is between only two people. The terms *IM* and *chat* are often used interchangeably. VoIP service uses the Internet to place voice and video phone calls.

2. **Compare Different Forms of Asynchronous Online Communication**

   Email is an asynchronous, store-and-forward technology. You shouldn't expect that your email is private. You can access email by using webmail or a desktop email program. Use the To, Cc, and Bcc fields to address your messages and the subject line to tell the receiver what the message is about.

3. **Discuss the Impact of Social Media in Society**

   Social networking and sharing allow you to keep in touch, create content, share ideas, and benefit from the expertise of others. You no longer need to rely on experts for news or advice.

4. **Locate User-Generated Content in the Form of a Blog or Podcast**

   Blogs can be created on websites such as Blogger and WordPress. Podcasts can be found using a podcast client or by searching websites such as YouTube or podcasts.com. RSS feeds push frequently updated content to subscribers.

5. **Discuss How Wikis and Other Social Media Sites Rely on the Wisdom of the Crowd**

   Wikis are unique because anyone can edit their content. Many types of social websites, including wikis, rely on the wisdom of the crowd rather than experts. Social review sites let users review hotels, movies, games, books, and other products and services; social bookmarking sites allow you to save and share your bookmarks or favorites online; and social news sites are different from traditional media news sites in that at least some of the content is submitted by users.

6. **Explain the Influence of Social Media on E-commerce**

   Businesses leverage social media through social media marketing strategies such as contests, fan pages, and review sites. B2B (business-to-business), B2C (business-to-consumer), and C2C (consumer-to-consumer) are three forms of e-commerce.

Summary continues on the next page

Summary *continued*

7. Develop a Brand Marketing Strategy Using Social Media and Other Online Technologies
A successful organization in today's digital world needs to have an online presence that includes both a traditional website and social media. Important tools to use include Facebook Pages, Twitter, and local business pages on search engines, including Google, Yahoo!, and Bing. Search engine optimization (SEO) is used to make a website easier to find by both people and software that indexes the web and to increase the webpage ranking in search engine results.

Multiple Choice

Answer the multiple-choice questions below for more practice with key terms and concepts from this chapter.

1. Which form of online communication happens in real time?
   a. Blog
   b. Chat
   c. Email
   d. Forums

2. Which technology allows calls to be transmitted over the Internet instead of via traditional phone lines or cellular towers?
   a. Instant messaging
   b. Forums
   c. Message boards
   d. VoIP

3. A(n) _____ is used to prevent automated software from creating online accounts.
   a. captcha
   b. email signature
   c. store-and-forward technology
   d. SMS

4. Which field is like an FYI and generally means that a reply isn't expected?
   a. Bcc
   b. Cc
   c. Fw
   d. To

5. Websites that enable you to create content, connect, network, and share are called _____.
   a. asynchronous
   b. MMORPG
   c. social media
   d. viral

6. Facebook and LinkedIn are examples of _____.
   a. forums
   b. MMORPGs
   c. social networks
   d. wikis

7. Your _____ is all the information that someone could find out about you by searching the web, including social networking sites.
   a. avatar
   b. digital footprint
   c. profile
   d. screen name

8. Which type of social media site are Twitter and Tumblr?
   a. Bookmarking
   b. Forum
   c. Microblog
   d. Wiki

9. What service is used to distribute web feeds to subscribers?
   a. Captcha
   b. Podcast
   c. SMS
   d. RSS

10. _____ is the practice of using social media sites to sell products and services.
    a. B2B
    b. SEO
    c. SMM
    d. Twitter

True or False

Answer the following questions with T for true or F for false for more practice with key terms and concepts from this chapter.

_____ 1. Chat is a service that allows phone calls to be transmitted over the Internet instead of traditional phone lines.

_____ 2. Email is not private and can be read by others.

_____ 3. Using the Short Message Service (SMS), you can send brief electronic messages between mobile devices.

_____ 4. Social media enables users to create user-generated content, connect, network, and share.

_____ 5. A viral video spreads computer viruses.

_____ 6. User-generated content includes videos and photos posted online but not what is written and said.

_____ 7. You must download a podcast to a media player in order to listen to it.

_____ 8. Like a wiki, a blog usually has many authors.

_____ 9. Crowdsourcing means obtaining the collective opinion of a crowd of people rather than the individual opinion of an expert.

_____ 10. E-commerce is the practice of using social media sites to sell products and services.

Fill in the Blank

Fill in the blanks with key terms from this chapter.

1. _____ online communication happens in real time.

2. A(n) _____ is an online, asynchronous conversation, also known as a discussion board.

3. Tools called _____ are used to communicate and collaborate on the web and enable you to be a creator, not just a consumer, of content.

4. Your _____ is all the information that someone could find out about you by searching the web, including social networking sites.

5. A(n) _____ is an online journal.

6. The _____ consists of all the blogs on the web and the connections between them.

7. A(n) _____ is a digital media file of a prerecorded radio- or TV-like show that's distributed over the web.

8. A(n) _____ is a website that allows users to edit content, even if it was written by someone else.

9. _____ sites let users review hotels, movies, games, books, and other products and services.

10. _____ is used to make a website easier to find by both people and software that indexes the web and to increase the webpage ranking in search engine results.

Running Project ...

... The Finish Line

Use your answers from the previous sections of the chapter project to discuss the impact of social networking on society. How has it changed the way we keep in touch with others? Do business? How has it personally changed the way you connect with others? Write a report responding to the questions raised throughout the chapter. Save your file as **lastname_firstname_ch08_project** and submit it to your instructor as directed.

Do It Yourself 1

Instant messaging and chatting are important tools businesses use to provide services to customers. Some schools also offer virtual advisors and librarians that you can chat with live online. From your student data files, open the file *vt_ch08_DIY1_answersheet* and save the file as **lastname_firstname_ch08_DIY1_answersheet**

If your school or local library offers this service, use it to ask about the success of this service. Take a screenshot of your conversation and paste it into your answer sheet. If you don't have a local library that uses chat or IM, use the Internet to find another library that does. Have you ever used this type of service in researching a topic? What type of help can this particular library chat service provide? What are the hours the service is available? What other online resources does the library offer? Type up your answers, save the file, and submit your work as directed by your instructor.

Do It Yourself 2

Many websites require you to provide an email address to register and use the site. In this activity, you will create a free Yahoo! email account. From your student data files, open the file *vt_ch08_DIY2_answersheet* and save the file as **lastname_firstname_ch08_DIY2_answersheet**

1. Go to yahoo.com and if you're already logged in to Yahoo!, click your name and sign out. Click *Sign In* and then click *Sign up for a new account*. Fill in the form. Click *Create Account*. What are the rules for creating a password on this site?

2. After you successfully create your account you will be redirected to the Yahoo! homepage. Click *Hi, yourprofilename*. On the Hello page, click *Personal info page*. Click *CHANGE COVER IMAGE* and select a new cover. Close the CHANGE COVER IMAGE panel. Under Preferences, enter your location information. If you choose, add a profile picture or other information. Take a screenshot of your profile page, paste the image into your answer sheet, and save and submit your file as directed by your instructor.

File Management

Social sharing sites allow you to put your videos and images online. To help organize this content, these sites use social tagging. For this activity, you'll create tags for a group of images. From your student files, open the file *vt_ch08_FM_answersheet* and save the file as **lastname_firstname_ch08_FM_answersheet**

1. Using File Explorer or Finder, navigate to the student data files for this chapter. Look at the 21 images in the *vt_ch08_file_management* folder. In your answer sheet, for each image, list at least two tags that you would use to tag the file. Try to use the same tags for multiple files.

Image	Tag 1	Tag 2

2. Go to the Flickr website and search for the three tags that you used the most often in your table. Do you find images that are similar to the ones you tagged? Do you think you did a good job of tagging them? Take a screenshot of one of the images you found and paste it into your answer sheet. Save your file and submit it as directed by your instructor.

Critical Thinking

Social networks are often criticized in the media for their privacy settings. In this exercise you will examine the privacy policy of Facebook to determine the appropriate settings to use for your own profile. You do not need to have a Facebook account to do this exercise. From your student data files, open the file *vt_ch08_CT_answersheet* and save the file as **lastname_firstname_ch08_CT_answersheet**

Go to www.facebook.com/about/basics. Read through the various topics on this page. How does Facebook protect your privacy? What are the default privacy settings, and do you think they do a good job protecting you? If you have a Facebook account, have you set your privacy settings to keep your personal information protected? When was the last time you checked and updated them? Have the terms of service changed since you first joined this network? Type up your answers, save your answer sheet, and submit it as directed by your instructor.

Ethical Dilemma

Your digital footprint says a lot about you, but not everything is true or accurate. When you're a student, you may not think about the impact your digital life will have on future employment. Potential employers may search the web looking for information on job applicants. From your student data files, open the file *vt_ch08_ethics_answersheet* and save the file as **lastname_firstname_ch08_ethics_answersheet**

Is it ethical for a potential employer to use the Internet this way? Is it legal? What if an angry ex-boyfriend or ex-girlfriend posted some things pretending to be you? How might this affect your chances for employment? Do you think it's okay to post things that make you look good, even if they're not true? Use the Internet to look up Internet defamation. Look up the definitions of *libel* and *slander*. How do they differ? What are the legal consequences of each? Type up your answers, save the file, and submit your work as directed by your instructor.

On the Web

Using social news sites is a great way to find out what other people think is important. From your student data files, open the file *vt_ch08_web_answersheet* and save the file as **lastname_firstname_ch08_web_answersheet**

Visit Slashdot, reddit, or Digg. What are some of the recent stories? How do these compare to the headlines today in traditional mass media? Select two stories that you think are interesting or important and write a short summary of each. Why did you select these stories? Type up your answers, save the file, and submit your answer sheet as directed by your instructor.

Collaboration

With a group of three to five students, research the history of social networks and create a timeline showing five to seven important milestones of this development.

Instructors: Divide the class into groups of three to five students.

The Project: As a team, research the history of social networks. Create a timeline showing five to seven important milestones of social networks. Use at least three references. Use Google Drive or Microsoft Office to prepare your research and provide documentation that all team members have contributed to the project.

Outcome: Use a free online timeline generator, a drawing program, a word processor, or a presentation tool to create your timeline and present it to your class. The presentation may be no longer than 3 minutes and should contain five to seven milestones. Turn in a final version of your presentation named **teamname_ch08_timeline** and your file showing your collaboration named **teamname_ch08_collab** Be sure to include the name of your presentation and a listing of all team members. Submit your presentation to your instructor as directed.

Application Project

Office 2016 Application Projects
PowerPoint 2016: Browsers

Project Description: In this project, you will create a presentation about desktop browsers. In this presentation, you will apply design and color themes. You will also insert and format a chart and apply animations to objects on your slides, as well as transitions between slides. If necessary, download student data files from **pearsonhighered.com/viztech**.

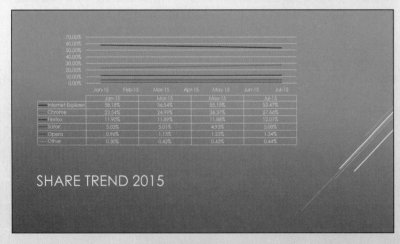

Step	Instructions
1	Start PowerPoint. From your student data files, open *vt_ch08_ppt*. Save the file as **lastname_firstname_ch08_ppt**
2	Apply the Slice theme, green variant, to the presentation.
3	On Slide 1, using your name, type **Firstname Lastname** in the subtitle placeholder.
4	On Slide 2, change the bullets to Arrow bullets and set the line spacing to 1.5.
5	Apply the Appear animation and set a duration of 00.50 to the bulleted list on Slide 2.
6	On Slide 3 in the title placeholder, type **SHARE TREND 2015**
7	On Slide 3, in the content placeholder, add a line chart. In the range A1:G5 enter the following data to create the chart:

Month	Internet Explorer	Chrome	Firefox	Safari	Opera	Other
January 2015	58.18%	23.54%	11.90%	5.03%	0.96%	0.39%
March 2015	56.54%	24.99%	11.89%	5.01%	1.15%	0.42%
May 2015	55.15%	26.37%	11.88%	4.93%	1.23%	0.43%
July 2015	53.47%	27.66%	12.01%	5.08%	1.34%	0.44%

Step	Instructions
8	Change the chart to Layout 5. Delete the Chart Title and Axis Title.
9	Insert a new Title and Content slide after Slide 3. On Slide 4, in the title placeholder, type **SOURCE** In the content placeholder, type **Netmarketshare.com** and remove the bullet.
10	Apply the Split transition to all slides in the presentation.
11	Insert the footer **Firstname Lastname,** using your name, on the notes and handout pages for all slides in the presentation. View the presentation in Slide Show, view from beginning to end, and then return to Normal view.
12	Save the presentation and close PowerPoint. Submit the presentation as directed.

Application Project

Office 2016 Application Projects
Excel 2016: Broadband Internet Growth

Project Description: In this project, using data from the World Bank, you will format a spreadsheet and create and format a chart showing broadband growth from 2000 to 2013. If necessary, download student data files from **pearsonhighered.com/viztech.**

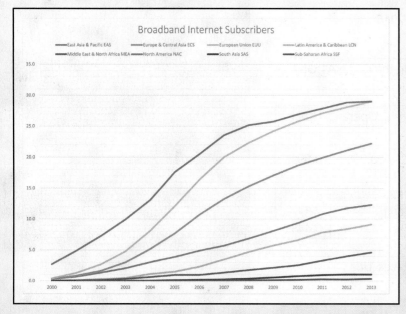

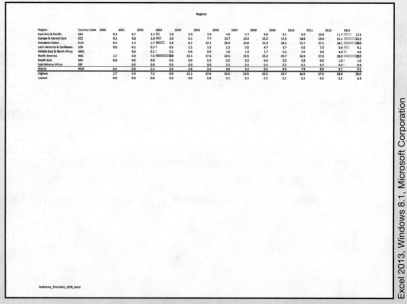

Step	Instructions
1	Start Excel. From your student data files, open the Excel file *vt_ch08_excel*. Save the file as **lastname_firstname_ch08_excel**
2	On the Regions sheet, select the range C2:P10. Apply the Number Format to the selected range. Decrease the decimals displayed to 1.
3	Select A1:P1 and apply the Heading 4 cell style.
4	Adjust the widths of columns A and B to fit the contents.
5	Select A10:P10 and apply a Top and Double Bottom Border to the range.
6	In cell A11, type **Highest** In cell A12, type **Lowest**
7	In cell C11, use a function to calculate the highest number of broadband subscriptions in the range C2:C9; do not include the world data. Copy the formula from C11:P11.
8	In cell C12, use a function to calculate the lowest number of broadband subscriptions in the range C2:C9. Copy the formula from C12:P12.
9	Select the range A1:P9 and insert a line chart. Move the chart to a new sheet named **Line Chart** Format the chart Style 8.
10	Change the chart title to **Broadband Internet Subscribers**
11	On the Regions sheet, apply the Gradient Blue Data Bar conditional formatting to the range F2:F9 and apply the Gradient Orange Data Bar conditional formatting to the range P2:P9.
12	Change the orientation of the Regions worksheet to Landscape. Adjust the Scale option to change the Width to 1 page.
13	Insert a header with the sheet name in the center cell. Insert a footer with the file name in the left cell. Return to Normal view.
14	Ensure that the worksheets are correctly named and placed in the following order in the workbook: Line Chart, Regions, Source. Save the workbook and then exit Excel. Submit the workbook as directed.

Nmedia/Fotolia

Networks and Communication

In This Chapter

The Internet is the largest computer network in the world, but it is actually a network of networks. On a much smaller scale, most of the computers that you use at school and in the workplace are part of a network, and you may also have a network at home. When you have finished this chapter, you'll be able to identify and use different kinds of computer networks.

Objectives

1 Discuss the Importance of Computer Networks

2 Compare Different Types of LANs and WANs

3 List and Describe the Hardware Used in Both Wired and Wireless Networks

4 List and Describe Network Software and Protocols

5 Explain How to Protect a Network

Running Project

In this chapter, you'll learn about computer networks and communication. Look for instructions as you complete each article. For most articles, there is a series of questions for you to research. At the conclusion of this chapter, you'll submit your responses to the questions raised.

Pixelrobot/Fotolia

From Sneakernet to Hotspots

Objective

1 Discuss the Importance of Computer Networks

A **computer network** is two or more computers that share resources. **Network resources** can be software, hardware, or files. Computer networks can save you both time and money and make it easier to work, increasing productivity. Before computers were connected in networks, moving files between them involved physically putting them on a disk and carrying the disk to the new machine. This is wistfully referred to by some as *sneakernet*.

Peer-to-Peer Networks

Figure 9.1 shows a small peer-to-peer network like one you might have set up at home. In a **peer-to-peer (P2P) network**, all computers are considered equal—each device can share its resources with every other device, and there's no centralized authority. The computers might, for example, share music files and a printer. Although they can share an Internet connection, they don't necessarily have to connect to the Internet at all. Computers in a P2P network belong to a **workgroup**.

Most P2P networks are found in homes or small businesses. P2Ps don't require a specialized NOS (network operating system). Desktop and mobile operating systems include the networking features to set up and join a P2P network.

P2Ps are easy to set up and configure and provide basic file and print sharing. For example, if you have a printer in your house that's connected to your desktop computer, you can easily share the printer with your notebook computer through your home network. The drawback to this type of setup is that the computer that's sharing a resource must be turned on for the other computers in the network to access its resources—if your desktop computer is turned off or in sleep mode, then the notebook will be unable to print.

Windows makes setting up a home network an easy task. When you add a new computer to your home and turn it on, Windows will automatically detect the other devices that are already on your network. Windows Network and Sharing Center enables you to view and configure your network settings (Figure 9.2).

FIGURE 9.1 A simple peer-to-peer network enables devices to share resources.

Pearson Education, Inc.

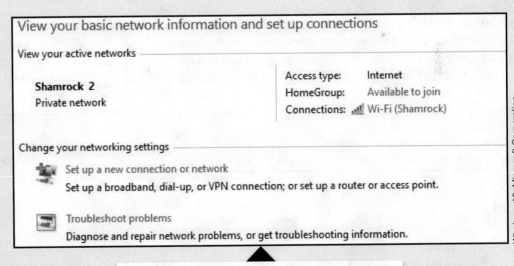

FIGURE 9.2 Windows Network and Sharing Center

Windows 10, Microsoft Corporation

In File Explorer, in the Navigation pane, click *Network* to view the devices on your network. Figure 9.3 shows a mixed home network consisting of both Windows and Mac computers, a smart TV, and a router. Other devices that you can have on a home network include printers, tablets, smartphones, and video game consoles.

Windows includes a simple networking feature called a **homegroup**, which consists of the computers on your home network running Windows 7 or higher that are configured with the same homegroup password. Once you create a homegroup, Windows will create a password that you can use to join all your other Windows computers to the homegroup. Members of a homegroup automatically share their pictures, music, video libraries, and printers with each other without any additional configuration. In Figure 9.4, you can see a homegroup in the File Explorer window. In the Navigation pane, my MacBook laptop—DEBRAS-AIR—is visible under Network but does not appear under Homegroup, because Macs and other computers not running Windows can't join a homegroup.

To share resources with other computers, you must use a workgroup. Although the Mac, running OS X, is visible in the Windows network, it must be configured to share files with Windows computers. Setting up sharing in a workgroup is not difficult but takes a bit more work than setting up a homegroup. Computers in a workgroup need to have the same workgroup and account information configured. By default, Windows computers belong to the workgroup called *workgroup*. A Mac can view both Mac and Windows computers in a mixed network through Finder (Figure 9.5), but Mac computers need to be configured to share resources with Windows computers. A Linux computer can also view and access workgroup resources with some configuration.

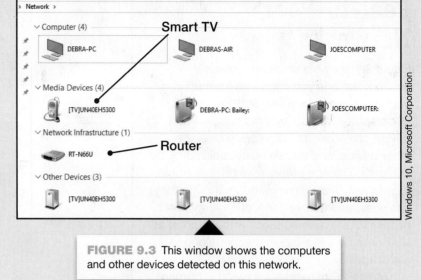

FIGURE 9.3 This window shows the computers and other devices detected on this network.

FIGURE 9.4 A Homegroup and Other Network Computers

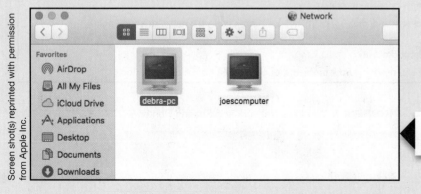

FIGURE 9.5 This Mac network includes both Windows and Mac computers.

Client–Server Networks

P2P networks are suitable for homes and very small businesses, but they have two major drawbacks. They're limited to a small number of devices, and they provide no centralization of resources and security. In most business settings, a better choice is a **client–server network**—a network that has at least one server at its center (Figure 9.6).

A **server** is a multiuser computer system that runs a network operating system (NOS) and provides services— such as Internet access, email, or file and print services—to client systems. The personal computers and other devices that connect to the server are called **clients**. Server computers range from very small to massive enterprise-level systems that serve hundreds of thousands of clients. The server provides a way to centralize the network management, resources, and security. In a client–server network, users log in to the network instead of to their local computers and are granted access to resources based on their logins.

FIGURE 9.6
A Client–Server Network with a Centralized Server

Cutimage/Fotolia

Running Project

Select a computer network that you use (school, home, or work). Is it a P2P or client–server network? How do you connect to it? What resources do you access or share on this network?

3 Things You Need To Know	Key Terms
• A computer network is two or more computers that share resources, such as software, hardware, or files. • A peer-to-peer (P2P) network is a network in which all computers belong to the same workgroup and are considered equal. • A client–server network is a network that has at least one server at its center that provides centralized management, resources, and security.	client client–server network computer network homegroup network resource peer-to-peer (P2P) network server workgroup

Examine Network and Sharing Settings

HOW TO VIDEO

In this activity, you'll examine your current network settings and share resources on your network. (Note that in a school network, security settings may prevent you from being able to perform parts of this exercise.) If necessary, download student data files from **pearsonhighered.com/viztech**. From your student data files, open the *vt_ch09_howto1_answersheet* file and save the file as **lastname_firstname_ch09_howto1_answersheet**

1 From the Windows desktop, right-click the network icon on the taskbar and click *Open Network and Sharing Center*. Take note of the Connections listed in the right pane. In the left pane, click *Change adapter settings*. How many network connections do you have on this computer? Which ones are connected? Take a screenshot and paste it into your answer sheet.

Windows 10, Microsoft Corporation

2 Locate the connection that you are currently using and double-click it to open the status window. Is this connection wired or wireless? What speed is the connection? Click the *Details* button. What is the IPv4 address of this connection? What other information can you locate here? Take a screenshot and paste it into your answer sheet. Close the open dialog boxes and windows.

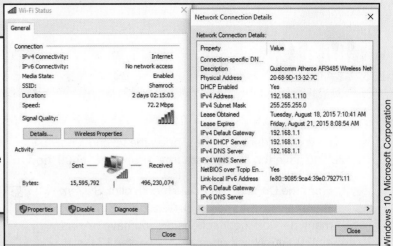

Windows 10, Microsoft Corporation

3 Open File Explorer and click *Network* in the Navigation pane. List the other devices in your network. What resources do you access or share from or with these devices? Take a screenshot and paste it into your answer sheet. Close File Explorer.

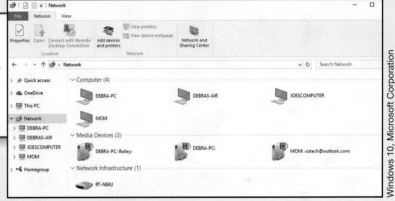

Windows 10, Microsoft Corporation

4 Right-click on the desktop, point to *New*, and click *Folder*. Name the folder **myshare**. Right-click the *myshare* folder and point to *Share with*. By default, who is this folder shared with? Click *Specific people* to open the File Sharing control panel window. Click the down arrow next to Add. Who can you share this folder with? Choose *Everyone* and click *Add*. By default, what permissions are granted to Everyone? Take a screenshot and paste it into your document. Click *Cancel* and then delete the folder. Save your answer sheet, including screenshots, and submit as directed.

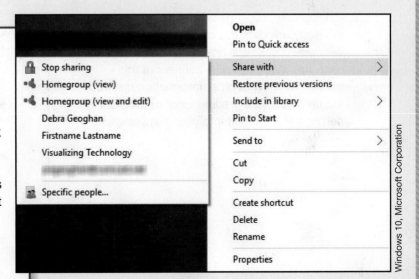

Windows 10, Microsoft Corporation

MAC

If you are using a Mac:
From your student data files, open the *vt_ch09_howto1_answersheet_mac*
file and save the file as **lastname_firstname_ch09_howto1_answersheet_mac**

1. From the Dock or the Apple menu, click *System Preferences* and then click *Network*. How many network connections do you have on this computer? Which ones are connected? Take a screenshot and paste it into your answer sheet.

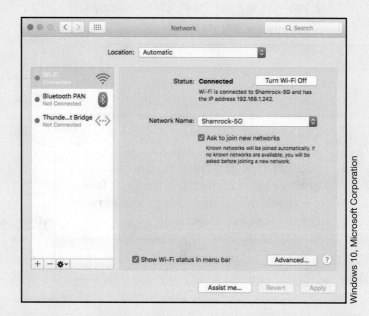

Windows 10, Microsoft Corporation

2. If necessary, click the connection that you are currently using. Is this connection wired or wireless? Click *Advanced*. Click and review each tab. What is the IP address of this connection? What other information can you locate here? Take a screenshot of the TCP/IP settings and paste it into your answer sheet.

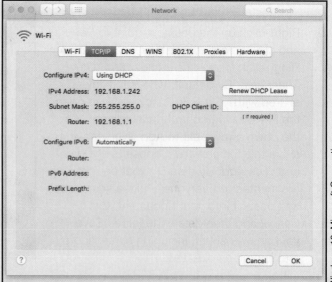

Windows 10, Microsoft Corporation

3. Open Finder. Click the *Go* menu, then click *Network*. List the other devices in your network. What resources do you access or share from or with these devices? Take a screenshot and paste it into your answer sheet.

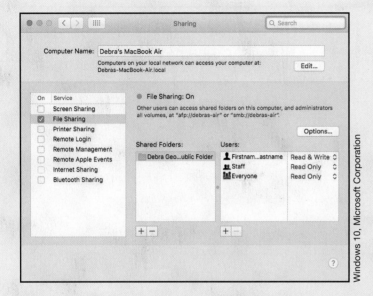

4. In Finder, click *Desktop*. Click *File*, click *New Folder*, and name the new folder **myshare**. Return to the System Preferences window and click *Sharing*. What resources are you sharing? If necessary, check *File Sharing*. What folders are shared?
5. Click *Options* and, if necessary, select *Share files and folders using SMB* to make your shares accessible to Windows computers on your network. Click *Done*. In the Sharing window, click the + sign, navigate to your new folder, and then click *Add* to share your new folder. Take a screenshot and paste it into your answer sheet. If you have a Windows computer on the same network, see if you can access your Mac files from it. Save your file, including screenshots, and submit it as directed.

Tomasz Zajda/Fotolia

LANs and WANs

Objective 2

Compare Different Types of LANs and WANs

Networks come in many different shapes and sizes. In this article, we discuss some of the most common types of networks found in both homes and businesses.

SIMULATION Networks

Small Networks

A **local area network (LAN)** is a network in which all connected devices or nodes are located in the same physical location. On a small scale, a home network is a LAN. In a business, a LAN might consist of a single room, a floor, a building, or an entire campus. A home LAN is probably a peer-to-peer network, but a business LAN is more likely to be a client–server network that consists of computers, printers, and servers as well as the network hardware that connects them. Devices on a LAN are connected using switches (Figure 9.7) or wireless access points.

A small network that consists of devices connected by **Bluetooth**—a technology that connects peripherals wirelessly at short ranges—is referred to as a **personal area network (PAN)**. Bluetooth has a very limited range of only about 10 to 100 meters (30 to 300 feet). Bluetooth is designed to be easy to use, enabling devices to talk to each other securely over short distances. The most common Bluetooth used for personal electronics has a range of 30 feet and a data transfer rate of up to 3 Mbps. Each device in a PAN can connect to up to seven other devices at a time. Some common devices that use Bluetooth include mice, keyboards, interactive whiteboards, headsets, smartphones, cameras, media players, video game consoles, speakers, and printers (Figure 9.8).

A LAN that uses Wi-Fi to transmit data is known as a **wireless LAN (WLAN)**. Wi-Fi uses radio waves to provide wireless, high-speed network connections; it has a much larger range, higher speeds, and better security, and it supports more devices than Bluetooth, but it is also more expensive and complicated to set up.

Vladimirs/Fotolia

FIGURE 9.7 A switch connects a client to a LAN.

Dean Bertoncelj/Shutterstock

FIGURE 9.8 A Personal Area Network Using Bluetooth Devices: Mouse, Keyboard, Headset

Lan Topologies

A home LAN uses the same Ethernet standards and equipment used in larger business networks. **Standards**—specifications that have been defined by an industry organization—ensure that equipment made by different companies work together. The **Ethernet** standard defines the way data is transmitted over a local area network.

Network data transmission speed is measured in bits per second. Ethernet networks transmit signals over twisted-pair cable, fiber-optic cable, and Wi-Fi at data transmission speeds of 10 Mbps to 10 Gbps. Most home networks use 100 Mbps or 1 Gbps Ethernet—also called Gigabit Ethernet. The maximum speed depends on the type of media and capability of the network hardware on the LAN.

The devices, or nodes, on the LAN can be connected in three physical layouts: bus, ring, or star **topology** (Figure 9.9). In a bus topology, the nodes are all connected via a single cable. The data travels back and forth along the cable, which is terminated at both ends. In a ring topology, the devices are connected to a single cable, but the ends of the cable are connected in a circle, and the data travels around the circle in one direction. Both buses and rings are simple networks that were popular in the past; you are not likely to find a pure bus or ring network today. Modern LANs use a physical star topology—or a hybrid star–ring or star–bus topology. In a star topology, every node on the network is attached to a central device such as a switch or wireless access point. This connection device allows nodes to be easily added, removed, or moved without disrupting the network.

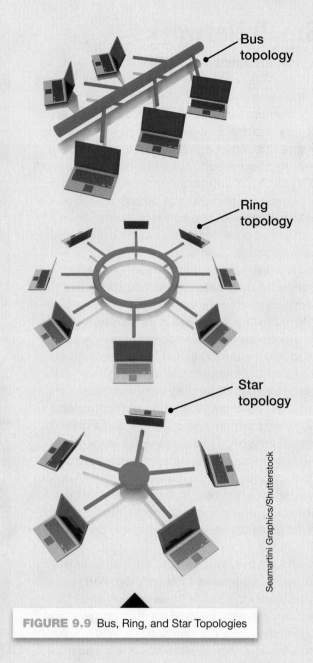

Bus topology

Ring topology

Star topology

Seamartini Graphics/Shutterstock

FIGURE 9.9 Bus, Ring, and Star Topologies

Large Networks

A **wide area network (WAN)** is a network that spans multiple locations and connects multiple LANs over dedicated communication lines using **routers**—devices that connect two or more networks together. A college that has multiple campuses uses WAN connections between them (Figure 9.10). WAN technologies are much more expensive than LAN technologies. At home, the WAN you connect to is the Internet, and the port on your router that connects to the modem may be labeled the *WAN* or *Internet* port, distinguishing it from the LAN ports your other devices connect to.

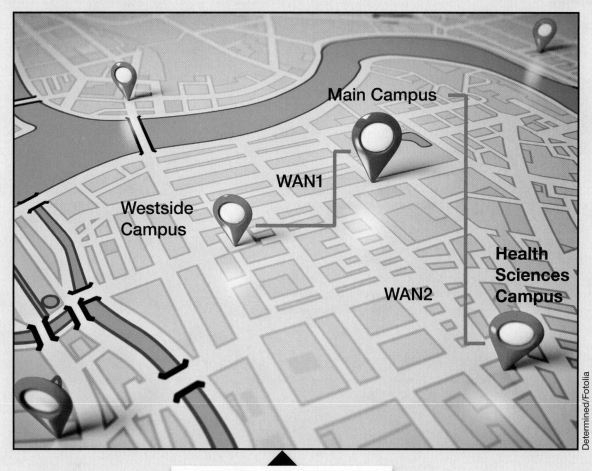

FIGURE 9.10 A WAN connects LANs located at different campuses.

Determined/Fotolia

What if you need to connect to your work network from home or while on the road? Because you're located in a different location, you must use a WAN connection to access your work network. It isn't practical for a business to provide its employees dedicated WAN lines for every offsite location. Instead, companies use a special type of connection called a **virtual private network (VPN)** (Figure 9.11). A VPN creates a private network through the public network—the Internet—allowing a remote user to access a LAN securely without needing a dedicated line. VPNs use encryption to ensure that data is secure as it travels through the public network. This is much less expensive and more practical for businesses than providing a dedicated line to each remote employee.

Somewhere between a LAN and a WAN is an enterprise network. In a business that is large and has many computers to manage, there may be multiple LANs located in the same location. These LANs are connected to each other using routers—technically making them WANs. This hybrid is sometimes called a **campus area network (CAN)**.

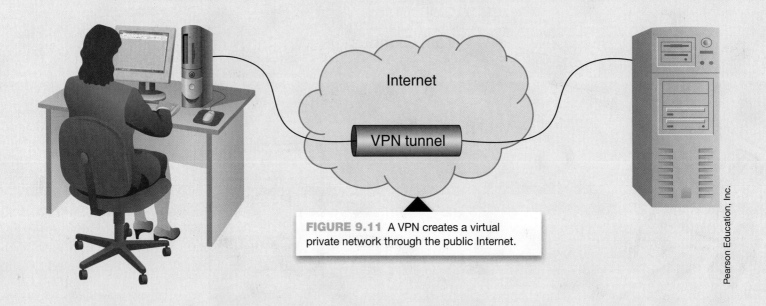

FIGURE 9.11 A VPN creates a virtual private network through the public Internet.

Pearson Education, Inc.

Companies that have massive amounts of information to move and store may have a **storage area network (SAN)** between the data storage devices and the servers on a network, making the data accessible to all servers in the SAN. Users are not part of the SAN but are able to access the information stored in the SAN through the LAN servers.

A network that covers a single geographic area—such as the CBS Mobile Zone in central Manhattan—is called a **metropolitan area network (MAN)**.

Cellular networks use cell towers to transmit voice and data over large distances. Modern 4G networks have speeds that make these networks a practical way for people on the move to connect to network resources, including the Internet and corporate VPNs, from almost anywhere in the world.

Running Project

Make a list of networks that you use. Include home, cellular, work, and school networks. Label each as a LAN, WAN, or one of the other network types described in this article. List the devices you use to connect to each. What resources do you access?

5 Things You Need To Know

- A local area network (LAN) is a network that has all its nodes located in the same physical location.
- Wireless network types include Bluetooth personal area networks (PANs), Wi-Fi wireless LANs (WLANs), and cellular networks.
- Ethernet is the standard that defines the way data is transmitted over a LAN. Topology describes the physical layout of a network.
- A wide area network (WAN) is a network that spans multiple locations and connects multiple LANs.
- A VPN creates a private network through the public network (Internet).

Key Terms

Bluetooth

campus area network (CAN)

cellular network

Ethernet

local area network (LAN)

metropolitan area network (MAN)

personal area network (PAN)

router

standard

storage area network (SAN)

topology

virtual private network (VPN)

wide area network (WAN)

wireless LAN (WLAN)

Silvano Rebai/Fotolia

Silvano Rebai/Fotolia

Hardware

List and Describe the Hardware Used in Both Wired and Wireless Networks

VIZ CLIP

Home Networking Hardware

Every network has two major components: hardware to create the physical connections between devices and software to configure the resources and security. In this article, we look at the hardware needed to create different types of networks.

Network Adapters

The hardware needed to set up a peer-to-peer network is much less complicated than what is needed in a client-server network. The simplest P2P network can consist of two devices sharing files by using a wireless connection or a single cable. For example, you can send data from your smartphone directly to your colleague's phone, or transfer music from your computer to your media player through a USB cable. Connecting larger home networks with many types of devices requires additional hardware.

Each device that connects to a network must have some type of **network adapter**—a communication device used to establish a connection with a network. Most personal computers today come with a built-in Ethernet adapter. This type of connection, called an RJ-45 port, looks like a large phone jack (Figure 9.12). The cable used for this type of connection is called twisted-pair, Ethernet cable, Cat-5e, or Cat-6. Depending on the size of the network you're connecting to, the other end of the cable might plug into a wall jack or a port on a switch, a router, or a modem. Many devices have built-in wireless adapters, but for those that don't, a USB adapter is an easy fix (Figure 9.13).

The advantages to using a wired network connection include speed, location, and security. Wired Ethernet connections can reach speeds of 1,000 megabits per second, also known as Gigabit Ethernet. Most home Ethernet connections use Fast Ethernet connections, which equal 100 Mbps. No wireless technology can currently reach the 1 Gbps speed, but Wi-Fi and cellular networks can equal or exceed the 100 Mbps speed. Another advantage is that a wired connection is less subject to interference and can travel long distances without slowing. Buildings and other structures can slow or even prevent a wireless connection from working. Finally, a wired connection is more secure than a wireless connection, especially if the wireless connection is not configured with strong security settings.

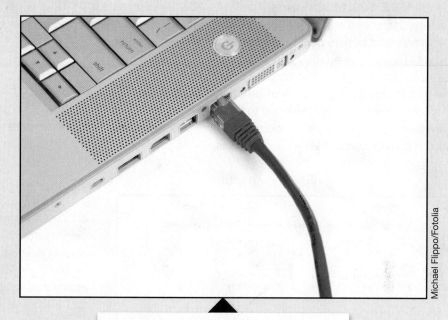

Michael Flippo/Fotolia

FIGURE 9.12 A Built-in Ethernet Adapter Connected to an Ethernet Cable

Oleksiy Mark/Fotolia

FIGURE 9.13 A USB Wireless Adapter

There are several types of wireless network adapters. The Wi-Fi networks found in homes and public hotspots use the **IEEE 802.11** standards. The Wi-Fi Alliance certifies wireless devices to ensure interoperability. Most notebook computers and tablets come with a built-in wireless adapter, and a USB wireless adapter can easily be connected to a desktop, smart TV, or game console that does not have one built in. Wireless printers can be connected directly to a network, eliminating the need to be shared from an individual computer. Table 9.1 compares the speeds of the most common types of Wi-Fi connections.

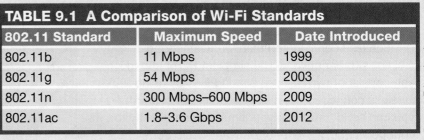

TABLE 9.1 A Comparison of Wi-Fi Standards

802.11 Standard	Maximum Speed	Date Introduced
802.11b	11 Mbps	1999
802.11g	54 Mbps	2003
802.11n	300 Mbps–600 Mbps	2009
802.11ac	1.8–3.6 Gbps	2012

Pearson Education, Inc.

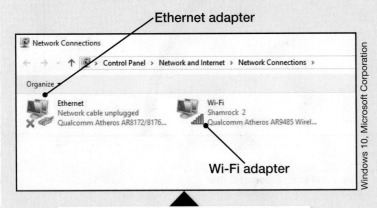

Ethernet adapter

Wi-Fi adapter

Windows 10, Microsoft Corporation

FIGURE 9.14 This Network Connections window shows both wired and wireless network adapters on this Windows computer.

When two wireless devices connect to each other directly, they create an **ad hoc network**. In an **infrastructure wireless network**, devices connect through a wireless access point. At home, a wireless access point is built into your wireless router.

A 3G or 4G adapter can be built into a mobile device or can be connected by USB to a computer, allowing you to use a cellular network for network access.

To view the network adapters that are installed on your Windows computer, right-click the network icon on the taskbar and click *Open Network and Sharing Center*. In the left pane, click *Change adapter settings*. This opens the Network Connections window, which lists all the network adapters on the machine and the status of each. From here, you can manage your connections. The computer in Figure 9.14 has both a wired Ethernet adapter and a wireless Wi-Fi adapter. Computers can have multiple types of network adapters, and you might also find Bluetooth or cellular adapters listed in this window. To view the network adapters on a Mac, open System Preferences from the Dock or Apple menu and then click *Network*. The Mac in Figure 9.15 has three adapters: Wi-Fi, Bluetooth, and Thunderbolt Bridge—which lets two Macs communicate through the Thunderbolt port.

Screen shot(s) reprinted with permission from Apple Inc.

FIGURE 9.15 This Network window shows three network adapters on this Mac.

Network Connectivity Hardware

Creating networks with many resources and devices requires some additional hardware. The first device on a network is usually the device that connects to the Internet. If you are using a dial-up connection, this is an analog **modem**—short for modulator-demodulator. Cable and DSL have special digital modems, and fiber networks use **optical network terminals (ONTs)**. You can connect your computer directly to a modem or an ONT, but you can share the connection with other devices more easily with some basic network hardware.

A business network consists of routers, switches, wireless access points, and firewalls. Your home router serves all these functions. A router connects two or more networks together—for example, your home network and the Internet. A router uses address information to correctly route the data packets it receives.

In a home network, the router is a convergence device that serves several functions: It shares the Internet connection, provides IP addresses to the other devices on the network, and, if configured correctly, provides security for your network.

Routers make up the backbone of the Internet and are responsible for sending data packets along the correct route to their destination (Figure 9.16). If you think of the Internet as a map of highways, you'll realize that there are many different ways to get from one place to another. When you plan a trip, you take not only the distances into consideration but also traffic congestion and construction. You might make a detour if you run into a problem along the way. The shortest route is not always the fastest route. Routers serve the same function, routing data packets around traffic, collisions, and other impediments.

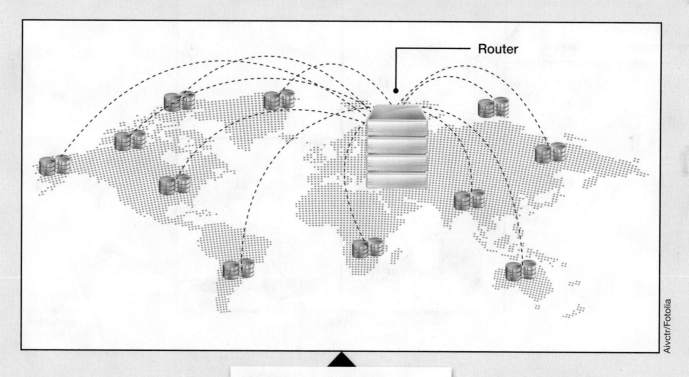

Aivctr/Fotolia

FIGURE 9.16 A router sends data packets to their destinations.

A home router also includes a built-in **switch**—a device that connects multiple devices on a LAN—and can also serve as a **wireless access point (WAP)**—a device that allows wireless devices to join a network. Within the network, a switch uses address information to send data packets only to the port that the appropriate device is connected to. To set up a Wi-Fi network, you need a wireless access point—a large wireless network may have many WAPs installed, but one or two WAPs can usually provide enough coverage in a home network. Figure 9.17 shows a home network that includes both wired and wireless devices.

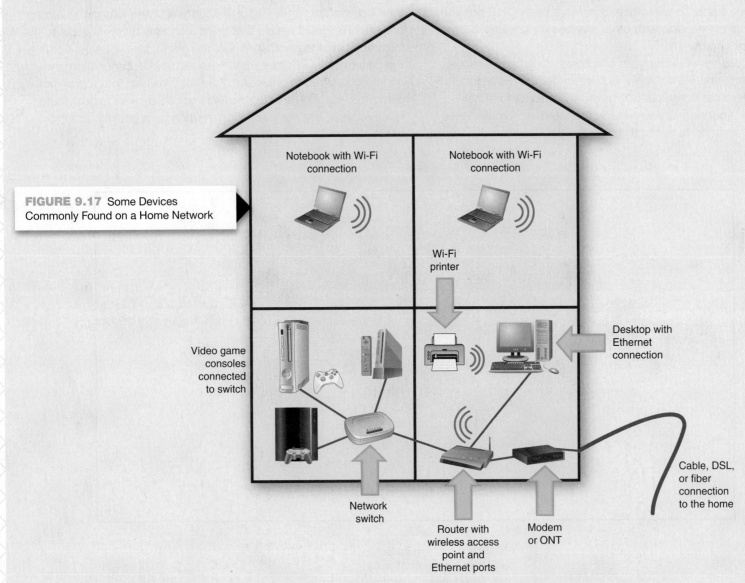

FIGURE 9.17 Some Devices Commonly Found on a Home Network

Notebook with Wi-Fi connection

Notebook with Wi-Fi connection

Wi-Fi printer

Video game consoles connected to switch

Desktop with Ethernet connection

Network switch

Router with wireless access point and Ethernet ports

Modem or ONT

Cable, DSL, or fiber connection to the home

Pearson Education, Inc.

A **firewall** blocks unauthorized access to a network. There are both software firewalls, such as the one included with your operating system (Figure 9.18), and hardware firewalls. A hardware firewall may be part of a router or a stand-alone device. Firewalls can check both outgoing and incoming data packets and can be configured with filters to allow or deny various kinds of traffic based on IP address, protocol type, domain name, or other criteria. For example, a firewall might block access to certain websites or deny Internet access to certain computers during certain hours. Incoming packets that try to access restricted data will be denied access to the network.

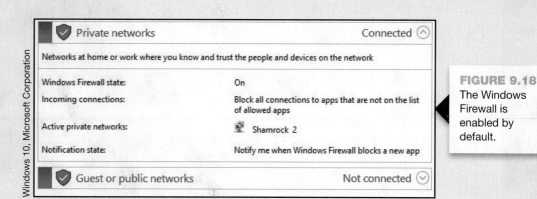

Windows 10, Microsoft Corporation

Private networks	Connected ⌃
Networks at home or work where you know and trust the people and devices on the network	
Windows Firewall state:	On
Incoming connections:	Block all connections to apps that are not on the list of allowed apps
Active private networks:	Shamrock 2
Notification state:	Notify me when Windows Firewall blocks a new app
Guest or public networks	Not connected ⌄

FIGURE 9.18
The Windows Firewall is enabled by default.

Running Project

Open the Network Connections window, as described in this article. If you are using a Mac, open Network Preferences. What adapters are installed on your computer? What type of networks do they connect to? Which of them are connected now? Include a screenshot of the window.

VizCheck—In MyITLab, take a quick quiz covering Objectives 1–3.

4 Things You Need To Know

- Each device that connects to a network must have a network adapter.
- The first device on a network connects to the Internet and is typically a modem or an optical network terminal (ONT).
- A router connects two or more networks together; switches and wireless access points connect multiple devices on a network.
- A firewall blocks unauthorized access to a network.

Key Terms

ad hoc network

firewall

IEEE 802.11

infrastructure wireless network

modem

network adapter

optical network terminal (ONT)

switch

wireless access point (WAP)

Software and Protocols

Objective

4

List and Describe Network Software and Protocols

Network hardware allows devices to physically connect to each other, but software and protocols enable them to communicate with and understand each other. In this article, we look at network operating systems, communication software, and protocols that make a network work.

VIZ CLIP

Connecting to a Public Wi-Fi Hotspot

Peer-to-Peer Network Software

No special software is required to create a simple peer-to-peer network. When Windows is installed on a computer, it includes a feature called Client for Microsoft Networks, which allows it to remotely access files and printers on a Microsoft network. To verify that the Client for Microsoft Networks is installed on your computer, open the Network and Sharing Center from the taskbar, click *Change adapter settings* in the left pane, right-click the active adapter, and click *Properties* to open the properties dialog box for the connection (Figure 9.19).

Using the workgroup feature of Windows allows you to share and remotely access files on a Windows network. OS X includes Windows File Sharing, and its network discovery tool should locate your Windows computers automatically in Finder. To configure Windows File Sharing (SMB) on a Mac, open System Preferences, click *Sharing*, select *File Sharing*, and then click *Options* (Figure 9.20). If your network consists of computers running the same OS, the computers are able to detect and share resources with each other with little or no configuration on your part.

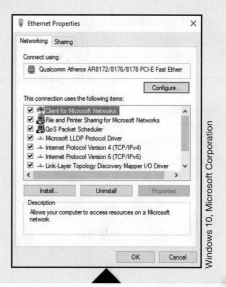

FIGURE 9.19 The Ethernet Properties dialog box shows the Client for Microsoft Networks installed.

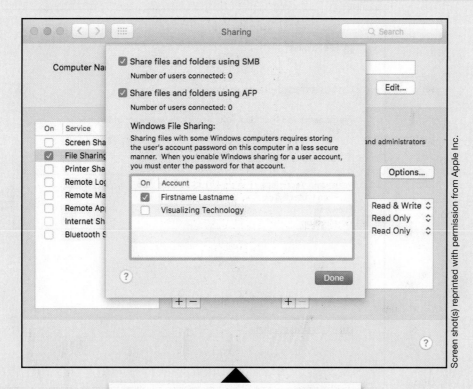

FIGURE 9.20 Configure a Mac for Windows file sharing.

To share a resource from a Windows computer with computers in your workgroup, right-click the item to be shared and choose *Share with* (Figure 9.21a). Click *Specific people* to open the File Sharing dialog box. In the File Sharing dialog box, choose the users you want to give access to from the drop-down list box and click *Add* (Figure 9.21b). You can grant read or read/write access to this folder. You can also remove users from this list.

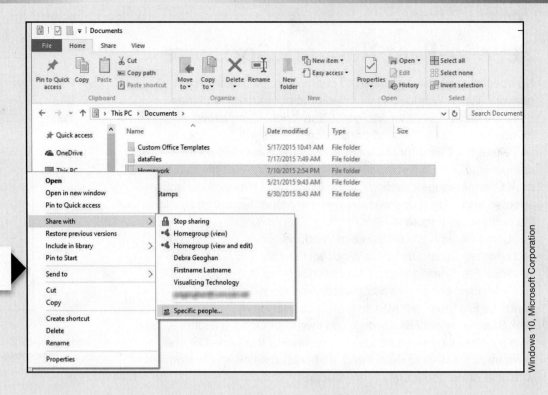

FIGURE 9.21a Right-click and select *Share with* to grant access to your files.

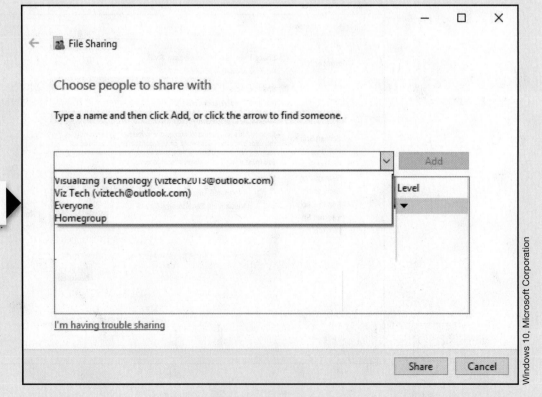

FIGURE 9.21b Choose the users and permission in the File Sharing dialog box.

With two Macs, using an OS X feature called AirDrop is an easy way to wirelessly share files. Simply open Finder and click the *AirDrop* folder on both computers. Once you see each other in your AirDrop folders, you can drag and drop files to share them (Figure 9.22). There is no configuration or password necessary to use AirDrop, and once the file has been accepted, the connection is broken.

FIGURE 9.22 AirDrop easily shares files between Macs.

Client–Server Network Software

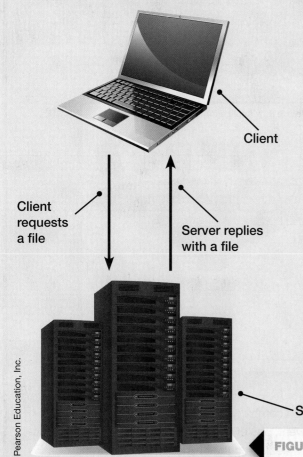

Client

Client requests a file

Server replies with a file

Server

FIGURE 9.23 A Client Request to a Server

As the name implies, both client software and server software are needed on a client–server network. The client software makes requests, and the server software fulfills them (Figure 9.23).

In a network where the servers run the Microsoft Server NOS, Windows clients don't need any special client software for basic file and print services. Instead, they use the same Client for Microsoft Networks used in peer-to-peer networks to connect to the servers. A **domain** is a network composed of a group of clients and servers under the control of one central security database on a special server called the domain controller. You log in to the domain to have access to all the servers in the domain—in a network with multiple servers, you don't need to log in to each one individually. The domain security database includes your user information—who you are, what your password is, and what your access and restrictions are.

For many types of servers, a special client is needed. When you use your web browser to access your email, the browser serves as an email client. The browser can also act as an FTP client when you download a file, a database client when you access your bank transactions, and an HTTP client when you access a webpage. Other client software you may use includes VPN software, desktop email programs, instant messaging/chat programs, and mobile banking apps.

Server software is also known as a **network operating system (NOS)**—a specialized operating system that controls the software and hardware on a network.

It enables multiple client devices to communicate with the server and each other and to share resources, run applications, and send messages. An NOS centralizes resources and security and provides services such as file and print services, communication services, Internet and email services, and backup and database services to the client computers.

Servers are classified by the type of services they provide. Some common services are file and print services, email, database, web, chat, audio/video, and applications. Whenever you log in to a website such as Facebook or Gmail (Figure 9.24), you're connecting to a server.

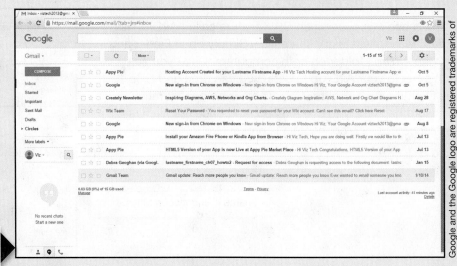

FIGURE 9.24 Using a Web Browser as an Email Client to Connect to an Email Server

Google and the Google logo are registered trademarks of Google Inc., used with permission.

GREEN COMPUTING
Server Virtualization

Technically, the term server refers to the server software on a computer, not to the hardware it runs on. So a network server computer might actually run mail server, web server, and file and print server software. The advantage to this is that a single physical computer can be several different servers at once. Server computers are high-end, with fast processors and lots of storage. Sometimes, the computer's capabilities aren't fully utilized, and its processors are idle much of the time. Virtualization takes advantage of such unused resources. A common configuration would be running both a Microsoft Exchange email server and an Apache web server on the same computer. Each virtual server runs in its own space; the virtual servers share the hardware but do not interact with each other in any way. To the client, they appear to be separate servers.

Server virtualization is a big component of cloud computing. A company that offers IaaS (Infrastructure as a Service) can set up virtual servers for many small companies on a large enterprise server. This saves money and reduces the amount of hardware needed for each business. Keeping servers in one location can also save in cooling and electric costs and reduce the e-waste generated by each company. IaaS is good not only for small companies—Joyent, one of the largest IaaS providers, hosts the social network LinkedIn and the online retailer Gilt Groupe.

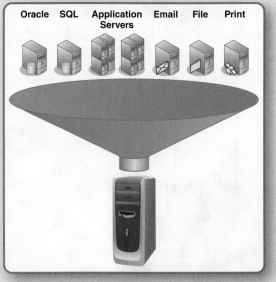

Pearson Education, Inc.

Network Protocols

Network hardware enables devices to connect to each other, and network protocols enable them to communicate. **Protocols** define the rules for communication between devices. These rules determine how data is formatted, transmitted, received, and acknowledged. Without protocols, devices could be physically connected and still unable to communicate.

Think about a meeting between two people. When you walk into the meeting, you greet the other person, perhaps shake hands, and exchange names. Mutually agreed-upon protocols determine how you begin the conversation. Network protocols also define how a conversation between devices begins, which ensures that both are ready to communicate and agree on how to proceed. During the meeting, you also follow rules: what to say, how to say it, what language to speak, and what's appropriate and what's not. Protocols define how devices converse in much the same way. Finally, at the end of your meeting, you stand up, shake hands, say goodbye, and depart; similarly, protocols define the method to end an electronic conversation.

Although there are hundreds of different protocols, the most important ones belong to the **TCP/IP protocol stack**. This is a suite of protocols that define everything from how to transfer files (FTP) and webpages (HTTP) to sending (SMTP) and receiving (POP) email. **TCP** stands for **Transmission Control Protocol**, and it's responsible for ensuring that data packets are transmitted reliably. **IP**, or **Internet Protocol**, is responsible for addressing and routing packets to their destination. Both pieces are needed for data to move between devices. Table 9.2 lists some of the important protocols in the TCP/IP stack and their functions.

Lsantilli/Fotolia

TABLE 9.2 Some Important Network Protocols in the TCP/IP Stack

Protocol	Function
TCP (Transmission Control Protocol)	Ensuring that data packets are transmitted reliably
IP (Internet Protocol)	Addressing and routing packets to their destination
HTTP (Hypertext Transfer Protocol)	Requesting and delivering webpages
FTP (File Transfer Protocol)	Transferring files between computers
POP (Post Office Protocol)	Receiving email
SMTP (Simple Mail Transfer Protocol)	Sending email
DHCP (Dynamic Host Configuration Protocol)	Requesting and receiving IP addresses from a DHCP server
DNS (Domain Name System)	Resolving a domain name such as **www.ebay.com** to an IP address

Pearson Education, Inc.

The TCP/IP protocol stack runs on the Internet, and because of this, it's also the protocol stack that runs on most LANs. TCP/IP is the default protocol stack installed on Windows, Mac, and Linux computers, and it's what allows them to communicate with each other easily. Figure 9.25 shows the properties for the Ethernet adapter. You can see that both TCP/IPv6 and TCP/IPv4 are installed. Currently, TCP/IP version 4 is used on the Internet and most LANs. Although many older devices don't support TCP/IP version 6, it is currently being implemented and will eventually replace version 4 altogether. By default, Windows computers are set to obtain an IP address automatically, using DHCP. The computer sends out a DHCP request that's answered by a DHCP server—most likely your router at home. Every computer on the network must have a unique IP address. This automatic configuration makes it easy to create a home network.

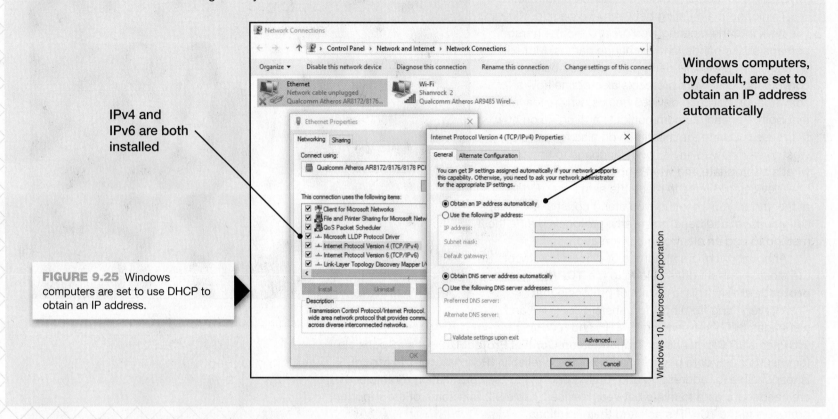

IPv4 and IPv6 are both installed

Windows computers, by default, are set to obtain an IP address automatically

FIGURE 9.25 Windows computers are set to use DHCP to obtain an IP address.

Windows 10, Microsoft Corporation

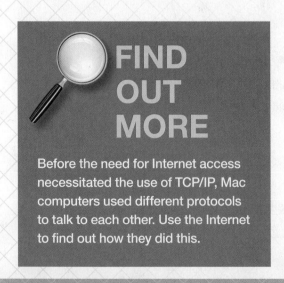

FIND OUT MORE

Before the need for Internet access necessitated the use of TCP/IP, Mac computers used different protocols to talk to each other. Use the Internet to find out how they did this.

CAREER SPOTLIGHT

Dotshock/Shutterstock

United States Department of Labor

NETWORK ADMINISTRATOR—You'll find computer networks in every type of business, and knowing how to access network resources is a critical skill for most employees.

A **network administrator** is the person responsible for managing the hardware and software on a network. The job may also include troubleshooting and security. Although not required, a two- or four-year college degree is helpful in this field, as are certifications. According to Salary.com, the average salary for a person in this field with two to five years' experience is about $64,000. As with any technical field, you should expect to continue your training to keep up with the changes in technology. An entry-level person may be called a network technician rather than an administrator.

Because networks and connectivity are critical for most businesses, experts in making networks secure and reliable will always be in demand. The *Occupational Outlook Handbook* at **bls.gov/ooh** predicts that network-related jobs will grow faster than the average for all occupations over the next decade, so considering a career in this field might be a good choice for you.

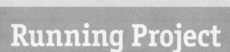

Running Project

Make a list of the networks you use. Include home, cellular, work, and school networks. List the software clients that you use to connect to each. What resources do you access? Do you use different clients to access different resources?

As with any computer system, the hardware of a network is useless without the software to make it work. In a network, that software also includes protocols to define the rules of communication. Together, the hardware, software, and protocols allow devices to share resources securely, efficiently, and (hopefully) easily.

5 Things You Need To Know

- Computers in a peer-to-peer network are able to detect and share resources with each other with little or no configuration.
- A domain is a network composed of a group of clients and servers under the control of the domain controller.
- Client devices log in to a server and request access to resources.
- Server software allows clients to communicate with the server to share resources, run applications, and send messages.
- Protocols define the rules for communication between devices. TCP/IP is the protocol stack that runs on the Internet and on most LANs.

Key Terms

domain

IP (Internet Protocol)

network administrator

network operating system (NOS)

protocol

TCP (Transmission Control Protocol)

TCP/IP protocol stack

Check Your System Security Software

Security software is important for protecting your computer from malicious attacks. In this activity, you'll examine your computer to determine what type of security software is installed on it and whether your computer is properly protected. From your student data files, open the file *vt_ch09_howto02_answersheet* and save the file as **lastname_firstname_ch09_howto02_answersheet**

1 Right-click the Start button and click *Control Panel*. If necessary, change to View by Category. Under *System and Security*, click *Review your computer's status and resolve issues*. If necessary, click the arrow to open the *Security* section. What information is located here? What is your status for each category? Are there any important notices? What software is reported for virus protection and spyware?

2 If necessary, click the arrow to open the *Maintenance* section. What's your status for each category? Are there any important notices? Take a screenshot of the *Security and Maintenance* window (Windows 8.1 Action Center) and paste it into your answer sheet.

Review recent messages and resolve problems

No issues have been detected by Security and Maintenance.

Security		⌃
Network firewall		On
🛡 Windows Firewall is actively protecting your PC.		
Virus protection		On
🔲 Windows Defender is helping to protect your PC.		
Spyware and unwanted software protection		On
🔲 Windows Defender is helping to protect your PC.		
Internet security settings		OK
All Internet security settings are set to their recommended levels.		
User Account Control		On
UAC will notify you when apps try to make changes to the computer.		
🛡 Change settings		
Windows SmartScreen		On
Windows SmartScreen is helping to protect your PC from unrecognized apps and files downloaded from the Internet.		
🛡 Change settings		

Windows 10, Microsoft Corporation

3

In the navigation pane on the left, click *Change Security and Maintenance settings* (Windows 8.1: click *Change Action Center settings*). Take a screenshot of the settings window and paste it into your answer sheet. Close the settings window.

Turn messages on or off

For each selected item, Windows will check for problems and send you a message if problems are found.
How does Security and Maintenance check for problems?

Security messages

- ☑ Windows Update
- ☑ Internet security settings
- ☑ Network firewall
- ☑ Microsoft account
- ☑ Windows activation

- ☑ Spyware and unwanted software protection
- ☑ User Account Control
- ☑ Virus protection
- ☑ SmartScreen

Maintenance messages

- ☑ Windows Backup
- ☑ Automatic Maintenance
- ☑ Drive status
- ☑ Device software
- ☑ Startup apps

- ☑ Windows Troubleshooting
- ☑ HomeGroup
- ☑ File History
- ☑ Storage Spaces
- ☑ Work Folders

4

In the navigation pane on the left, click *Change Windows SmartScreen settings*. How does SmartScreen protect you? Take a screenshot of the SmartScreen dialog box and paste it into your answer sheet. Close any open windows and dialog boxes. Type up your answers. Save your file and submit your work as directed by your instructor.

Windows SmartScreen   ✕

What do you want to do with unrecognized apps?

Windows SmartScreen can help keep your PC safer by warning you before running unrecognized apps and files downloaded from the Internet.

- ⦿ Get administrator approval before running an unrecognized app from the Internet (recommended)
- ○ Warn before running an unrecognized app, but don't require administrator approval
- ○ Don't do anything (turn off Windows SmartScreen)

OK   Cancel

Some info is sent to Microsoft about files and apps you run on this PC.
Privacy statement

MAC

If you are using a Mac, from your student data files, open the file *vt_ch09_howto02_answersheet_mac* and save the file as **lastname_firstname_ch09_howto02_answersheet_mac**

1. Open *System Preferences* and then click *Security & Privacy*. Click the *General tab*. Examine the General tab and record your settings for each section. Take a screenshot of the General tab and paste it into your answer sheet.

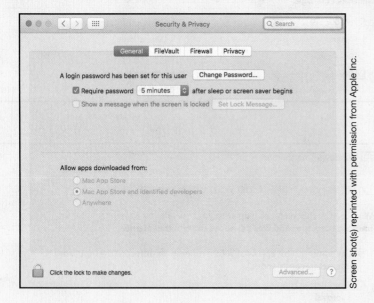

Screen shot(s) reprinted with permission from Apple Inc.

2. If necessary, click to unlock the padlock, and then click *Advanced*. What settings display?

3. Examine the Privacy tab and record your settings for each section. How do Location Services affect your privacy? Do you have any apps configured to use location services? Take a screenshot of the Privacy tab and paste it into your answer sheet.

Screen shot(s) reprinted with permission from Apple Inc.

4. Close any open windows and dialog boxes. Type up your answers. Save your file and submit your work as directed by your instructor.

Zinkevych/Fotolia

Protecting Your Network

5 Explain How to Protect a Network

Not long ago, network security was a concern only to network administrators in large businesses; today, with networks everywhere, it has become a larger problem. Just as you use layers of security at home—fences, door locks, alarm systems, and even guard dogs— the same approach should be used with network security.

Layer 1: The Fence

In a network, the fence is the hardware at the access point to your network (Figure 9.26). In a home network, the hardware firewall is probably part of your router. In a business, the firewall is a stand-alone device. The firewall examines the data packets as they enter or leave your network and will deny access to traffic based on rules the network administrator defines. It also shields your computers from anyone directly accessing them from the Internet, hiding them from hackers looking for an easy target.

Layer 2: Door Locks

In a network, door locks are represented by the network configuration that determines what's shared and who's granted access to it. Your user names should have strong passwords that are hard to crack, and each user should be granted access only to what they need. Using no passwords or using passwords that are easy to guess—such as birthdays or pets' names—is equivalent to leaving your doors unlocked.

Windows (Figure 9.27) and OS X (Figure 9.28) enable you to create standard users or administrators, and they also include parental controls for child accounts. For normal use, it is best to use a standard user account, which has less access to change system and security settings. An administrator account should be used only when necessary and should be protected by a strong password. In a business environment, only IT staff should have administrator accounts on computers.

FIGURE 9.26 A firewall protects the network.

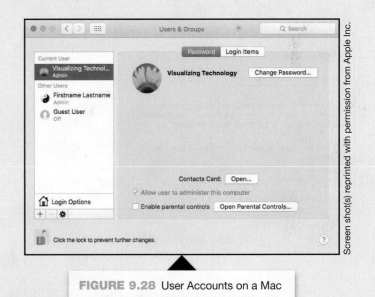

FIGURE 9.28 User Accounts on a Mac

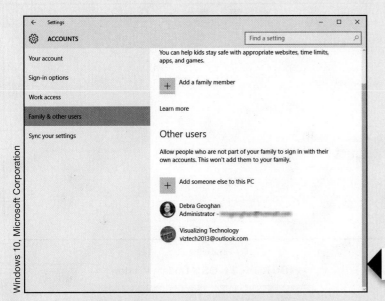

FIGURE 9.27 User Accounts on a Windows Computer

Layer 3: Alarm Systems

The alarm system on a computer network includes software-based firewalls and antivirus and antimalware software on the individual computers on the network. Windows Defender is installed on Windows computers to protect against computer viruses and other malware (Figure 9.29). Your individual computers should be protected by software firewalls such as those included with Windows or OS X. If an intruder somehow breaches your network, software will detect and prevent unauthorized actions.

Layer 4: Guard Dogs

The network administrator—on a home network, that's you—needs to be diligent in keeping the systems on the network up to date and secure. Windows (Figure 9.30) and OS X (Figure 9.31) automatically check for and install updates, but other software applications can also have potential vulnerabilities and should be kept up to date as well. Unpatched systems are easy targets for hackers and can allow them access into your network.

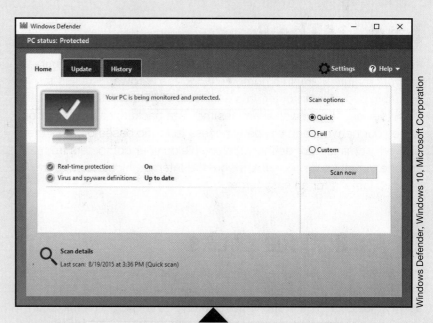

FIGURE 9.29 Each computer on the network should have its own up-to-date security software installed.

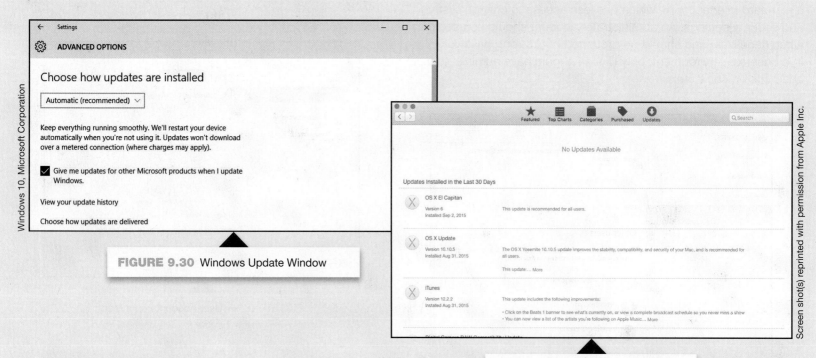

FIGURE 9.30 Windows Update Window

FIGURE 9.31 OS X Update Window

ETHICS

The term **piggybacking** means using an open wireless network to access the Internet without permission. Many times, people intentionally use open wireless access. If an access point is left unsecured, they figure, "Why not?" In some places, it's illegal to use a network without authorization, but many statutes—if they exist at all—are vague. It's difficult to detect when someone is piggybacking. Still, it's unethical to use someone's connection without his or her knowledge.

To make things more confusing, some free hotspots—such as in cafes and hotels—might be accessible beyond the premises. So, a person sitting in a car parked on the street might be able to access the coffee shop hotspot intended for patrons of the shop.

The practice of **wardriving**—driving around and locating open wireless access points—is closely related. There are communities on the Internet where wardrivers post maps of the open networks they find, along with free software that makes it easy to locate wireless networks. Wardrivers don't actually access the wireless networks, so the practice isn't illegal—but is it ethical?

Running Project

Think about the user names and passwords you use on the computer networks that you use most often—such as school and work networks. Are there strong password rules you must follow? How often do you change your passwords? When was the last time you changed your school, home, and work passwords?

4 Things You Need To Know

- A firewall examines data packets as they enter or leave a network.
- User names should have strong passwords that are hard to crack, and each user should be granted access only to what he or she needs.
- Individual computers on a network should be protected with firewalls and antivirus and anti-malware software.
- Systems on a network must be kept up to date and secure.

Key Terms

piggybacking

wardriving

VizCheck—In MyITLab, take a quick quiz covering Objectives 4–5.

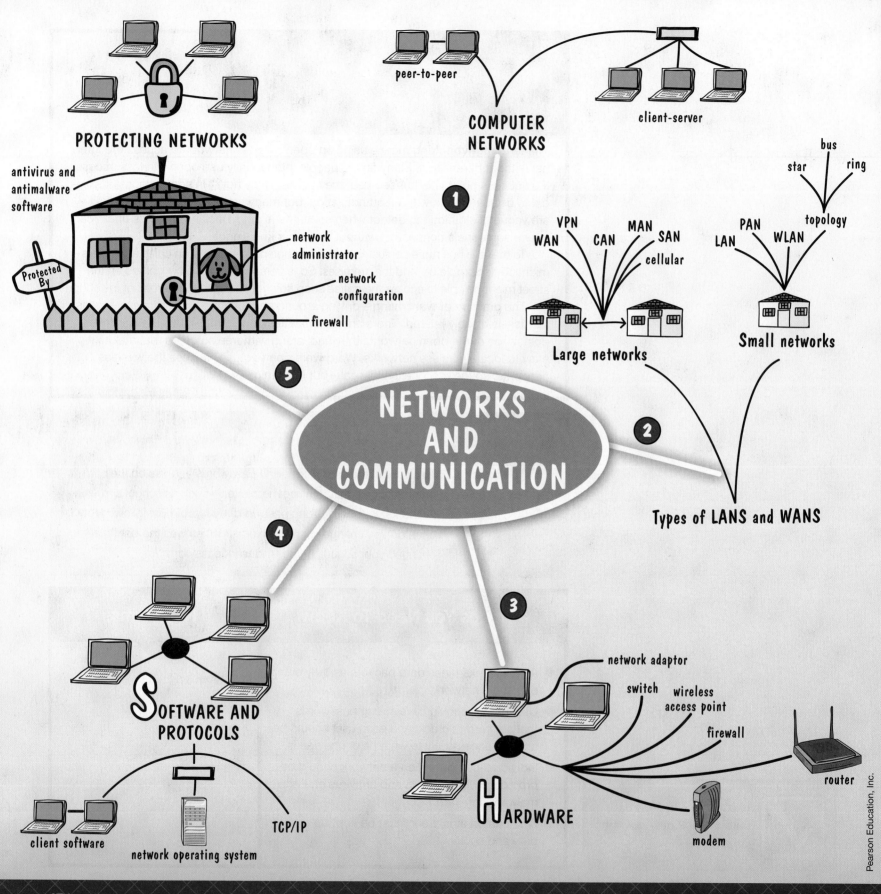

PROTECTING NETWORKS

antivirus and
antimalware
software

network
administrator

network
configuration

firewall

Protected By

COMPUTER NETWORKS

peer-to-peer

client-server

1

NETWORKS AND COMMUNICATION

bus
star ring
VPN MAN topology
WAN CAN SAN PAN
cellular LAN WLAN

Large networks

Small networks

2

Types of LANS and WANS

5

4

3

SOFTWARE AND PROTOCOLS

client software

network operating system

TCP/IP

HARDWARE

network adaptor

switch wireless
access point

firewall

router

modem

Pearson Education, Inc.

Objective Recap

1. Discuss the Importance of Computer Networks
2. Compare Different Types of LANs and WANs
3. List and Describe the Hardware Used in Both Wired and Wireless Networks
4. List and Describe Network Software and Protocols
5. Explain How to Protect a Network

Key Terms

ad hoc network **454**
Bluetooth **447**
campus area network (CAN) **450**
cellular network **451**
client **441**
client–server network **441**
computer network **438**
domain **461**
Ethernet **448**
firewall **457**
homegroup **440**
IEEE 802.11 **454**
infrastructure wireless network **454**
IP (Internet Protocol) **463**
local area network (LAN) **447**
metropolitan area network (MAN) **451**
modem **455**
network adapter **453**
network administrator **465**
network operating system (NOS) **461**

network resource **438**
optical network terminal (ONT) **455**
peer-to-peer (P2P) network **439**
personal area network (PAN) **447**
piggybacking **473**
protocol **463**
router **449**
server **441**
standards **448**
storage area network (SAN) **451**
switch **456**
TCP (Transmission Control Protocol) **463**
TCP/IP protocol stack **463**
topology **448**
virtual private network (VPN) **450**
wardriving **473**
wide area network (WAN) **449**
wireless access point (WAP) **456**
wireless LAN (WLAN) **447**
workgroup **439**

Summary

1. Discuss the Importance of Computer Networks

A computer network is two or more computers that share resources: software, hardware, or files. Computer networks save us both time and money and make it easier to work, increasing productivity. A peer-to-peer (P2P) network is a network in which all computers are members of a workgroup and are considered equal. A client–server network is a network that has at least one server at its center and provides a way to centralize the network management, resources, and security.

2. Compare Different Types of LANs and WANs

A local area network (LAN) is a network that has all nodes located in the same physical location. Devices on a LAN are connected using switches. A wireless LAN (WLAN) uses Wi-Fi to transmit data, and a personal area network (PAN) uses Bluetooth. Ethernet defines the way data is transmitted over a local area network, and topology is the physical layout of a network. A wide area network (WAN) is a network that spans multiple locations and connects multiple LANs over dedicated lines using routers. A VPN creates an encrypted private network through the public network (Internet), allowing remote users to access a LAN securely without dedicated lines. A campus area network (CAN) connects multiple LANs located in the same location. A network that covers a single geographic area is called a metropolitan area network (MAN). A storage area network (SAN) connects data storage devices and servers on a network. Cellular networks use 3G and 4G cell towers to transmit voice and data.

3. List and Describe the Hardware Used in Both Wired and Wireless Networks

Each device that connects to a network must have a network adapter. The first device on a network is usually the device that connects to the Internet: a modem or an optical network terminal (ONT). A business network consists of routers, switches, wireless access points, and firewalls. A home router serves all these functions. A router is a device that connects two or more networks together. It uses address information to correctly route the data packets it receives. A switch is a device that connects multiple devices on a LAN. A wireless access point (WAP) is a device that allows wireless devices to join a network. A firewall is a device that blocks unauthorized access to a network.

4. List and Describe Network Software and Protocols

Clients log in to a server and request access to resources. A web browser can act as an FTP client, a database client, and an HTTP client. Other client software you may use includes VPN software, desktop email programs, instant messaging or chat programs, and mobile banking apps. Server software—also known as a network operating system (NOS)—is a multiuser operating system that controls the software and hardware on a network.

Summary continues on the next page

Protocols define the rules for communication among devices and determine how data is formatted, transmitted, received, and acknowledged. The most important protocols belong to the TCP/IP protocol stack and define everything from how to transfer files (FTP) and webpages (HTTP) to sending (SMTP) and receiving (POP) email. TCP stands for Transmission Control Protocol, and it's responsible for ensuring that data packets are transmitted reliably. IP stands for Internet Protocol, and it's responsible for addressing and routing packets to their destination.

5. Explain How to Protect a Network

Use a layered approach to security. Protect the access point to your network with a firewall. Ensure correct network configuration—that is, what is shared and who is granted access to it. Secure individual computers with software-based firewalls as well as antivirus and anti-malware software. Be diligent in keeping the systems on the network up to date and secure.

Multiple Choice

Answer the multiple-choice questions below for more practice with key terms and concepts from this chapter.

1. Computers in a peer-to-peer network belong to a _____.
   a. client-server group
   b. domain
   c. personal area network
   d. workgroup

2. A _____ is a computer that connects to, or requests services from, another computer.
   a. client
   b. node
   c. server
   d. workgroup

3. A PAN is a small network that consists of devices connected by _____, a technology that connects peripherals wirelessly at short ranges.
   a. Bluetooth
   b. cellular
   c. Ethernet
   d. Wi-Fi

4. In which topology does data travel back and forth along the cable, which is terminated at both ends?
   a. Bus
   b. Ring
   c. Star
   d. Hybrid

5. Which type of network spans multiple locations and connects multiple networks?
   a. LAN
   b. MAN
   c. VPN
   d. WAN

6. The device needed to connect two or more networks together is called a(n) _____.
   a. access point
   b. modem
   c. optical network terminal
   d. router

7. A(n) _____ is created when two wireless devices connect to each other directly.
   a. ad hoc network
   b. infrastructure wireless network
   c. personal area network (PAN)
   d. virtual private network (VPN)

8. A(n) _____ blocks unauthorized access to a network.
   a. firewall
   b. modem
   c. ONT
   d. switch

9. Which type of network consists of a group of clients and servers under the control of one central security database?
   a. Domain
   b. Homegroup
   c. IEEE 802.11
   d. Workgroup

10. Which protocol is responsible for ensuring that data packets are transmitted reliably?
    a. IP
    b. POP
    c. SMTP
    d. TCP

True or False

Answer the following questions with T for true or F for false for more practice with key terms and concepts from this chapter.

_____ 1. In a client–server network, all computers are considered equal.

_____ 2. It's not possible to share files between computers running Windows and Linux.

_____ 3. Most LANs are configured in a physical star or hybrid topology.

_____ 4. A metropolitan area network (MAN) covers a single geographic area.

_____ 5. Computers can have more than one network adapter installed at a time.

_____ 6. When devices connect through a wireless access point, they form an infrastructure wireless network.

_____ 7. A router is a device that connects two or more networks together.

_____ 8. You must install special software to create a peer-to-peer network.

_____ 9. TCP/IP is the default protocol installed on Linux computers.

_____ 10. Using an open wireless network to access the Internet without permission is called wardriving.

Fill in the Blank

Fill in the blanks with key terms from this chapter.

1. _____ include the software, hardware, and files that are shared in a network.

2. In a(n) _____ network, all computers are considered equal.

3. Devices in a(n) _____ connect using Bluetooth

4. In a(n) _____, wireless devices connect directly to each other.

5. _____ ensure that equipment that is made by different companies will be able to work together.

6. _____ is the most commonly used standard on local area networks.

7. The _____ standards define the way data is transmitted over a Wi-Fi network.

8. A(n) _____ is a communication device used to establish a connection with a network.

9. _____ define the rules for communication between devices.

10. The protocol responsible for addressing and routing packets to their destination is _____.

Running Project ...

... The Finish Line

Assume that you just moved into a new apartment with several roommates. Use your answers to the previous sections of the project to help decide the best type of network setup to use so you can all share an Internet connection and printer as well as stream media files. Describe the hardware and software requirements for your setup. What other devices might you also connect to the network?

Write a report describing your selections and responding to the questions raised throughout the chapter. Save your file as **lastname_firstname_ch09_project** and submit it to your instructor as directed.

Do It Yourself 1

Network security is an important topic for all network users to understand. In this exercise, you will create a mind map to illustrate network security. A mind map is a visual outline. More information about using mind maps can be found in Appendix B. From your student data files, open the file *vt_ch09_DIY1_answersheet* and save the file as **lastname_firstname_ch09_DIY1_answersheet**

Use an online mind mapper tool such as Mindmeister (mindmeister.com), or Mindomo (mindomo.com) to create a mind map that visualizes network security. Your map should have three or four major branches, and each branch should have at least two leaves. When you are finished your map, take a screenshot of this window and paste it into your answer sheet, or, if available, export your mind map as a PNG or JPG file. Save the file and submit the assignment as directed by your instructor.

Do It Yourself 2

In this exercise, you'll examine a network you use and the devices that are part of it. There is no answer sheet for this assignment; you will create your own file.

Use a program such as MS Paint, Visio, PowerPoint, or Prezi to create a diagram of a network you use. If you don't have a home network, you may draw a friend's network or one you work on at school or work. Label the computers and other devices, including printers, game consoles, media devices, and routers. Save the file as **lastname_firstname_ch09_DIY2** and submit it as directed by your instructor.

File Management

In this activity, you'll examine sharing settings on your computer. From your student data files, open the file *vt_ch09_FM_answersheet* and save the file as **lastname_firstname_ch09_FM_answersheet**

1. Open File Explorer. In the Navigation pane, click *Network*. Are there any items listed under Network? If so, what are they? (On a Mac, use Finder; on the Go menu, click Network.) Take a screenshot of this window and paste it into your answer sheet.

2. Search Help and Support or Google for *Map network drive*. What's the purpose of mapping a drive? To what other places can you create shortcuts? Type up your answers, include the screenshot, save the file, and submit the assignment as directed by your instructor.

Critical Thinking

You work for a small accounting office. Your boss wants to ensure that everyone in the office knows the basics of keeping the office network secure. There is no answer sheet for this assignment; you will create your own file.

Use the Internet and the information you learned in this chapter to create a list of five rules that employees should follow to ensure the security of the office computers. Use a word processor or drawing software to create a poster that can be displayed in the office to remind the employees of these rules. Save the file as **lastname_firstname_ch09_ct** and submit your work as directed by your instructor.

Ethical Dilemma

From your student data files, open the file *vt_ch09_ethics_answersheet* and save the file as **lastname_firstname_ch09_ethics_answersheet**

A help desk technician received a call from an upset customer, Samantha. Samantha had been accessing the Internet at home with her tablet for months but was suddenly unable to connect. The technician asked her some questions to help her troubleshoot the problem. Did she try turning off her router and turning it back on? No—she didn't have a router. What about a wireless access point? No—she didn't have one of those either. Did she call her ISP for help? You guessed it—she didn't have one of those either! After some more questions, the technician finally realized that Samantha had been piggybacking off her neighbor's wireless network.

Samantha was very upset to have lost her Internet connection, and a few days later, when her neighbor returned from vacation, it was restored. Her neighbor was unaware that Samantha had been using the connection. Is it acceptable for Samantha to continue to use her neighbor's network now that she understands what she's doing? Look up the laws where you live. Is it legal? Is it ethical? Would you do it? Type up your answers, save the file, and submit it as directed by your instructor.

On the Web

IPv6 is designed to replace IPv4. In this exercise, you will learn more about each IP version and why the change is important. From your student data files, open the file *vt_ch09_web_answersheet* and save the file as **lastname_firstname_ch09_web_answersheet**

Go to the Internet Society website, **internetsociety.org**, and search for IPv6. What are some of the advantages of switching to IPv6? What was World IPv6 Day, and what were the results? How does the number of IPv6 addresses compare to the number of IPv4 addresses? Type up your answers, save the file, and submit it as directed by your instructor.

Collaboration

Instructors: Divide the class into small groups and provide each group with a large piece of paper or poster board or access to computers.

The Project: As a team, prepare a Venn diagram that compares the features of peer-to-peer and client-server networks. Use at least three references. Use Google Drive or Microsoft Office to prepare your research and provide documentation that all team members have contributed to the project.

Outcome: Prepare a Venn diagram using a large piece of paper or a computer drawing program. The diagram must have at least four items in each of the three areas of the diagram. Present your findings to the class. Be sure to include a listing of all team members. Turn in your diagram named **teamname_ch09_collab** Submit your presentation to your instructor as directed.

Application Project

my**it**lab grader

Office 2016 Application Projects

Excel 2016: Mobile Cellular Subscriptions

Project Description: In this project, using data from the World Bank, you will format and summarize a large spreadsheet showing mobile cellular subscription growth from 2000 to 2014. If necessary, download the student data files from **pearsonhighered.com/viztech**.

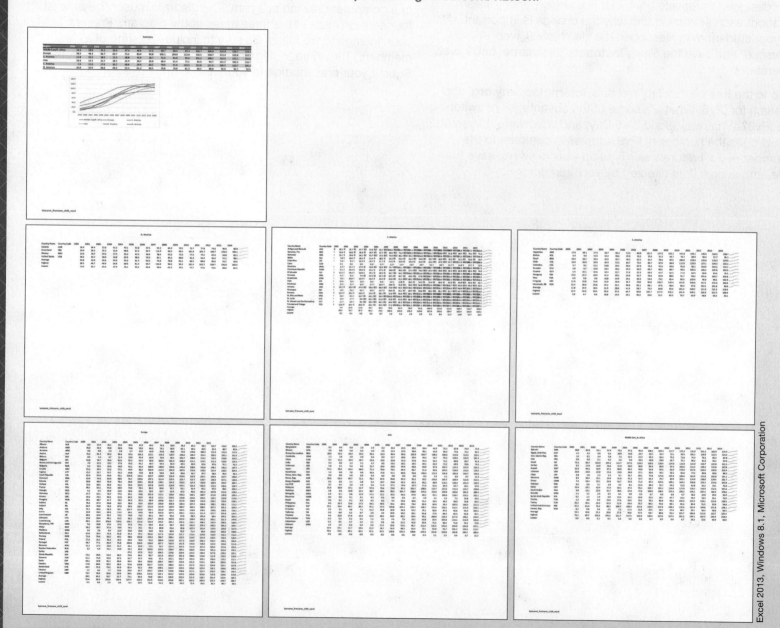

Excel 2013, Windows 8.1, Microsoft Corporation

Step	Instructions
1	Start Excel. From your student data files, open the Excel file *vt_ch09_excel*. Save the file as **lastname_firstname_ch09_excel**
2	Insert a header with the sheet name in the center cell. Insert a footer with the file name in the left cell. Return to Normal view.
3	On the N. America sheet, select the range C2:Q5. Apply the Number Format to the selected range and decrease the decimals displayed to 1.
4	In cell C6, use the AVERAGE function to average the values in the range C2:C5. Copy the formula from C6:Q6.
5	In cell C7, use a function to calculate the highest number of cellular subscriptions of the range C2:C5. Copy the formula from C7:Q7.
6	In cell C8 use a function to calculate the lowest number of cellular subscriptions of the range C2:C5. Copy the formula from C8:Q8.
7	In the range R2:R5, using the data range C2:Q5, insert line Sparklines. Apply Sparkline Style Accent 2 (no dark or light).
8	Copy the Average row C6:Q6 from the N. America sheet. Use the Paste link function to paste it into row 2 of the Summary sheet. Repeat the process to copy the average row for the remaining regions on the Summary sheet.
9	On the Summary sheet, format the values B2:P7 with the Number Format and decrease the decimals displayed to 1.
10	Select the range A1:P7 and insert the recommended line chart. Move the chart so the top left corner is in the top left corner of cell B10. Format the chart Style 4.
11	On the Summary worksheet, format the data in the range A1:P7 as a table with headers using Table Style Medium 16. Sort the 2014 column from the largest to the smallest value.
12	On the C. America sheet, apply the Gradient Light Blue Data Bar conditional formatting (under Gradient Fill) to the range C2:Q21.
13	On the Europe sheet, click cell A2, and then freeze the panes of the worksheet so that when you scroll down, the headings in row 1 remain visible.
14	Select all worksheets. Prepare the worksheets for printing by changing the orientation to Landscape. Adjust the Scale option to change the Width to 1 page. Ungroup the worksheets and hide the Source worksheet.
15	Ensure that the worksheets are correctly named and placed in the following order in the workbook: Summary, N. America, C. America, S. America, Europe, Asia, Middle East, N. Africa. Save the workbook and close Excel. Submit the workbook as directed.

Application Project

*my**itlab** grader*

Office 2016 Application Projects
Word 2016: Secure Passwords

Project Description: In this project, you will format a document with columns, outline and shade text, create and apply styles, work with images and SmartArt graphics, and insert and format a table. If necessary, download the student data files from **pearsonhighered.com/viztech**.

Creating a Secure Password

We are all responsible for system security!

Password Policy

IT Services provides you with security and tech support for all school systems. In order to ensure the security of college resources, all users are required to create a secure password that must be changed at the start of each semester.

No dictionary words

Mixed case letters

Numbers

Creating Your Password

Here are some guidelines for creating (and remembering) a secure password. You must use a combination of letters and numbers. You must use at least one uppercase and one lowercase letter. Your password must be between 8-12 characters. Try using a combination of words that you can easily remember, but that someone else cannot easily guess. So don't use your kid's name (or your pet's, spouse's...) Everybody knows who your favorite sports team is (because you wear the team shirt to class every day). Instead, go for less obvious choices. One idea: pick a famous song lyric and use the first letter of each word. So, for example, Mary Had a Little Lamb becomes MHaLL. Mix up the case and add a few numbers and you have MhAlL345.

Tech	Extension
Sue	X5421
Charlie	X5422

For help with your password or other security questions, contact IT Services. (702) 555-1234.

vt_ch09_word_solution.docx

Excel 2013, Windows 8.1, Microsoft Corporation

Step	Instructions
1	Start Word. From your student data files, open *vt_ch09_word*. Save the file as **lastname_firstname_ch09_word**
2	To the title of the document, *Creating a Secure Password*, apply the Title style and apply the Fill – Blue, Accent 1, Shadow text effect. Center the title and change the font size to 36.
3	To the text *We are all responsible for system security!* apply the Heading 1 style and center align.
4	Select the subtitle *Password Policy* and all the remaining text in the document. Modify the selected text so that it displays in two columns.
5	Immediately to the left of the subtitle *Creating Your Password*, insert a column break.
6	Position the insertion point at the end of the paragraph that begins *Here are some guidelines...* Insert a 2x3 table. Apply the Grid Table 6 Colorful - Accent 3 table style. Enter the following in the table: Tech Extension Sue X5421 Charlie X5422
7	Center align the subtitle *Password Policy* and change the font size to 22. Change the font color of the selected text to Green, Accent 6, Lighter 40% and format as bold.
8	Create a new style based on the formatting of the subtitle *Password Policy*. Name the style **Password** Apply the Password style to the subtitle *Creating Your Password*.
9	Position the insertion point immediately to the left of the paragraph beginning *IT Services*. Insert the image *vt_ch09_image1* from your student data files.
10	With the image selected, change the text wrapping to tight. Resize the image height to 1.5 inches, lock aspect ratio.
11	Add a box border to the paragraph beginning *For help with your password* and then change the shading to Green, Accent 6, Lighter 80%.
12	Position the insertion point at the end of the paragraph that begins *IT Services provides* in the first column. Insert a SmartArt graphic using the Vertical Box List style from the List category.
13	Increase the height of the graphic to 3.5 inches. Apply the Intense Effect style to the SmartArt graphic. Change color to Colorful Range - Accent Colors 5 – 6.
14	Display the text pane for the SmartArt graphic and insert the following text as the three bullet items and then close the text pane: No dictionary words Mixed case letters Numbers
15	Insert the file name in the footer. Save the document and close Word. Submit the document as directed.

Appendix A

Microsoft® Office 2016 Applications Chapter Guide
Visualizing Technology, Fifth Edition

CHAPTER	APP 1	PROJECT	APP 2	PROJECT
1. What Is a Computer?	Word Level 1	Intern Report	PPT Level 1	Business Technology Plan
2. Application Software	PPT Level 1	Introduction to PowerPoint design	Excel Level 1	Comparing Office Application Suite Costs
3. File Management	Excel Level 1	Municipal Waste	Word Level 1	Importance of File Management
4. Hardware	Word Level 2	Ergonomics	PPT Level 2	Comparing Printers
5. System Software	PPT Level 2	Should You Upgrade Your OS?	Excel Level 2	Worldwide Smartphone Sales
6. Digital Devices and Multimedia	Excel Level 2	Worldwide Digital Camera Sales	Word Level 2	Making the Most of Your Cellphone Camera
7. The Internet	Word Level 2	Cellular Internet Service	PPT Level 2	Internet Services
8. Communicating and Sharing: The Social Web	PPT Level 3	Browsers	Excel Level 3	Broadband Internet Growth
9. Networks and Communication	Excel Level 3	Mobile Cellular Subscriptions	Word Level 3	Secure Passwords

	WORD	POWERPOINT	EXCEL	ACCESS
Level 1	Enter and edit text Format text Insert and format graphics Check spelling and grammar Create headers and footers	Enter and edit text Format text Insert and format graphics Check spelling and grammar Create headers and footers Apply slide transitions Organize slides	Create and edit workbooks Format workbooks (themes) Format data (fonts, cell styles, number formats) Use basic formulas and functions Create headers and footers	Enter and edit table data Create forms and reports
Level 2	Level 1 skills plus: Format page and paragraphs (margins, line spacing, etc.) Find and replace text Use lists Create footnotes	Level 1 skills plus: Apply and modify themes Format text Use lists	Level 1 skills plus: Use absolute cell references Create column and pie charts	Level 1 skills plus: Generate queries
Level 3	Level 1 and 2 skills plus: Format graphics Create tables Use columns Incorporate borders and shading Create SmartArt	Level 1 and 2 skills plus: Insert and format graphics Use SmartArt Create tables Use charts Create animations	Level 1 and 2 skills plus: Use multiple sheets Apply more complex functions Use conditional formatting Create sparklines Sort and filter	N/A

Appendix B

Mind Maps

A mind map is a visual tool that's useful for taking notes and studying. It helps you organize information using images and keywords and see how the pieces are related to each other. To draw a mind map:

1. Write the main topic in the center of the page and then put a circle around it.
2. For each major subtopic, draw a line radiating out from the center.
3. Draw branches off the subtopics as you dig deeper into the material.
4. Draw dotted connecting lines between branches that are related.

Use single words and simple phrases, color, and images to help clarify the material.

Mind maps are used throughout this book to outline the basic structure of each chapter, but you can build on those beginning maps to delve deeper into the material. The figure below shows the mind map for Chapter 4. We can build on it by adding more detail to the branches.

The printer branch is a good place to expand. What topics and concepts would you list on the printer branch? Look at the chapter, and you'll see many choices that you might put here. The next figure shows some ideas you might include on your map of this branch. We could draw a connection between PictBridge on the printer branch and the digital camera on the input branch as well as the solid-state storage (memory card) on the storage branch.

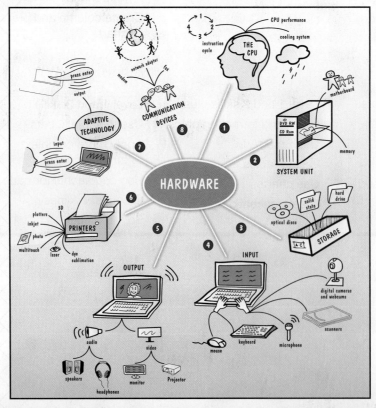

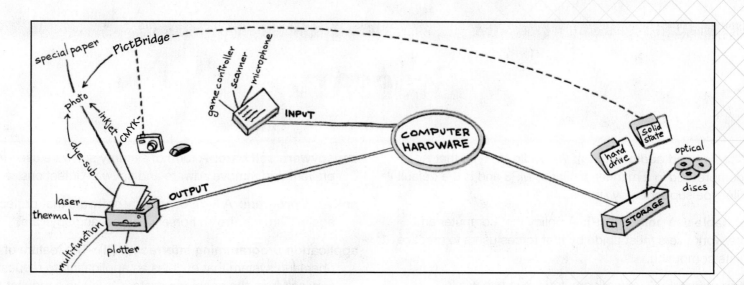

Because mind maps are used to help you remember and connect information, there's no right or wrong answer. Some people like to hand-draw mind maps; others use software to make maps cleaner. Mind maps help you review material and see connections between the topics. They're one tool you could use to take notes and study.

Glossary

AAC (advanced audio coding): An audio file type that is compressed in a manner similar to MP3 and is the default file type supported by iTunes.

acceptable use policy (AUP): A policy that computer and network users must abide by that forces users to practice safe computing.

ad hoc network: A network created when two wireless devices connect directly to each other.

adapter card: A card that plugs directly into an expansion slot on a motherboard and enables you to connect additional peripheral devices to a computer. Also called an expansion card.

adaptive technology: Software and hardware used by individuals with disabilities to interact with technology. Also called assistive technology.

add-on: An application that extends the functionality of a web browser.

adware: A type of malware that shows ads in the form of pop-ups and banners.

Agile Development: An incremental and iterative process that uses short iterations or sprints, with the project team stopping and reevaluating the direction of a project every two weeks.

AGP (Accelerated Graphics Port): The standard analog video port on computers manufactured before 2009.

algorithm: A set of steps to solve a problem.

all-in-one computer: A compact desktop computer with the system unit integrated into the monitor.

Analytical Engine: A mechanical computer designed, but not built, in the early 19th century by mathematician Charles Babbage that could be programmed using punch cards.

Android: A mobile Linux operating system that runs on many smartphones and tablets.

antispyware software: A form of security software used to prevent and remove adware and spyware infections.

antivirus program: A form of security software that protects against viruses, Trojan horses, worms, and spyware.

application programming interface (API): The feature of an operating system that enables an application to request services from the operating system, such as a request to print or save a file.

application software: A program that performs a useful task for the user, such as productivity, entertainment, and education software.

arithmetic logic unit (ALU): The part of a processor that performs arithmetic (addition and subtraction) and logic (AND, OR, and NOT) calculations.

ARPANET: The network developed by the U.S. Department of Defense in the 1960s that eventually became the Internet.

artificial intelligence: The branch of science concerned with making computers behave like humans.

ASCII (American Standard Code for Information Interchange):
An 8-bit binary code set with 256 characters.

assembly language: A programming language that is written with statements closer to language that humans speak, which must be converted into machine language by an assembler before the computer can execute it.

asynchronous online communication: A form of online communication that does not require the participants to be online at the same time—for example, email.

autofocus: A camera feature that automatically adjusts the focal length by using a small motor to move the lens in or out.

avatar: A virtual body used online in virtual worlds and games.

back up: The process of copying files to another location for protection.

bandwidth: The data transfer rate of a network, measured in kilobits per second (Kbps), megabits per second (Mbps), or gigabits per second (Gbps).

beta testing: The process of testing a program under actual working conditions.

beta version: A pre-release version of software.

big data: The collection of large amounts of data from multiple sources—both internal and external—used for ongoing analysis and decision making.

binary (base 2) number system: A number system that has only two digits, 0 and 1.

binary code: A system that represents digital data as a series of 0s and 1s that can be understood by a computer.

bioinformatics: A field of study in which information technology is applied to the field of biology.

biometric scanner: A scanner that measures human characteristics such as fingerprints and eye retinas.

BIOS (Basic Input/Output System): A program stored on a chip on a motherboard that is used to start up a computer.

bit: A binary digit; the smallest unit of digital information.

bitcoin: An anonymous, digital, encrypted currency.

blog (weblog): An online journal.

blogosphere: All the blogs on the web and the connections among them.

Bluetooth: A technology that connects peripherals wirelessly at short range.

Blu-ray disc (BD): An optical disc with about five times the capacity of a DVD, which it was designed to replace. The single-layer disc capacity is 25 GB, and the double-layer disc capacity is 50 GB.

Boolean operator: A term (AND, OR, or NOT) that defines the relationship between words or groups of words and is used to create a search filter.

booting: The process of loading the operating system when starting up a computer.

bot: A computer that is infected with malware and is part of a botnet under the control of a master. Also called a zombie.

botnet: A network of computer zombies, or bots, controlled by a master, which can be used to send out spam and viruses or to launch a denial-of-service attack.

bridge table: In a relational database, a table that breaks a many-to-many relationship up into two one-to-many relationships.

broadband: Internet access that exceeds 10 Mbps as defined by the FCC.

browser hijacker: A form of malware that changes your home page and redirects you to other websites.

bug: A flaw in software programming.

burst mode: A feature on some digital cameras that enables you to take several pictures in quick succession by holding down the shutter button.

business intelligence (BI) tool: An application used to analyze data in information systems so it can be used to make decisions.

byte: Consists of 8 bits and used to represent a single character in modern computer systems.

cable Internet access: Internet access provided by cable companies.

cache memory: Fast memory that stores frequently accessed information close to the processor.

campus area network (CAN): A network that consists of multiple LANs located in the same location and connected to each other using routers.

captcha (Completely Automated Public Turing Test to Tell Computers and Humans Apart): A series of letters and numbers that are distorted in some way so that they are difficult for automated software to read but relatively easy for humans to read.

caption: The text of the audio in a video.

CD (compact disc): The oldest type of optical disc in use today, with a storage capacity of about 700 MB.

cell: The intersection of a row and a column in a spreadsheet.

cellular network: A network that uses cell towers to transmit voice and data over large distances.

central processing unit (CPU): The brain of a computer, housed inside the system unit on the motherboard. It consists of two parts: the arithmetic logic unit and the control unit.

chat: A real-time online conversation between multiple people at the same time in a chat room.

ciphertext: Text that has been encrypted.

clickjacking: A social network attack in which clicking on a link allows malware to post unwanted links on your page.

clickstream data mining: Analyzing the links customers click as they visit a website.

client: A computer that connects to, or requests services from, another computer called a server.

client–server network: A network that has at least one server at its center. Users log in to the network instead of to their local computers and are granted access to resources based on their logins.

client-side program: A program in which the coding is within a webpage, downloaded to the client computer, and compiled and executed by a browser or plug-in.

clock speed: The speed at which a processor executes the instruction cycle.

cloud computing: A type of computing that moves processing and storage off your desktop and business hardware and puts it in the cloud—on the Internet. Cloud computing consists of three parts: Infrastructure-as-a-Service (IaaS), Platform-as-a-Service (PaaS), and Software-as-a-Service (SaaS).

cloud service provider (CSP): A company that provides cloud (Internet-based) computing services: Infrastructure-as-a-Service (IaaS), Platform-as-a-Service (PaaS), and Software-as-a-Service (SaaS).

cloud: Another term for the Internet.

cluster: One or more sectors on a disk where data is stored.

CMOS (complementary metal oxide semiconductor): A volatile form of memory that uses a small battery to provide it with power to keep the data in memory even

when the computer is turned off. It stores settings that are used by the BIOS.

CMYK: The standard ink colors used by printers: cyan, magenta, yellow, and key (black).

codec: Short for compression/decompression. An algorithm that reduces the size of digital media files.

CODIS (Combined DNA Index System): A system that searches across multiple local, state, and national DNA profile databases. It consists of five indices: Forensic, Arrestee, Detainee, Offender, and Missing Persons.

cognitive computing system: An information system that learns from its interactions and interacts with humans using normal language.

communication device: A device that serves as both an input and output device and enables you to connect to other devices on a network or to the Internet.

compact system camera (CSC): An advanced point-and-shoot camera with interchangeable lenses and other DSLR features.

compiler: A program that converts programming code into machine language that a computer can read and execute.

compression: The process of making files smaller to conserve disk space and make the files easier to transfer.

computer fraud: A scheme perpetrated over the Internet or by email that tricks a victim into voluntarily and knowingly giving money or property.

computer network: Two or more computers that share resources such as software, hardware, and files.

computer program: A sequence of instructions for a computer to follow, written in a language that the computer can understand and including any data the computer needs to perform the instructions.

computer programming (coding): The process of converting an algorithm into instructions the computer can understand.

computer: A programmable machine that converts raw data into useful information.

control panel applet: A program in the Control Panel that is used to configure, monitor, or troubleshoot settings, hardware, and software.

Control Panel: A Windows feature that allows you to change, configure, monitor, or troubleshoot most system settings, hardware, and software.

control structure: A structure (sequence, selection, and loop) used in flowcharts and pseudocode to show the logic and the processing flow of an algorithm.

control unit: The part of the processor that manages the movement of data through the CPU.

convergence: The integration of technology on multifunction devices such as smartphones.

convertible notebook: A type of notebook computer that has a screen that can swivel to fold into what resembles a notepad or tablet.

cookie: A small text file placed on a computer when you visit a website that helps the website identify you when you return.

Creative Commons (CC) licensing: A form of licensing that enables people to easily change their copyright terms from the default of "all rights reserved" to "some rights reserved."

crowdfunding: Project funding from multiple small investors rather than few large investors.

crowdsourcing: Trusting the collective opinion of a crowd of people rather than the individual opinion of an expert.

CRT monitor: A legacy display technology that uses a cathode ray tube to excite phosphor particles coating a glass screen to light up the pixels.

cyberbullying: A form of computer harassment that happens between two minors.

cybercrime: Criminal activity on the Internet.

cyber-harassment: A form of computer harassment that happens between two adults.

cyber-stalking: A form of computer harassment that is serious in nature, with a pattern of harassment and a credible threat of harm.

cyber-terrorism: An unlawful attack against computers or networks that's done to intimidate a government or its people for a political or social agenda.

data breach: A situation in which sensitive data is stolen or viewed by someone who is not authorized to do so.

data bus: A wire on a motherboard over which information flows between the components of a computer.

data dictionary: The part of a database that defines all the fields and the type of data each field contains.

data flow diagram (DFD): A diagram that shows the flow of data through an information system.

data mining: The process of discovering relationships between data items.

data normalization: The process of reducing data redundancy in a database.

data type: The kind of data that you can enter in a field.

data validation: Rules designed to reduce data-entry errors by preventing invalid data from being entered. Rules may include data type, data length, acceptable values, and required fields.

data warehouse: A central repository for all the data that an enterprise uses, including internal databases and external sources such as vendors and customers.

data: The unprocessed, or raw, form of information.

database administrator (DBA): A person who manages database systems.

database management system (DBMS): Software used to create and manage data in a database.

database: A collection of information that is organized in a useful way. Database records are organized into one or more tables.

datacenter: A facility designed to house a company's servers and other equipment in a secure and controlled environment; sometimes called a server farm.

debugging: The process of detecting and fixing errors—or bugs—in a computer program.

decision support system (DSS): An information system designed to help make decisions in situations where there's uncertainty about the possible outcomes of those decisions.

default program: The program that's associated with a particular file type and that automatically opens when a file of that type is double-clicked.

defragmenter: A disk utility that reorganizes fragmented files on a disk.

denial-of-service attack: An attack that sends out so much traffic that it could cripple a server or network.

desktop computer: A personal computer that fits into a workspace such as a desk or counter.

device driver: A piece of software that acts as a translator, enhancing the capabilities of the operating system by enabling it to communicate with hardware.

dial-up: Internet access over ordinary telephone lines.

digital device: A device that represents audio or video data as a series of 0s and 1s.

digital footprint: All the information that someone could find out about you by searching the web, including social networking sites.

digital rights management (DRM): A technology that is applied to digital media files, such as music, eBooks, and videos, to impose restrictions on the use of these files.

digital single-lens reflex (DSLR) camera: A digital camera that uses interchangeable lenses, can be manually focused, and can cost thousands of dollars. DSLR cameras give the user more control than point-and-shoot cameras.

DisplayPort: A digital video standard designed to replace DVI and VGA.

distributed computing: Processing of a task that is distributed across a group of computers.

DLP (digital light-processing) projector: A projector that uses hundreds of thousands of tiny swiveling mirrors to create an image.

DNS (Domain Name System): The service that allows you to use a friendly name, such as google.com, instead of an IP address, such as 74.125.224.72, to contact a website.

document management system (DMS): Software that enables a company to save, share, search, and audit electronic documents throughout their life cycle.

domain name: The part of a URL that precedes the TLD and is sometimes called the second-level domain. The domain name represents a company or product name and makes it easy to remember the address.

domain: A network composed of a group of clients and servers under the control of one central security database on a special server called the domain controller.

donationware: A form of freeware where the developers accept donations, either for themselves or for a nonprofit organization.

drive controller: A component located on the motherboard that provides a drive interface, which connects disk drives to the processor.

drive-by-download: A situation that occurs when you visit a website that installs a program in the background without your knowledge.

DSL (digital subscriber line): Internet access over telephone lines designed to carry digital signals.

DVD (digital video disc/digital versatile disc): An optical disc that can hold more information than a CD. A single-layer (SL) DVD can hold about 4.7 GB of information. A double-layer (DL) DVD has a second layer to store data and can hold about 8.5 GB.

DVI (digital visual interface): An older, digital video standard that was designed to replace VGA.

dye-sublimation printer: A printer that uses heat to turn solid dye into a gas that is then transferred to special paper.

e-commerce: Business on the web; often broken into three categories—B2B, B2C, and C2C, where *B* stands for *business* and *C* stands for *consumer*.

EIDE (Enhanced Integrated Drive Electronics): A legacy drive interface found on the motherboards of older personal computers.

email: A system of sending electronic messages using store-and-forward technology.

embedded computer: A specialized computer found in ordinary devices, such as gasoline pumps, supermarket checkouts, traffic lights, and home appliances.

embedded operating system: A specialized operating system that runs on GPS devices, ATMs, smartphones, and other devices.

encryption: The process of converting unencrypted plain text into code, called ciphertext.

ENIAC (Electronic Numerical Integrator and Computer): The first working, digital, general-purpose computer.

enterprise server: A large computer that can perform millions of transactions in a day.

e-reader: A tablet designed primarily for reading.

ergonomics: The study of the relationship between workers and their workspaces.

Ethernet: The most commonly used standard that defines the way data is transmitted over a local area network.

EULA (end-user license agreement): A license agreement between a software user and the software publisher.

e-waste: Electronic waste, including old computers, cell phones, TVs, VCRs, and other electronic devices, some of which are considered hazardous.

expansion card: A card that plugs directly into an expansion slot on a motherboard and enables you to connect additional peripheral devices to a computer. Also called an adapter card.

expansion slot: An interface on a motherboard that expansion cards plug in to.

expert system: An information system programmed to make decisions in real-life situations (for example, diagnosing diseases based on symptoms).

feasibility study: A study created by a project team that includes the creation of the terms of reference (project charter) that state the objectives and scope of the project, the timeline for the project, risks, participants, deliverables, and budget. The four types of feasibility are economic, technical, operational, and political.

fiber-to-the-home (FTTH): Internet access over fiber-optic cables.

field: A single piece of information in a record in a database. For example, in a phone book record, the fields would be name, address, and phone number.

fifth-generation language (5GL): A system that a user can use without actually writing code. Primarily used in artificial intelligence applications and in combination with Platform-as-a-Service (PaaS) application development.

File Explorer: The window you use to navigate the file system and work with files, libraries, or folders on a Windows computer.

file extension: The second part of a file name. The extension is assigned by the program that is used to create the file and is used by the operating system to determine the type of file.

file fragmentation: Unorganized files that are broken into small pieces and stored in nonadjacent, or noncontiguous, clusters on the disk.

file management: The processes of opening, closing, saving, naming, deleting, and organizing digital files.

file name: The property of a file that's used to identify it using a name and file extension.

file property: Information about a file, such as authors, size, type, and date, which can be used to organize, sort, and find files more easily.

file system: Keeps track of what files are saved and where they're stored on the disk.

Finder: The tool you use to work with files and folders in OS X.

FiOS (Fiber Optic Service): The primary fiber broadband Internet service in the United States, provided by Verizon.

firewall: A device or software that blocks unauthorized access to a network or an individual computer.

FireWire: A hot-swappable port that can connect up to 63 devices per port. It also allows for peer-to-peer communication between devices, such as two video cameras, without the use of a computer. Also known as IEEE 1394.

first-generation language (1GL): A machine language written in binary that can be understood by a computer.

fixed-focus: A type of camera that has a preset focal length.

flash drive: A small, portable, solid-state drive. Also called a key drive, thumb drive, pen drive, or jump drive.

flash memory: A technology used by solid-state storage devices, such as flash drives and memory cards, that stores data on a chip.

flat database: The simplest type of database, which consists of a single list of items.

flowchart: A graphic view of an algorithm.

focal length: The distance at which subjects in front of the lens are in sharp focus.

folder: A container used to store and organize files on a computer.

form: A database object used to enter data into a database table.

formatting: The process of preparing a disk to store files by dividing it into tracks and sectors and setting up the file system.

forum: An online, asynchronous conversation, also known as a discussion board.

fourth-generation language (4GL): A computer language that's designed to be closer to natural language than a 3GL. Many 4GLs are used for accessing databases.

freeware: Software that can be used at no cost for an unlimited period of time.

fuzzy logic: A process used in artificial intelligence applications which recognizes that not everything can be broken down to true or false answers.

game controller: A type of input device that is used to interact with video games.

Gantt chart: In project management, a chart that shows the schedule and progress of a project.

geocaching: An electronic scavenger hunt played around the world. Geocachers hide geocaches and post GPS coordinates on the Internet.

geotagging: Adding location information to a digital photo.

gigahertz (GHz): A measure of the speed at which a processor executes the information cycle. 1 GHz is equal to 1 billion cycles per second.

GIS (geographic information system): An information system that combines layers—or datasets—of geographically referenced information about Earth's surface.

GPS (Global Positioning System): A system of 24 satellites that transmit signals that can be picked up by a receiver on the ground and used to determine the receiver's current location, time, and velocity through triangulation of the signals.

GPU (Graphics-Processing Unit): A processor found on a video card that can contain multiple cores.

graphical user interface (GUI): The interface between a user and a computer. A GUI allows a user to point to and click on objects, such as icons and buttons, to initiate commands.

green code: Computer code written efficiently so the program runs on the hardware with minimal impact.

green computing: The efficient and eco-friendly use of computers and other electronics.

grid computing: Distributed computing using a group of computers in one location.

hacking: The act of gaining unauthorized access to a computer system or network.

hacktivism: Hacking to make a political statement.

hard drive: The primary mass-storage device in a computer that stores data magnetically on metal platters. Also called a hard disk or hard disk drive.

hardware: The physical components of a computer.

hashtag: A word or phrase preceded by a # symbol that is used to organize and make tweets searchable.

HDMI (High-Definition Multimedia Interface): A digital port that can transmit both audio and video signals. It is the standard connection for high-definition TVs, video game consoles, and other media devices.

headphones: Output devices that convert digital signals into sound. They come in several different sizes and styles, ranging from tiny earbuds that fit inside your ear to full-size headphones that completely cover your outer ear.

heat sink: A part of the cooling system of a computer, mounted above the CPU and composed of metal or ceramic to draw heat away from the processor.

hierarchy: The folder structure created by an operating system in which there are folders within folders, known as subfolders or children.

home page: (1) The webpage that appears when you first open your browser. (2) The main or starting page of a website.

homegroup: A simple way to network a group of Windows computers that are all on the same home network.

hotfix: A software update that addresses an individual problem when it is discovered. Also called a patch.

hotspot: A public wireless access point often available in a public location such as an airport, school, hotel, or restaurant.

hot-swappable: A device that can be plugged in and unplugged without turning off the computer.

HTML (Hypertext Markup Language): The authoring language that defines the structure of a webpage.

Human Genome Project (HGP): A research project that determined the sequence of chemical base pairs that compose DNA and mapped the approximately 20,000–25,000 human genes.

hyperlink: A connection between pieces of information in documents written using hypertext.

hypertext: Text that contains links to other text and allows you to navigate through pieces of information by using the links that connect them.

IAFIS (Integrated Automated Fingerprint Identification System): A national fingerprint and criminal history system maintained by the FBI and used by local, state, and federal law enforcement. The largest biometric database in the world.

iCloud: A cloud storage and sync service from Apple.

identity theft: A form of cybercrime in which someone fraudulently uses your name, Social Security number, or bank or credit card number.

IEEE 1394: See FireWire.

IEEE 802.11: The standards that define the way data is transmitted over a Wi-Fi network.

image stabilization: A feature on some digital cameras that compensates for camera shake and therefore takes sharper images.

index: A list that Windows maintains that contains information about the files located on your computer to improve search speed.

inference engine: A set of rules for applying a knowledge base to each particular situation.

information processing cycle (IPC): The process a computer uses to convert data into information. The four steps of the IPC are input, processing, storage, and output.

information system: The people, hardware, and software that support data-intensive applications such as financial accounts, human resources, and other business transactions.

information: The processed, useful form of data.

infrastructure wireless network: A wireless network in which devices connect through a wireless access point.

Infrastructure-as-a-Service (IaaS): Part of cloud computing: the use of Internet-based servers.

inkjet printer: A printer that spray droplets of ink onto paper.

input device: A device used to enter data into a computer system so that it can be processed.

instant messaging (IM): A real-time online conversation.

instruction cycle: The steps a CPU uses to process data: fetch, decode, execute, store. Also known as the fetch-and-execute cycle or the machine cycle.

integrated circuit: A chip that contains a large number of tiny transistors that are fabricated into a semiconducting material called silicon.

integrated development environment (IDE): A complete system for developing software, typically consisting of a code editor, one or more compilers, one or more SDKs, and a debugger.

Internet backbone: The high-speed connection points between networks that make up the Internet.

Internet Crime Complaint Center (IC3): An organization that provides a website for victims to report cybercrimes.

Internet Exchange Points: The backbone of the modern Internet.

Internet of Things (IoT): The connection of the physical world to the Internet. Objects are tagged and can be located, monitored, and controlled using small embedded electronics.

Internet service provider (ISP): A company that offers Internet access.

Internet: The global network of computer networks.

Internet2: A second Internet designed for education, research, and collaboration.

iOS device: An Apple device—iPad, iPhone, or iPod—that runs the iOS mobile operating system.

iOS: A mobile operating system that runs on iPods, iPhones, and iPads.

IP (Internet Protocol) address: A unique numeric address assigned to each node on a network.

IP (Internet Protocol): The protocol responsible for addressing and routing packets to their destination.

Joint Application Development (JAD): A collaborative system development process that involves the end user throughout the design and development of the project, through a series of JAD sessions.

joystick: An input device mounted on a base that consists of a stick, buttons, and sometimes a trigger.

keyboard: An input device that translates keystrokes into a signal a computer understands; the primary input device for entering text into a computer.

keylogger: A computer program or hardware device that captures information a user enters on a keyboard.

keypad: A small alternative keyboard that has a limited set of keys.

knowledge base: Part of an expert system that contains expert knowledge and accumulated experience in a particular field.

laptop: A portable personal computer. Also referred to as a notebook.

laser printer: A printer that uses a laser beam to draw an image on a drum. The image is electrostatically charged and attracts a dry ink called toner. The drum is then rolled over paper, and the toner is deposited on the paper. Finally, the paper is heated and pressure is applied, bonding the ink to the paper.

LCD (liquid crystal display): A flat-panel display type found on most desktop and notebook computers that consists of two layers of glass glued together with a layer of liquid crystals between them. When electricity is passed through the individual crystals, it causes them to pass or block light to create an image.

LCD projector: A projector that passes light through a prism, which divides the light into three beams—red, green, and blue—which are then passed through an LCD screen.

legacy technology: Old technology that's still used alongside its more modern replacement because it still works and is cost-effective.

library: A tool used to gather files that are located in different locations on a Windows computer.

Linux: An open source operating system distribution that contains the Linux kernel and bundled utilities and applications.

local area network (LAN): A network in which all connected devices or nodes are located in the same physical location.

logic bomb: An attack that occurs when certain conditions are met.

logic error: An error in programming logic that results in an unexpected outcome.

lossless compression: A compression algorithm that looks for redundancy in a file and creates an encoded file by removing redundant information. When the file is decompressed, all the information from the original file is restored.

lossy compression: A compression algorithm used on files that contain more information than humans can typically detect (typically images, audio, and video files).That extra information is removed from the file. It's not possible to fully decompress this file, as the information has been removed from the file.

LTE (Long-Term Evolution): A means of connecting to the Internet using cellular networks that provide 4G service.

Mac: A personal computer manufactured by Apple. Also referred to as a Macintosh.

machine language: A programming language written in binary that can be understood by a computer.

machinima: The art of creating videos using screens captured from video games.

macro: A small program used to automate tasks in applications such as Word and Excel.

mainframe: A large multiuser computer that can perform millions of transactions in a day.

malware: A computer program that's designed to be harmful or malicious.

management information system (MIS): An information system that includes software, hardware, data resources (such as databases), decision support systems, people, and project management applications.

many-to-many relationship: A database relationship in which multiple records in one table link to multiple records in another table.

massively multiplayer online role-playing game (MMORPG): An online game in which players interact with people in real time in a virtual world using an avatar, or virtual body.

memory card: A storage medium that uses flash memory to store data.

memory: Temporary storage that a computer uses to hold instructions and data.

metasearch engine: A search engine that searches other search engines.

metropolitan area network (MAN): A network that covers a single geographic area.

microblogging: A form of blogging in which posts are limited to a small number of characters and users post updates frequently. Twitter is a microblog site.

microbrowser: A web browser optimized for small-screen devices, such as smartphones and tablets. Also called a mobile browser.

micropayment: A small charge for additional lives, levels, or other features from within an app.

microphone: An input device that converts sound into digital signals and is used to chat in real time or as part of voice-recognition applications used in video games and for dictating text.

microprocessor: A complex integrated circuit that contains the central processing unit (CPU) of a computer.

Microsoft Windows: The operating system used on most personal computers.

midrange server: A server used to perform complex calculations, store customer information and transactions, or host an email system for an organization. These servers can support hundreds of simultaneous users and are scalable, allowing for growth as a company's needs change.

minicomputer: The smallest multiuser computer. Users connect to a minicomputer via dumb terminals, which have no processing capabilities of their own.

mobile application (mobile app): A program that extends the functionality of a mobile device.

mobile browser: A web browser optimized for small-screen devices, such as smartphones and tablets. Also called a microbrowser.

mobile device: A portable device such as a smartphone or tablet.

mobile operating system: An embedded operating system that runs on mobile devices such as smartphones and tablets and is more full-featured than other embedded OSs.

modem: A communication device used to connect a computer to a telephone line, most often for dial-up Internet access. *Modem* is short for modulator-demodulator.

monitor: A video output device that works by lighting up pixels on a screen. Each pixel contains three colors—red, green, and blue (RGB)—and all colors can be created by varying the intensities of these three colors.

Moore's Law: An observation made by Gordon Moore in 1965 that the number of transistors that can be placed on an integrated circuit had doubled roughly every two years.

motherboard: The main circuit board of a computer, which houses the processor (CPU) and contains drive controllers and interfaces, expansion slots, data buses, ports and connectors, the BIOS, and memory. It provides a way for devices to attach to the computer.

mouse: An input device that may include one or more buttons and a scroll wheel that works by moving across a smooth surface to signal movement of the pointer.

MP3 (MPEG-1 Audio Layer 3): A common audio file type used for music files. MP3 is a lossy form of compression that works by removing some of the detail.

MP3 player: A handheld device that allows you to carry with you thousands of songs and podcasts, so you can listen to them wherever you are. Also called a portable media player if it supports photos and videos.

multi-core processor: A processor that consists of two or more processors integrated on a single chip.

multidimensional database (MDB): A type of database optimized for storing and utilizing data. It may be created using input from existing relational databases, but it structures the information into multidimensional data cubes.

multifunction device: A printer device with a built-in scanner and sometimes fax capabilities. Also known as an all-in-one printer.

multimedia: The integration of text, graphics, video, animation, and sound content.

multitasking: Doing more than one task at a time.

multiuser computer: A system that allows multiple, simultaneous users to connect to it, allowing for centralized resources and security.

municipal Wi-Fi: Wireless Internet access available in some cities and towns.

near field communication (NFC): A technology that enables devices to share data with each other by touching them together or bringing them within a few centimeters of each other.

netbook: A lightweight, inexpensive notebook computer designed primarily for Internet access; with built-in wireless capabilities, a small screen, and limited computing power and storage.

Network Access Point (NAP): One of the sites that make up the Internet backbone.

network adapter: A communication device used to establish a connection with a network. The adapter may be onboard, an expansion card, or a USB device and may be wired or wireless. Also called a network interface card (NIC).

network address translation (NAT): A security feature of a router that shields the devices on a private network from the public network (the Internet).

network administrator: The person responsible for managing the hardware and software on a network.

network interface card (NIC): See network adapter.

network operating system (NOS): A specialized operating system found on servers in a client–server network that provides services requested by the client computers, such as file services, printing services, centralized security, and communication services.

network resource: The software, hardware, or files shared on a network.

neural network: A system that simulates human thinking by emulating the biological connections—or neurons—of the human brain.

Next Generation Identification (NGI): A national fingerprint and criminal history system maintained by the FBI that has replaced IAFIS.

nonvolatile: A form of storage that does not require power to preserve stored information.

notebook: A portable personal computer. Also referred to as a laptop.

object-oriented database (OODB): A type of database in which data is stored as objects, which are used by modern programming languages, such as C++ and Java. Often used to create databases that have more complicated types of data, such as images, audio, and video.

object-oriented programming (OOP): A programming model that defines objects and the actions or methods that can be performed on them.

office application suite: A suite of productivity applications—such as a word processor, spreadsheet, presentation program, database, and personal information manager—integrated into a single package.

office support system (OSS): An information system that consists of software and hardware that improve productivity of employees by automating common tasks.

OLED (organic light-emitting diode): A monitor composed of extremely thin panels of organic molecules sandwiched between two electrodes.

OneDrive: Free online storage associated with a Microsoft account.

one-to-many relationship: The most common type of relationship in a relational database, in which a single record in one table is related to multiple records in another table.

one-to-one relationship: A database relationship in which a single record in one table is related to exactly one record in another table. The records are linked by a common primary key.

online analytical processing (OLAP): A system that enables a user to selectively extract and view data from different points of view and can be used for data mining or discovering relationships between data items.

open source: Software that has its source code published and made available to the public, enabling anyone to copy, modify, and redistribute it without paying fees.

operating system (OS): System software that provides the user with an interface to communicate with the hardware and software on a computer. The OS also manages system resources.

optical disc: A form of removable storage where data is stored by using a laser to either melt the disc material or change the color of embedded dye. A laser reads the variations as binary data.

optical network terminal (ONT): The device that connects a LAN to a fiber network.

OS X: The operating system installed on Apple Mac computers.

output device: A device that returns processed information to the user.

overclock: To run a processor at speeds higher than it was designed to perform.

parallel processing: The process of using multiple processors, or multi-core processors, to divide up processing tasks.

patch: A software update that addresses an individual problem when it is discovered. Also called a hotfix.

path: The sequence of folders to a file or folder.

payload: An action or attack by a computer virus or other malware.

PCI (Peripheral Component Interconnect): The most common type of expansion slot on a motherboard.

PCIe (PCI Express): A faster version of PCI that is used to connect a video card and other peripherals.

peer-to-peer (P2P) network: A network in which each computer is considered equal. Each device can share its resources with every other device, and there's no centralized authority.

peripheral devices: Components that serve the input, output, and storage functions of a computer system.

personal area network (PAN): A small network that consists of devices connected by Bluetooth.

personal computer (PC): A small microprocessor-based computer used by one person at a time.

personal information manager (PIM): A program used to manage email, calendars, and tasks that is often part of an office suite.

pharming: A form of cybercrime that redirects you to a phony website even if you type the correct address into your browser.

phishing: A form of cybercrime in which email messages and IMs that appear to be from those you do business with— such as your bank, credit card company, social network, auction site, online payment processor, or IT administrator— are designed to trick you into revealing information.

photo printer: A printer designed to print high-quality photos on special photo paper. Photo printers can be inkjet printers or dye-sublimation printers.

PictBridge: An older industry standard that allows a camera to connect directly to a printer, usually by a USB connection or special dock.

piggybacking: Using an open wireless network to access the Internet without permission.

pipelining: A method used by a single processor to process multiple instructions simultaneously. As soon as the first instruction has moved from the fetch stage to the decode stage, the processor fetches the next instruction.

pixel: Short for picture element. A single point on a display screen. Each pixel contains three colors: red, green, and blue (RGB).

plasma monitor: A large display type that works by passing an electric current through gas sealed in thousands of cells inside the screen. The current excites the gas, which in turn excites the phosphors that coat the screen to pass light through an image.

Platform-as-a-Service (PaaS): Part of cloud computing: an online programming environment used to develop, deploy, and manage custom web applications.

platform-neutral: An application that can run on all modern personal computing systems.

plotter: A printer that uses one or more pens to draw an image on a roll of paper.

Plug and Play (PnP): An operating system feature that allows you to easily add new hardware to a computer system. When you plug in a new piece of hardware, the OS detects it and helps you set it up.

plug-in: A third-party program that extends the functionality of a browser.

podcast client: A program used to locate, subscribe to, and play podcasts.

podcast: A prerecorded radio- or TV-like show that you can download and listen to or watch anytime.

point-and-shoot camera: The simplest, least expensive digital camera type, which has the fewest features.

port: A connection point that is used to attach a peripheral device to a motherboard.

portable apps: Application software that can be run from a flash drive.

portable media player: A handheld device that allows you to carry with you audio files, photos, and videos, so you can enjoy them wherever you are. Also called an MP3 player.

primary key: A field that uniquely identifies a record in a database table.

procedural programming: A programming model that uses a step-by-step list of instructions.

processor: See central processing unit (CPU).

program development cycle: A set of steps that a programmer follows to create a computer program.

project management software: An application designed to help complete projects, stick to a budget, stay on schedule, and collaborate with others.

project manager (PM): The leader of a project team, who coordinates the team and keeps the project on track.

projector: A video output device typically used when making a presentation or sharing media with a group in such places as classrooms, businesses, and home theaters because they can produce larger output than a monitor.

protocol: The rules for communication between devices that determine how data is formatted, transmitted, received, and acknowledged.

PS/2 port: A legacy port used to connect a keyboard and mouse to a computer.

pseudocode: The expression of the steps of an algorithm using English-like statements that focus on logic, not syntax.

punch card: A stiff piece of paper that conveys digital information by the presence or absence of holes.

QR (Quick Response) code: A two-dimensional bar code found in ads and on merchandise tags that can be scanned using an app on a mobile device to learn more about the item.

query language: A language used to design a database query.

query: A database object that pulls out records that meet specific criteria. A query retrieves specific data from one or more tables to answer a question.

RAM (random access memory): A volatile form of memory that holds the operating systems, programs, and data the computer is currently using.

ransomware: A form of malware that prevents you from using your computer until you pay a fine or fee.

Rapid Application Development (RAD): An iterative development process that uses prototyping and user testing of the designs. RAD tools use object-oriented programming (OOP) and reusable code modules to speed up the process.

record: A row of data in a database table that describes a particular entry in the database—for example, a customer or product.

relational database: The most common type of database, which consists of multiple tables related by common information.

relational keyword: A keyword used in SQL statements to manipulate, query, and update data in relational databases; examples of relational keywords are SELECT, FROM, WHERE, and AND.

report: A database object that displays data from a table or a query in a format that is easy to read and print.

resolution: The number of horizontal by vertical pixels—for example 1280×1024 or 1920×1080—on a display screen.

retail software: The user pays a fee to use the software.

RFID tag: A tag that can be read by an RFID (radio-frequency identification) scanner. It contains a tiny antenna for receiving and sending a radio-frequency signal.

ROM (read-only memory): A nonvolatile form of memory that does not need power to retain data.

rootkit: A set of programs that allows someone to gain control over a computer system while hiding the fact that the computer has been compromised.

router: A device that connects two or more networks together. It uses address information to route the data packets it receives to the correct locations.

RSS (Really Simple Syndication): A format used for distributing web feeds that change frequently—for example, blogs, podcasts, and news—to subscribers.

runtime error: An error that occurs when a program is running and data or a command that is entered causes it to crash.

SATA (Serial Advanced Technology Attachment): The standard internal drive interface.

satellite Internet access: A means of connecting to the Internet using communication satellites.

scanner: An input device that can increase the speed and accuracy of data entry and convert information into a digital format that can be saved, copied, and manipulated.

screen capture: A software tool used to create a video of what happens on a computer screen.

search engine optimization (SEO): The method used to make a website easier to find, by both people and software, that indexes the web and increases the webpage ranking in search engine results.

search engine: A database that indexes the web.

second screen: Using a computer or mobile device while watching television to interact with other viewers or view enhanced content.

second-generation language (2GL): An assembly language that must be converted into a machine language by an assembler before a computer can execute it.

Secure Sockets Layer (SSL): A protocol that encrypts information before it is sent across the Internet.

security suite: A package of security software that includes a combination of features such as antivirus, firewall, and privacy protection.

serial and parallel ports: Legacy ports used to connect peripheral devices to a computer.

server: A multiuser computer system that runs a network operating system (NOS) and provides services—such as Internet access, email, or file and print services—to client systems.

server-side program: A program that runs on a web server instead of the client computer. No special software is needed by the client.

service pack: A large planned update that addresses multiple problems or adds multiple features and includes previous patches and hotfixes.

Settings window: A Windows feature that enables you to change common settings.

shareware: Software offered in trial form or for a limited period that allows the user to try it out before purchasing a license.

shill bidding: Fake bidding by a seller or his or her accomplice to drive up the price of an auction item.

shutter lag: The time between pressing the shutter button and the camera snapping the picture.

smart appliance: A home appliance that monitors signals from the power company, and when the electric grid system is stressed, can react by cutting back on power consumption.

smart grid: A network for delivering electricity to consumers that includes communication technology to manage electricity distribution efficiently.

smart home: A house that uses automation to control lighting, heating and cooling, security, entertainment, and appliances.

smartphone: A multifunction device that blends phone, PDA, and portable media player features.

social bookmarking site: A site that allows you to save and share your bookmarks or favorites online.

social media marketing (SMM): The practice of using social media sites to sell products and services.

social media: Websites that use Web 2.0 technologies that enable you to create user-generated content, connect, network, and share.

social network: An online community where people with common interest can communicate and share content with each other; a social network combines many of the features of other online tools.

social news site: An online news site that allows community members to submit content they discover on the web and puts it in one place for everyone to see and to discuss.

social review site: A website where users review hotels, movies, games, books, and other products and services.

software developer: A person who designs and writes computer programs.

software development kit (SDK): A bundle of libraries and tools that are developed for a particular platform.

Software-as-a-Service (SaaS): Part of cloud computing: the delivery of applications—or web apps—over the Internet.

solid-state drive (SSD): A small drive often used in small electronic devices, such as media players and cell phones, as well as in notebooks and netbooks.

solid-state storage: A non-mechanical form of storage that uses flash memory to store data on a chip.

sound card: An expansion card that provides audio connections for both audio input devices and output devices.

spam: Unsolicited and unwanted email messages, also called junk mail.

spamming: The sending of mass, unsolicited emails.

speaker: An output device that converts digital signals from a computer or media player into sound.

speech recognition: A feature that enables users to use a device by speaking commands.

Spotlight: The search tool in OS X.

spreadsheet: An application that creates electronic worksheets composed of rows and columns. Spreadsheets are used for mathematical applications, such as budgeting, grade books, and inventory.

spyware: A form of malware that secretly gathers personal information about you.

SSID (service set identifier): The name of a wireless network.

stakeholder: A person who has an interest in and will be affected by the successful completion of a project.

standard: A specification that has been defined by an industry organization to ensure that equipment that is made by different companies will be able to work together.

storage area network (SAN): A network between the data storage devices and the servers on a network that makes the data accessible to all servers in the SAN.

streaming: Media, such as video or audio, that begins to play immediately as it is being received and does not require the whole file to be downloaded to your computer first.

Structured Query Language (SQL): The most common query language used to create database queries.

stylus: A special pen-like input tool that enables you to write directly on a touch screen.

subnotebook: A notebook computer that is thin and light and that has high-end processing and video capabilities.

supercomputer: A very expensive and powerful computer system that is used to perform complex mathematical calculations, such as those used in weather forecasting and medical research.

switch: A device that connects multiple devices on a LAN and uses address information to send data packets only to the port that the appropriate device is connected to.

synchronous online communication: A form of online communication that requires the participants to be online at the same time—for example, chat and instant messaging.

syntax error: An error in the way code is written.

syntax rule: A rule that defines the correct construction of commands in a programming language.

system development life cycle (SDLC): The traditional model for system development, which consists of five phases—planning, analysis, design, implementation and testing, and maintenance—where each phase is completed in order before the next can begin.

System Preferences: An OS X feature that allows you to change system settings.

system requirements: The minimum hardware and software specifications required to run a software application.

system software: The software that makes a computer run.

system unit: The case that encloses and protects the power supply, motherboard, CPU, and memory of a computer.

table: A database object in which data is stored. It's arranged in rows and columns.

tablet: A handheld mobile device that falls somewhere between a computer and a smartphone.

tagging: Labeling images or files with keywords to make it easier to organize and search for them.

TCP (Transmission Control Protocol): The protocol responsible for ensuring that data packets are transmitted reliably on a network.

TCP/IP protocol stack: A suite of protocols that define everything from how to transfer files (FTP) and webpages (HTTP) to sending (SMTP) and receiving (POP) email. TCP/IP is the protocol stack that runs on the Internet, and because of this, it's also the protocol stack that runs on most LANs.

telephoto lens: A type of zoom lens that makes an object appear closer.

text messaging: Sending brief electronic messages between mobile devices using Short Message Service (SMS).

thermal printer: A printer that creates an image by heating specially coated heat-sensitive paper, which changes color where the heat is applied.

third-generation language (3GL): A computer language for which a compiler is needed to convert the code into machine language that a computer can understand and execute. Most modern programming languages, both procedural and object-oriented programming (OOP), fall in this category.

three-dimensional (3D) printer: A printer that can create objects such as prototypes and models.

Thunderbolt: A port that carriers both PCIe and DisplayPort video signals on the same cable, so it can be used to connect many different types of peripherals to a computer.

Thunderbolt combines two 10 Gbps channels and can daisy-chain up to six devices using one connection.

time bomb: A form of logic bomb in which the attack is triggered by a specific time and date.

top-level domain (TLD): The suffix, such as .com or .edu, that follows the domain name in a URL and represents the type of website you're visiting.

topology: The physical layout of a computer network.

touchpad: An input device typically found on a notebook computer instead of a mouse. You move a finger across the touch-sensitive surface, and the computer detects and translates your motion.

touchscreen: An input device that can accept input from a finger or a stylus.

transaction-processing system (TPS): An information system that links together the multiple operations that make up a transaction and ensures that all operations in a transaction are completed without error.

transistor: A tiny electric switch used in second-generation computers.

Trojan horse: A program that appears to be a legitimate program but is actually something malicious.

Turing machine: A machine that can perform mathematical computations.

Turing test: A measure of a computer's ability to display intelligent behavior.

ubiquitous computing (ubicomp): Technology that recedes into the background and becomes part of the environment.

Unicode: An extended ASCII set that is the standard on the Internet and includes codes for most of the world's written languages, mathematical systems, and special characters. It has codes for more than 100,000 characters.

UNIX: A multiuser OS developed in the 1970s that is still used on servers and some specialized workstations.

URL (uniform resource locator): An address, such as http//google.com, that consists of three main parts: the protocol (http), domain name (google), and top-level domain (.com).

USB (Universal Serial Bus): A standard port type that is used to connect many kinds of devices, including printers, mice, keyboards, digital cameras, cell phones, and external drives. Up to 127 devices can share a single USB port.

USB hub: A device used to connect multiple USB devices to a single USB port.

User Account Control (UAC): A Windows security feature that notifies you before allowing changes to be made on your computer.

user account: An account that grants a user certain rights and access to a computer system.

user interface: The part of an operating system that you see and interact with.

user-generated content: Web content created by ordinary users.

utility software: A type of system software used to perform computer maintenance.

vacuum tube: A tube that resembles an incandescent light bulb and was used in first-generation computers.

VGA (video graphics array): A legacy, analog video standard.

video card: An expansion card that provides the data signal and connection for a monitor or projector. It may also include input ports to connect a TV tuner or another video device to the system.

video game system: A computer that is designed primarily for playing games.

viral video: A video that becomes extremely popular because of recommendations and social sharing.

virtual private network (VPN): A private network through the public network (Internet) that allows remote users to access a LAN securely.

virus: A program that replicates itself and infects computers. It needs a host file, such as a game, to travel on.

VoIP (Voice over IP): A service that allows phone calls to be transmitted over the Internet instead of traditional phone lines.

volatile: A form of storage that requires power to preserve stored information.

volunteer computing: A form of distributed computing that relies on the processing power of hundreds or thousands of volunteers' personal computers.

wardriving: The practice of driving around and locating open wireless access points.

wearable: A computer worn on the body.

Web 2.0: Technologies used to communicate and collaborate on the web that enable you to be a creator, not just a consumer, of content.

web browser: A program that interprets HTML to display webpages.

webcam: A specialized video camera that provides visual input for online communication, such as web conferencing or chatting.

webcasting: Broadcasting on the web.

webpage: Information on the Internet written in HTML, which can be viewed with a web browser.

website: One or more related webpages, all located in the same place.

wide area network (WAN): A network that spans multiple locations and connects multiple LANs over dedicated lines using routers.

wide-angle lens: A type of zoom lens that widens the view, making objects appear smaller and farther away.

Wi-Fi Protected Setup (WPS): A technique for setting up a secure wireless home network using a push button, personal identification number (PIN), or USB key to automatically configure devices to connect to your network.

Wi-Fi: A type of network found in homes and public hotspots, which uses radio waves to provide wireless, high-speed network connections.

wiki: A website that allows users to edit content, even if it was written by someone else.

WiMAX Mobile Internet: A means of connecting to the Internet using cellular networks that provide 4G service.

wireless access point (WAP): A device that allows wireless devices to join a network.

wireless encryption: A feature that adds security to a wireless network by encrypting transmitted data.

wireless LAN (WLAN): A network that uses Wi-Fi to transmit data.

word processor: An application that is used to create, edit, and format text documents. The documents can also contain images.

workgroup: A group of devices in a peer-to-peer network.

workstation: A high-end desktop computer or one that's attached to a network in a business setting.

World Wide Web: The hypertext system of information on the Internet that allows you to navigate through pieces of information by using hyperlinks that connect them.

worm: A form of self-replicating malware that doesn't need a host to travel. It travels over networks and spreads over network connections without any human intervention.

zero-day exploit: An attack that occurs on the day an exploit is discovered, before the publisher of the compromised software can fix it.

zombie: A computer that is infected with malware and is part of a botnet under the control of a master. Also called a bot.

zoom: Making objects appear closer or farther away.

Index

B

C

F

Facebook, 393, 393 fig. 8.11, 421–423, 422 fig. 8.30, 423 fig. 8.31
facial recognition/matching, 68
fax machines, 211, 211 fig. 4.51
Federal Aviation Administration (FAA), 37
fees, software, 83
fetch-and-execute cycle, 165
Fiber Optic Service (FiOS), 339
fiber-to-the-home (FTTH), 339
fields, 59
File Explorer (Windows)
  file navigation, 115–116, 115 fig. 3.1
  file organization, 120 table 3.1, 122–124
  system specs, 79, 79 fig. 2.24–2.25
file fragmentation, 256, 258
File History (Windows), 133, 133 fig. 3.13, 260–262
file management, 113–152
  backing up files, 132–136
  careers, 151
  compression, 138–143, 140 fig. 3.19–3.20
  computer navigation, 115–118
  default program association, 148–150
  defined, 114
  mind map, 152
  organization, 119–125
  paperless offices, 137
  search options, 144–147
  storage, mobile devices, 118
file(s). *See also* file management
  extensions, 127–128, 128 table 3.4
  image formats, 288, 288 table 6.3
  names, 127–128, 127 fig. 3.9, 127 table 3.3
  properties, 129–131, 129 fig. 3.10, 130 fig. 3.11, 131 fig. 3.12
  type associations, 150, 150 fig. 3.30–3.31
file system, 255
File Transfer Protocol (FTP), 463 table 9.2
financial software, 61, 66
Finder (OS X), 118, 118 fig. 3.5, 120, 120 fig. 3.8, 121 table 3.2, 124–125
FiOS (Fiber Optic Service), 339
firewalls, 259, 457, 457 fig. 9.18, 471, 471 fig. 926
FireWire cables/connectors, 173, 173 fig. 4.15, 284
first-generation computers, 11, 12 table 1.1
5G networks, 340
fixed-focus cameras, 278
flash drives, 119, 119 fig. 3.7, 178, 178 fig. 4.20, 179–181
flash memory, 178
Flickr, 289–290, 397, 397 fig. 8.15
Flowers, Tommy, 12 table 1.1
focal length, 278
folders
  compressing, 142–143
  creating, 114–125
  defined, 115
formatting, disk, 255, 255 fig. 5.18
forms, 59
forums, 391, 391 fig. 8.10
4G networks, 339–340, 339 fig. 7.5
fourth-generation computers, 13, 13 fig. 1.6
freeware, 83, 85
FTP (File Transfer Protocol), 463 table 9.2
FTTH (fiber-to-the-home), 339

G

Game Bar (Windows 10), 307
game controllers, 30, 191, 191 fig. 4.34
games, video, 30, 69, 340
Gantt charts, 62
genealogy software, 70, 70 fig. 2.21
geocaching, 31
geotagging, 289, 289 fig. 6.13
gigahertz (GHz), 166
Global Positioning System (GPS), 29, 29 fig. 1.14
Google Apps for Business, 88 table 2.1
Google Chrome, 344, 344 fig. 7.10
Google Drive, 348–351
Google Now, 302
Google Scholar, 368
Google searches, 355–356, 355 fig. 7.17
Gore, Al, 332
GPS (Global Positioning System), 29, 29 fig. 1.14
GPU (graphics-processing unit), 166
Grab tool (Mac), 9
graphical user interface (GUI), 229
graphics-processing unit (GPU), 166
green computing
  defined, 15
  e-waste, 303
  paperless offices, 137
  power management, 235
  server virtualization, 462
  smart homes, 15
  smart shopping, 213
  social awareness, 399